February 2024

The Jewish Experience of the First World War

To Yael-Louise,
I hope you find
inspiration and courage
in this fascinating
collection of stories.
I felt greatly honoured
to have participated
in this project.
With warmest
best wishes,

Edward

Edward Madigan · Gideon Reuveni
Editors

The Jewish Experience
of the First World War

Editors
Edward Madigan
Department of History
Royal Holloway, University of London
Egham, UK

Gideon Reuveni
Department of History
University of Sussex
Falmer, UK

ISBN 978-1-137-54895-5   ISBN 978-1-137-54896-2   (eBook)
https://doi.org/10.1057/978-1-137-54896-2

Library of Congress Control Number: 2018951052

This Palgrave Macmillan imprint is published by the registered company Springer Nature
Limited
The registered company address is: The Campus, 4 Crinan Street, London, N1 9XW,
United Kingdom

Acknowledgements

This book was inspired by a conference that took place in London in June 2014 in anticipation of the centenary of the outbreak of the First World War. The conference was a joint venture between several organizations, and a product of the hard work of a number of individuals. At the beginning of 2014, Elizabeth Selby of the Jewish Museum London informed us about the forthcoming 'For King and Country' exhibition designed to mark the centenary. Around the same time, Ben Berkow and Toby Simpson of the Wiener Library also expressed interest in the topic. This led to the idea of holding the conference in London in conjunction with the exhibitions on the Jewish experience of the First World War being staged by these leading guardians of Jewish memory. We would very much like to thank Elizabeth and Toby for all their patience and hard work in helping us to organize the conference, and for the institutional support provided by the Jewish Museum London and the Wiener Library for this event. We would also like to express our gratitude to the Austrian Cultural Forum, to the Institute for German Jewish history in Hamburg, and to the Jewish Military Museum in London, all of whom helped to sponsor the event.

On behalf of the Centre for German Jewish Studies at the University of Sussex, we would like to thank Diana Franklin, the manager of the centre, for her invaluable assistance. Unfortunately, not all participants at the conference were able to contribute to the volume, but their comments and input were very helpful in shaping the intellectual parameters of the book. We are also very grateful to Carmel Kennedy and

Emily Russell of Palgrave Macmillan for their support and patience in helping us bring an occasionally quite challenging project to fruition. Finally, we would like to extend our sincere gratitude to each of the individual authors whose work has been included in the pages that follow. Their collective insights have greatly enriched the fields of Jewish history and First World War studies and we are very much in their debt.

Edward Madigan
Gideon Reuveni

CONTENTS

NOTES ON CONTRIBUTORS

Tim Corbett is a historian, editor, and translator specialising in the modern cultural history of Jews in Austria. He completed his Ph.D. at Lancaster University in 2015 and is currently preparing his first monograph, a history of Vienna's Jewish cemeteries. He has published and translated numerous articles on Central European Jewish history, translated a book by Arndt Engelhardt, and been the recipient of numerous international fellowships and awards. He currently holds the inaugural Prins Foundation Postdoctoral Fellowship at the Museum of Jewish Heritage in New York.

Michal Friedlander is Head of the Judaica department at the Jewish Museum Berlin. She is the author of numerous articles on different aspects of Jewish material culture and the co-editor of *10 + 5 = Gott—Die Macht der Zeichen* (2004), and *Kosher & Co.—Über Essen und Religion* (2010). In 2013, she co-curated 'The Whole Truth—Everything you always wanted to know about Jews', an exhibition which sparked international debate. Friedlander's current research focuses on the concept of the Jewish object.

Anat Kidron is senior lecturer, head of the Land of Israel Department and dean of the Faculty of Humanities at Ohalo Academic College of Education and Sport. She also lectures in the departments of Jewish History and Israel Studies at the University of Haifa and acts as academic coordinator of the Schumacher Institute for the Study of Christian Activity in Palestine in the modern era. She has written a number of articles on the mandatory period and the early years of Israeli statehood and her first book, *Between Nationality and Locality: The Jewish community in Haifa During the British Mandate*, was published in Hebrew in 2012.

Edward Madigan is Lecturer in Public History and First World War Studies at Royal Holloway, University of London. His work combines cultural, military, and social history and he is particularly interested in the British and Irish experience and memory of the First World War. From 2012 to 2013 he sat on the UK Government's Centenary Events Planning Group and he currently sits on the editorial board of the 14–18 Online Encyclopaedia and the executive committee of the International Society for First World War Studies. His publications include *Faith Under Fire: Anglican Army Chaplains and the Great War* (Palgrave, 2011) and, with John Horne, *Towards Commemoration: Ireland in War and Revolution, 1912–1923* (2013) and he is currently researching the British experience of the Irish War of Independence.

Ruth Nattermann is a postdoctoral fellow at the Historical Seminar of the Ludwig-Maximilians-Universität, Munich, academic assistant at the Universität der Bundeswehr, Munich, and scientific coordinator of the international DFG-network "Gender-Nation-Emancipation: Women and Families in the 'long' Nineteenth Century in Italy and Germany". Her postdoctoral project focuses on Jewish women in the Italian women's movement from 1861 to 1945 and her wider research interests include Italian fascism and Italian-Jewish and German-Jewish history. Among her recent publications is "Zwischen Pazifismus, Irredentismus und nationaler Euphorie. Italienische Jüdinnen und der Erste Weltkrieg", which appeared in *Jüdische Publizistik und Literatur im Zeichen des Ersten Weltkriegs*, a volume edited by Petra Ernst and Eleonore Lappin-Eppel and published in 2016.

Philipp Nielsen received his Ph.D. from Yale University in 2012. He is Assistant Professor of Modern European History at Sarah Lawrence College, New York, and a former research fellow and current Associated Researcher at the Center for the History of Emotions at the Max Planck Institute for Human Development in Berlin. His research interests include German-Jewish history, German political and architectural history, and the history of emotions. He has published articles on notions of responsibility and compromise in conservative inter-war politics in

Germany and on debates about adequately "democratic architecture" in West Germany in the 1950s and 1960s.

Sarah Panter studied Modern History and Political Science at the University of Freiburg and the University of Michigan, Ann Arbor. She received her Ph.D. from the University of Freiburg in 2013 and is now Research Associate at the Leibniz Institute of European History in Mainz. Her publications include her first book, *Jüdische Erfahrungen und Loyalitätskonflikte im Ersten Weltkrieg*, and, as guest-editor, *European History Yearbook: Mobility and Biography* (vol. 16, 2015). Her research interests focus on modern Jewish history in Europe and the United States, ethnic minorities during the First World War, transnational lives and mobility studies.

Gideon Reuveni is director of the Centre for German-Jewish Studies at the University of Sussex. In his scholarly work, Reuveni has sought out the fringes of the historical discipline, to reach those areas of research and theory where the historical method meets literature, anthropology, cultural studies, and economics. He has published widely on such diverse topics as historiography, sport, reading culture, and Jewish economic history. His most recent book is *Consumer Culture and the Making of Jewish Identity*, which won the National Jewish Book award in 2018.

Björn Siegel is a researcher at the Institute for the History of the German Jews in Hamburg. He completed his M.A. and Ph.D. at the Ludwig Maxmilian University of Munich and is a former fellow at the Franz Rosenzweig Minerva Research Centre at the Hebrew University (Israel) and lecturer at the Centre for German-Jewish Studies, University of Sussex. He has been awarded numerous scholarships (DAAD; Max-Weber-Foundation; USHMM) and his publications include *Austrian Jewry Between East and West: The Austrian Jewish Alliance 1873–1938* (2010) and, with Beate Meyer, *Kurt Fritz Rosenberg: Einer der nicht mehr dazugehört* (2012). His research interests focus on Jewish migration and philanthropy as well as Jewish maritime studies.

Christopher Smith completed his Ph.D. thesis on London Jewry and the First World War at King's College London in 2017. Prior to this, he taught early modern history at King's College London, and he has been published in 'Reviews in History'. He is currently working on a study of the impact of war and rationing on Anglo-Jewish food, and his research interests include the social and cultural history of Britain during the First

World War and the experiences of minority communities in Britain in the early twentieth century.

Gavin Wiens is a doctoral candidate in the Department of History at the University of Toronto. His research examines the presence of dual loyalties among German soldiers between the mid-nineteenth century and the end of the First World War and stresses the importance of viewing the Kaiser's army as a decentralized and diverse institution in which ethnic and religious minorities and state-based groups retained distinct identities that frequently aroused the concern of the military authorities in Berlin. His other research interests include war and society since the eighteenth century and the relationship between Europe's monarchs and military power.

Vanda Wilcox completed a D.Phil. at the University of Oxford in 2006 and now teaches modern European history at John Cabot University and Trinity College, Rome Campus. Her publications include her first book, *Morale and the Italian Army During the First World War*, and *Italy in the Era of the Great War*, an edited volume published in 2018. She has also published articles and book chapters on various aspects of the First World War era in Italy, including soldiers' emotions, the construction of national identity in wartime, the Italian invasion of Libya and post-war memory and commemoration.

Esther Yankelevitch received her Ph.D. in 2004 from the University of Haifa, Israel, where she is now a lecturer and a research associate in the Israel Studies Department. Her research focuses on Jewish settlement in the Galilee and Tiberias during the late Ottoman and Mandate periods and on Agricultural Education. Her publications include her first book: *"Goodbye Mr. Fiat": Nathan Fiat and the Kadoorie Mount Tabor Agricultural School 1937–1959*, which was published in 2013.

Emma Zohar is Lecturer at the Holocaust Studies Programme at Western Galilee College, Akko, Israel. She is a graduate of the University of Haifa and a Ph.D. candidate at the Avraham Harman Institute of Contemporary Jewry at the Hebrew University of Jerusalem. Her doctoral thesis focuses on young Jewish activists in inter-war Poland, and her broader research interests include education, culture, and the everyday life of Polish Jewry between the world wars. From 2015 to 2016, she was a visiting research fellow at the Centre for German-Jewish Studies at the University of Sussex.

LIST OF FIGURES

**'Thou Hast Given Us Home and Freedom, Mother England':
Anglo-Jewish Gratitude, Patriotism, and Service During and After
the First World War**

LIST OF TABLES

The First World War and the Jews

Gideon Reuveni and Edward Madigan

The people of the states that mobilized in the summer of 1914 were not quite as naïve or enthusiastic about the prospect of war as either contemporary accounts or later historiography would have us believe.[1] Indeed, over the previous decade or so, a small number of recognized experts on modern warfare, including the Polish-Jewish banker Jan Bloch and the French strategist Jean Colin, had foreseen the military

---

[1] For analyses of the myth of widespread war enthusiasm, see Gerhard Hirschfeld (2011), "The Spirit of 1914': A Critical Examination of War Enthusiasm in German Society', in Lothar Kettenacker and Torsten Riotte, eds. *The Legacies of Two World Wars: European Societies in the Twentieth Century* (New York, Berghahn), 29–40; David Silbey (2004), *The British Working Class and Enthusiasm for War* (Abingdon, Frank Cass) 1–15; and Jay Winter (1992), Nationalism, the Visual Arts and the Myth or War Enthusiasm in 1914, *History of European Ideas* 15:1–3, 57–62.

G. Reuveni
Department of History, University of Sussex, Falmer, UK
e-mail: G.Reuveni@sussex.ac.uk

E. Madigan (✉)
Department of History, Royal Holloway, University of London, Egham, UK
e-mail: Edward.Madigan@rhul.ac.uk

dynamics of the conflict with remarkable prescience.[2] Amid the popular roar of patriotic fervour that greeted the outbreak of war, there were also many who understood that a major conflict between industrialized powers would undoubtedly lead to suffering and destruction on a grand scale.[3] Yet the brutally harsh experience of the war, and the extraordinary impact it had on world affairs, still seemed to confound all expectations.[4] For who, in the years of antebellum peace, could have anticipated the historically unparalleled upheaval of the 'war to end all wars'? At the level of the state, the global conflagration would ultimately lead to the collapse of no fewer than four dynastic empires that had ruled much of Europe and the Middle East for centuries and ensure the long-term destabilization of international relations. In societal terms, the war brought about widespread social dislocation and economic ruin, while the male populations of the belligerent states were profoundly impacted by the loss over ten million combatants in the fighting and the physical and psychological trauma of millions more. Away from the battlefront, the conflict also gave rise to unprecedented civilian encounters with violence, hunger, disease, and bereavement. Thus, although the First World War did not mark a complete rupture in European or world history, its impact on the belligerent states and the communities of which those states were composed was nothing short of cataclysmic. The essays gathered together in this volume seek simply to explore the diverse ways in which Jewish communities experienced this cataclysm.

---

[2] Paul Reynolds (2013), 'The Man Who Predicted the Great War', *History Today*, 63:5. On Bloch's relationship with, and influence on, the staff officers of the British army, see especially Michael Welch (2001), 'The Centenary of the British Publication of Jean de Bloch's Is War Now Impossible? (1899–1999)', *War in History*, 7:3, 273–294. Jean Colin's *Les Transformations de la Guerre* was first published in 1911 and translated into English the following year, see Edward Madigan (2013), "Sticking to a Hateful Task': Resilience, Humour, and British Understandings of Combatant Courage, 1914–1918', *War in History*, 20:1, 84–86.

[3] On the complexity of popular responses to the outbreak of war in Britain, Germany, and France; see Catriona Pennell (2012), *A Kingdom United: Popular Responses to the Outbreak of the First World War in Britain and Ireland* (Oxford, Oxford University Press); Jeffrey Verhey (2000), *The Spirit of 1914: Militarism, Myth and Mobilization in Germany* (Cambridge, Cambridge University Press); and Patrick J. Flood (1990), *France 1914–1918: Public Opinion and the War Effort* (Basingstoke, Palgrave), 43–56.

[4] Dan Todman (2005), *The Great War: Myth and Memory* (London, Hambledon), 7.

With the advent of war in 1914, Jews in Europe and across the wider world were forced to support, or at least acquiesce in, the national war efforts of their respective homelands. Expressing this support often meant overlooking or renouncing long-standing relationships with their co-religionists in 'enemy' states and publicly standing with majority populations that had traditionally treated them with indifference or contempt. And yet many Jewish clergymen, journalists, and other commentators used their public platforms to rally support for the war, and millions of Jewish men enlisted in the armies of the various empires that entered the fray on both sides. Although most Jewish men of military age had little choice over whether they served or not, the pro-war statements and activity of Jewish civilians were much more voluntary and often inspired both by genuine patriotic conviction and an acute sense of their vulnerability as members of a minority in the ultra-nationalistic climate of the war years. One of the most striking and well-known examples of Jewish war fervour from the early months of the conflict is the famous, or infamous, German *Hymn of Hate*, the closing lines of which read as follows:

> French and Russian, they matter not,
> A blow for a blow, a shot for a shot,
> We fight the battle with bronze and steel,
> And the time that is coming Peace will seal.
> You we will hate with a lasting hate,
> We will never forego our hate,
> Hate by water and hate by land,
> Hate of the head and hate of the hand,
> Hate of the hammer and hate of the crown,
> Hate of seventy millions choking down.
> We love as one, we hate as one,
> We have one foe and one alone –
> ENGLAND!

The song was written by Ernst Lissauer, who also coined the slogan *Gott strafe England* (God punish England), which became a semi-official German *Schlachtruf* (battle cry) during the war years.[5] Lissauer was a

[5] For more on Lissauer, see Guide to the Papers of Ernst Lissauer (1882–1937), 1722–1967 AR 25209/MF 700 evadible online in the Leo Baeck Institute archive http://findingaids.cjh.org/?pID=121527#secIII-6-B.

playwright, poet, and journalist, regarded by his contemporaries as 'the most German of all Jewish poets'. An informative account of the composition of the *Hymn* can be found in Stefan Zweig's memoir, *The World of Yesterday*, in which the author depicts Lissauer as a warm-hearted, honest man for whom Germany was the entire world. When the war broke out, Lissauer's first act was to hurry to the local barracks to enlist. 'I can well imagine the laughter of the sergeants and corporals', Zweig writes, 'when this fat boy came puffing up the stairs'.[6] Lissauer was promptly rejected as unfit for military service. This plunged him into despair but made him determined that since he could not serve his country with his body he would serve Germany with his talent. As Zweig goes on to explain, 'everything that the newspapers and the German army published was gospel truth for Lissauer. His country had been attacked, and the worst criminal was that perfidious Sir Edward Grey, the British Foreign Minster'.[7] This feeling, that England was Germany's arch enemy, and responsible for the war, ultimately found very direct and public expression in Lissauer's *Hymn of Hate*. As James Gerard, the American ambassador in Berlin during the war, observed, everyone was familiar with the *Hymn*. It was not extraordinary that one man in a country at war should produce a composition of this kind, Gerard noted in his memoir, but 'it is extraordinary as showing the state of mind of the whole country, that the Kaiser should have given him the high order of the Red Eagle as a reward for having composed this extraordinary document'.[8]

The German-Jewish community celebrated Lissauer as 'one of our own' and he became a national hero overnight. Although it would come to be quite widely criticised and derided in Germany as well as in Britain, the *Hymn of Hate Against England* nonetheless expressed the desire of German Jews to prove their loyalty and love for Germany in 1914 through deep abhorrence for the enemy. Two days after the outbreak of the war, the Central Association of German Citizens of Jewish Faith declared in the Jewish and national press 'that every German Jew is ready to sacrifice property and blood as duty demands'.[9] The German branch of the World Zionist Organization

---

[6] Stefan Zweig (1943), *The World of Yesterday: An Autobiography* (London, Cassel and Company), 179.

[7] Ibid., 180.

[8] James Gerard (1917), *My Four Years in Germany* (New York, Grossert & Dunlap), 224.

[9] *Im Deutschen Reich* (September 1914), 339.

followed, printing its own powerful call to arms in its weekly newspaper, *Jüdische Rundschau*. 'German Jews!', the announcement said, 'In the spirit of the old Jewish commandments, we call on you, with all your heart, and all your soul and with all your assets to give yourself to serve the Fatherland'.[10] The renowned philosopher Hermann Cohen even assigned a distinctively German-Jewish meaning to the war. Writing in 1915 he proclaimed, 'so we as Jews, too, are proud to be Germans in this epic era, in which the fate of nations is at stake, for we have become aware of the task that should convince all our fellow Jews throughout the world of the religious significance of Germanness, of its impact, of the legal claims that it exerts on Jews among all the nations of the world, both for their religious development and for all their cultural activity'.[11] Along similar lines, the thirty-six-year-old Zionist thinker Martin Buber interpreted the war in terms of 'cultural redemption', hoping that it would unite Germans and Jews around a common historical mission of bringing culture to the Middle East.[12]

This type of almost unconditional surrender to the national war effort, and a sense of the civilizing mission that accompanied it, was by no means limited to Jews living in Germany. On the other side of the conflict, in England, Jewish community leaders and intellectuals took a similar stance, emphasizing unequivocal Jewish loyalty to the state and casting the war as a great clash of civilizations. 'England has been all she could be to Jews, the Jews will be all they can be to England' proclaimed the *Jewish Chronicle*.[13] For Leopold Greenberg, the editor who wrote these words, and Anglo-Jewish writers and intellectuals such as Israel Zangwill and Lucien Wolf, Jewish interests were unquestionably at stake in the global conflict. In an address entitled *Jewish Ideals and the War*, delivered and published in December 1914, Wolf depicted the war as 'a war of ethical opinion'. The German people, he observed, 'have become saturated with a philosophy which has sought to rationalize and

[10] *Jüdische Rundschau: Allgemeine jüdische Zeitung* (7 August 1914), 333.

[11] Herman Cohen (1915), *Deutschtum und Judentum, mit grundlegenden betrachtungen über staat und internationalismus* (Gießen, Verlag von Alfred Töpelamann), 37.

[12] Ulrich Sieg (2002), *Jüdische Intellektuelle im Ersten Weltkrieg: Kriegserfahrungen, weltanschauliche Debatten und kulturelle Neuentwürfe* (Berlin, Akademia Verlag). For further examples see: *Rolf Vogel (1914), Ein Stück von uns: deutsche Juden in deutschen Armeen 1813–1976; eine Dokumentation (Mainz, Hase und Koehler).

[13] The *Jewish Chronicle*, 7 August 1914, 5.

justify their domination instinct and ambitions ... this teaching is the absolute negation of all that modern [British] political philosophers [...] have taught [and] it is not less diametrically opposed to Jewish thought, instinct and ideals'.[14] He, therefore, called upon all British Jews to rally behind the war effort 'until the power of what is called German militarism is crushed'.[15] Only then, Wolf asserted, could Jews across Europe be sure that their political, civil, and religious rights were safeguarded. Importantly, however, Jewish intellectuals in the Central Powers, such as Herman Cohen and Martin Buber, also interpreted the global conflict as a 'Jewish war'. Indeed, even in the United States, which would remain ostensibly neutral until April 1917, the war was seen by some in the Jewish community as a moment in which Jewish patriotism should be confidently asserted.

Yet by no means all Jewish commentators shared this sense of dramatic purpose and patriotic optimism with regard to the war, and as the conflict progressed, dissenting voices became more prevalent. The German-Jewish writer, Samy Gronemann, for one, viewed Lissauer's *Hymn of Hate* as 'patriotic kitsch of the most evil kind'.[16] The Galician journalist and ethnologist Binjamin Segel reproached his co-religionist, the French philosopher Henri Bergson, in a similar vein. In the annual meeting of the French *Académie des Sciences Morales et Politiques* in December 1914, Bergson claimed that Europe had been plunged into war by a brutal and mechanistic German spirit with no greater motivation than pure materialistic gain.[17] This statement, Segel noted, was 'particularly painful', not only because it undermined Bergson's standing as a serious philosopher who was well respected by his German colleagues,

---

[14] Lucian Wolf (1915), *Jewish Ideals and the War: An Address Delivered by Lucien Wolf on 7 December 1914* (London, Central Committee for National Patriotic Organizations).

[15] Ibid.

[16] See in Joachim Utz (1990), 'Der Erste Weltkrieg im Spiegel des deutschen und englischen Haßgedichts', in Jan Assmann and Dietrich Harth, eds. *Kultur und Konflikt* (Frankfurt am Main, Suhrkamp Verlag), 373. Gronemann also write about Lissauer in chapter XIX of his memoirs: Sammy Gronemann (2014), *Erinnerung an meine Jahre in Berlin* (Hamburg, Eropäische Verlaganstalt). More broadly on the topic see in Christoph Jahr (1994), 'Das Krämervolk der eitlen Briten: Das deutsche Englandbild im Ersten Weltkrieg', in Christoph Jahr, Uwe Mai, and Kathrin Roller, eds. *Feindbilder in der deutschen Geschichte. Studien zur Vorurteilsgeschichte im 19 und 20 Jahrhundert* (Berlin, Metropol-Verlag), 115.

[17] Henri Bergson (1920), *The Meaning of the War* (London, T. Fisher Unwin Ltd).

but because he was a Jew. For Segel, Bergson's address was nothing more than a distorted expression of patriotic feeling, which did not contain 'as much as a spark of Jewish sentiment'.[18]

To be sure, the manner in which the Great War pitted Jews on either side of the front-lines against each other was regarded by many contemporaries as a profound tragedy. As early as November 1914, the Jewish-American poet Florence Kiper Frank published her well-known poem *The Jewish Conscript*, which opens with the lines:

> They have dressed me up in a soldier's dress,
> With a rifle in my hand,
> And have sent me bravely forth to shoot
> My own in a foreign land.[19]

As combatants in the armed forces of all of the mobilized belligerents, Jews often struggled to reconcile divided loyalties and, in some cases, had to defend themselves against the states for which they fought. In the Eastern and Middle-Eastern theatres, in particular, where millions of Jews lived under German, Russian, and Ottoman occupation, Jewish communities often bore a terrible and disproportionate share of the human suffering wrought by the war. In the words of a 1916 report produced by the *American Jewish Committee* on the condition of Jews in the Eastern war zones: 'of all the people that have suffered deeply from the present war, none have borne a greater burden than the Jews—in physical and economic loss, in moral and spiritual torment'.[20] The text of the report also contains an interesting section on the wartime plight of Jews living under Ottoman rule, a topic that Esther Yankelevitch explores in this volume. At the heart of her chapter is the story of the expulsion of the Jews of Jaffa and Tel-Aviv to more remote settlements, such as Tiberias, Saffed, and Damascus in the spring

---

[18] Benjamin Segel (1920), *Der Weltkrieg und das Schicksal der Juden: Stimme eines galizischen Juden* and seine Glaubensgenossen in der neutralen Länder insbesondere in Amerika (Berlin, Stilke Verlag), 143.

[19] Florence Kiper Frank (1914), 'The Jewish Conscript', *Poetry Magazine of Verse*, 66.

[20] American Jewish Committee (1916), *The Jews in the Eastern War Zone* (New York, American Jewish Committee), 7. The American Jewish Committee was founded in 1906 to address the need to defend Jewish civil rights in the United States and throughout the world. It should be added that the report also deals with the situation of Jews in Palestine under Ottoman rule.

of 1917. Yankelevitch analyses the work of the Galilee migration committee that operated in the region during the war, aiding an exiled population in acute crisis and ultimately alleviating their hardships.

The war years were a period of quite profound social dislocation for civilians living in or near the zones of conflict and the Jewish communities in the Middle East were certainly impacted by the military fortunes of the Ottoman and British forces. One contemporary rabbi even referred to the war as a 'Third Exile', noting that the Turks declared war on the 9th of the Hebrew month Av 'the saddest and darkest day in Israel's history', the anniversary of the destruction of the Temple.[21] Indeed, according to this particular account, the destruction wrought by the Great War was even more calamitous for the Jews than the first and second captivities. This sense of the horribly unprecedented nature of the war was quite common among contemporaries who felt they were witnessing the overturning of all norms and conventions.

Yet although the conflict clearly had a major impact on Jewish communities across the globe, we still know relatively little about these experiences and the ways in which they shaped Jewish lives in the twentieth century. The dearth of historiographical interest in the Jewish experience of the First World War becomes all the more apparent when compared with the relative wealth of research concerning Jewish life, and the destruction of Jewish life, in the 1930s and over the course of the Second World War. As the chapters in this volume should demonstrate, however, investigations of Jewish encounters with diverse wartime phenomena, such as mass mobilization, profound social dislocation, enforced exile, and the performance of patriotic loyalty both offer us insights into the impact of the First World War and enhance our understanding of the Jewish experience of the twentieth century. Given that the Second World War started with a similar division of Eastern Europe between Germany and what was then the Soviet Union, for example, an exploration of the impact of German occupation during the First World War becomes even more intriguing.[22] As we learn from Philipp Nielsen's

---

[21] Sabeti B. Rohold (1915), *The War and the Jews: Bird's Eye View of The World's Situation and The Jews Place in It* (Toronto, The Macmillan Company of Canada), 11.

[22] This connection was not lost on contemporaries in the 1940s. See, for example, Eliezer Kalier's (1943) detailed account of the German occupation of his home town in Poland with the telling title: *The Fathers of the Nazis. Memoirs of the German occupation in Poland during the First World War* [in Hebrew] (Tel Aviv, Achdot Publishing), or the pamphlet of the Research Institute on Peace and Post-War Problems of the American Jewish

chapter here, the German military authorities regarded the Jews as natural allies in the struggle for *Kultur* against *Gesellschaft* in their wartime vision for the East. Taking the 'gifts' of liberation and emancipation offered by the German government as a starting point, Nielsen shows how, at least initially, occupied Eastern Europe appeared as a sort of promised land to Jews in Germany and Central Europe.

The centenaries of the conflict seem to have had a positive impact on the historiographical record and the field is now slowly changing, but until very recently research into the Jewish experiences of the 'war to end all wars' was scarce and carried out on the margins of both Jewish and First World War studies.[23] For obvious reasons, Jewish historiography of the twentieth century had traditionally been much more preoccupied with the Second World War than with the earlier global conflict. This proactivity created an interesting discrepancy between what seems to be prevailing view among 'general' historians, who commonly regard the First World War as a turning point in modern history marking the birth of the twentieth century, and Jewish scholars, who read modern Jewish history in terms of 'before and after' the Holocaust. By advancing our understanding of the highly diverse Jewish experience of the First World War—be it through the travails of Jewish soldiers, Jewish mothers, or rabbis in different national and imperial settings—this volume

Committee (1942) entitled *The Two World Wars – A Comparison and Contrast, Jewish Post-War Problems: A Study Course* (New York, Research Institute on Peace and Post-War Problems).

[23] Since 2014 there has been a growing number of publications on Jewish engagement with the war. The most prominent English-language collections are Petra Ernst, Jeffrey Grossman, and Ulrich Wyrwa. eds. (2016), *The Great War. Reflections, Experiences and Memories of German and Habsburg Jews (1914–1918)* a special issue of the online journal *Quest. Issues in Contemporary Jewish History* available at http://www.quest-cdecjournal. it/index.php?issue=9; and Marsha L. Rozenblit and Jonathan Karp. eds. (2017), *World War I and the Jews: Conflict and Transformation in Europe, the Middle East, and America* (New York, Berghahn Books). Both of these publications should be regarded as pioneering texts. Beyond the very useful introduction to *World War I and the Jews* by Rozenblit and Karp, the first three articles of this collection by Marsha Rozenblit, David Engel and Carole Fink provide stimulating overviews of the main topics at hand, along with very informative bibliographical references. A forthcoming volume, which we did not have the opportunity to review while preparing this book for publication is: Jason Crouthamel, Michael Geheran, Tim Grady, and Julia Barbara Köhne, eds. *Beyond Inclusion and Exclusion: Jewish Experiences of the First World War in Central Europe* (New York, Berghahn books).

calls for a reappraisal of the place and significance of this seminal conflict in modern Jewish history. Thus, for example, Emma Zohar, in her chapter, examines the transformations experienced by Jewish communities in Poland during the war years and argues that the German occupation triggered a fairly radical political liberalization among Polish Jews, which arguably laid the ground for the 'golden years' of Jewish culture and education in the interwar period. Her research clearly reveals the degree to which the war influenced civilian mentalities, but the impact of the conflict was arguably most visceral in the hearts and minds of the servicemen who had been 'at the sharp end' of combat. Studying the engagement of the Russian-Jewish community of London's East End with military service in the so-called Jewish Battalion, Christopher Smith demonstrates how this specially formed unit helped to shape British-Jewish identities. According to Smith, service in the Jewish Battalion proved to be a powerful source of civic pride for London's Russian Jews, inculcating them with a sense of shared struggle alongside wider society, and thus becoming a baptism of fire for a formerly very inward-looking community.

Perhaps one of the more compelling findings that emerges when the Great War is approached as a Jewish event is the way Jewish individuals, families, and communities struggled to reconcile divided loyalties, and a number of chapters in this volume specifically address this question. Gavin Wiens discusses the infamous *Judenzählung*, conducted in the autumn of 1916. Commissioned by the German military High Command in October 1916, this census of Jewish military service was designed to address accusations of a lack of patriotism among German Jews. While the census disproved the charges, its results were not made public, thus fueling rather than allaying anti-Jewish sentiment in Germany. In the existing historiography, the *Judenzählung* is frequently depicted as a turning point in German-Jewish relations. Questioning this interpretation, Wiens notes that if one considers the *Judenzählung* in isolation and with the benefit of hindsight and knowledge of the crimes of the National Socialist regime, this is certainly true. In his view, however, the *Judenzählung* should be seen as one of many measures introduced in the second half of the war in response to concerns about the cohesion of the German army. Interestingly, this approach not only demonstrates the preoccupation with the question of dual loyalties following the outbreak of war in 1914, but also reveals that by the end of the war the German army had learned to disaggregate the soldiers under their command into two groups, one 'reliable', the other not, with Jews belonging to the latter group.

Moving from the perspective of the state to that of the Jews themselves, Sarah Panter explores the degree to which the war forced Jewish communities and individuals to carefully balance their sense of civic loyalty with transnational bonds of Jewish identity and solidarity. In common with Wiens, Panter contends that, during the war, 'inclusion' and 'exclusion' were marked by ambiguity and suggests that we should thus avoid oversimplified generalizations. According to Panter, though, this ambiguity gave rise to what she calls the 'ethnicisation of citizenship', a process that strengthened Jewish identity without necessarily undermining the Jewish sense of belonging to the countries they fought for. Taking the experiences of Jewish soldiers on both sides of the Atlantic into account, she observes that after returning home from the war, many Jewish soldiers became active in Jewish communal life and in veterans' organizations. Such activism, Panter argues, promoted an image of Jewish soldiers as manly heroes and patriots. Exploring the service of Jews in the Italian armed forces, Vanda Wilcox reveals the ways in which this experience reflected the divisions within the Italian-Jewish community between an 'assimilationist' majority on the one hand and a youthful revivalism which was leaning towards Zionism on the other. Notwithstanding these differences, from May 1915 both sides committed themselves energetically to patriotic war service. According to Wilcox, the experience of military service in wartime created a Jewish sense of belonging that was fully compatible with Italian patriotism, validating a patriotic understanding of self and community that was rooted in emancipation. As Edward Madigan explains in his chapter on Anglo-Jewish responses to the war, this type of loyalty was deeply embedded in feelings of gratitude for perceived fair treatment at the hands of state and society in the decades before 1914. Madigan explores the Anglo-Jewish framing of patriotic obligation in reciprocal terms and highlights the degree to which military service, in particular, was depicted as the repayment of a debt to a country that had traditionally treated Jews well. Thus, the war record of Jewish servicemen, and the Anglo-Jewish war dead in particular, came to be presented as irrefutable proof of patriotic commitment in the face of a marked wartime and post-war rise in antisemitic sentiment in Britain.

To be sure, the question of Jewish loyalty did not originate during the First World War. The conflict simply intensified and made more tangible an issue that had a long and illustrious history, compelling both Jews and non-Jews to consider the notion of Jewish belonging. Not only were Jews forced to fight other Jews, the war also challenged the concept of the so-called 'hyphenated Jew'; the idea that one could be Jewish and yet something else. In so doing, the war called the very notion of what it means to be a Jew in the modern world into question. As a result, many Jewish men and women, in Europe, in the Middle East, and across the Atlantic, felt that they were forced into a kind of a twilight zone of identity and were left with an empty sense of being somehow different from their compatriots but not quite in unison with their co-religionists.[24] At the same time, and for a brief moment in Jewish history, the Great War created a new Jewish world full of opportunities, offering different, sometimes opposing versions of how to be Jewish in both the old and the emerging centres of Jewish life across the globe. The United States became a new powerful hub of Jewish life, while the Soviet Union and the emerging Jewish settlements in Palestine revealed themselves as further promised lands for the struggling Jewish masses in Central and Eastern Europe.[25] This development did not escape the keen eyes of contemporary Jewish observers. As Björn Siegel notes, for example, the influential national Jewish aid organization *Israelitische Allianz zu Wien* welcomed the outbreak of the war as a great opportunity to finally end Jewish persecution and oppression in Eastern Europe and promote emancipation. As Siegel argues, however, the war would ultimately force the *Allianz* to forgo its initial *mission civilisatrice* of international humanitarianism and adjust its work according to the demands of the war effort, and, mainly, to the Austrian national interest.

Looking ahead to the post-war period, the Viennese journal *Jüdische Kriegsarchiv*, which had been founded in 1915 as a forum to discuss Jewish war matters, proclaimed in its first issue that the war would generate 'new possibilities for free development [for Jews], while new dangers will arise'.[26] In order to take advantage of the former, and to avoid the latter, the *Jüdische Kriegsarchiv* contended that it was absolutely

---

[24] Hannah Arendt (1946), 'Privileged Jews', *Jewish Social Studies* 8, 30.

[25] Yuri Slezkine (2004), *The Jewish Century* (Princeton, Princeton University Press).

[26] No Author mentioned, 'An die Leser!' *Jüdisches Archiv Mitteilungen Des Komitees Jüdisches Kriegsarchiv* 1 (1915), 1. See also Max Gottschalk, ed. (1942), *How The Jewish Communities Prepared for Peace During the First World War* (New York, Research Institute on Peace and Post-War Problems).

necessary to acquire precise information about the situation of Jews during the war, based on which Jewish individuals and communities were
supposed to prepare and conduct themselves in the post-war period.
Creating this body of knowledge was one of the main aims of this periodical. It is, however, doubtful if the writer of these lines could have
genuinely imagined the new world that would ultimately emerge out of
the ruins of the war, the chaotic reality of which confounded most pre-
dictions made in the first year of the conflict.

Several chapters in this volume deal with the turbulent post-war years.
Tim Corbett, Ruth Nattermann, and Michal Friedlander each explore
different aspects of Jewish memory and commemoration both during
and after the war. According to Corbett, attempts to create a coherent Austrian nation in the post-war years were closely interlinked with
the commemoration of the war. His chapter demonstrates that while
there were many similarities between the ways Jews and other Austrians
commemorated the conflict, Jewish memorialization was removed
from the public eye and discursively marginalized, nurturing the view
of Jewishness and Austrianness as mutually opposing concepts. Ruth
Nattermann's chapter sheds valuable light on what she calls 'The Female
Side of War'. Focusing on Italian-Jewish women's experience and memory of the conflict, she ultimately argues that the experience of antisemitism during the Fascist period led to a delusive memorialization of the
Great War as an era of complete national unity. Michal Friedlander examines various German-Jewish objects of remembrance, with a particular
focus on commemorative plaques and 'nailed' emblems, that highlighted
Jewish service and sacrifice during the war years. The making of such
memorial objects, she contends, was motivated by an unbridled sense of
commitment to the German state. Yet, as objects of ritual mourning for
Jewish communities and bereaved individuals, they also served as mirrors
in which communities could reflect, within the apparent safety of their
own walls, on their self-image as German-Jewish patriots.

The twenty years between the end of the Great War and the beginning of the Second World War comprise one of the most fascinating and
dramatic periods in Jewish history. Seen from the post-Holocaust perspective, the interwar years appear as a brief, well-defined era between
the seemingly 'golden age of security'[27] that ended with the First World

---

[27] Zweig (1943), *The World of Yesterday*, Chapter 1.

War and a new beginning after the terror wrought by the rise of Nazism and the final solution. Moreover, while after the Second World War it seemed that there was no future for Jewish life in Europe, we now know that this is far from being the case. Despite recent troubling events in some European countries, as a whole Jewish life in Europe is thriving. Thus, without in any sense undermining the significance of the Holocaust, it appears that the Jewish world of today is, to a large extent, a product of the First World War.

As an 'in-between period', the interwar years were a time in which all forms of Jewish life coexisted. For the first time in Jewish history, substantial numbers of Jews resided in the new and the old worlds. The rapidly growing Jewish settlement in what Theodor Herzl, founder of political Zionism, called the *Altneuland* (Old-New land), made the idea of a Jewish national homeland in Palestine an attractive prospect for many Jews. And there can be no denying that the First World War was something of watershed moment in the history of Zionism.[28] Notwithstanding its initial leanings towards the Central Powers, shortly after the beginning of the war, the Zionist movement was quick to change its orientation to support the Triple Entente, a move that was rewarded with the British promise for a Jewish homeland in Palestine in 1917. As Anat Kidron demonstrates in her chapter, the crisis brought about by the advent of war was used by the Zionist movement as an effective means through which to attract international support for the idea of a Jewish state in Palestine. Kidron further argues that the distinction between an old (non-Zionist) and a new (Zionist) settlement in Palestine was used to promote the image of Zionism as a progressive movement that would help to modernize the Middle East, consolidating its dominance in Palestine as the sole representative of the Jews living in this region.

In this regard, the war prompted the creation of a novel situation in Jewish history in which Jewish life was divided, for the first time, between three major centres, one in Europe, another in America, and the third in an evolving Jewish polity in the Holy Land. While the rise of Zionism and a flourishing Jewish Palestine strengthened a new Jewish identity across Europe and the United States, it did not diminish other national affiliations and the feelings of belonging of many Jews to the countries in which they were born and came of age. The First World

---

[28] Michael Berkowitz (1997), *Western Jewry and the Zionist Project, 1914-1933* (Cambridge, Cambridge University Press).

War was thus a crucial moment for the preservation, reconstruction, and recreation of modern Jewish identities, the legacies of which continue into our own time.

All of the Jewish political, cultural, and religious movements that were active in the years between the wars sought to offer different answers and ways of coping with the changing realities of the time. The interwar period, of course, witnessed the emergence of radically new ideologies and forms of government; communism and fascism prevailed, and new nation-states emerged while old empires were declining and new ones were forming. As such, it was a period in which Jews experienced modernity in all its dizzying forms and manifestations; a time of new hopes and utopian fantasies, but also a period of despair and extraordinary hardship as the economic situation deteriorated and Jewish exclusion intensified, culminating in the disaster we now call the Holocaust. Indeed, for Jews, the period between the two world wars was truly an age of extremes.

The essays collected in this volume explore the variety of social and political phenomena that combined to the make the First World War a key turning point in the Jewish experience of the twentieth century. For many Jewish contemporaries, the significance of the Great War was evident and from its outset, the war was seen as a watershed in Jewish history. Indeed, in 1915, the Viennese *Jüdisches Kriegsarchiv* depicted the world war as a landmark in the development of mankind that would reshuffle Jewish destiny.[29] In a similar vein, the Hebrew language daily newspaper *Hatzfira*, published in Warsaw, announced in 1917: 'the Great Commonwealth War that confused the world had put the Jewish world under one star. From the time the Hebrew people went into exile there was no one single historical event, which could include and encompass the entire Jewish people in all places of dispersion, as this global war did'.[30] Indeed, later scholars, such as Hannah Arendt, noted that even before totalitarian politics consciously destroyed the very structure of European civilisation, 'the explosion of 1914 and its severe consequences of instability had sufficiently shattered the façade of Europe's political system to lay bare its hidden frame'.[31] This cataclysm, according to Arendt, would have grave consequences for the Jewish minority.

---

[29] 'An die Leser!', 1.

[30] No author given, 'Historical position', *Hatzfira* (26 March 1917), 1.

[31] Hannah Arendt (1973), *The Origins of Totalitarianism* (San Diego, A. Harvest), 267.

Much of this may seem obvious to some readers, but until recently scholars had done relatively little to address the multifaceted dimensions of the Jewish experience of the Great War.[32] The thirteen chapters collected in this volume seek to make a small but meaningful contribution in this direction. They do not constitute a master narrative but instead offer a range of perspectives on a highly significant moment in modern Jewish history. It is our hope that this book will open up new avenues of research and prompt scholars from different disciplines to further explore this transformative chapter of the Jewish past, so that the Jewish experience of the First World War will receive due recognition, both in the history of war and in the history of the Jewish people.

[32] See footnote 22 for some very recent publications on the topic.

PART I

Eastern Fronts

Between Light and Darkness: Jewish Education in Time of War

Björn Siegel

During a ceremony commemorating Jewish war service held in November 1866, just months after the end of the Austro-Prussian War, Adolf Jellinek, chief rabbi of the Viennese-Jewish community, praised the loyalty of the Austrian soldiers to the Habsburg dynasty and appealed for continued Jewish loyalty to the Crown in order to preserve the internal strength of the Empire.[1] On the battlefields, he claimed, the Austrian soul had emerged and triumphed beyond national and religious boundaries.[2] Even though Austria had lost the war, he saw a splendid future for the Austrian-Hungarian Empire under Franz Joseph I and under

---

[1] Adolf Jellinek (1867), *Gedächtnisrede auf die im letzten Kriege gefallenen Soldaten israelitischer Religion am 15. November 1866 geahlten* (Wien), 6. For the role of Jewish soldiers in the war 1866, see István Deák (1990), *Beyond Nationalism: A Social and Political History of the Habsburg Officer Corps 1848–1918* (New York, Oxford University Press), 50–55, 172–173.

[2] [..., aber im Kampfgewühle schlägt nur das Herz des Österreichers; ...] Jellinek (1867), *Gedächtnisrede*, 6–7.

B. Siegel (✉)
Institute for the History of the German Jews, Hamburg, Germany
e-mail: bjoernsiegel@gmx.de

© The Author(s) 2019
E. Madigan and G. Reuveni (eds.),
The Jewish Experience of the First World War,
https://doi.org/10.1057/978-1-137-54896-2_2

the slogan 'united, peaceful and fraternal'.[3] Almost fifty years later, Austro-Hungarian Jewry would again be confronted with the outbreak of a war and questions of loyalty, patriotism and participation. In 1914 Austro-Hungarian Jews once again enthusiastically endorsed the imperial declaration of war, this time against Serbia, and supported their 'deified Monarch to protect and defend the honour of the fatherland'[4] as the popular weekly paper the *Oesterreichische Wochenschrift* declared. Across the internal religious divide, and despite their diverse political convictions, Jews of the Danubian Monarchy demonstrated their devotedness to the throne and dynasty.[5] In its annual report of April 1914, the *Israelitische Allianz zu Wien* (IAzW), an influential national Jewish aid organization founded in 1872–1873, had described the ongoing pogroms in the Russian Empire, the ritual murder trial against Menahem Mendel Beilis in Kiev and growing antisemitism and persecution in the 'East' at the beginning of the year. The paper thus welcomed the outbreak of the war as a great opportunity to finally end Jewish persecution and oppression in Eastern Europe.[6] Despite its international organizational structure and transnational collaborations and contributors, the Vienna *Allianz* adhered to the idea of Jewish loyalty to throne and Empire and openly declared its dedication to the Austrian fatherland. This chapter examines the role of the *Allianz* (or IAzW) in the Austro-Hungarian Empire during the war years and explores the organization's ambivalent position between internationalism and nationalism.

---

[3] [... einig, friedlich, brüderlich ...'] Jellinek (1867), *Gedächtnisrede*, 8–9.

[4] Anonymus (1914), 'Der Kaiser ruft!' *Dr. Bloch's Oesterreichische Wochenschrift*, 31:3, 529.

[5] For a selection, see Anonymous (1914), 'Der Tod des Thronfolgerpaares', *Jüdische Zeitung: National-Jüdisches Organ*, 8:27, 1; Anonymous (1914), 'Der Krieg', *Neue National-Zeitung*, 16:15, 113; and Anonyous (1914), 'Aus der Woche', *Die Wahrheit: Unabhängige Zeitschrift für Jüdische Interessen*, 29, 3–5.

[6] Israelitische Allianz zu Wien (1914), *XLI. Jahresbericht der Israelitischen Allianz zu Wien erstattet an die XLI. ordentliche Generalversammlung am 20 April 1914* (Wien), 6–15. For a general overview of the history of the Vienna Allianz, see Björn Siegel (2010), *Österreichisches Judentum zwischen Ost und West: Die Israelitische Allianz zu Wien 1873–1938* (Frankfurt am Main, Campus Verlag).

War Alliances and the New 'Enemies'

With the outbreak of the Great War in the summer of 1914 many Jewish organizations were confronted with the challenge of rising nationalism. The majority of Jews across Europe tended to support the national causes of their home countries and many ostensibly international Jewish organizations were forced to adjust to these new circumstances. Jewish aid organizations which had worked on a transnational level for decades found these changes particularly challenging. The Vienna *Allianz*, which was founded along the lines of the ideas of the French *Alliance Israélite Universelle* (AIU) and had established well-organized links with other international Jewish institutions, provides a good example of an organization torn between national and international interests.

In the decades before 1914, influential members of the Jewish community of Vienna, including Adolf Jellinek and the former president of the Jewish community, Joseph Ritter von Wertheimer, had become strong supporters of certain progressive ideas that had originally been formulated in Paris. In 1860, the newly established French AIU had openly declared that it would fight for Jewish emancipation and integration across the globe based on the universal ideas of equality and freedom. Its formulated *mission civilisatrice* aimed to spread French republican ideals fused with ideas of Jewish modernization beyond the French borders. The French language, modern education and a combination of religious and secular teaching were the essence of the AIU's programme, which promoted its understanding of a modern Judaism and a modern Jewish identity.[7] Aron Rodrigue has emphasized that three major issues dominated the AIU's self-proclaimed mission, 'educational reform to socialize the Jews, vocational instruction to turn them to 'useful' trades, and the transforming of rabbinical training to produce new spiritual leaders of the community'.[8]

Jellinek, who was chief rabbi of the Viennese-Jewish community between 1865 and 1893, clearly adopted and promoted some of the

---

[7] Joan Gardner Roland (1969), *The Alliance Israélite Universelle and French Policy in North Africa 1869–1918* (New York), 3, 5–8; Aron Rodrigue (1990), *French Jews, Turkish Jews: The Alliance Israélite Universelle and the Politics of Jewish Schooling in Turkey 1860–1925* (Bloomington), 20–23; and Eli Bar-Chen (2002), 'Prototyp jüdischer Solidarität: Die Alliance Israélite Universelle', *Simon-Dubnow-Institutsjahrbuch*, 1, 277–296.

[8] Rodrigue (1990), *French Jews, Turkish Jews*, 7.

contemporary ideas of equality, modern education and emancipation, which had influenced the establishment of the AIU. He even saw in the foundation of a universal Jewish association a clear symbol of modernity which reflected his strong belief in progress and a better future.[9] He called for a 'century of love, humanity and freedom' and stressed the importance of a brotherly alliance with other leading Jewish communities in Western Europe. Consequently, he was convinced that the Jewish communities of Western Europe had a religious and social obligation to defend Jewish rights and push for Jewish modernization as part of the more general processes of modernization.[10] Moreover, he declared that the propagation of religious truth and modern education were the main missions of Israel and should be made available not only to Jews but to all mankind. He thus proclaimed education and knowledge as essential pillars of modern Judaism, and, in turn, of a modern Jewish identity.[11] Wertheimer, who had demanded political equality and cultural-religious modernization, was also deeply influenced by French ideas and openly absorbed and adopted them. In common with Jellinek, Wertheimer perceived the idea of an international alliance fighting for universal rights as a perfect symbol of modernity.[12] He also supported the reorganization of Jewish education and learning and publicly declared that the neutralization of the so-called 'poison of prejudices' (antisemitism) could be achieved and the 'period of darkness' could be overcome.[13]

[9]Adolf Jellinek (1878), *Der Israelitische Weltbund (L'Alliance Israélite Universelle): Rede am 1. Tage des Hüttenfestes 5639 gehalten* (Wien), 5.

[10]Adolf Jellinek (1879), *Rede zur Förderung der israel. Allianzen: Samstag, den 19 Juli 1879 im israelitischen Bethaus der Inneren Stadt gehalten* (Wien), 5–7.

[11]Jellinek (1878), *Der Israelitische Weltbund*, 7.

[12]Israelitische Allianz zu Wien (1913), *XL. Jahresbericht der Israelitischen Allianz zu Wien erstattet an die XL. ordentliche Generalversammlung am 16 April 1913 nebst einem Rückblick auf die vierzigjährige Wirksamkeit des Vereins 1872–1912* (Wien), 8; Moritz Güdemann (1887), *Ansprache im Auftrage des Vorstandes der israel. Allianz zu Wien gehalten an der Bahre des sel. Herrn Präsidenten Josef Ritter von Wertheimer am 18 März 1887* (Wien), 1; and Gerson Wolf (1868), *Joseph von Wertheimer: Ein Lebens- und Zeitbild. Beiträge zur Geschichte der Juden Oesterreich's in neuester Zeit* (Wien), 150–151.

[13]Wertheimer saw especially in increasing Antisemitism in the 1880s a problematic process and worked for the preservation of a progressive and equal society. Josef von Wertheimer (1886), *Gesinnungstüchtigkeit des jüdischen Stammes in humaner und staatlicher Beziehung und dessen Leistungsfähigkeit auf allen Gebieten des menschlichen Wissens und Könnens: Zur Wahrung der menschen- und staatsbürgerlichen Rechte der Juden durch Thatsachen erhärtet* (Wien), 40–57; Josef von Wertheimer (1883), *Jüdische Lehre und*

Influenced by the AIU's ideas and its self-declared *mission civilisatrice*, education emerged as a key element in the strategy of the Viennese-Jewish elite to counterbalance anti-Jewish sentiment, strengthen Jewish emancipation and integration and modernize Jewish communities, especially in the so-called 'East', which comprised the Eastern territories of the Danube Monarchy and neighbouring countries such as the Russian Empire or Romania. The strong support for the new progressive ideas by Viennese Jews was labelled not only as a fight for Jewish rights, but also as a struggle for more generally proclaimed human rights. Jellinek and Wertheimer, therefore, called for a strong alliance of Western European Jewries in support of the ideals of emancipation, integration and modern education, which also influenced other leading Viennese Jewish figures. These 'modern' political and humanitarian ideas especially united the Viennese religious elite, but also influenced the economic and cultural elites in the Habsburg metropolis and reshaped the traditional Jewish identity. The highly acculturated elite, which was comprised of bankers, journalists, communal workers and religious authorities, was convinced that the Habsburg Empire had a duty to guide their so-called 'half-wild' neighbours into modernity and become the advocate of culture and justice in the 'East'. They argued that Vienna, located at the edge of 'enlightened' and 'civilized' Western Europe had a natural duty to spread modernity into the 'East'. The Viennese Jews were, therefore, eager to establish a national organization following the model of the Anglo-Jewish Association (AJA), which had been founded in London in 1871. Even though leading figures such as Wertheimer propagated a brotherly union between Paris, London and Vienna, the Viennese community leaders—in common with their British counterparts—were committed to the notion that a national organization was better placed to serve universalist ideas.[14] In 1872, leading Jewish aid organizations organized a conference in Brussels which prompted the Viennese Jewish delegation

---

jüdisches Leben mit besonderer Beziehung auf die Juden in Oesterreich und auf die Pflichten gegen Vaterland und Mitmenschen (Wien), 3–31.

[14]For the relations between AIU, AJA and IAzW, see Josef von Wertheimer (1882), *Zur Emanzipation unserer Glaubensgenossen: Excurs* (Wien), 25–26, 28; Zosa Szajkowski (1957), 'Conflicts in the Alliance Israélite Universelle and the founding of the Anglo-Jewish Association, the Vienna Allianz and the Hilfsverein', *Jewish Social Studies* 19:1–2, 29–50.

to form an independent association.[15] The Viennese-Jewish elite subsequently founded the IAzW in 1872/73 and began promoting their own understanding of modernity. The Viennese *Allianz* placed a strong emphasis on the improvement and reform of Jewish education in the Danubian Monarchy, and especially in the Eastern crownlands of Galicia and Bucovina, and supported the fight against any kind of oppression and persecution of Jews.[16] Despite the foundation of a national organization, the board of the Vienna *Allianz* strongly supported the continuation of close links between the Western-European Jewish centres. Indeed, Moritz Friedländer, secretary of the Vienna *Allianz* and later of the Baron Hirsch Stiftung (BHS), declared the inner unity of the alliances as essential elements in the fight for modernity and progress, especially in Galicia.[17] Wertheimer referred to the cooperation between Vienna and Paris as 'notre entente cordiale',[18] which would secure the 'regeneration' of Galicia, the 'East' and other regions of the world. Wertheimer and Jellinek even presented Paris, London and Vienna as centres in which the process of modernization had already begun to take place and progress based on an enlightened and modern education were immanent. The three Jewish centres grouped under the slogan of the 'West' became an important signifier for the unity of a modern and progressive European Jewry and formed a central point of reference for Viennese-Jewish identity. In turn, the newly founded Jewish foundations in Paris, London and Vienna—the AIU, the AJA and the Vienna *Allianz*—became symbols of the Western-European unity of ideals which were essential in the processes of Jewish modernization through education and *Kultur*. In 1879, Jellinek gave a speech in which he stressed the unity of the universalist mission of these foundations and insisted that

---

[15]Archive of the Alliance Israélite Universelle [henceforth AAIU], Autriche I A 1–3, Folder I A 1, Lettre of the IAzW to the AIU (Vienna, 4 December 1872), No. 4074, 1.

[16]For the problematic situation of Galicia, see Klaus Hödl (1994), *Als Bettler in die Leopoldstadt: Galizische Juden auf dem Weg nach Wien* (Vienna), 17–39; Piotr Wróbel (1994), 'The Jews of Galicia Under Austrian-Polish Rule 1869–1918', *Austrian History Yearbook*, 25, 99–132.

[17]AAIU, Autriche I A 1–3, Folder I A 3 Vienne Alliance, Lettre of the IAzW to the AIU (Vienna, 7 March 1887/9 March 1887), No. 9235, 1.

[18]AAIU, Autriche I A 1–3, Folder I A 3 Vienna Alliance, Lettre of the IAzW to the AIU (Vienna, 17 February 1887/21 February 1887), No. 9152, 1.

every "son of Juda" should support them.[19] A broad base of support in the different countries was perceived as an important step towards the fulfilment of the vision, or visions, formulated by the founders of these organizations. Consequently, the IAzW also supported the foundation of the *Hilfsverein der deutschen Juden*, which was founded in Berlin in 1901 and seen as another potentially powerful partner in the 'West'.[20]

With the outbreak of the First World War, however, members of the Viennese-Jewish elite were directly confronted with a rise in nationalist sentiment and a growing necessity to distance themselves from their religious brethren in the 'West', with whom they had formerly been so close. Even though the Paris-based AIU had elected Dr. Alfred Stern and Dr. Arthur Kuranda, two influential members of the Viennese-Jewish community and supporters of the IAzW, onto its own board in July 1914, the Vienna *Allianz* had to renounce its close cooperation with the French group after the outbreak of the war.[21] In an open letter published in the Austrian press, the IAzW declared that despite the similarity of the organizational name and the strong cooperation with Paris, the Vienna *Allianz* was an Austrian association that served humanitarian and patriotic ideals and was supported and recognized as such by the Imperial state authorities.[22] The burden of wartime nationalism clearly pressured the IAzW to renounce its close cooperation with Paris, London and other Jewish centres. While the Viennese-Jewish elite could easily support the fight against Tsarist Russia and declare the war in the East as

---

[19] Jellinek (1879), *Rede zur Förderung der israel. Allianzen*, 10. Despite the propagated unity of ideals, some problems and tensions also crystallized before the First World War, see e.g. AAIU, Autriche II A 4–7, Folder II A 4 Gutmann-Friedländer, Lettre of the IAzW to the AIU (Vienna, 6 November 1895/10 November 1895), No. 7671/2, 1–6.

[20] AAIU, Autriche II A 4–7, Folder II A 5 1897–1901, Lettre of the IAzW to the AIU (Vienna, 5 July 1901/7 July 1901), No. 7401, 1–3.

[21] AAIU, Autriche II A 4–7, Folder II A 7 1910–1914, Lettre of the IAzW to the AIU (Vienna, 22 June 1914/24 June 1914), No. 9861, 1.

[22] [„…, dass die Israelitische Allianz zu Wien ein ausschliesslich österreichischer Verein ist, dessen humanitäre und patriotische Wirksamkeit den höchsten Staatsstellen – mit denen wir bei der Führung unserer Hilfsaktionen in ständigem Kontakt stehen – wohl bekannt ist und der mit den Vereinen verwandten Namens in feindlichen Ländern in gar keiner organischen Verbindung jemals gestanden hat.'] Russian Special Archive-Military Archive Moskwa [henceforth RSA-MAM], Fond 675 Opis 1 Dela No. 164, 17 April 1916–01 August 1916: Lettre of the IAzW to Dr. Otto Schwarz (Bohemia) (Vienna, 20 April 1916), 15kb.

part of the struggle for Jewish rights, equality and emancipation, the declaration of war against France and the United Kingdom remained problematic.

In July 1914, the Vienna *Allianz* justified the issue of the Austrian ultimatum against Serbia in a letter to its French co-organization and declared that Austria-Hungary, as the defender of European values and modern human rights, had to be supported in its struggle against Eastern despotism and inhumanity. Indeed, the 'historic opportunity' to end Jewish oppression and persecution by Tsarist Russia was clearly referenced and almost celebrated. In an allusion to the Russian alliance with the western empires, moreover, the letter criticised the general French and British support of the 'Eastern evil', thereby revealing the strain the advent of war put on relations between formerly close and mutually supportive Jewish organizations in Europe.[23] The IAzW even announced that Paris and London, though they once had guided European Jewry into the modern age, had lost their progressive status due to the Franco-British alliance with Russia.

Binjamin Segel, a Galician-born author and journalist who aimed to connect 'East' and 'West', described the war as an 'unnatural and perverse Alliance between extremists' that brought together the 'absolutist regime on the lowest level of European culture' and the 'most freedom loving nations in Europe'.[24] In his analysis, Segel came to the conclusion that France was driven by revenge and Great Britain by economic jealousy.[25] For his part, Jonas Kreppel, a Galician-born author and publicist, identified French chauvinism, Russian war interests and British greed as the driving forces behind the alliance between the Entente powers.[26] Unsurprisingly, Moritz Güdemann, chief rabbi of Vienna during the war years, also developed similar ideas; in his view, Great Britain was driven by economic jealousy, Russia—as the modern Philistine or Goliath—by Medieval barbarism, and France by hate and revenge. Thus, Güdemann

---

[23] AAIU, Autriche III A 8–11, Folder III A 8 1901–1914, Lettre of the IAzW to the AIU (Vienna, 24 July 1914/27 July 1914), No. 9967/2, 1–4.

[24] Binjamin Segel (1915), *Der Weltkrieg und das Schicksal der Juden: Stimme eines galizischen Juden an seine Glaubensgenossen in den neutralen Ländern insbesondere in Amerika* (Lemberg), 8.

[25] Ibid., 83.

[26] Jonas Kreppel (1915), *Der Weltkrieg und die Judenfrage* (Wien), 7.

declared that France and Great Britain had betrayed their own ideals of freedom and humanity.[27] Great Britain, in particular, was perceived by Güdemann as a ruthless and perfidious enemy, and a jealous and scurrilous partner,[28] and he fervently hoped that German and Austro-Hungarian victory would bring world peace.[29]

JEWISH REFUGEES IN 'EAST' AND 'WEST'

In 1914, Austro-Hungarian Jews flocked to their flag(s) and supported dynasty and Empire in what was popularly interpreted as a fight against discrimination and oppression. In common with their counterparts in the German Empire, Jewish soldiers volunteered in high numbers, with approximately 300,000 serving in the Austro-Hungarian forces, and, in contrast to the German case, were even officially accepted in the army hierarchy.[30] The authorship of the grim but very popular *Österreichisches Reiterlied,* or Austrian Cavalry Song, by Jewish writer Hugo Zuckermann, along with his own service and ultimate death in the ranks of the Austrian army, reflected the broader participation of Austro-Hungarian Jews in the war effort.[31] In common with Jewish communities in other states, the Habsburg Jews thus supported the national war effort and stressed their patriotism and loyalty to the nation. However, as Marsha L. Rozenblit has argued, Habsburg Jews 'were patriotic, to be sure, but to a supranational Austria, a territorial, dynastic state, not a nation either in the French sense of a nation of equal citizens or in the ethno-national sense so pervasive in Central Europe'.[32]

---

[27] Max Güdemann (1915), 'Der jetzige Weltkrieg und die Bibel', *Monatsschrift für Geschichte und Wissenschaft des Judentums,* 23, 5–6.

[28] Ibid., 10.

[29] Ibid., 12.

[30] For more information on Jews in the Army, see Michael Berger (2010), *Eisernes Kreuz Doppeladler Davidstern: Juden in deutschen und österreichisch-ungarischen Armeen. Der Militärdienst jüdischer Soldaten durch zwie Jahrhunderte* (Berlin), 107–114; Erwin A. Schmidl (1991), 'Davidstern und Doppeladler: Jüdische Soldaten in Österreich (-Ungarn)', *Österreich in Geschichte und Literatur,* 35:1, 20–27.

[31] George E. Berkley (1988), *Vienna and Its Jews: The Tragedy of Success 1880s–1980s* (Ann Arber), 135–136; David Rechter (2001), *The Jews of Vienna and the First World War* (London), 24–27.

[32] Marsha L. Rozenblit (2001), *Reconstructing a National Identity: The Jews of Habsburg Austria during World War I* (Oxford), 17.

Despite their clear use of belligerent language, the leading figures of the Viennese-Jewish elite tried to avoid direct confrontations with their formerly close Western colleagues. Instead they tended to attack Russia and later Romania, states which they depicted as the arch-enemies of all Jews. The same persistent images thus dominated the discourse on the war, demonstrating the degree to which stereotypes and prejudices were used to elicit support and construct unity. The field of education was highlighted and praised in the many commentaries as the most important difference between progressive Austria-Hungary and 'degenerate' and backward Russia. The Eastern focus and the widely perceived culture gap between Central and Eastern Europe fueled the ambitions of the Viennese-Jewish elite to expand their already existing cultural mission to the 'East'. In contrast to the French AIU, the Viennese organization had for some time focused on the Eastern provinces of the Habsburg Empire and the 'East' in general. While the ideas of the AIU were openly adopted in the pre-war years, their actual implementation reflected the impact of nationalism and Jewish acculturation in Vienna as well as the influence of the multidimensional Jewish identity in the Habsburg Empire. Questions about centralization, authority and representation remained important for the Viennese communal elite and were even reinforced by the early events of the First World War. In general keeping with AIU ideas, e.g. to protect, educate and even modernize 'Oriental Jews', respectively Jews from the Ottoman Empire or the Near East, e.g. from Morocco or Persia/Iran, the Vienna *Allianz* began focusing its efforts on the 'Eastern Jews' in Galicia and Bucovina with a view to possibly extending their cultural mission to the Jews in Central Russia and Romania. As with the 'Oriental Jews', the 'Eastern Jews' were perceived by the Viennese-Jewish elite as culturally backward and religiously 'degenerated'. The Vienna *Allianz* consequently formulated its own cultural mission to help their Eastern co-religionists.

With the outbreak of war, and the changing borders brought about by the military successes of the Central powers, the IAzW had to focus on its internal problems and spheres of influence. As the majority of Austrian Jews lived in the Eastern provinces of Galicia and Bucovina, this region became a major focus of attention and emerged as a testing ground for the organization's educational mission. The Viennese-Jewish elite wanted to demonstrate that the Eastern-Jewish communities could be guided into modernity by the introduction of a modern educational system, a fundamental process of vocational restructuring and a fully implemented social and religious emancipation. The general economic decline of the region, growing antisemitism, nationalistic clashes and the dominance of orthodox or Chassidic groups were perceived by the Viennese-Jewish elite as major reasons for the contemporary cultural stagnation of these provinces and their Jewry. The elite of the Vienna *Allianz* hoped to solve the problems of the region by transferring Viennese-Jewish ideals to the East. By educating the 'Eastern-Jewish masses' in modern schools, by introducing religious reform measures, by lobbying for a strong local acculturation, it was hoped that Eastern Jews could be given the opportunity to partake in the process of European modernization as an integral part of Eastern Europe.

In close cooperation between the Vienna *Allianz* and the Baron Hirsch Stiftung (BHS), an organization founded by Baron Maurice de Hirsch in order to transform Jews 'into capable citizens, and thus furnish humanity with much new and valuable material',[33] there emerged a vision of occupied Eastern Europe as a sphere of influence of the Habsburg Empire. This vision very much followed the strategies which had already been implemented in the years before the war. In 1901, for example, fifty Jewish schools were operating in Galicia (48) and Bucovina (2) and a total of almost 10,000 children (the majority of whom were male) were enrolled in the foundation's schools.[34] Contemporary commentators were soon praising the BHS as an important institution which transferred Western ideals of education and knowledge into the 'darkness' of Galicia.[35] During the war years, the Vienna *Allianz* strengthened its affiliation with the German language and Viennese-Jewish identity and promoted a strong alliance between Vienna and Berlin. When the Ottoman Empire joined the war as an ally of Germany and Austria-Hungary in November 1914, the Austro-Hungarian Ambassador, in cooperation with the Vienna *Allianz,*

---

[33] Baron Maurice de Hirsch (1891), 'My Views on Philantrophy', *North American Review*, CCCCXVI, 2.

[34] Hödl (1994), *Als Bettler in die Leopoldstadt,* 96–97. For Baron de Hirsch's work in the Austrian-Hungarian Empire, see Kurt Grunwald (1966), *Türkenhirsch: A Study of Baron Maurice de Hirsch Entrepreneur and Philanthropist* (Jerusalem), 68–69; Salomon Adler-Rudel (1963), 'Moritz Baron Hirsch: Profile of a Great Philanthropist', *Leo Baeck Institute Yearbook* VIII, 40–42.

[35] Aleksander von Gutry (1916), *Galizien: Land und Leute* (München and Leipzig), 102–103.

even called for a stronger dedication towards the modernization of the Jewish 'Orient' and for a replacement of French cultural influence.[36] The well-established school network of the Paris-based AIU, which had a long tradition in the Ottoman Empire and had educated the elite of Ottoman Jewry according to French-Jewish values, emerged on the one hand as a guiding example. On the other hand, however, it also came to be seen as an enemy structure which had to be replaced by a German/Austrian version. Consequently, the Vienna *Allianz* began to transfer money to Jewish communities in Palestine and other parts of the Ottoman Empire which contained Austrian or Hungarian citizens in order to help and strengthen their influence.[37]

Despite such activities, however, the reality of the educational mission of the IAzW remained far from its envisioned ideal. While the Jewish communities in Galicia celebrated and supported the Austro-Hungarian Army, which was positively described in letters sent through the army postal service, the war record of the army was quite different, at least in the opening phases of the conflict.[38] In the first month of the war, the Austro-Hungarian forces had to deal with massive military defeats and Russian troops not only triumphed on the battlefield and occupied Eastern Galicia and parts of the Bucovina, they also closed or destroyed many schools founded by the Viennese-Jewish organization. Neither Lemberg (or Lviv/Lwów) nor Przemyszl could be defended, which symbolized the pressure being exerted by the advancing Russian forces and the rather precarious military situation of the Austro-Hungarian army.[39] Reports on the first experiences of Russian troops on Galician soil documented war crimes, Jewish persecution, the destruction of synagogues

---

[36] Archive of the Ministry of Foreign Affairs Vienna [henceforth AMFA-V (Österreichisches Haus-, Hof- und Staatsarchiv—Archiv des Aeusseren)], Mappe XLII/5 Israelitische Goldschmid-Schule und Rabbinerseminar Danon, Lettre of Dr. A. J. Baraw (Embassy in Constantinopel/Istanbul) to Baron Burian (Ministry of Foreign Affairs), (Istanbul, 24 March 1916), No. 24/P, 1–3.

[37] For more details on financial support of Jewish communities in Palestine during the war, see AMFA-V, PA XII Turkey, Karton 379, Liasse XLII/1–7, Lettre of the IAzW to the Ministry of Foreign Affairs (Vienna, 5 May 1916), No. 1550, 1.

[38] Eugen Tannenbaum (1915), *Kriegsbriefe deutscher und österreichischer Juden* (Berlin), 3–6.

[39] For more information on Jewish experiences in Galicia and Bucovina, see Frank M. Schuster (2008), '... wie ein Blitz aus heiterem Himmel': Der Erste Weltkrieg in Galizien und der Bukowina aus jüdischer Sicht', *Transversal* 9:2, 33–58.

and other atrocities.[40] The French AIU did intervene at the French Foreign Ministry in order to ease the problems suffered by Jews in war-torn Galicia, but coordinated efforts were no longer possible.[41] An IAzW delegate who coordinated the financial help in Galicia described in his travel letter the dramatic destruction in Eastern Galicia where there was 'not a single Jewish home that had not been destroyed'.[42] Reports on Russian intolerance and strict military government spread across the Empire and the image of Russian anti-educational policies became especially prominent. Moreover, the prevalent propaganda which portrayed the Russians as 'evil antisemites' *par excellence* led to an enormous migration movement. Rumours of antisemitic pogroms and persecutions due to accusations of espionage against Jews and other national groups, including Poles and Ukrainians, prompted the flight of many inhabitants of the Eastern provinces to the West. A Russian order, which Austro-Hungarian forces captured, called for a strict anti-Jewish policy due to the disloyalty of these communities and demanded their active expulsion.[43] The Austro-Hungarian military elite quickly realized that the destruction and persecution in the Eastern provinces demanded a coordinated response. Moreover, the generally wanton destruction of the Russian forces also became a perfect tool of propaganda against the Russian enemy. In 1915, the War Propaganda Corps stated that it had collected documents and photos that 'could be used in a Jewish journalistic manner' as propaganda material.[44]

Due to the proximity of the front-line in the Eastern regions and the Russian occupation of parts of Galicia and Bucovina, Jewish refugees flooded into many cities in the Western hemisphere of the Empire, which

---

[40] Segel (1915), *Der Weltkrieg und das Schicksal der Juden*, 36, 44–47.

[41] Central Archive for the History of the Jewish People [henceforth CAHJP], HM2/2764 b, Conjoint Committee Report 6–8 on the Jews of Russia, Galicia, Roumania 1916, Report VII. 17 May 1916–27 June 1916, 1.

[42] RSA-MAM, Fond 675 Opis 1 Delo No. 404, Lemberg: Lettre of an IAzW delegate to the IAzW (Lemberg, 19 July 1915), 1.

[43] AMFA-V, PA I Allgemein, Karton 931, Liasse Krieg 13 a-k, Greultaten 1914–1918, Mappe 13 a, Telegramm of Graf Thun (n.pl., 15 March 1915), No. 2429, 1–2.

[44] The letter thus not only documented an ongoing information war between the Allies and Central Powers, but also persistent Jewish stereotypes across the war lines. AMFA-V, PA I Allgemein, Karton 931, Liasse Krieg 13 a-k Greultaten 1914–1918, Mappe 13 h, Der Vertreter des k.u.k. Ministeriums des Äusseren beim k.u.k. Armee-Oberkommando, Herr Freiherr von Burián (Teschen, 21 November 1915), No. 6972, 2.

made Jews very visible in the public sphere. A report published in 1915 by the *Israelitische-Theologische Lehranstalt* documented the enormous destruction of houses, synagogues, etc. by 'Russian hordes' in the 'East' and the visibility of Jewish refugees on the streets of Vienna.[45] Jewish migration from the East, and especially from Galicia, was already quite common before 1914, but the migrations during the war drastically changed the general setting.[46] By 1915, approximately 77,000 Jewish refugees had arrived in Vienna, while 20,000 had reached Budapest and 15,000 had come to Prague.[47] The Vienna *Allianz* joined the B'nai B'rith, the Austrian-Israelite Union and other newly established welfare institutions, in an attempt to cope with the enormous refugee crisis.[48] A Central Welfare institution for refugees from Galicia and Bucovina [*Zentralstelle der Fürsorge für die Flüchtlinge aus Galizien und der Bukowina*] was established under Rudolf Schwarz-Hiller in order to coordinate and organize Jewish aid.[49] All of these national Jewish aid organizations attempted to solve the myriad problems and react to the consequences of the war. International organizations, which, in the early years of the war, were usually based in neutral countries such as the United States, continued to transfer money and helped to ease the plight of their co-religionists in the regions most affected by the war. The American Jewish Relief Committee for Sufferers from the Wars and the Joint Distribution Committee, both of which were based in New York,

---

[45] Israelitisch-Theologische Lehranstalt (1915), *XXII. Jahresbericht der Israelitisch-Theologischen Lehranstalt in Wien für das Schuljahr 1914/1915* (Wien), 94.

[46] For an overview on Galician-Jewish migration to Vienna, see Hödl (1994), *Als Bettler in die Leopoldstadt*, 133–154.

[47] David Rechter (2014), 'Die große Katastrophe: Die österreichischen Juden und der Krieg', in Marcus G. Patka, ed. *Weltuntergang: Jüdisches Leben und Sterben im Ersten Weltkrieg* (Vienna), 19–21; Berkley (1988), *Vienna and Its Jews*, 137–140; and Rechter (2001), *The Jews of Vienna and the First World War*, 68–69.

[48] Rechter (2001), *The Jews of Vienna and the First World War*, 32–33.

[49] After the Italian declaration of war the institution was renamed 'Zentralstelle für Kriegsflüchtlinge.' Rechter (2001), *The Jews of Vienna and the First World War*, 74–76; Beatrix Hoffmann-Holter (1995), *'Abreisemachung': Jüdische Kriegsflüchtlinge in Wien 1914–1923* (Vienna), 43–47; and Hans Jäger-Sustenau (1973), 'Der Wiener Gemeinderat Rudolf Schwarz-Hiller: Kämpfer für Humanität und Recht', *Zeitschrift für die Geschichte der Juden*, 10:1–2, 10–12.

were just two of such international organizations that helped the IAzW and other Austrian-Jewish organizations to keep up their campaigns.[50]

In the very first weeks of the war, the Austro-Hungarian authorities began setting up refugee camps in the Western crownlands, including parts of Bohemia, Moravia and Austria, along the lines of ethnic affiliations and organized according to an Imperial law issued on 11 August 1914.[51] These actions aimed to channel migration, provide the state authorities with a framework to deal with the refugee problem and avoid a mass-concentration of Jewish refugees in one place. The authorities were particularly concerned that a strong presence in Vienna and other urban centres should be avoided, which resulted in an official closure of Vienna to refugees in 1914 by the Viennese authorities.[52] It offered the government an opportunity, as David Rechter has noted, 'to showcase the unity of the monarchy's people in the war effort, thereby counteracting, it was hoped, centrifugal nationalist tendencies'.[53] Interestingly, along with Poles, Ukrainians, Italians and Slovenes, Jews were perceived as an ethnic group, and were thus housed in specifically Jewish refugee camps in places such as Bruck an der Leitha, Nikolsburg, Pohrlitz, Gaya and Deutschbrod.[54] However, the Viennese Jewish community was reluctant to adopt Zionist ideas in order to counteract the Jewish refugee problem. As Rechter has emphasized: 'welfare work was thus an important element in the wartime realignment of the balance of power within Jewish Society, in particular the emergence of Jewish nationalism as a major force'.[55]

In the eyes of the liberal elite of the Viennese community the refugees, Jewish and non-Jewish alike, had to be treated as an imperial

---

[50] RSA-MAM, Fond 675 Opis 1 Delo No. 127, 11 June 1915: Lettre of the IAzW to the American Jewish Relief Committee for Sufferers from Wars (New York), (Vienna, 30 June 1915), 135kb–137kb.

[51] Hoffmann-Holter (1995), '*Abreisemachung*', 31–33.

[52] Despite such an official policy, refugees continued to come to Vienna. Hoffmann-Holter (1995), '*Abreisemachung*', 35.

[53] David Rechter (1997), 'Galicia in Vienna: Jewish Refugees in the First World War', *Austrian History Yearbook* 28, 115.

[54] Rozenblit (2001), *Reconstructing a National Identity*, 73; Hoffmann-Holter (1997), '*Abreisemachung*', 34.

[55] Rechter (2001), *The Jews of Vienna and the First World War*, 83.

problem by the state authorities.[56] While the Vienna *Allianz* held the Austro-Hungarian Empire responsible for the maintenance of the refugee camps, they were eager to deal with the organization of the camps and, in particular, to provide refugees with cultural, social and religious services. This dilemma or tension between confessional help and state authority reflected the general position of the Jews. Indeed, as Rechter has observed, 'it could be argued that they had no realistic alternative, given their dual commitment to being at one and the same time both proud Jews and faithful Austrian citizens'.[57] In common with other camps, in which the Catholic and Protestant churches provided religious and educational services, the Vienna *Allianz* established itself as the major authority on Jewish matters. The state, which could barely deal with the unprecedented refugee crisis, in which Jewish refugees made up 157,000 out of a total of almost 390,000 in 1915, enthusiastically accepted the cooperation of the Vienna *Allianz*. In 1917, the IAzW announced that it was supporting 72,000 Jewish refugees in Bohemia, 36,000 in Moravia, 40,000 in Vienna, 10,000 in Upper Austria, 4000 in Styria and approximately 20,000 in the Hungarian part of the Empire.[58]

EDUCATION IN WARTIME

The commitment of the Vienna *Allianz* to providing relief for so many thousands of Jewish refugees has to be seen as part of its loyal support for the Habsburg state which was still perceived as the main guarantor of freedom and security for Jews. In June 1915, Aron Lewi, Chief Rabbi of Sambor in Galicia, inaugurated a synagogue in the refugee camp in Bruck a.d. Leitha and gave a sermon that appeared to follow the traditional worldview of the IAzW. In dramatic words, he described the war as a fight against the 'darkness' of oppression and persecution, thus strongly suggesting that the conflict was a just war.[59] Support for the refugees was also naturally understood as a religious obligation to help

---

[56] Hoffmann-Holter (1997), '*Abreisemachung*', 95–101.

[57] David Rechter (2002), 'Ethnicity and the Politics of Welfare: The Case of Habsburg Austrian Jewry', *Simon-Dubnow-Institutsjahrbuch* 1, 265.

[58] Rozenblit (2001), *Reconstructing a National Identity*, 66–67.

[59] Aron Lewin (1915), *Festpredigt anläßlich der Einweihung der Synagoge im k.k. Barackenlager für jüdische Kriegsflüchtlinge aus Galizien und der Bukowina in Bruck a.d. Leitha gehalten am 27 Juni 1915* (Wien), 2–3, 10–11.

persecuted religious brethren according to long-standing ideas of solidarity and support. In addition, in a letter to the regional bureau of the Vienna *Allianz* in the Galician town of Kolomea, which had a very large Jewish community, the board of the Viennese organization made it clear that the military service of the Jewish male population, the general support of the imperial war effort by the Jewish female population and the philanthropic measures of the IAzW, were seen as 'holy duties' for the fatherland.[60] Demonstrations of patriotism and effective support for the war effort were seen as integral elements for ending discrimination and antisemitic attacks. The righteousness of the imperial cause seemed so self-evident that some Austro-Hungarian rabbis even referred to the conflict as a 'holy war'.[61]

Along with the promotion of this interpretation of the war as a moral conflict, the IAzW followed the educational mission it had established in the years before the war and opened schools and offered evening classes for religious education in the Jewish refugee camps. Even though the Jewish community in Vienna had to deal with tremendous challenges, including antisemitism, the mass influx of refugees and a growing Zionist influence, it remained faithful to its pre-war mission. In the eyes of the Viennese-Jewish elite, the great cultural gap between Western and Eastern Jews had by no means disappeared and still persisted during the war years. According to the annual report of the IAzW published in 1916, for example, the 'Jewish refugees are so entirely different in their religious habits and social practices, it is as if they come from another world'.[62] In another example of this sort of commentary, a 1915 report on the refugee camp in Brünn/Brno mentioned the 'autochthonic dresses – Kaftan and ringlets' as just one element of the differences which distinguished Jewish refugees from the East from Western Jewry.[63]

[60] RSA-MAM, Fond 675 Opis 1 Delo No. 368, Kolomea: Lettre of Samuel Scheirmann (religious teacher in Kolomea) to the IAzW (Kolomea, 2 June 1916), 1.

[61] Rozenblit (2001), *Reconstructing a National Identity*, 44–45.

[62] RSA-MAM, Fond 675 Opis 1 Delo No. 57, Insp. Sperber: Report on Leipnik, Ossek a.d. Becwa, Wesselicko, Trschitz and Klein Lasnik (Vienna, 3 November 1916), No. 6488, 2.

[63] Tätigkeitsbericht, *Tätigkeitsbericht des Zentralbüros zum Schutze der galizischen Flüchtlinge jüd. Galubensbekenntnisses in Brünn für die Zeit vom 15.12.1914 bis 31 Oktober 1915* (Brünn), 3.

Thus, the influence of pre-war attitudes and ideas persisted and the ambition to educate and modernize the Eastern religious brethren remained a central theme in the various annual reports. Some of these declared that despite the social and religious difficulties and inhuman living conditions of the Jewish war refugees in the Western camps, these people would return to their homes enlightened and modernized when the triumphant Austrian Army reconquered the 'East'. In addition, the IAzW, acting in cooperation with the BHS, opened a number of schools designed to further their educational mission. In the refugee camp at Nikolsburg in Moravia, 332 boys and 330 girls were educated, while in the city of Nikolsburg 68 boys and 58 girls were given access to education. Likewise, in the refugee camp at Pohrlitz, the figures were 203 boys and 204 girls, while in the city of Pohrlitz it was 66 to 61, and in the refugee camp Gaya 209/212, while, in Kanitz, a total of 43 boys and girls were educated.[64] Moreover, rabbis, kosher butchers, cantors and other prominent Jewish community figures were employed at the refugee camps and in communities in order to help and educate.[65] Despite the catastrophic hygienic and social circumstances in the various refugee camps, members of the IAzW continued to adhere to their formulated ideas about education and culture and promoted agricultural training

---

[64] Israelitische Allianz zu Wien, *XLIII. Jahresbericht der Israelitischen Allianz zu Wien …1916*, 10.

[65] Austrian State Archive-General Administration Archive [henceforth ÖStA-AVA], Neuer Kultus: Akatholischer Teil, Israelitischer Kultus (auch jüdischer Kultus), Signatur D 3 Kultusgemeinden, Militärseelsorger, Rabbiner, Schächter, Karton 7 Kultusgemeinde, Rabbiner, Militärseelsorger, Schächter in genere 1848–1918: Lettre of the Imperial Ministry (K.K. Ministerium für Kultus und Unterricht) (Vienna, 3 April 1917), No. 11445, topic: Flüchtlingsseelsorge/Oberrabbiner Dr. Josef Rosenfeld, 1; ÖStA-AVA, Neuer Kultus: Akatholischer Teil, Israelitischer Kultus (auch jüdischer Kultus), Signatur D 3 Kultusgemeinden, Militärseelsorger, Rabbiner, Schächter, Karton 7 Kultusgemeinde, Rabbiner, Militärseelsorger, Schächter in genere 1848–1918: Lettre of the Imperial Ministry (K.K. Ministerium für Kultus und Unterricht) (Vienna, 3 April 1917), No. 11206, topic: Isr. Flüchtlingsfürsorge, Bestellung von Vorbetern und Schächtern, 1; ÖStA-AVA, Neuer Kultus: Akatholischer Teil, Israelitischer Kultus (auch jüdischer Kultus), Signatur D 3 Kultusgemeinden, Militärseelsorger, Rabbiner, Schächter, Karton 7 Kultusgemeinde, Rabbiner, Militärseelsorger, Schächter in genere 1848–1918: Lettre of the Imperial Ministry (K.K. Ministerium für Kultus und Unterricht) (Vienna, 21 September 1915), No. 28935, topic: Seelsorge in den Barakenniederlassung in Bruck a/L., 1.

and other vocational skills in the refugee camps and communities, such as in Frankstedt.[66]

Several *Allianz* reports emphasized the fact that the Jewish refugees should not be regarded as 'annoying aliens' or 'intrusive beggars', but as citizens of the Austro-Hungarian Empire who had a moral right to imperial support.[67] Yet despite such claims and appeals, some memoranda also documented the problematic relations between Jewish refugees and the local population in the regions to which they had fled. In a report on Moravian Weisskirchen and Keltsch, the IAzW realized that in many rural areas the local communities perceived the refugees as 'aliens' with 'extra mouths to feed'. Such negative images and perceptions were not generally assuaged by sympathetic sermons and speeches given by local military figures and Christian clergymen.[68] Persistent stereotypes and prejudices remained relevant and led to an intensification of the IAzW's efforts to ease war-related problems. In 1916, a school inspector of the BHS travelled to different refugee camps and communities and documented the continuing lack of understanding on the part of local populations. He stressed that the Jews had suffered because of their loyalty to throne and dynasty which made the persisting scepticism and exclusion in the Western communities an 'underserved challenge' and a 'heavy burden'.[69] Kreppel also emphasized that Jews—here Galician Jewry— had made great sacrifices for Austria-Hungary, a fact that he argued should be recognized as proof of their patriotism and loyalty to dynasty and Empire.[70] However, an increasingly intense antisemitism nonetheless emerged across the Habsburg Empire.[71]

---

[66] Here the source demanded that the 'Eastern Jews' should not just hang around, but should work for their own cultural and occupational 'elevation'. RSA-MAM, Fond 675 Opis 1 Delo No. 57, Insp. Sperber: Report on Frankstedt (Vienna, 4 May 1917/5 May 1917), No. 2588, 1–2.

[67] RSA-MAM, Fond 675 Opis 1 Delo No. 57, Insp. Sperber: Report on Gewitsch (Vienna, 3 May 1917/4 May 1917), No. 2586, 4.

[68] RSA-MAM, Fond 675 Opis 1 Delo No. 57, Insp. Sperber: Report on Mährisch Weisskirchen u. Keltsch (Vienna, 12 November 1916/16 November 1916), No. 6805, 4.

[69] RSA-MAM, Fond 675 Opis 1 Delo No. 57, Insp. Sperber: Report of the Kreisschulinspektors of the Baron Hirsch Stiftung (Vienna, 1 October 1916/27 October 1916), No. 6400, 6.

[70] Jonas Kreppel (1915), *Der Weltkrieg und die Judenfrage* (Wien), 21–22.

[71] Rechter (2014), 'Die große Katastrophe: Die österreichischen Juden und der Krieg', 22–23.

The defeats suffered by the Austro-Hungarian Army in the early months of the war, and, in particular, the initially highly successful Brusilov Offensive of 1916 and other Russian incursions, desolated the Eastern parts of the Habsburg Empire. Schools were destroyed, teachers drafted into the army and the Jewish population dispersed, and the existing Jewish school network in Eastern Galicia was essentially dissolved. However, the military victories brought about by close cooperation with the German forces in the later years of the war led to changing attitudes in Viennese-Jewish circles. In 1916, a report produced by the *Allianz* declared the rebuilding of their school system, which had been destroyed during the Russian occupation.[72] In 1917, the reconquest of Eastern Galicia was seen as an important step in the expansion of the financial and social support of Jewish refugees and victims in the 'East'. A report of an association for Jewish war orphans which strongly cooperated with the *Zentralstelle*, the Viennese community, the BHS and IAzW, declared that the reconquest of these territories meant that more help was needed.[73] The Vienna *Allianz* was particularly glad of the expansion of Austrian influence beyond the old borders of the Habsburg Empire, which it welcomed as the first step towards finally implementing the old dream of Jewish emancipation and modernization in Eastern Europe.

After the Romanian declaration of war in 1916, the Viennese-Jewish community intensified its efforts to promote the Austro-Hungarian fight for freedom and equality as a morally righteous endeavour.[74] The IAzW even declared that their vision would bring freedom and emancipation to their co-religionists in Russian Poland, free them from Tsarist oppression and guide them into modernity.[75] The reconquest of Galicia and Bucovina demanded a re-establishment of their former offices in Brody, Stanislau, Kolomea, Przemysl, Jaroslau and Sambor, and later also in Czernowitz and Rzeszow. Krakow became the headquarters for

---

[72] Israelitische Allianz zu Wien (1916), *XLIII. Jahresbericht der Israelitischen Allianz zu Wien erstattet an die XLIII. ordentliche Generalversammlung am 5 Juni 1916* (Wien), 6.

[73] ÖStA-AVA, Neuer Kultus: Akatholischer Teil, Israelitischer Kultus (auch jüdischer Kultus), D 16 Kkoscher, Stiftungen, Vereine, Karton 58 Vereine -1918: Verein zur Rettung verlassener jüdischer Kinder Galiziens und der Bukowina, *II. Tätigkeitsbericht pro 1917 erstattet und genehmigt in der Generalversammlung am 12.02.1918* (Wien), 7.

[74] Rozenblit (2001), *Reconstructing a National Identity*, 52–53.

[75] Israelitische Allianz zu Wien (1916), *XLIII. Jahresbericht der Israelitischen Allianz zu Wien ...*, 6.

West-Galicia, Przemysl for East-Galicia and Czernowitz for Bucovina.[76] In early 1917, the IAzW had realized that a potential declaration of war by the United States endangered important transfers of money from overseas, which had enabled the Vienna *Allianz* to establish kindergartens and schools in the occupied territories as well as restructuring its destroyed schools in the Eastern provinces of the Habsburg Empire.[77] Such a development was seen by the IAzW authorities as a threat to their efforts and measures to help and educate their Eastern co-religionists and promote their vision beyond the actual borders of the Austrian-Hungarian Empire.[78] The money coming from the United States was regarded as a particularly important element in the maintenance of welfare and educational measures in the regions of Lublin, Radom, Piotrokow and Kielce. Thus, the IAzW brought together leading members of the communities, associations and foundations of these regions to discuss contemporary problems and possible solutions.[79] As a result of their military successes, the Austro-Hungarian forces had occupied Southern Poland and effectively opened this region to the influence of the Vienna *Allianz*.[80] In 1918, the IAzW demanded the delivery of heating material to its formerly closed and newly established schools in order to fulfil the formulated ideals.[81] However, the US declaration of war reduced not only American but international support and money transfers in general. The annual report of the IAzW announced

---

[76] Ibid., 16.

[77] Rechter (2001), 'Ethnicity and the Politics of Welfare', 266–267.

[78] For the problematic relation with the USA and the threat of its entrance to the war, see RSA-MAM, Fond 675 Opis 1 Delo No. 134, Kopierbuch 27 December 1916–28 February 1917: Lettre of the IAzW to the Jüdische Flüchtlingskomitee (Direktor J. Kipman, Lublin, Russ. Poland) (Vienna, 12 February 1917), 764kb–765kb.

[79] Israelitische Allianz zu Wien (1916), *XLIII. Jahresbericht der Israelitischen Allianz zu Wien ...*, 22–23; RSA-MAM, Fond 675 Opis 1 Delo No. 140, 17 October 1916–26 December 1916: Lettre of the IAzW to the Jüdische Hilfskomittee/J. Kipman (Lublin, Russ. Poland) (Vienna, 23 October 1916), 45kb–46kb.

[80] Jörg Wiesner (1960), 'Die Politik der Mittelmächte in Polen während der Besetzung im Ersten Weltkrieg', *Ostdeutsche Wissenschaft*, 7, 130–133.

[81] ÖStA-AVA, Neuer Kultus: Akatholischer Teil, Israelitischer Kultus (auch jüdischer Kultus), D 16–17 Koscher, Stiftungen, Vereine, Karton 60 Stiftungen, Beiträge an der katholischen Geistlichkeit, Kultus: Lettre of the Baron Hirsch Stiftung Wien—Zuweisung von Kohle, behufs Beheizung der Büroräume, (Vienna, 22 January 1918), No. 2705 (Baron Hirsch Stiftung (Vienna, 18 September 1918), Abschrift No. 283, 1–3.

a total discontinuation of financial help for war victims in the Austrian-Hungarian Empire. Moreover, antisemitism within the Empire and in the occupied Polish territories increased and made the task of implementing the ideals of the IAzW even more difficult.[82]

After the short-lived period of peace following the Treaty of Brest-Litovsk, the final dissolution of the Habsburg Empire after the end of the war in 1918 confronted the Vienna *Allianz* with the apparently total destruction of its educational network in the East. The newly established Polish, Romanian and Czechoslovakian governments closed all existing schools, banned any activity of the Viennese organization in the former crownlands, and confiscated the financial funds of the school foundations. Already in the last months of the war antisemitism had increased within the Monarchy and anti-Jewish riots in Galicia and elsewhere had undermined the envisioned modernity of the Vienna *Allianz*.[83] Even though the IAzW celebrated the peace treaty with Romania in 1918 as the liberation of 'the last slaves of Europe [the Romanian Jews]',[84] the final Austro-Hungarian capitulation and the break up of the Habsburg Empire, along with the attendant breakdown of imperial state structures led to the collapse of the IAzW. Without its international connections, its financial resources, its established educational network and its regional branches, the Vienna *Allianz* lost its international status and prestige. In 1925, the first post-war annual report of the IAzW declared that the envisioned emancipation and integration of Jews in the 'East', by which it meant Romania and Ukraine, were still the central agenda of the IAzW. The war, however, had reduced the IAzW to the status and scope of a local organization. The new Austrian state, which was described in the report as 'small, unimportant and pitiful', could no longer fight for universal rights and serve the formulated ideals of the IAzW.[85]

---

[82] After the declaration of war the Joint and other US institutions stopped their support of Austrian-Hungarian efforts to ease war related problems. However, through the diplomatic channels the Dutch Embassy money transfers, which aimed to support war victims in occupied territories, continued. Israelitische Allianz zu Wien (1918), *45. Jahresbericht der Israelitischen Alianz zu Wien erstattet in der 45. ordentlichen Generalversammlung am 10. Juni 1918* (Wien), 4–8.

[83] Rozenblit (2001), *Reconstructing a National Identity*, 108–111.

[84] RSA-MAM, Fond 675 Opis 1 Delo No. 255, Rum.-Jüd. Frage: Lettre of the IAzW to the Ministry of Foreign Affairs (Vienna) (Vienna 4 March 1918), 1–2.

[85] Israelitische Allianz zu Wien (1925), *XLVI. Jahresbericht der Israelitischen Allianz zu Wien erstattet an die XLVI. ordentliche Generalversammlung am 21. Mai 1925* (Wien), 5.

In addition, the establishment of the Joint Distribution Committee's Vienna bureau degraded the IAzW and reflected the ongoing loss of influence of the once proud Viennese institution.[86] The Viennese agenda to bring 'light' into the 'East' and to transfer the ideas of modernity by educating and modernizing the 'Jewish masses' of Galicia and Bucovina, as well as the Polish territories, had come to an end. The once influential and internationally recognized organization had lost its status, its cooperating partners and its supporters, and had thus become a victim of the First World War, a conflict it had enthusiastically embraced in 1914.[87]

CONCLUSION

The story of the *Israelitische Allianz zu Wien* between 1914 and 1918 demonstrates the degree to which the First World War impacted the trajectory of Jewish history in general and the history of the Viennese aid organizations in particular. The advent of war very much forced the Vienna *Allianz*, which had been founded along the lines of international solidarity and humanitarianism as well as ideas of modernity and the propagation of *Bildung* and culture, to readjust its identity and mission(s). Many of the leading representatives of the organization interpreted the war as an opportunity to finalise the processes of emancipation and integration that were already underway. The Vienna *Allianz* thus publicly endorsed the Austro-Hungarian declaration of war and readily supported the subsequent national war effort. This very public expression of patriotism and loyalty to the Habsburg throne and dynasty, however, clashed with the formerly institutionalized transnational relationships with other Jewish aid organizations in Europe. In contrast to formerly promoted ideas of international humanitarianism, a distinctive *mission civilisatrice*, which had been established before the war, was enlarged and redesigned according to national sentiments. It aimed at educating the Jewish 'East' according to Viennese ideals, and, in the process, guiding Eastern Jews into modernity as well as securing the Austro-Hungarian influence in Eastern Europe. Education emerged as a major tool for the institutionalization and implementation of the Vienna *Allianz*'s power

---

[86] Ibid., 7.

[87] The IAzW continued to exist after 1918, but it was a very much reduced organization and it never regained its former influence.

in the Jewish communities of the Habsburg Empire as well as the occupied territories. The foundation of schools and other educational institutions which could secure a 'cultural domination' was presented by the Viennese elite as an additional share in the national war effort. By organizing the relief work for the majority of Jewish refugees in the Habsburg Empire, the Vienna *Allianz* adhered to its self-propagated ideas of national unity and solidarity and education policies. While the *Allianz* gave up its international collaboration and connections, which had developed over the course of almost three decades prior to 1914, and joined the national and patriotic efforts to win the war, this loyalty did not ultimately pay off. After the war, the Vienna *Allianz* not only lost its *Heimat*, the multi-ethnic Habsburg Empire, but it was also unable to re-establish harshly severed relations with its European partners, based in the now victorious states. Indeed, the legacy of the unprecedented political and cultural clashes of the war years was about to haunt not only the Vienna *Allianz* but also the entire European continent.

Eastern Promises: Jewish Germans in the German Administration of Eastern Europe During the Great War

Philipp Nielsen

Among the photos taken on the Eastern Front during the First World War that emerge from the archives, there is one that is particularly striking. Taken some time in the spring of 1916, it shows two German officers wearing gas masks and posing for the camera. Their uniforms are a bit tight around the waist; the dog sitting at their feet shakes his head in a blur. So far, so conventional. Yet the officer on the right wears a distinctive emblem around his neck, a large Star of David. This is Army Rabbi Aaron Tänzer from Göppingen, then serving with the Staff of IV Army Corps, part of the newly created Army of the Bug, or *Bugarmee*, in

P. Nielsen (✉)
Sarah Lawrence College, New York, NY, USA
e-mail: pnielsen@sarahlawrence.edu

P. Nielsen
Center for the History of Emotions, Max Planck
Institute for Human Development, Berlin, Germany

© The Author(s) 2019
E. Madigan and G. Reuveni (eds.),
The Jewish Experience of the First World War,
https://doi.org/10.1057/978-1-137-54896-2_3

43

Jablon.[1] What seems, in retrospect, to be an image full of foreboding—featuring Jews, the Eastern Front, German uniforms, and gas—was, in early 1916, an image full of promise. The feeling of ambiguity, at best, and outright hostility, at worst, which had marked German both Jewish and non-Jewish attitudes towards Eastern European Jews before the war, and which had, in turn, complicated Jewish-German relations, was replaced, at least for a while, by almost uniform endorsement.

With the outbreak of the war, Eastern Europe briefly appeared as a sort of promised land to Jews in Germany and Central Europe. In the 1914 declaration 'To the Jews of Poland!', the German army pledged to liberate Eastern European Jews,[2] and, despite some serious short-comings, the German occupation brought freedom from the Russian regime.[3] German combatant officers and chaplains set up soup kitchens and conducted religious services. From being regarded as posing a danger to 'Germanness' or *Deutschtum* in the pre-war writings of Heinrich von Treitschke, Eastern European Jews were transformed into outposts of that very *Deutschtum*.[4] As Jesko von Puttkammer, former governor of the German colony of Cameroon and not known there for particularly liberal policies, put it in a newspaper article in December 1915, Eastern European Jews embodied 'the Germanic idea' in the fight against the

---

[1] Stadtarchiv (StA) Göppingen—Nachlass Aron Tänzer: Dr. A. Tänzer, *Als Feldrabbiner bei der Bugarmee*, 7; LBI NY ME640—Aron Tänzer, *Kriegserinnerungen*, 13. The army was named after the river Bug.

[2] See 'An die Juden in Polen!' 1 September 1914, reprinted as Annex I in Zosa Szajkowski (1969), 'The German Appeal to the Jews of Poland, August 1914', *Jewish Quarterly Review* 59, 317–318.

[3] On the German occupation in Eastern Europe, see Vejas Gabriel Liulevicius (2000), *War Land on the Eastern Front: Culture, National Identity, and the German Occupation in World War I* (Cambridge, Cambridge University Press), 126, 191–192; Jürgen Matthäus (1998), 'German *Judenpolitik* in Lithuania During the First World War', *Leo Baeck Institute Yearbook* 43:1, 155–174; Steven E. Aschheim (1983), 'Eastern Jews, German Jews and Germany's *Ostpolitik* in the First World War', *Leo Baeck Institute Yearbook* 28:1, 351–368; Egmont Zechlin (1969), *Die deutsche Politik und die Juden im Ersten Weltkrieg* (Göttingen, Vandenhoeck & Ruprecht), 278–284; and for a recent overview, see Tracey Hayes Norrell (2010), 'Shattered Communities: Soldiers, Rabbis, and the Ostjuden under German Occupation: 1915–1918' (PhD diss., University of Tennessee, Knoxville).

[4] For Treitschke see Heinrich von Treitschke (1879), 'Unsere Aussichten', *Preussische Jahrbücher* 44, 572–573; for the way German-Jewish associations promoted this position, see Aschheim (1983), 'Eastern Jews, German Jews', 355–357.

Slavs.[5] These Germans 'in the diaspora', were, he insisted, 'an outstanding, not to be underestimated bulwark against Russiandom and the dangers of the East'.[6]

The wartime visions of the Imperial German state and German Jews, and indeed those for a post-war settlement, coalesced more closely in Eastern Europe than anywhere else. The German declaration of a war of *Kultur* against *Gesellschaft* opened a rhetorical and, in many cases, real door for Eastern European Jews into German plans. This chapter will trace Jewish participation in the administration of German-occupied Eastern and Central Europe and explore the role played by Jewish soldiers as active participants in the German military, rather than as objects of the military's actions.[7] As such, it contributes to the growing historiography on the relationship between, and the experiences of, Jews and non-Jews, both German and otherwise, in Eastern Europe during the period of the First World War.[8] Taking the promises of liberation and

[5] Jesko von Puttkammer (1915), 'Eine Kulturfrage im Osten', *Der Tag*; on Puttkammer see, for example, Christian S. Davis (2012), *Colonialism, Antisemitism, and Germans of Jewish Descent in Imperial Germany* (Ann Arbor, University of Michigan Press), 182.

[6] von Puttkammer (1915), 'Eine Kulturfrage'.

[7] Derek Penslar (2011) has proposed a similar shift in perspective in his 'The German Jewish Soldier: From Participant to Victim', *German History* 29:3, 404–422, and in his book (2013) that followed *Jews and the Military: A History* (Princeton, Princeton University Press), 5–10, see also Tim Grady's (2017) *A Deadly Legacy: German Jews and the Great War* (New Haven, Yale University Press), 2–3.

[8] In addition to the already cited works of Penslar, Grady and Liulevicus, see also Steven E. Aschheim (1982), *Brothers and Strangers: The East European Jew in German and German Jewish Consciousness, 1800–1923* (Madison, The University of Wisconsin Press); Michael Berger (2009), *Eisernes Kreuz und Davidstern* (Berlin trafo); Michael Berger and Gideon Römer-Hilbrecht, eds. *Juden und Militär in Deutschland: Zwischen Integration, Assimilation, Ausgrenzung und Vernichtung* (Baden-Baden, Nomos); Charles Ingrao and Franz A. J. Szabo, eds. (2008), *The Germans and the East* (West Lafayette, Purdue University Press); David J. Fine (2012), *Jewish Integration in the German Army in the First World War* (Berlin, de Gruyter); Tim Grady (2011), *The German-Jewish Soldiers of the First World War in History and Memory* (Liverpool, 2011); Ulrike Heikaus and Julia B. Köhne, eds. (2014), *Krieg! Juden zwischen den Fronten, 1914–1918* (München, Jüdisches Museum München); Robert L. Nelson (2011), *German Soldier Newspapers of the First World War* (Cambridge, Cambridge University Press); Ulrich Sieg (2001), *Jüdische Intellektuelle im Ersten Weltkrieg: Kriegserfahrungen, weltanschauliche Debatten und kulturelle Neuentwürfe* (Berlin, Akademie Verlag); as well as editions such as those Sabine Hank and Hermann Simon (2013), *Feldrabbiner in den deutschen Streitkräften des Ersten Weltkriegs* (Berlin, Hentrich & Hentrich); and idem (2002), *Feldpostbriefe Jüdischer Soldaten* (Teetz, Hentrich & Heinich).

emancipation offered by the German government as a starting point, the chapter explores in depth the experience of three Jewish individuals and their non-Jewish counterparts serving in the German army and administration in the East who attempted to implement these promises. The three were Adolf Warschauer, a noted German archivist from Posen who was recruited by Governor General of Warsaw Hans Hartwig von Beseler in 1915 to run the Polish archives; Army Rabbi Leopold Rosenak from Bremen, serving under the *OberOst* (short for *Oberbefehlshaber der gesamten deutschen Streitkräfte im Osten*, the Commander-in-Chief of all German Forces in the East headquarters) Field Marshal Paul von Hindenburg and his quartermaster Erich Ludendorff from 1916 until the end of the war; and, lastly, the aforementioned Aron Tänzer. Rather than offering a comprehensive or representative overview, these three individuals serve as case studies for the experience of Jews in the three different kinds of administration in the East: civil administration in the General Government, military administration in *OberOst*, and an army group at the front.

THE PECULIAR POSITION OF MILITARY RABBIS ON THE GERMAN EASTERN FRONT

During the First World War, military rabbis were included in the army's pastoral staff for the first time in German history. Initially accepted only as volunteers by the Prussian army, from August 1915 on they also received a financial allowance in accordance with those granted to military chaplains not permanently in the army's service.[9] Notwithstanding the issue of pay, the rabbis were ranked and treated, in common with Protestant and Catholic chaplains, as 'general [*allgemeine*] officers' and 'senior military officials'. Army chaplains did not have a clearly determined officer rank, though the pay they received suggests that they were regarded as equivalent to colonels.[10] Over the course of the war,

---

[9] The allowance was granted retroactively in September that year, see Arnold Vogt (1984), *Religion im Militär: Seelsorge zwischen Kriegsverherrlichung und Humanität, eine militärgeschichtliche Studie* (Frankfurt a.M., Peter Lang), 586–587, 606; Bayerisches Hauptstaatsarchiv München: MOB Akten 1. Weltkrieg, 13847—Prussian Ministry of War to the Royal Bavarian Ministry of War, 21 September 1915.

[10] Vogt (1984), *Religion im* Militär, 75, 205.

thirty rabbis served on different fronts and with various army groups where they were attached to the army staffs.[11] Jewish services at the front, which had been such memorable exceptions in previous wars, now became much more routine, but the frequency with which they were held fluctuated as military chaplains, both Jewish and non-Jewish, were stretched thin in relation to the soldiers for whom they had to provide pastoral care. In addition, more often than not chaplains were based in hospitals in rear areas, usually at quite a remove from the front-line. Occasionally, when the only service available was a Shabbat service by a military rabbi, Christian infantrymen attended these[12]; in other instances, Protestant and Jewish chaplains conducted services together.[13]

Aron Tänzer's surviving diaries and correspondence offer insights into the way individual rabbis could experience their peculiar position in the East.[14] Born in 1871 in Pressburg, then part of the Austro-Hungarian Empire, he had studied in Berlin and Bern in the years before the war. Following his doctoral degree, and after various positions in Germany and Austro-Hungary, he settled in Göppingen near Stuttgart in 1907 as the rabbi of this southwest German community. At this point he received German citizenship.[15] Following the outbreak of war, Tänzer immediately volunteered to become a military rabbi. On 29 July 1915, as the status of rabbis was being fully recognized, he was called to report to the headquarters of IV Army Corps. With just two weeks remaining

[11] Vogt (1984), *Religion im Militär*, 599; Berger (2009), *Eisernes Kreuz und Davidstern*, 141; and Hank and Simon, *Feldrabbiner*, 14.

[12] CJA 1.75 D Ta 1—Aron Tänzer: 13368—'1. Bericht des Feldrabbiner der Bugarmee Dr. A. Tänzer aus Göppingen', September 1915, Bl. 2; Heinrich Walle (1983), 'Deutsche Jüdische Soldaten, 1914–1945', in Militärgeschichtliches Forschungsamt, ed. *Deutsche Jüdische Soldaten, 1914–45* (Herford, Verlag E.S. Mittler), 41; and Vogt (1984), *Religion im Militär*, 479, 594–595.

[13] CJA 1.75 C Ve 1—Verband der deutschen Juden: 13020—Leopold Rosenak (1915), 'Bericht des über meine Tätigkeit vom 27 August bis 24. Sept., 26 Sept 1915', Bl. 135–136; see also David J. Fine (2011), 'Jüdische Soldaten und Religion an der Front', in Heikaus and Köhne (2014), *Krieg!*, 140.

[14] For the published wartime memoir and diaries see Peter C. Appelbaum (2014), *Loyalty Betrayed: Jewish Chaplains in the German Army During the First World War* (London, Valentine Mitchell).

[15] Karl-Heinz Rueß (1988), 'Dr. Aron Tänzer – Leben und Werk des Rabbiners', in Aron Tänzer, *Die Geschichte der Juden in Jebenhausen und Göppingen. Mit erweiterten Beiträgen über Schicksal und Ende der Göppinger Judengemeinde, 1927–1945 Neu herausgegeben von Karl Heinz Rueß* (Weißenhorn, Anton H. Konrad), 622–625.

until his departure, he frantically prepared for what he assumed would
be expected of him as a German Imperial officer and learnt how to
ride a horse and fire his newly purchased revolver.[16] Army chaplains,
whatever their confession, did not usually carry weapons and instead
wore a brassard with a red cross on white background to indicate their
non-combatant status.[17] Nonetheless, at least one photo exists of Tänzer
proudly posing with a pistol belt over his white fur winter coat,[18] and in
his memoirs about the war, Tänzer claimed that the weapons training he
received before going to the front served him well.[19]

Tänzer's actual work, however, included little shooting but a lot of
riding, as he pointed out when defending the cost of riding lessons three
years into the war.[20] In his letters, Tänzer mostly wrote of organizing
religious services, of distributing mail and care packages (the so-called
Liebesgaben, filled with cigarettes and newspapers), of arranging kosher
provisions and, perhaps the most difficult aspect of his ministry, notifying
the parents of fallen soldiers. For Tänzer, these tasks had a very personal
dimension, as his two oldest sons, Paul and Fritz, were also serving at
the front.[21] He was particularly moved by his visits to military hospitals,
where 'even though I wear my insignia of a rabbi visible for everybody,
all soldiers treat me with the greatest cordiality and gratitude'.[22]

Tänzer's appointment was the result of German military success on
the Eastern Front over the course of 1915. The German armies had
stemmed the Russian advance in the autumn of 1914 and the spring of
the following year brought another series of spectacular victories, which
saw German and Austro-Hungarian troops advancing deep into formerly
Russian territory.[23] The region they captured included the historic Pale

---

[16] StA Göppingen: Dr. A. Tänzer, *Als Feldrabbiner*, 7; LBI NY ME640—Aron Tänzer,
Kriegserinnerungen, 13.

[17] Vogt (1984), *Religion im Militär*, 587.

[18] 'Der Armeerabbiner der Bug-Armee Dr. Aron Tänzer – Göppingen an der Ostfront
bei Pinsk', *Israelitisches Familienblatt*, 14 January 1916, Issue 2, 3.

[19] LBI NY ME640—Tänzer, *Kriegserinnerungen*, 13.

[20] CJA 1.75 D Ta 1—Aron Tänzer: 13368—'2. Bericht des Feldrabbiners bei der
Bugarmee', 3 October 1915, Bl. 17–18.

[21] Rueß (1988), 'Dr. Aron Tänzer', 641.

[22] CJA 1,75 D Ta 1—Aron Tänzer: 13368—'4. Bericht des Feldrabbiners der Bugarmee
Dr. A Tänzer', 7 October 1915, Bl. 23–23.

[23] Roger Chickering (2004), *Imperial Germany and the Great War, 1914–1918*, 2nd ed.
(Cambridge, Cambridge University Press), 56; Liulevicius (2000), *War Land*, 17–20.

of Settlement, the area to which Jewish settlement had been restricted under the Russian Empire. It was the heartland of European Jewry, and by the autumn of 1915 some three million Jews were living under the German army's authority.[24] The position of rabbis in the military structure on the Eastern Front is particularly interesting given the size of the local Jewish population. Needed as interlocutors, bridging the divide between German troops and local civilians, rabbis served with the headquarters of the different army groups.[25] In an ironic twist, after Jewish ascent in the military hierarchy had been blocked for the preceding thirty years, rabbis now suddenly became the highest-ranking Jewish officers.

The first year of the war proved to be a mostly positive experience for Tänzer. In November 1915, he established a kosher soup kitchen in the town of Biala, something he later considered the most important legacy of his time in Poland. Both Jews and Christians came to eat, and the capacity of the kitchen soon needed to be expanded.[26] In fact the first soup kitchen of this kind, established by Tänzer's colleague Leopold Rosenak in Kovno, was named after the *OberOst* quartermaster General Erich Ludendorff, who fondly recalled this detail in his memoirs published immediately after the war.[27]

Rosenak's biography has striking parallels with that of Tänzer. He was born three years earlier, in 1868, in Nadasz, a small town just outside of Pressburg. In common with Tänzer, Rosenak completed his doctorate at the university of Bern, and in 1886 he became the first rabbi to be formally appointed to the Jewish community in Bremen. In contrast to Tänzer, however, Rosenak had already been involved in Eastern European Jewish matters before the war as Bremen was one of the major embarkation points for Jews emigrating from Eastern Europe to England or the United States.[28]

Rosenak immediately joined the forces on the outbreak of war in 1914 and was sent to the Eastern Front. His daughter Minnie commented

[24] For a contemporary estimate see 'Zur Statistik der Juden in Polen', in *Süddeutsche Monatshefte* 13:5 (February 1916), 848.

[25] Vogt (1984), *Religion im Militär*, 586–587.

[26] StA Göppingen—Arnold Tänzer to his wife Bertha, 26 November 1915.

[27] Erich Ludendorff (1919), *Meine Kriegserinnerungen, 1914–1918* (Berlin, Ernst Siegfried Mittler und Sohn: Verlagsbuchhandlung), 154.

[28] Minnie Rosenak (1988), 'Rabbiner Dr. Leopold Rosenak: Vom Feldrabbiner zum politischen Engagement', *Leo Baeck Institute Bulletin* 79, 4–5.

tersely that 'while before the Ghetto had marched through Germany, now the German army marched to the Ghetto'.[29] Initially attached to the staff of the 12th Army, in 1916 Rosenak was transferred to the 10th Army, which was stationed at the Kovno headquarters of *OberOst*. He was present at headquarters most of the time and he would eventually be formally attached to the *OberOst*. In his letter of appointment on 29 May 1916, *OberOst* Hindenburg informed Rosenak that one of his tasks would be to advise him on questions concerning the care of the Jewish population under German occupation and matters relating to the Jewish school system.[30] Just three days later Hindenburg sent Rosenak to The Hague to negotiate a delivery of potatoes to the occupied territories in the East.[31] In June 1916, Rosenak was awarded the Iron Cross Second Class for distinguished service,[32] and in August 1916 he was asked to join the *Ausschuß der fahrbaren Kriegsbüchereien an der Front* (Committee on Mobile Field Libraries). His Protestant counterpart on the staff of *OberOst*, Ludwig Hoppe, who had invited him, wrote:

> Having got to know you as a member of your religious community who takes a lively interest in our work, it would be our pleasure to demonstrate that the unification of all patriotic forces is a project that is very dear to us by electing you to our committee.[33]

Tänzer's experiences also suggest that serving his religious community and his country could go hand in hand and be appreciated as such by his non-Jewish comrades and superiors.[34] He was awarded the Iron Cross Second Class in June 1916, the same month as Rosenak. Just a

---

[29] Ibid., 5.

[30] LBI Jer 468—Leopold Rosenak: Hindeburg to Rosenak, 20 May 1916.

[31] Ibid.: Administration of the *Reichskartoffelstelle* to Senate of the City of Bremen, 23 May 1916; on the positive relationship between Rosenak and the OberOst see also Minnie Rosenak and the letters she cites, see Rosenak (1988), 'Rabbiner Dr. Leopold Rosenak', 8–11; That someone had to be sent at all, however, was the result of the disastrous agricultural decisions and policies of OberOst in 1916, see Liulevicius (2000), *War Land*, 68–69.

[32] LBI Jer 468—Rosenak: Generalleutnant von Koith to Rosenak, Kovno, 30 June 1916.

[33] Ibid.: Divisionspfarrer Ludwig Hoppe to Leopold Rosenak, 24 August 1916.

[34] For the very similar experience of Rabbi Georg Salzberger, see Michael Berger (2009), 'Jüdische Militärseelsroge: Davidstern und Feldgrau, Jüdische Soldaten, Feldrabbiner und religiöse Praxis im Dienst', in Berger and Römer-Hillebrecht, *Juden und Militär in Deutschland*, 92.

few months later, he received the relatively prestigious Knight's Cross First Class of the Order of Frederick of Württemberg, and in December the Knight's Cross of the Order of Franz-Josef by the Austro-Hungarian army.[35] Although Tänzer does not mention the acts or types of service for which he received these awards, the receipt of the Knight's Cross strongly suggests that he served with distinction while under enemy fire and was thus regarded by his superiors as being especially committed to his role at the front.

The official recognition Tänzer and Rosenak received for their military service in the form of medals does not indicate a complete absence of antisemitism at the front. The nature of antisemitic prejudice was, in fact, one of seven discussion topics at the first 'Conference of the Army Rabbis in the East' held in Vilna in March 1916. The general consensus of the rabbis present was that instances of discrimination were still too sporadic to warrant an intervention by the *Central-Verein deutscher Staatsbürger jüdischen Glaubens* (Central Association of Germans of the Jewish Faith). Indeed, Tänzer himself claimed to know of only one such case. The rabbis nonetheless agreed that everyone confronted with antisemitism should fight it openly, not least to defend the honour of all German Jews.[36]

Any antisemitism encountered by Jewish soldiers and officers, especially in the first years of the war, was generally appraised in the context of comparatively extreme Russian antisemitism and the Tsarist pogroms and deportations. In a letter written in August 1915, for example, Rosenak referred to 'Russian atrocities' and the defiling of a synagogue in Soldau.[37] He also described the contributions the local Jewish population had to make to the German occupiers as mild 'in comparison to the Russian yoke'.[38] In general, the rabbis saw it as their task

[35] See CJA 1.75 D Ta 1—Aron Tänzer: 13366—*Vorschlagsliste zur Verleihung eines Württembergischen Kriegsorderns*, 4 June 1916, Bl. 20; ibid., Feldrabbiner Dr. Arthur Levy to Tänzer, 22 June 1916, Bl. 4; ibid., Dr. Alexander Lourié to Tänzer, 25 December 1916, Bl. 21; StA Göppingen—Arnold Tänzer to his wife Bertha, 6 September 1916.

[36] CJA 1.75 D Ta 1—Aron Tänzer: 13367—Protocol of the 1st Conference of the Army Rabbis of the East, Vilna, 6 and 7 March 1916, Bl. 7–8.

[37] CJA 1.75 C Ve 1—Verband der deutschen Juden: 13020—Leopold Rosenak to *Verband der deutschen Juden*, Soldau, August 1915, Bl. 120–121.

[38] CJA 1.75 C Ve 1—Verband der deutschen Juden: 13020—Leopold Rosenak, 'Bericht des über meine Tätigkeit vom 27 August bis 24. Sept. 1915', Bl. 136.

to explain the oppression of Eastern European Jewry to the German soldiers who would encounter the local population. In November 1915 Tänzer, for example, began to lecture German officers on the history of Eastern European Jews.[39] These lectures represented a wider attempt by German Jews to stake out a claim for Eastern European Jews in future German plans for Poland.

THE GENERAL GOVERNMENT
OF WARSAW AND TEACHING THE HISTORY OF THE EAST

After German troops entered Warsaw in August 1915, the Imperial government established a General Government of Poland headquartered in the city. The new German administration began on a note of goodwill; Russification policies were reversed and the Polish-speaking university in Warsaw that had been replaced by a Russian language university in 1870 was reopened.[40] Even if the future of the occupied territories remained unclear, not least due to competing views within Germany as well as between Germany and Austria-Hungary, the atmosphere was reasonably positive and, for the time being, Poles were appointed to run local and regional administrations.[41]

Governor General Hans Hartwig von Beseler travelled extensively to acquaint himself with his new domain. Writing to his wife Clara from one such excursion in September 1915 he exclaimed: 'In the cities Jews, Jews and Jews.'[42] His impression of them was not necessarily negative, though, and, for their part, Eastern European Jews did their best to impress the new authorities favourably. In February 1916, Beseler wrote of encountering Jews who had fled from further East: 'In a refugee camp the poor Jews who had been driven from Brest-Litovsk brought me bread and salt and their spokesman declared an exuberant "Hoch!" on Germany:

[39] StA Göppingen—Arnold Tänzer to his wife Bertha, 7 November 1915, 2 June 1916, 2 April 1917, 27 January 1918.

[40] Bundesarchiv (BArch) N 30 (Hans Hartwig von Beseler/Briefe 1915)/53—Beseler to his wife, 16 October 1915; see also Anita Prazmowska (2010), *Poland: A Modern History* (London, I.B. Tauris), 66–67. One of the first things the German General Government in Warsaw in the Second World War would do, was to close that very same university.

[41] Prazmowska (2010), *Poland*, 66; Antony Polonsky (2012), *The Jews in Poland and Russia: Volume III, 1914–2008* (Oxford, The Littman Library of Jewish Civilization), 14.

[42] BArch N 30 (Beseler/Briefe 1915)/53—Beseler to his wife, 29 September 1915.

that was after he had thanked me for the loving care with which the Germans treated them and gave them bread. Take care in whom you trust [*Trau, schau, wem*]! But it was nonetheless nice.'[43] In an article published in December 1915, the former governor of Cameroon, Jesko von Puttkammer, was even more emphatic and departed from the usual description of Eastern European Jews as physically weak, though with potential. Instead, he praised the 'tall, lean, muscular and energetic [...] Maccabean figures' he had encountered on a visit to Poland.[44]

Arthur Kahn of the *Verein für die Bodenkultur unter den Juden Deutschlands*, founded at the end of nineteenth century to promote agricultural initiatives among Germany's Jews, displayed a similar, if slightly more guarded enthusiasm. Kahn was as enamoured with Jewish agricultural settlements as von Puttkammer. In Germany proper, they had served to maintain the Jewish village communities and thus the 'age-old site of the religious and political conservatism of the Jews'. Now, by settling Jewish war invalids on estates in the East, Eastern European Jews could be familiarized with German agriculture. This population that was '*German friendly, and a loyal and reliable population group*' in the occupied territory would thereby become '*the strongest German bulwark against any hostile Slavdom*'.[45]

In common with Kahn and the rabbis, the letters German-Jewish soldiers wrote home from the East often convey their sense that Eastern European Jews needed to learn from the German occupiers. Alongside occasional allusions to romantic encounters with a more spiritual Judaism, the authors of these letters quite frequently comment on the utter poverty and squalor in which their co-religionists lived, even if among the other ethnic linguistic groups Jews were described as the cleanest.[46]

---

[43] BArch N 30 (Beseler/Briefe 1915)/54—Beseler to his wife, 20 February 1916.

[44] Jesko von Puttkammer (1915), 'Eine Kulturfrage'.

[45] Arthur Kahn (1915), 'Jüdische Bauern', *Die Jüdische Presse: Konservative Wochenschrift*. Emphasis in the original.

[46] On the romantic encounter with Eastern Judaism, for example by Arnold Zweig or Martin Buber, see Paul Mendes-Flohr (1999), *German Jews: A Dual Identity* (New Haven, Yale University Press), 66–88; on the fascination as well as overall rejection on actual encounter Aschheim (1982), *Brothers and Strangers*, 148–153; Aschheim (1982), 'From Myth to Counter-Myth: The Romanticization of the Eastern Jew (1880–1914)', *Immigration and Minorities* 1:3, 306–319; and Leslie Morris (1998), 'Reading the Face of the Other: Arnold Zweig's and Hermann Struck's *Das ostjüdische Antlitz*' in Sara Friedrichsmeyer, Sara Lennox, and Susanne Zantop, eds. *The Imperialist Imagination:*

In light of such reactions, the educational effort of the German rabbis stationed in the East was meant to improve German attitudes towards the local Jews. Beyond giving lectures, they also published educational stories. In one article of July 1916, titled 'A Dream' and written by Rabbi Dr H. Wiesel, a Jew from Vilna encounters an occupying German soldier. True to the impressions conveyed in the letters of Jewish soldiers and probably also a sign of enduring pre-war stereotypes, the Jew is portrayed as the stereotypical *Ostjude*— down-trodden, weak, and humble. Fully expecting to be struck down by the soldier, as a Russian soldier would have done, the German soldier, only identified as 'genius', instead declares that he is delivering the spirit of freedom, justice, benevolence, and charity. Following this short German sermon, God enters the scene. He praises the 'genius' for his words and anoints him as his official messenger to reveal God's wonders to the world. To make absolutely clear that the 'genius' is, in fact, Germany, the dream ends with the words: 'Since you act as you do, you have understood my spirit. Hence, o Germany, you will triumph.'[47]

Under pressure from the steamrolling Russian Brusilov offensive that threatened the German front throughout the summer of 1916, German Jewish soldiers may have needed reminding what would lie in store for their co-religionists in the event of defeat. Such stories may also have been designed to put any German antisemitism into context once more. Whether using the image of the *Ostjude*, so fraught with antisemitic stereotypes, was the best way to achieve any of these goals is another matter. In fact, non-Jewish German soldier newspapers carried similar yet non-fictional stories about liberating Jews from Russian antisemitism. In these depictions, the Eastern European Jews'

German Colonialism and Its Legacy (Ann Arbor: University of Michigan Press), 189–203; for a combination of spiritual revival and German style emancipation see Hermann Cohen (1916), 'Der polnische Jude,' *Der Jude* 1, 154. As an example for the letters see, Otto Köhler to Siegmund Feist, the director of the Jewish Orphanage in Berlin, 15 January 1915, in Hank and Simon, eds. (2002), *Feldpostbriefe Jüdischer Soldaten*, 357, or ibid., Leo Jaretzki to Feist, 23 August 1915, 295.

[47] Rabbiner Dr. H Wiesel (1916), 'Ein Traum', in *Feldbriefe Posener Rabbiner an die jüdischen Soldaten der Provinz Posen*, 1st Series, Tamus 5676, July 1916 (Frankfurt a.M., M. Lehrberger & Co.), 13–15; archived in CAHJP P24: Arnold Tänzer.

similarity to Germans and difference from Slavs was highlighted: the Jews were 'good looking', 'industrious', and usually spoke a German dialect.[48]

The 'Dream' is also revealing with regard to the ways in which military rabbis interpreted the war for other reasons. Rabbis, according to the existing literature, were much more circumspect about war and violence and more beholden to the ideas of universalism and peace in Judaism than their Christian counterparts.[49] Yet the narrative of 'A Dream', with its conflation of Germany's destiny and God's will, is very close to the wartime sermons of Protestant ministers. Thus, at least in their appeals to soldiers on the Eastern Front, rabbis did not shy away from invoking God as an ally of Germany well into the war.

Though no 'genius', Governor General von Beseler certainly seems to have conceived of his mission as one that could ultimately benefit the Eastern European Jewish population as well as German war aims. Beseler considered the local Jews 'useful members of a modern state' and 'important for the development of the Polish national economy'. He also saw their emancipation as both a fundamental human right and a solution to the 'Jewish problem' for which he favoured a local solution. He opposed Jewish emigration, be it to Germany, the United States, or Palestine.[50] Instead, the German administration hoped to turn Polish Jews into outposts of *Deutschtum* by making German the language of instruction in Jewish schools.[51] This was also something von Puttkammer had called for in order to draw Eastern European Jews into the German cultural orbit in the future.[52] The proposal did not elicit universal enthusiasm among Polish Jews themselves, however, and, at least in private, Beseler had his doubts about how German or, rather, Prussian, the Eastern European Jews really were:

---

[48] Robert Nelson (2002), '"Unsere Frage ist der Osten" Representations of the Occupied East in German Soldier Newspapers, 1914–1918', *Zeitschrift für Ostmitteleuropa-Forschung* 51:4, 523–525.

[49] See Sieg (2011), *Jüdische Intellektuelle*, 132–134, 151–154.

[50] BArch N 30 (Hans Hartwig von Beseler/Jüdische Angelegenheiten in Polen)/27—marginal comments on a pamphlet sent to him by the 'Deutsche Vereinigung für die Interessen der osteuropäischen Juden' in October 1915, Bl. 6–11.

[51] Polonsky (2012), *The Jews in Poland and Russia*, 13.

[52] von Puttkammer (1915), 'Eine Kulturfrage'.

The Jews play the German, but despite the fathomless mistreatment think back with a certain nostalgia to the Russian 'Tshin', who for a few roubles would look the other way.[53]

Importantly, the Governor General had no such doubts about the German-Jewish employees in his staff, whose Jewishness for him was not even worth remarking upon. Beseler appointed Adolf Warschauer to organize the Polish archives. Warschauer, born in the province of Posen in 1855, had made a name for himself as head archivist in Posen and Danzig as well as the publisher of several journals on the German history of Eastern Central Europe.[54] On several occasions, Beseler invited Warschauer to dine with him. After the first time, Warschauer wrote to his wife that he had wanted to flee the invitation since he felt 'small and ugly, the only civilian among 50 officers and generals'.[55] Indeed, in the photos surviving from his time in Warsaw, Warschauer, even in uniform, always looks small and lost, though not without pride, among his military superiors.[56] Ultimately, he did not act on his instincts to avoid that first dinner engagement and instead stayed for what turned out to be a delightful evening. The conversation was animated and the wine flowed freely enough for the archivist to wake up the next morning with a slight hangover. He informed his wife that he did not want her to brag about the episode, but she could tell their children that 'one of our greatest military heroes'—Beseler, who had led the conquest of Antwerp before being posted to Warsaw—had 'valued their father sufficiently to have him sit right next to him at the table'.[57]

Warschauer was particularly proud that Beseler and the other officers had been well informed about his work.[58] Indeed, the Governor General was not only informed but also impressed by it, and continued to be so

[53] BArch N 30 (Beseler/Briefe 1915)/53—Beseler to his wife, 16 October 1915, Bl. 22.

[54] Adolf Warschauer (1926), *Deutsche Kulturarbeit in der Ostmark: Erinnerungen aus vier Jahrzehnten* (Berlin, Reimar Hobbing), 11–15; See Mathias Seiter (2009), 'Jewish Identities Between Region and Nation: Jews in the Borderlands of Posen and Alsace-Lorraine, 1871–1914' (PhD diss., University of Southampton), 55–67, 73.

[55] CAHJP P267: Adolf Warschauer—Warschauer to Bertha Warschauer, 15 December 1915; Warschauer (1926), *Deutsche Kulturarbeit*, 272–273.

[56] See CAHJP P267: Warschauer: Box 4—Photographs.

[57] CAHJP P267: Warschauer—Warschauer to his wife, 15 December 1915.

[58] CAHJP P267: Warschauer—Warschauer to his wife, 15 December 1915.

as he wrote to a friend of his, the chair of geography at the Berlin university *Geheimrat* Albrecht Penck, in November 1916.[59] Warschauer had an equally cordial relationship with Count Hutten-Czapski, a Prussian-Polish aristocrat now serving as the General Government's political expert, who often invited him for dinner at the palace he had taken as his residence in Warsaw.[60] In his memoirs, published in 1936, Hutten-Czapski described Warschauer as a close friend and trusted council, as a man with a 'wide mental horizon' who 'possessed strong patriotic feelings'.[61]

THE RUSSIAN REVOLUTION AND A NEW EAST

Around the time that Beseler wrote to Penck, the improving military situation in the East and the changes on the home front made planning for the future paramount. The Brusilov offensive was beaten back, Romania was defeated in December 1916, and the Russian revolution of February 1917 sapped Russian fighting morale, tipping the scales decisively in favour of the forces of the Central Powers.[62] Hindenburg's and Ludendorff's ascension to the Supreme Command, combined with the Russian revolution, also decisively altered the political dynamics of the Eastern Front. Prince Leopold of Bavaria became the new *OberOst* and Major General Max Hoffmann was appointed his chief of staff. Hoffmann had served with Ludendorff since the beginning of the war and was sure to follow his superior's policies.[63] The increased if not absolute control over German policies in the East exercised

[59] BArch N 30 (Beseler/Briefe 1916)/54—von Beseler to Geh.Rat. Penck, Warsaw, 17 November 1916, Bl. 74–75; according to Adolf Warschauer's memoirs, von Beseler at the dinner in December 1915 praised his work, Warschauer (1926), *Deutsche Kulturarbeit*, 291–292; after the war Penck became prominent and active for using cartography to further German *völkisch* claims in Eastern Europe, see Kristin Kopp (2012), *Germany's Wild East: Constructing Poland as Colonial Space* (Ann Arbor, University of Michigan Press), 144–150.

[60] CAHJP P267: Warschauer—Warschauer to his wife Bertha, 23 March 1916.

[61] Bogdan Graf von Hutten-Czapski (1936), *Sechzig Jahre Politik und Gesellschaft*, vol 2 (Berlin, Verlag von E.S. Mittler & Sohn), 265; on Hutten-Czapski and his network of Jewish acquaintances in pre-1914 Berlin see Werner E. Mosse (1989), *The German-Jewish Economic Elite, 1820–1935: A Socio-Cultural Profile* (Oxford, Clarendon Press), 192–196.

[62] Chickering (2004), *Imperial Germany*, 74–75, 168.

[63] Liulevicius (2000), *War Land*, 177.

by Ludendorff, directly through the Supreme Command and indirectly through Hoffmann, worried Governor General von Beseler. He realized the potential attraction the Russian revolution might have on the Polish population that had become ever more dissatisfied by the exploitative German economic policies, particularly should the German authorities fail to take Polish aspirations into account.[64] He had no great faith in Ludendorff's intellectual capabilities—Hindenburg for him was a mere puppet—to devise an adequate response to these concerns.[65]

In November 1916, Beseler issued a decree in the name of the Central Powers that established the Kingdom of Poland, a move which merely created more strife. The question of who would govern Poland and how closely it would be tied to Germany and Austria divided the Germans, the Austrians, and, naturally, the Polish nationalists.[66] Since Polish nationalists had been somewhat antagonistic towards Jewish emancipation, the declaration also troubled German Jews, who aimed to improve a lot of their Eastern co-religionists.[67]

That was not their only cause for worry, however. In October 1916, the Prussian war ministry ordered its officers to report back the numbers of Jews in their units, an undertaking that has loomed large in the secondary literature.[68] The military rabbis in the East were not, however,

---

[64] Ibid., 195–199; Prazmovska (2010), *Poland*, 66–67.

[65] BArch N 30 (Beseler/Briefe 1917)/55—von Beseler to his wife, 15 April 1917; on Ludendorff essentially being in command and Hindenburg being little more than a puppet, see Chickering (2004), *Imperial Germany*, 73–75; Pyta sees Hindenburg as much more in control, cf. Wolfram Pyta (2009), *Hindenburg: Herrschaft zwischen Hohenzollern und Hitler* (Munich, Pantheon), 231–231, 299–302.

[66] See also Liulevicius (2000), *War Land*, 195; Chickering (2004), *Imperial Germany*, 86. It also set off an international jockeying for Polish support by promises towards a future independent Poland, see Prażmovska (2010), *Poland*, 68.

[67] See 'Juden-Polen-Deutsche', *Der Jude*, December 1916, 569–576; 'Königreich Polen', *Neue Jüdische Monatshefe*, 1:3 (10 November 1916), 57–58; also Prazmovska (2010), *Poland*, 41, 104; and Polonsky (2012), *The Jews in Poland and Russia*, 12, 15–16; even French and British Jews were worried about the antisemitism of the Polish national movement as represented by Roman Dmowski who had come to London in 1915 to secure the Entente's support, see Eugene C. Black (1992), 'Squaring a Minorities Triangle: Lucien Wolf, Jewish Nationalists and Polish Nationalists', in Paul Latawski, ed. *The Reconstruction of Poland, 1914–23* (Basingstoke, Macmillan), 22–23.

[68] For a detailed history see Werner T. Angress (1978), 'The German Army's "Judenzensus" in 1916: Genesis-Consequences-Significance', *Leo Baeck Institute Yearbook* 23:1, 117–137; Jacob Rosenthal (2007), *'Die Ehre des jüdischen Soldaten:' Die*

EASTERN PROMISES: JEWISH GERMANS ...   59

united in their assessment of the effects of the so-called *Judenzählung* or Jewish census. Rosenak reported from the headquarters of *OberOst* that the letters he received from Jewish soldiers had gone from enthusiastic before the census to depressed and resigned afterwards.[69] Yet Sali Levi, an army rabbi stationed in Vilna, wrote a report to the *Verband der deutschen Juden* essentially confirming that the integrity of the front-line community (or *Frontgemeinschaft*) still held, and politics and the ministry were the problem. According to Levi, some of the Christian officers who were supposed to conduct the count were outright ashamed to do so and the Jewish front-line soldiers he was in touch with took the order calmly. Jewish soldiers serving in the rear, however, who now found themselves confronted with the stigma of shirking, even though they had often served at the front before, were more likely to have their pride hurt by the census.[70] Governor General von Beseler's attitude towards Jews, at least, had not changed. In February 1917, he responded to a letter from a Professor Reincke of Kiel. Reincke had forwarded Beseler a letter of complaint about the pro-Jewish attitude of the German administration in Poland. Beseler described the letter writer as a 'fanatic Pole and antisemite', rejected his positions, and reaffirmed the German commitment to the full legal and religious emancipation of Jews in Poland.[71]

Something that had an unarguably direct impact on the lives of Eastern European Jews, however, was the so-called 'Hindenburg Plan'.

Judenzählung im Ersten Weltkrieg und ihre Folgen (Frankfurt am Main, Campus Verlag); for a few examples of the census as a watershed, see Clemens Picht (1997), 'Zwischen Vaterland und Volk: Das deutsche Judentum im Ersten Weltkrieg', in Wolfgang Michalka, ed. *Der Erste Weltkrieg: Wirkung, Wahrnehmung, Analyse* (Weyarn, Seehamer), 748; Avraham Barkai (2002), *'Wehr Dich!': Der Centralverein deutscher Staatsbürger jüdischen Glaubens, 1893–1938* (Munich: C.H. Beck), 60; as one of many symptoms oft he reviving antisemitism, Peter Pulzer (1992), *Jews and the German State: The Political History of a Minority, 1848–1933* (Oxford, Blackwell), 205–206; in support of my claim of the more limited impact of the 'Jewish Census' on frontline soldiers, see also: Tim Grady (2011), *The German-Jewish Soldiers of the First World War in History and Memory* (Liverpool, Liverpool University Press), 33, 48–49.

[69] CJA 1.75 Ve 1—Verband der deutschen Juden: 13020—Rosenak to *Verband der deutschen Juden*, 24 December 1916, Bl. 220.

[70] CJA 1.75 Ve 1—Verband der deutschen Juden: 12850—Sali Levi to *Verband der deutschen Juden*, 16 February 1917, Bl. 123.

[71] BArch N 30 (Beseler/Briefe 1917)/55—von Beseler to Reincke, 19 February 1917, Warsaw, Bl. 18–19.

The new General Staff demanded an all-out effort by the German state, including the occupying authorities in Eastern Europe to fully utilize all resources under German command.[72] This involved a much more active and indeed aggressive recruitment of foreign labour, not least in the East and among Jews. The recruitment practices, as well as the working conditions in Germany, created tensions between the occupying forces and the local population.[73] In response, the German army rabbis sought greater involvement in the management of foreign workers.[74] The *OberOst* Quartermaster, Hans von Brandenstein, reiterated his determination to review all economic policies necessitated by the war effort with due consideration for the religious sentiments of the local population. The army would continue to supply the Jews with ritual food such as matzo, and particularly 'to be considerate of the religious holidays which have become so important to the Jewish population'.[75]

During this period, the military rabbis continued to provide pastoral care for soldiers and prepared an updated field prayer book, since the one in use had been conceived with a short war in mind.[76] In March 1917, Rosenak gave a lecture to the army rabbis assembled for their fourth conference, this time in Bialystok, on the importance of field sermons. He felt that such sermons served both a secular and a religious purpose in keeping the soldiers in an optimistic state of mind, fortifying them against antisemitism, strengthening their faith and warding off the vapid attractions of materialism which they would face upon their return home. It was felt that the spirituality of Eastern European Jewish life that the soldiers had encountered on active service might help in this

---

[72] Chickering (2004), *Imperial Germany*, 76–77.

[73] Liulevicius (2000), *War Land*, 72, 180; Matthäus, 'German *Judenpolitik* in Lithuania', 169–171; and Chickering (2004), *Imperial Germany*, 84.

[74] CJA 1.75 D Ta 1—Aron Tänzer: 13367—Protocol of the Conference of the Army Rabbis of the East in Vilna on 20 and 21 November 1917, Bl. 27–29, 29.

[75] LBI Jer 468—Rosenak: Oberquartiermeister von Brandenstein to Rosenak, 11 September 1917; the promise was kept, see Matthäus, 'German *Judenpolitik* in Lithuania', 171.

[76] CJA 1.75 D Ta 1—Aron Tänzer: 11367—Protocol of the Conference of the Army Rabbis of the East in Vilna, 20 and 21 November 1917, Bl. 27–29; ibid., Protocol of the Conference of the Army Rabbis of the East in Vilna, 2–4 July 1917, 25–26; and ibid., 4th Conference of the Army Rabbis in the East in Bialystok, 5 March 1917, Bl. 22–24.

regard.[77] Rosenak concluded with this oblique reference to antisemitism and did not bring up the issue again at any of the subsequent conferences. The same was true for the spiritual lessons Eastern European Jewry might offer. In most of Rosenak and Tänzer's descriptions, the local Jews appear mostly as poor and wretched rather than as models for German Jews.[78]

The Russian revolution significantly influenced German planning for the future of Eastern Europe. After the declaration of unlimited submarine warfare in April 1917 had failed to change German fortunes in the West, the German military's dreams continued to rest in the East. At the same time, relations between the military leadership and the civilian government on the German home front deteriorated sharply. The struggle ended with a victory for Hindenburg and Ludendorff over Chancellor Bethmann-Hollweg, who was dismissed by Kaiser Wilhelm II in July 1917.[79] The parliament's peace initiative, in turn, launched by the newly united majority of Social Democrats, Catholic Zentrum and Left Liberals the same month, was undercut by the Russian Kerensky offensive and its sudden collapse. The counteroffensive saw the German forces advance rapidly and in September 1917, Riga fell into German hands. The German position in the East appeared now so unassailable that overall victory seemed once more within reach and the attraction of a peace without 'annexations and reparations' was replaced by ambitious imperial visions for Eastern Europe.[80]

The military rabbis continued to be integrated into these visions. Yet whether they were integrated into German plans out of expedience or sentiment, the difference to the occupation twenty-five years later is striking indeed. Already in April 1917, OberOst's chief of staff, Major General Max Hoffmann, had assured the Komitee für den Osten, which had been founded at the beginning of the war to lobby for the interests of Eastern European Jews, that OberOst treated Jews under its authority

[77] CJA 1.75 D Ta 1—Aron Tänzer: 13367—4th Conference of the Army Rabbis in the East in Bialystok, 5 March 1917, Bl. 22–24.

[78] See for example CJA 1.75 D Ta 1—Aron Tänzer: 13368— 'Der Armeerabbiner der Bugarmee Dr. A Tänzer über sein Tätigkeit in den MOnaten August bis Dezember 1915', 12 December 1915, Bl. 3–8; LBI Jer 468—Rosenak: Rosenak to his wife from Byalistok, September 1915.

[79] Chickering (2004), Imperial Germany, 161–162.

[80] Ibid., 169–170, 174; Liulevicius (2000), War Land, 205–206.

like any other ethnic group.[81] In fact, Hoffmann went to great lengths to explain that although some Jewish associations were of the opinion that Jews in *OberOst* needed to be treated simply as a religious denomination, that was unrealistic. To reflect the actual situation and ensure equal treatment of Jews, they needed to be considered a distinct ethnic group. This was also the position of the *Komitee für den Osten*.[82] And while the Hague Statutes governing what an occupation power could do had thus far barred *OberOst* from officially striking any discriminatory laws off the books, now that this had happened under the new Russian government, the emancipation would of course also apply to the Russian territories under German control and thus formalize the equal treatment.[83]

Despite his fears following the 'Jewish census', Rosenak's war experience also continued to be one of active participation and recognition. In July 1917, the National Liberal *Reichstag* deputy Hartmann Freiherr von Richthofen, who had voted with his party against the 'peace resolution', explored the option of awarding Rosenak an honorary professorship, apparently with the support of Rosenak's superior, Major General Hoffmann.[84] And 'in reference to your praiseworthy and successful work in the previous year' the *OberOst*'s Quartermaster von Brandenstein sent Rosenak in October 1917 once more to The Hague to negotiate the delivery of seeds for the occupied territories in the East.[85] In April 1918, the rabbi received another military decoration, the Honour Cross of the Duke of Saxony-Meiningen.[86] Had it not been for the German revolution, Rosenak would have served as a delegate to The Hague again in late 1918.[87]

The rigours of military service notwithstanding, Aron Tänzer had a largely positive war experience until well into 1918. In January of that

---

[81] Aschheim, *Brothers and Strangers*, 157.

[82] Ibid., 158.

[83] CAHJP M72/1—Oberbefehlshaber Ost to Komitee für den Osten, 30 April 1917.

[84] LBI Jer 468—Rosenak: Hartmann Freiherr von Richthofen to Rosenak, Berlin, 27 July 1917.

[85] LBI Jer 468—Rosenak: Oberquartiermeister *OberOst* Oberst von Brandenstein to Rosenak, 28 October 1917.

[86] LBI Jer 468—Rosenak: *Verleihungsurkunde*, the State Minister of Saxony-Meiningen to Rosenak, Rabbi at the Staff of *OberOst*, 24 April 1918.

[87] LBI Jer 468—Rosenak: General at the Staff (no name) to Rosenak, 3 August 1918.

year, he reported on the wonderful service he had held on the occasion of Kaiser Wilhelm's birthday and how beautiful the military parade had been on this occasion. The rabbi was especially pleased with the patronage of General Friedrich von Bernhardi, 'the famous general' as Tänzer described him, who came to see him after the service, praising him for his *History of the Jews in Brest-Litovsk* and asking for a copy of the book.[88] Published that month, the book was a timely piece of historical writing as German and Soviet representatives had been negotiating a peace treaty in Brest-Litovsk since December of the previous year. In January Tänzer also lectured for a fourth time to German officers about the history of Eastern European Jews.[89] A few weeks later he wrote a postcard from occupied Riga, which he referred to as 'this charming, absolutely German [*kerndeutsche*] city'. Tänzer told his wife that he was waiting to hear about his further orders in the East, now that peace with Russia was as good as certain.[90] He was in the city for another conference of the army rabbis of the East, the purpose of which was to determine their peacetime role in the territories expected to be under German control.[91]

Peace, though, was not yet certain. A week after Tänzer wrote to his wife the negotiations reached an impasse and hostilities resumed. The gamble of the Bolshevik leadership that workers' revolutions in Europe and the American entry into the war would bring down the German Empire did not pay off, at least in the short term. Instead, German troops advanced further into the Baltic territories, Belarus, and Ukraine. Soon the Russian capital of St. Petersburg was under threat, and on 3 March the Bolshevik leadership signed a peace treaty with Germany with even harsher terms and greater territorial losses than previously negotiated.

---

[88] StA Göppingen—Arnold (Aron) Tänzer to his wife Bertha, 27 January 1918 from Kowel. With the beginning of the war Tänzer had begun to sign his letters with Arnold rather than Aron; Bernhardi had caused waves with his *Germany and the Next War* published in 1911 and published in English in the United States in 1914. In this book he aggressively advocated for war. Dr. Aron Tänzer (1918), *Die Geschichte der Juden in Brest-Litowsk* (Berlin, Louis Lamm).

[89] StA Göppingen—Tänzer to his wife Bertha, 27 January 1918.

[90] StA Göppingen—Tänzer to his wife Bertha, 12 February 1918, emphasis my own.

[91] CJA 1.75 D Ta 1—Aron Tänzer: 13367—Conference of the Military Rabbis of the East, Riga, 12 and 13 February 1918, Bl. 30–32.

Even then fighting in the East did not entirely end as German troops got embroiled in revolutionary violence and partisan action.[92] Tänzer's two eldest sons were wounded in Ukraine in the summer of 1918, but despite his personal distress he expressed his admiration for 'our troops'.[93] Tänzer himself also served in Ukraine, now posted with Army Group Kiev, and he visited his son Paul in the military hospital there.[94] He continued to provide Jewish soldiers at the front with religious and material support where he could. He also continued to lecture German officers in the occupying army about the history of the local Jewish population.[95] Though physically drained his spirit was unbroken, and as late as July 1918 he proudly wrote to his wife that he had received his fourth military decoration, the Hanseatic Cross from the city of Hamburg.[96]

UNPREPARED FOR DEFEAT

Though exhausted by the war, the collapse of the German Empire caught Tänzer unprepared, still deep in Eastern Europe and just decorated with yet another medal at the beginning of November 1918.[97] Rosenak, who had been discharged in early October and had returned to Bremen, a major naval port, had probably the best inkling of what was about to happen.[98] For Warschauer, the German defeat interrupted what had been a slow and organized handover of authority from the General Government in Warsaw to a Polish government under German tutelage. Released from a German prison in Magdeburg, Józef Piłudski, head of the Polish Socialist Party and the key figure of the Polish independence movement, arrived in Warsaw on 10 November and declared himself head of state.[99] A day later, when the armistice on the Western Front was signed, German authority was also rapidly coming undone in the East. That afternoon, Adolf Warschauer was suddenly confronted by

[92] Liulevicius (2000), *War Land*, 210–211.

[93] StA Göppingen—Tänzer to his wife Bertha, 28 May 1918, 1 June 1918, 2 June 1918.

[94] StA Göppingen—Tänzer to his wife Bertha, 28 May 1918; CJA 1.75 D Ta 1: 13364—Tänzer to Supreme Command Army Group Kiev, 22 August 1918, Bl. 9.

[95] StA Göppingen—Tänzer to his wife Bertha, 2 June 1916, 7 November 1916, 2 April 1917, 27 January 1918.

[96] StA Göppingen—Tänzer to his wife Bertha, 14 July 1918.

[97] Rueß (1988), 'Dr. Aron Tänzer', 631.

[98] Rosenak (1988), 'Rabbiner Dr. Leopold Rosenak', 12.

[99] Prazmovska (2010), *Poland*, 87.

Polish troops in his archive and his superiors were not available to advise him on what to do, Governor General von Beseler having already rather abruptly left Warsaw.[100] With the help of his former Polish subordinates at the archive, Warschauer packed the German documents into crates for transportation to Germany at a later stage. On 15 November he boarded a train arranged for the remaining German bureaucrats and left for Berlin.[101] At that point, his old hometown, Posen, the city to whose history he had dedicated most of his life, had already been seized by Polish troops and become Poznan. With no home to return to, Warschauer and his wife settled in the German capital. To Warschauer, his service under Beseler remained 'one of the most valuable memories of [his] life'.[102] He closed his memoirs, written in 1926, with a quote from a letter by Beseler that he received upon his arrival in Berlin:

> Your efforts have not been in vain, even if, to my greatest regret, they have found such a sudden conclusion due to the sad events of the time. Yet I maintain the hope that the work we have begun will be completed at a later stage and with German assistance.[103]

CONCLUSION

Ultimately, however, the promise of the war would not be realized and Beseler and Warschauer's wish was not to come true. Instead, expectations dashed, promise turned to resentment. With the shifting borders and disappointed wartime alliances, neither soil nor culture seemed a promising ground on which to anchor nationalism anymore. With race as a defining factor in the rising tide of German nationalism, Jewish Germans lost their place in the visions for a German-dominated Eastern Europe. Rosenak felt this change first when his former superiors Hindenburg and Ludendorff both declined his entreaties to defend Jewish wartime service against the increasing antisemitism in 1921.[104] Tänzer and Warschauer

[100] Warschauer (1926), *Deutsche Kulturarbeit*, 314–15.

[101] Ibid., 317.

[102] Ibid., 318.

[103] Ibid.

[104] LBI Jer 468—Leopold Rosenak: Hindenburg to Rosenak, 25 February 1921; ibid., Rosenak: Ludendorff to Rosenak, 15 February 1921; Rosenak (1988), 'Rabbiner Dr. Leopold Rosenak', 15; Rosenak died two years later, only 55 years old, on a steamer returning from a trip to the United States, see ibid., 16.

initially continued to live within a relatively inclusive frontline community after their return to Germany. Tänzer was made an honorary member of Göppingen's War Veteran's organization, the *Veteranen- und Militär-Verein "Kampfgenossenschaft" Göppingen*, and also wrote the association's festschrift on the occasion of its 50th anniversary that year.[105] Warschauer continued to write about the history of German settlement in the East, and his work was praised by newspapers on the left and the right on the occasion of his 70th and 75th birthdays, as well as on his death in 1930.[106] Yet Tänzer, the only one of the three still alive in 1933, would experience overt exclusion and discrimination under National Socialism along with attempts to expunge his wartime record.[107]

These were later developments, however, and the fact that Tänzer went to great lengths to defend his wartime record and to receive the Honour Cross of Frontline Soldiers that the German government awarded to veterans of the First World War in 1934–1935—and reluctantly also to Jews—reveals the pride he felt about his service even then. For the Great War itself, however, the experiences of Tänzer, Rosenak, and Warschauer that formed the core of this chapter highlight that for all the stereotypes that the German government and officer class might have held about Jews, their promises of liberation for Eastern Jews and their willingness to work with German Jews in their own ranks had not been idle talk, even if they did not ultimately come to fruition. Beseler's and thus Warschauer's work in Warsaw remained incomplete, military rabbis did not reach full parity with Lutheran or Catholic chaplains by the end of the war, and their future in a peacetime army remained uncertain even before the capitulation. Yet the medals and honours bestowed on the rabbis as well as the cordial relations between them and their comrades and commanders reveal a significant degree of acceptance and appreciation.

---

[105] Dr. A Tänzer (1921), *Die Geschichte des Veteranen und Militärvereins 'Kampfgenossenschaft' in Göppingen, 1871–1921: Eine Festschrift zur Feier des 50jährigen Bestehens* (Göppingen, Buchdruckerei der Göppinger Zeitung).

[106] CAHJP P267: Adolf Warschauer—Box 2a., for example '70. Geburtstag des Geheimrats Warschauer', *Ostland*, October 15, 1925.

[107] StA—Österreicher to Tänzer, 28 November 1935; ibid.—Arnold Tänzer to Paul Tänzer, 21 August 1936.

Bread, Butter and Education: The *Yiddishist* Movements in Poland, 1914–1916

Emma Zohar

It need hardly be emphasized that the First World War brought significant changes to political and social life in Eastern Europe. The imperial regime that characterized society both in the Tsarist and Austro-Hungarian territories crumbled, and, on its ruins, new nation-states arose. The process of change was gradual, however, and lasted for approximately six years, from the outbreak of the war in the summer of 1914 to March 1921, when the Treaty of Riga essentially ended the war in Eastern Europe. From a geo-political perspective, this was clearly a period of frequent and often radical change. Yet quite apart from changes in the nature of occupation or the forms of government to which the population of the region was subjected, the events of the war caused a profound transformation in the familiar way of life people had known and experienced for generations before 1914. This was perhaps especially true for the various Jewish populations of what was then known as Congress Poland. These changes were notable in individual

E. Zohar (✉)
The Hebrew University, Jerusalem, Israel

© The Author(s) 2019   67
E. Madigan and G. Reuveni (eds.),
The Jewish Experience of the First World War,
https://doi.org/10.1057/978-1-137-54896-2_4

and communal life, and across wider society, in employment conditions, in the role of Jewish politics and in the Jewish political parties in general.

Under the Tsarist regime, the Jewish population of Poland had few civil rights, Jewish political parties' activity was restricted and therefore mostly secret, and the very legitimacy of Jewish participation in the political system was widely questioned.[1] Yiddish was not acknowledged as a formal language, despite the fact that in the 1897 census 98% of a population of over four million Jews declared Yiddish as their mother tongue.[2] After the 1905 revolution, a so-called liberalization process took place but it had very little, if any, influence on Jewish political rights.[3] In pre-war Poland the Jewish education system was closely supervised and mainly based on religious instruction,[4] while in the broader education system, there was a cap on the number of Jewish pupils. This general exclusion of Jews from access to education led to the establishment of illegal Jewish educational institutions in the decades before 1914, mainly by members of Jewish left-wing political movements.[5]

The German occupation of the Polish lands during the war years caused radical change and political liberalization. A significant awakening took place with regard to political activity and the number of parties that were founded or brought into Poland from elsewhere was very significant indeed. Most research on Polish Jewry during the First World War has focused on political patterns of change and on the international efforts to gain recognition for Jews as a national minority.[6]

---

[1] Shlomo Netzer (1980), *The Struggle of Polish Jewry for Civil and National Minority Rights: 1918–1922* [in Hebrew] (Tel-Aviv, The Diaspora Research Institute), 13–47.

[2] Jacob Lestchinsky (1922), *Yidishe Folk in Tsifern* (The Jewish People in Numbers) [in Yiddish] (Berlin, Klal-Farlag), Table 15.

[3] For more on Jewish politics under Tsarist rule, see Vladimir Levin (2016), *From Revolution to War: Jewish Politics in Russia, 1907–1914* [in Hebrew] (Jerusalem, Zalman Shazar).

[4] Shimon Frost (1998), *Schooling as a Socio-Political Expression: Jewish Education in Interwar Poland* (Jerusalem, The Magnes Press), 28.

[5] Sabina Levin (1997), *Chapters in the History of Jewish Education in Poland in the Nineteenth and Early Twentieth Centuries* [in Hebrew] (Tel-Aviv, The Diaspora Research Institute) 196–211.

[6] Marcos Silber (2001), 'The New Poland will Nurture All of Its Children: The Efforts in Central Europe to Achieve Autonomy for the Jews of Congress Poland During World War I' [in Hebrew], Tel-Aviv (Thesis Submitted for the Degree of Doctor of Philosophy, Tel-Aviv University); Jonathan Frankel (1988), 'An Introductory Essay—The Paradoxical Politics of Marginality: Thoughts on the Jewish Situation During the Years 1914–1921', *Studies in Contemporary Jewry* 4, 3–21.

This chapter will instead focus on the transformations experienced by Jewish communities and, in particular, on the cultural and educational changes led by Jewish political parties, which arguably laid the ground for the 'golden years' of Jewish culture and education in interwar Poland.[7] These themes will be explored by drawing on the rhetoric and activity of three Jewish political parties, two of which operated in the framework of the Tsarist Empire, while the third was established in German-occupied Poland. The Bund was a socialist party, founded in Vilnius in 1897, which demanded cultural autonomy for Eastern European Jews.[8] Poale Zion was founded in the Tsarist-designated Pale of Settlement in 1905, and its ideology was based on Zionist and socialist ideas. Poale Zion had branches across the worldwide Jewish diaspora but the Polish branch had limited autonomy to develop its own ideology.[9] Upon the outbreak of war in 1914, the branches of the Bund and Poale Zion on Polish territory separated from their Russian counterparts and began operating independently. The Folkspartei (or Jewish People's Party) was founded by the Warsaw-based lawyer and journalist, Noah Prilutski, in the midst of the wartime crisis in 1916. The party, which operated mainly in Warsaw and the surrounding areas, went on to become one of the most popular Jewish pressure groups. It demanded national minority rights for Jews, including cultural autonomy, as well as the recognition of Yiddish as the formal language of the Jewish minority in Poland.[10]

These three distinctive but related parties provide a good survey group for exploring Jewish issues in wartime Poland as they shared a common aspiration for cultural autonomy for Jews within the new

---

[7] Miriam R. Eisenstein (1950), *Jewish Schools in Poland 1919–1939: Their Philosophy and Development* (New York, King's Crown Press); Shimon Frost (1998), *Schooling as a Socio-Political Expression: Jewish Education in Interwar Poland* (Jerusalem, The Magnes Press).

[8] Regard the ideology of the Russian Bund, see Moshe Mishkinski (1981), *The Beginning of the Jewish Labor Movement in Russia* [in Hebrew] (Tel-Aviv, Hakibbutz Hameuchad); Jonathan Frankel (1989), *Prophecy and Politics: Socialism, Nationalism and the Russian Jews 1862–1917* [in Hebrew] (Tel-Aviv, Am Oved); and Yoav Peled (1997), *Class and Ethnicity in the Pale: The Political Economy of Jewish Worker's Nationalism in Late Imperial Russia* [in Hebrew] (Tel-Aviv, Hakibbutz Hameuchad).

[9] Matityahu Mintz (1986), *Friend and Opponent: Yitshak Tabenkin in Poalei-Zion Party 1905–1912* [in Hebrew] (Efa'al, Yad Tabenkin), 26.

[10] Kalman Ian Weiser (2001), 'The Politics of Yiddish: Noyekh Prilutski and the Folkspartey in Poland 1900–1926', New York (Thesis Submitted for the Degree of Doctor of Philosophy, Colombia University).

Polish state. The members of these parties accepted the permanence of the Jewish presence in Poland and aimed to improve the community's well-being in terms of the freedom to practice and promote Jewish culture, education and language. Although they are defined in the relevant historiography as 'national movements', they acted, and could be more accurately described, as 'ethnic movements'.[11] The main characteristic of an ethnic movement being a strong connection to the linguistic, educational and cultural aspects of the ethnic group it represents. In this sense, these parties differed from the larger Zionist movement, the main demand and concern of which was new territory for Jewish settlement. This chapter will outline and explore the main issues and activities in which these parties were involved in the first half of the Great War, and which thus, as far as they were concerned, had the most influence on the Jewish community's day-to-day life: the humanitarian crisis brought about by the war and the Jewish struggle for linguistic recognition and control of education.

THE JEWISH PARTIES' RELIEF AND WELFARE ACTIVITIES

The first central city in Congress Poland that was conquered and occupied by the German forces was Łódź. Intense battles had taken place near the city since the first days of the war,[12] and, as a result of this proximity to the front-line, the city was disconnected from the Tsarist market and industrial production came to a halt.[13] This had a very adverse affect on the economic and social circumstances of the Jewish population of Łódź, which was involved mainly in the textile and tanning businesses. In addition, artillery fire from nearby German guns damaged many buildings, including civilian properties, and the number of homeless refugees

---

[11] Ernest Gellner (1987), *Culture, Identity, and Politics* (Cambridge, Cambridge University Press).

[12] HaTsfira (25 August 1914), 'Yediot Mi Łódź' (News from Łódź) [in Hebrew]; HaTsfira (31 August 1914), 'Yediot Mi Łódź' (News from Łódź) [in Hebrew]; and Jacob Hertz (1958), *Di geschychte fun Bund in Lodz* (The History of the Bund in Lodz) [in Yiddish] (New York, Unzer Tsait), 237.

[13] Marcos Silber (2006), 'Ruling Practices and Multiple Cultures: Jews, Poles and Germans in Łódź During WWI', *Simon Dubnow Insitute Yearbook*, 5 (2006), 191; Emanuel Nowogródzki (2001), *The Jewish Labor Bund in Poland 1915–1939: From Its Emergence as an Independent Political Party Until the Beginning of World War II* [in Polish] (Rockville, Shengold Books), 3.

in the city rose sharply. The refugees tried to escape from the battle zone but disruption in public transport and damage to roads made this quite difficult.[14] Thousands of refugees and wounded soldiers nonetheless fled to the big cities such as Warsaw, which were further from the front. In addition to suddenly being forced to flee the battle zone, Jews suffered harassment and antisemitic attacks at the hands of soldiers of the various armies.[15] Those living in the path of the advancing Russian armies were also expelled from their homes and cities and forced to migrate. In response to this emerging humanitarian crisis, the permanent, usually wealthier residents of the less affected towns and cities began to set up welfare organizations to support the victims.[16] These organizations included hospitals and clinics, soup kitchens, accommodation and even schools and educational institutions for children.[17] The population that stayed within the battle zone suffered from a shortage of medical supplies and a lack of basic foodstuffs. A report on the situation in Łódź in the early stages of the war described the shortages in the city, where the food allowance was minimal at just 80 grams of bread and a small portion of buckwheat per person. The rising prices are described in the same report: a bag of wheat flour was sold for no less than 25 rubles, a loaf of bread for 50 kopeks and a portion of butter for 90 Kopeks, all significantly higher than pre-war prices.[18]

In order to maintain civil order, local civilian committees were organized in several cities, including Warsaw and Łódź, where they attempted to run day-to-day municipal life. In addition to tax collecting and operating the law courts, the committees also coordinated the activities of welfare organizations, including providing support for soldiers' families as well as paupers and refugees.[19] Examining the consequences of war in

[14] HaTsfira (12 August 1914), 'Yediot Mi Łódź' (News from Łódź) [in Hebrew].

[15] Jonathan Frankel (1988), 'An Introductory Essay—The Paradoxical Politics of Marginality: Thoughts on the Jewish Situation During the Years 1914–1921', *Studies in Contemporary Jewry* 4, 3–21; Arye Gelbard (1987), *Stirring Times: The Russian Bund in Revolutionary Days* [in Hebrew] (Tel-Aviv, The Diaspora Research Institute), 17.

[16] Semion Goldin (2000), 'Deportation of Jews by the Russian Military Command 1914–1915', *Jews in Eastern Europe* 1:41, 40–72.

[17] Alexander Guterman (1997), *The Warsaw Jewish Community Between the Two World Wars: National Autonomy Enchained by Law and Reality 1917–1939* [in Hebrew] (Tel-Aviv, The Diaspora Research Institute), 52–53.

[18] HaTsfira (29 November 1914), 'Yediot Mi Łódź' (News from Łódź) [in Hebrew].

[19] HaTsfira (28 August 1914), 'Yediot Mi Łódź' (News from Łódź) [in Hebrew].

Poland, it is clear that much of the population suffered from dislocation, sudden homelessness and malnutrition. These adverse conditions, combined with the legalization of political activity as a result of the German occupation, enabled the welfare work of the various political parties. The provision of welfare relief was, in fact, the beginning of their political activity during the war years. A description of the welfare activities of the Jewish political parties in Warsaw can be found in a post-war report on the Jewish communities and movements in the city. According to this report, Poale Zion were the first to establish a soup kitchen in Warsaw, which was open to the general public. The Bund also operated several soup kitchens in collaboration with the Polish socialist party PPS Left (*Polska Partia Socjalistyczna Lewica*). These latter establishments were open exclusively to the party members and activists.[20] Additionally, the Bund established and operated educational organizations and several different welfare institutions.[21]

This sort of welfare activity was not restricted to the capital and soon spread to other Polish cities. In Łódź each party founded soup kitchens for the local needy and began subsidizing grocery stores.[22] In Międzyrzecz (or Meseritz) the Bund's local branch operated a soup kitchen that was open to the general public. Later, the socialist parties in the city established a common welfare organization that operated soup kitchens exclusively for the city's proletariat.[23] The annual income of this establishment was around 20,000 marks, which was used both to run the kitchen and for other forms of charity.[24] Later in the war, the parties founded separate national welfare committees that operated and

[20]YIVO, P3/1114, Das juedische hilfskomite fuer Polen (The Jewish Help Committees in Poland) [in German]; Zalman Kratko (1975), 'Di yiddishe propessionele bavegong in congress poylen in der zeit fun der ershter velt milhume' (The Jewish Proffesional Movements in Congress Poland During First World War) [in Yiddish] *Gal-Ed* 2, 116.

[21]Konrad Zieliński (2004), 'Polski i żydowski ruch robotniczy w Królestwie Polskim w latach I wojny swiatowej' (Polish and Jewish Labor Movement in the Poland During the First World War) [in Polish], *Studia Judaica* 7:1, 53.

[22]Danota Dombrovska and Avraham Wein, eds. (1970), *Pinkas HaKehilot, Encyclopedia of Jewish Communities from Their Foundation Till After the Holocaust* [in Hebrew] (Jerusalem, Yad Vashem), 171.

[23]Lebens-Fragen (18 February 1916), 'Provintz- Międzyrzecz' (From the City Międzyrzecz) [in Yiddish].

[24]Lebens Fragen (9 March 1917), 'provinz- Białystok' (From the City Białystok) [in Yiddish].

coordinated welfare activities; the Poale Zion central committee founded the *Arbeiter Hiam*,[25] the Bund founded a mutual welfare committee, *Hilf Cammiten*[26] (in several cities the Bund also used the name *Arbeiter Hiam*).[27]

Unsurprisingly, the most vulnerable members of society were particularly badly affected, and many children found themselves orphaned and living in dire poverty. As M. Sanderovich related in his autobiography, he and his siblings suffered extreme hunger and poverty during the war:

> The first four years of my life were the worst. My father was recruited. We never heard from him ... my mother was left alone and had to provide for four little children. It was horrible times ... I was two years old and had nothing to eat for two whole days. Thanks to charity I survived.[28]

In order to support destitute children, the parties established schools and other institutions. In addition to modern education, the meals they received in these institutuions were often the only real sustenance that many children received during the course of the day.[29]

As the wartime situation deteriorated and the economic crisis deepened, many workers were exploited or lost their jobs. The various socialist parties soon intervened and organized strikes in most of the major cities.[30] The parties demanded an improvement in working conditions and insisted that workers be accorded basic rights, such as a limit to the number of hours in a given working day.[31] Later, with the establishment

---

[25] Victor Shulman (1946), *Di Yidn In Poyln* (The Jews in Poland) [in Yiddish] (New York, Unzer Tsait), 859.

[26] Hayim Solomon Kazdan (1966), 'In der tsait fun der ershter velt milhume 1914–1917' (In the Years of the First World War), in Herts Aronson, ed. (1966), *Nowogrodzki, Dobnow –Erlich eds. Di geshikhte fun Bund 3* (The History of the Bund 3) [in Yiddish] (New York, Unser Tsait), 34.

[27] Lebens Fragen (5 May 1916; 10 November 1916), 'provintz' (From the Cities) [in Yiddish].

[28] YIVO, Autobiography #3796.

[29] YIVO, P3/1114, Das juedische hilfskomite fuer Polen (The Jewish Help Committees in Poland) [in German].

[30] YIVO, 1400MG2, Box 38, Folder 430, Przeciw niszczeniu fabryk (Against the Destruction of Factories) [in Polish].

[31] Lebens Fragen (16 June 1916), 'Das vohl-platform fun socialistishen vohl blok' (The Election Platform of the Socialist-Block) [in Yiddish].

of the temporary Polish institutions that were set up by the German authorities, the parties demanded that workers be given access to health care.[32] Needless to say, the Jewish parties encountered financial difficulties during the war years, and most of them established charity funds that raised money for their activities, mainly from Jewish philanthropists in the United states.[33]

Another wartime issue in which the parties became involved, was law and order and the security of civil populations; in several cities, the threat of crime was so great that civilian militias were established. In Lublin, a Jewish militia was organized in order to defend the Jewish quarters. Writing many years after the war, a member of the militia named Tzvi Fractor recalled that the local commander of the Tsarist army had initiated the establishment of the militias a short time before the Austrian occupation of the city.[34] In Galicia, Jewish militias were mobilized in a number of cities to protect the Jewish population from the threat of pogroms.[35] In contrast, in Międzyrzecz a joint Polish-Jewish civil militia was organized.[36] These militias received formal recognition and responsibility after the war when many of them were absorbed into the new Polish army.

In Warsaw the attempt to organize a joint socialist militia in order to protect the proletariat and help the occupation forces failed due to disagreement among the involved parties, which included the PPS right (*Polska Partia Socjalistyczna Frakcja*), PPS Left, SDKPiL (*Socjaldemokracja Królestwa Polskiego i Litwy*), the Bund and Poale Zion.[37] It should be noted that even though the Folkspartei was not

[32] Zalman Kratko (1975), 'Di yiddishe propessionele bavegong in congress poylen in der zeit fun der ershter velt milhume' (The Jewish Professional Movements in Congress Poland During First World War) [in Yiddish], *Gal-Ed* 2, 119–120.

[33] Ibid.

[34] Tzvi Fractor (1957), 'The Jewish Militia in the Year 1915', in Meir Blumental and Nahman Kuzan, eds. *Encyclopaedia of the Diaspora-Lublin* (Jerusalem, New York Public Library), 327.

[35] Anshel Reiss (1970), 'The Jews of Eastern Galicia at the Rebirth of Poland' [in Yiddish], in Arieh Tartakower, ed. *Yearbook*, 3, 71–90.

[36] Lebens-Fragen (18 February 1916), 'Provintz- Międzyrzecz' (From the City Międzyrzecz) [in Yiddish].

[37] Anshel Reiss (1970), 'The Jews of Eastern Galicia at the Rebirth of Poland' [in Yiddish], in Arieh Tartakower, ed. *Yearbook*, 3 (1970), 71.

established until 1916, and was thus not involved in the welfare activity of the first year of the conflict, its leader, Noah Prilutski, was a central character in the Jewish scene in Warsaw at the beginning of the war.[38] As a respectable lawyer, Prilutski provided legal assistance and free legal aid to the needy. In order to provide his service as widely as possible he opened his private residence, Świętokrzyska 48, to the public.[39]

Welfare and civic aid activities were the main concern of the parties in Poland during the early stages of the war. These were essentially the first independent activities of the Bund and Poale Zion in Poland after they broke with the Russian mother-parties. The primary aim of these activities was to care for the Jewish population but, needless to say, party leaders also used their position as providers of welfare to spread their political message and raise support from the public. In spite of the social and humanitarian crisis brought about by the war and the general geo-political chaos, the political and cultural situation of Polish Jewry was somewhat improved during the first two years of the conflict. The German and Austrian conquest of Polish lands, along with the attendant Germanic occupation, introduced a tradition of relative political liberalism. This relatively liberal attitude toward ethnic and national minorities made for a striking contrast with the climate under Tsarist rule and marked a dramatic improvement for Jewish cultural and political life.

The Jewish Parties' Cultural and Educational Activities

In addition to the charity and welfare activities that the parties organized, they aimed to improve the linguistic, cultural and educational aspects of Jewish communal life. The relatively more liberal approach to minority culture that the Germans seemed to have introduced in Poland helped the Jewish parties, including the Bund, Poale Zion and the Folkspartei to try to realize this dimension to their political missions.

About six months after the occupation of Warsaw in August 1915, the Germans decided to establish a new municipal government in Poland's

---

[38] Yitshak Lev (1953), 'Poalei-Zion Left', in Yitshak Gruenbaum, ed. *Encyclopaedia of the Diaspora- Warsaw* (Jerusalem, New York Public Library), 97–98.

[39] Kalman Ian Weiser (2001), 'The Politics of Yiddish: Noyekh Prilutski and the Folkspartey in Poland 1900–1926', New York (Thesis Submitted for the Degree of Doctor of Philosophy, Colombia University), 194.

central cities. The first city chosen to hold an election was Warsaw. Unlike the system that obtained under the Tsarist regime, the Germans sought to establish an independent civil municipal government, which would be responsible for day-to-day life in the city. Since this was the first municipal election in Poland after the collapse of the Tsarist regime, the population and the political activists felt that this new council was about to be and to act as a national council.[40] The election was scheduled to take place in July 1916 and, in the months before, the political system was a veritable hive of activity, with a large number of parties and political movements being established, both among the non-Jewish as well as the Jewish sections of the population. It should be noted that not all three of the Jewish parties under review officially participated in this election. The Bund cooperated with the PPS Left to form the socialist committee list and won just one seat in the council. Unfortunately for the Jewish members, the first candidate in the list was a Polish candidate from the PPS, and no Bundist candidate was elected. Poale Zion did not participate at all in the election but decided to support the socialist committee.[41] Among the leaders of the city's Jewish community, the big winner in this election was Noah Prilutski, with his party, the Folkspartei, gaining four seats. This was a huge victory for a party that had only just been established. Despite the somewhat disappointing result of this election from a purely political perspective,[42] the Jewish community nonetheless benefitted from campaigning in the period before the election, especially in areas of culture and education. In fact, during the course of 1916, the Jewish political system as a whole underwent a clear ideological and organizational consolidation, not only in Warsaw but all over Poland. We can see the first harbinger of consolidation in the Jewish political parties' election platforms, where demands related to ethno-cultural aspirations were repeatedly made. These demands were focused

---

[40] Marcos Silber (1998/1999), 'Jews and Polish in Poland 1916' [in Hebrew], *Zmanim*, 85, 78–83.

[41] Emma Or-Tal Zohar (2011), 'The Bund and Poalei-Zion in Poland: The Cope with the Collapse of the Imperial Order and the Establishment of Poland as a Nation-State 1914–1921' [in Hebrew] (Haifa, Thesis Submitted for Master Degree, Haifa University).

[42] We can see that of 90 seats, 15 were Jewish. This, of course doesn't reflect at all the electoral power of the Jewish population in Warsaw; situation that was caused due to discrimination in the election methods. The statistics indicated that nearly 45% of the population in the city were Jewish those days.

on two main points: *Yiddisher Shprach* (Jewish language) and *Yiddishe Shtadt Shulen* (Jewish state schools).[43]

The first point, the adoption of a 'Jewish language' was one of the most important issues during the Warsaw city council election, and also for ordinary Polish Jews. Language has traditionally been recognized as one of the central and most important factors for defining nationality, especially when the given language is commonly used by an ethnic or national minority within a larger polity.[44] As was generally accepted during the period, and indeed today, the 'Jewish language' can be either Yiddish or Hebrew. All three of the key Polish Jewish parties chose to adopt Yiddish as their 'Jewish language', each for its own reason[45] and the language played a central role in their activities. The parties' main demand from the wartime authorities was that they formally recognize Yiddish as a second language in Poland.[46] The reason for this should be clear; in addition to helping the Jewish population cope and engage with the bureaucracy of the state in their own language, it would be an unambiguous statement that the new Polish state would be a home for two nations—the Polish as well as the Jewish. At first, the German authorities supported the idea of recognizing Yiddish as a formal language in the framework of the new Poland. This was largely due to their belief that Yiddish was a form of 'broken German' and their hope that the Jews would ultimately abandon Yiddish and adopt standard German in the future.[47] Consequently, almost all of these parties' newspapers,

---

[43] For example, Lebens Fragen (16 June 1916), 'Das vohl-platform fun sotsialistishen vohl-blok' (The Election-Platform of the Socialist-Block) [in Yiddish]; Prac. Reg. MBP w Łodzi, Blok socjalistyczny (The Socialist Block) [in Polish]; Der Moment (7 June 1916), 'Di yudishe folks-komitet' (The Jewish National Committee—The Folkspartey) [in Yiddish]; and Der Moment (12 June 1916), 'Di Farvohl bavegung. A oifruf tsu di yidishe elteren!' [in Yiddish].

[44] Miroslav Hroch (1994), *The Social Interpretation of Linguistic Demands in European National Movements* (Florence, European University Institute); Benedict Anderson (1983), *Imagined Communities* (London, Verso).

[45] The Yiddish was the most widespread language among the Jewish population in Poland those days; with more than 90% of Yiddish speaking as a mother tongue.

[46] Lebens Fragen (16 June 1916), 'Das vohl-platform fun sotsialistishen vohl-blok' (The Election-Platform of the Socialist-Block) [in Yiddish]; Der Moment (7 June 1916), 'Di yudishe folks-komitet' (The Jewish National Committee—The Folkspartey) [in Yiddish].

[47] Marcos Silber (2001), *The New Poland*, 156–157.

pamphlets and conferences were produced in Yiddish. Importantly, the schools, cultural activity and informal movements that were affiliated to the parties also used Yiddish as their main language, both during the war and in the years to come.

The second point was Jewish education for both youngsters and adults. Before the outbreak of the war, under the Tsarist regime, Jewish educational activities and the existence of proper Jewish schools were limited, restricted and under supervision.[48] After the German occupation and the advent of a more liberal approach to these issues in Poland, the Jewish population, and especially the political parties, began operating a wide range of educational and cultural institutions, which had been prohibited by the Tsarist regime. All of the Jewish parties established a network of schools in Poland, offered a variety of courses for adults and organized cultural events. It should be emphasized that the education system established in occupied Poland was of great importance for both the Jewish and non-Jewish population. The first decision made by the Warsaw's municipal committee appointed by the Germans in August 1915 was the initiation of compulsory education for the city's children. It was initially proposed that Jewish children would be integrated into the Polish municipal education system, but that Jews that did not wish their children to be educated in the Polish system would learn Polish in Jewish schools or *Heder*. Ultimately, however, this proposal did not come into effect, due to objections from different sources—German, Polish and Jewish.[49] It is beyond the scope of this chapter to outline the long political process to which this proposal was subjected, but, eventually, it was decided that a Jewish schools' council would be established and that Jewish schools would be funded by the city council. It was also decided that Yiddish would be the formal teaching language of Jewish schools in the city, but the choice between Yiddish and Hebrew as the main language would be left up to each local community.[50] It should be emphasized that this decision concerned only Warsaw and not the entire country. In Łódź, the Germans tried, unsuccessfully, to force German as the formal language in all schools.[51]

[48] Sabina Levin (1997), *Chapters in the History of Jewish Education in Poland*.

[49] Marcos Silber, 'The New Poland Will Nurture', 150.

[50] Ibid., 153.

[51] Ibid.

Jewish education was important from a purely practical perspective, but it was also central to the political and cultural ideologies of the various Jewish parties. During 1916, one of the main leaders of the Bund, Vladimir Medem,[52] published a series of articles in the Bund newspaper, *Lebens Fragen*, under the heading 'About the National School' (*Vegen der Folkshul*).[53] This series, which was divided into six parts, specifically referred to the Jewish proletariat's problem as a national minority in a nation state from a cultural-educational point of view. According to Medem, the national schools held the key for the survival of the Jewish nation in Poland as they would shape the children—the future of the Nation.[54] The primary demand from the state, as far as Medem was concerned, should thus be the establishment of a national school system and the adoption of the mother tongue of the majority in these schools.[55] Additionally, Medem argued that the state should fund and support these schools and force the children of the minority to enroll in them. In terms of a basic pedagogical approach, Medem felt that these schools should educate and prepare children for life in the 'real world' as Jewish workers in Poland.[56] He was quite clear that the school system should not deal with religious or political issues.[57]

---

[52] Vladimir Medem (1879–1923) was born in a converted to Christianity family. Medem studied Law at Kiev University, where he was exposed to socialist ideas. In 1900 he joined the Bund and soon became one of the party's leaders. In 1913 he was imprisoned by the tsarist regime due to his political activity, and was not discharged until the German had concurred Warsaw. Since then he started to act in the framework of the Polish Bund. He was the editor of the party's newspaper, the Lebens Fragen, where he published many of his thoughts and plans. In the early 1920s Medem immigrated to New York, where he acted as the main fundraiser for the polish Bund.

[53] Nowogródzki claims that this series of articles was signed under the name 'Komets Alef' (O) since the Yiddish version of them was translated by Maurycy Orzech, one the Bund's leaders, as Yiddish was not Medem's mother tongue. Emanuel Nowogródzki (2001), *The Jewish Labor Bund in Poland 1915–1939: From Its Emergence as an Independent Political Party Until the Beginning of World War II* [in Polish] (Rockville, Shengold Books), 342.

[54] Lebens Fragen (9 February 1916), 'Di Folkshul' (The National School) [in Yiddish].

[55] Lebens Fragen (3 November 1916), 'Vegen Di Folkshul IV- Der Shprah' (Regarding the National School 5—The Language) [in Yiddish].

[56] Lebens Fragen (11 October 1916), 'Vegen Di Folkshul II- Di Form' (Regarding the National School 2—The Program) [in Yiddish].

[57] Lebens Fragen (6 October 1916), 'Vegen Di Folkshul I- Tsilen un oifgeben' (Regarding the National School 1—Goals and Problems) [in Yiddish]; Lebens Fragen (27 October 1916), 'Vegen Di Folkshul III- Di mitlen' (Regarding the National School 3—Resources) [in Yiddish].

After the local election of the Warsaw city council in 1916 with Noah Prilutski as one of its members, the question of Jewish schools was very actively discussed in Jewish communities and in the political sphere. One of the actions that Prilutski promoted was a petition signed by 32,645 youngsters under the age of 18 and 40 Jewish leaders (including Vladimir Medem and other central Bund leaders) and addressed to the German authorities in occupied Warsaw. To support the petition, Prilutski added a letter describing the lack of a formal education system for Yiddish-speaking pupils. He claimed that the number of Yiddish-speaking children was increasing in Poland and that the need for Yiddish-speaking schools was crucial for the Jewish minority.[58] In addition to the activities in the ideological and political spheres, the leaders of the various parties became involved in establishing and operating independent Yiddishist education systems. These formal schools and informal education systems formed a central component of the parties' structure and acted as ideological instruments.

The parties began establishing such schools in 1915, with the first party school, the *Grosser Kinderhaim*, being founded by the Bund in Warsaw in the winter of 1915.[59] During the period of German occupation, Poale Zion also raised donations and established schools. The teaching language of these institutions was Yiddish and thus in keeping with the parties' ideology. By 1920, just five years after the *Grosser Kinderhaim* had been founded, several dozen Yiddish schools were operating in Warsaw, at which approximately two thousand pupils were enrolled.[60] At the same time, the parties began establishing schools in other cities with large Jewish populations, including Łódź and Białystok. These educational institutions would become central to the life of the Jewish political parties, and of course in the individual lives of Jewish activists, for years to come. Alongside these schools, the parties also set up a whole range of educational and cultural institutions, from kindergartens to primary and secondary schools, to informal organizations,

---

[58] Hayyim Solomon Kazdan (1947), *Di geshikhte fun yidishn shulvezn in umophengikn poyln* (The History of Yiddish Schools in Independent Poland) [in Yiddish] (Mexico, Gezelshaft Kultur Un Hilf), 33–34.

[59] Ibid., 23.

[60] Ibid., 25.

such as children's and youth movements, teachers' colleges (or seminars), sports teams and libraries.[61]

From reports produced by local branches, we can see that the Jewish parties' activists were very engaged during this period with the business of operating local educational organizations and events. In Łódź, a group of Bund members, teachers and students established a Yiddish kindergarten in the summer of 1915, which was considered the first Yiddish speaking kindergarten in the city.[62] During the same year, the local branch of the Bund ran a campaign focusing on the teaching language in local schools and advocated the establishment of national schools for the Jewish population. The Bund and Poale Zion would later join forces in order to provide a solution for the lack of a Yiddish speaking school system in the city. Together they raised money and founded a Yiddish school in which 280 pupils were enrolled.[63] It was rather unusual to see cooperation between the Bund and Poale Zion at such an early stage of the war, as the Russian section of the Bund was opposed to collaborating with other Jewish movements. This principle would change as the Polish Bund underwent a process of consolidation during the war.[64]

At the beginning of 1916, the Bund's local branch in Białystok founded a youth group for young Jewish workers, as well as a musical choir and a library with a reading room. This particular branch also continued to operate a workers' club in which the participants were introduced to socialist ideology and encouraged to develop a sense of cultural Jewish awareness. In addition to cultural activities, the Białystok branch had a discussion considering the local '*Yiddisher Falks-shul*' (the Yiddish

---

[61] More on the cultural organizations and institutions affiliated to the Bund, see also Jack Jacobs (2009), *Bundist- Counterculture in Interwar Poland* (New York, Syracuse University Press).

[62] Kazdan (1947), Di geshikhte fun yidishn, 52.

[63] Yiddishist educational activity in Congress Poland was chiefly directed by the Shul- un Folksbildung-fareyn (School and Public Education Association), an organization dedicated to the creation of a Yiddish model elementary school and the coordination of adult education programs. Though founded in 1915, the School Association was not legally recognized by German authorities until March 1916. The School Association's administration comprised Bundists, Poale Zionists, and non-party elements, including Shoyl Stupnitski and Noyekh Prilutski, who served as its president. Kazdan (1947), Di geshikhte fun yidishn, 53–54.

[64] Zohar (2011), 'The Bund and Poalei-Zion in Poland'.

People's school). Their main concern was the language of instruction in the school's curriculum. It was ultimately decided that Yiddish would be the main language of instruction while Hebrew would be incorporated as part of the general programme. It is important to note that members of the youth organization were part of this discussion and that their opinion seems to have been taken into account.[65] In Międzyrzecz, local Jewish leaders founded a library, from which workers could borrow books free of charge. They also set up an informal educational institution for younger children under the name 'Talmud Tora'.[66] In the city of Ostrow, a Bund's youth group founded a local library where the readers could not only find books but also newspapers and participate in lectures, educational courses and discussion groups.[67] In Pułtusk (or Ostenburg), the Bund's welfare organization, *Arbeiter Haim*, offered courses in both Yiddish and Polish. From time to time, the local branch also arranged musical performances for the Jewish workers on Saturdays.[68] In Łosice, the local branch opened a new library, which contained more than 100 books in the summer of 1916.[69] The Bund also ran libraries and workers' courses in Vilna, Góra Kalwaria, Garwolin, Łuków and Włocławek, where the local branch had also set up sports teams and competitions.[70] The evidence suggests, moreover, that these libraries played an important role in the education and cultural awareness of the younger generation of Polish Jews.[71] In these specially instituted libraries and reading rooms, Jewish youngsters were exposed to party

[65] Lebens Fragen (18 February 1916), 'provinz- Białystok' (From the City of Białystok) [in Yiddish].

[66] Lebens Fragen (18 February 1916), 'provinz- Międzyrzecz' (From the City of Międzyrzecz) [in Yiddish].

[67] Lebens Fragen (5 May 1916), 'provinz- Ostrow' (From the City of Ostrów) [in Yiddish].

[68] Lebens Fragen (10 November 1916), 'provinz- Pułtusk' (From the City of Pułtusk) [in Yiddish].

[69] Lebens Fragen (8 August 1916), 'provinz- Łosice' (From the City of Łosice) [in Yiddish].

[70] Lebens Fragen (8 August 1916; 3 November 1916), 'provinz' (From the Cities) [in Yiddish].

[71] Ido Bassok (2011), *Youthful Plots: Autobiographies of Polish-Jewish Youth Between the Two World Wars* [in Hebrew] (Tel-Aviv, The Diaspora Research Institute).

ideology and broader thinking and introduced to the sort of new ideas and new literature that was usually forbidden in their homes. Some of them also managed to practice their language skills (reading and writing in Yiddish) in the framework of these libraries and courses.[72]

As Poale Zion only began publishing a newspaper late in 1918, and just a few documents concerning the organization survive, it is difficult to trace the local work of the party. It nonetheless seems clear that the *Arbeiter Haimen* had an education department and that the party ran two schools in Warsaw and two in Łódź. The schools in the capital educated 230 Jewish pupils (80 in the school that was located in the suburb of Praga and 150 in the party's central school in Dzika street). We also know that the party's schools in Warsaw were well maintained and that the pupils were reasonably healthy even though they suffered from malnutrition. In common with their Bund counterparts, the local branches of Poale Zion instituted courses for workers in a range of subjects. In Łódź, for example, Jewish workers were given the opportunity to study Yiddish, Hebrew, Polish and German, as well as mathematics, geography, and Jewish history and literature. In Warsaw, the local branch added some practical courses, such as economics, book-keeping, stenography and health and safety.[73] It should be noted, however, that not all the Yiddishist schools were affiliated to the socialist parties. In Warsaw by the end of 1916, nine schools operated according to a curriculum established by Jacob Dinzon,[74] a Yiddish writer and educator, five of which were under the supervision of Noah Prilutski and H. D Nomberg[75] and defined as secular Yiddish schools.[76]

---

[72] Bina Garncarska-Kadary (1995), *In Search of Their Way—Poalei-Zion: The Left in Poland Up to World War II* [in Hebrew] (Tel-Aviv, The Diaspora Research Institute), 236.

[73] Ibid., 39–42.

[74] Jacob Dinzon (1858–1919), Born in Kaunas in 1858 to a Hasidic family, he moved to Warsaw in 1884, where he worked as a Yiddish writer and Y. L Perets' assistant. During the First World War Dinzon established a Yiddish school network in Warsaw.

[75] Hersh Dovid Nomberg was educated in Hebrew but was fluent in many languages. He settled in Warsaw in 1897 and was close to Y. L Perets, who inspired him to start writing in Yiddish. In 1916 he founded with Dinzon and Prilutski the 'Yiddish Writers and Journalists Union'. During the 20s he replaced Noah Prilutski as the Folkspartei member in the Polish sejm.

[76] Garncarska-Kadary (1995), *In Search of Their Way*, 40.

CONCLUSION

In conclusion, the advent of German occupation during First World War gave rise to a comparatively liberal political culture in Poland and, as such, marked a crucial turning point in the history of the region. Importantly, in this context, the freedom to engage in a wide range of political activities and to establish a distinctive cultural and educational infrastructure gave rise to the emergence of a more confident and self-aware Jewish community in Poland between the world wars. This political pluralism and the variety of opinions and parties it allowed to flourish not only influenced the Jewish community but also had a major impact on the newly independent Polish state more generally.

In other words, these political institutions provided a wide range of activities in a wide range of aspects; the community soon gathered around the parties and especially around their education systems. The parties' educational and cultural systems were part of the activists and their families from very early in their lives and in almost every field. All of these changes, improvements and transformations laid the basis for a new and modern Jewish community structure. This structure was based on political affiliation rather than on the geographic location as it had been before. During the inter-war years, these foundations allowed the Jewish political communities in Poland to flourish as the Jewish parties operated not only schools, but also youth movements, sports organizations, theatres, choirs and other leisure and cultural activities.[77]

---

[77] Garncarska-Kadary (1995), *In Search of Their Way.*

War and Nationalism in Palestine: The Jewish Migration Committee in the Galilee During the First World War

Esther Yankelevitch

On 25 September 1918, Australian troops marched into Tiberias, thus signalling the total conquest of northern Palestine by the British and bringing the First World War in the Middle East to an end. The Jewish leadership in the city responded by gathering to celebrate the end of 400 years of Ottoman rule, four years of war, and eighteen months of exile for the Jewish people, who had involuntarily migrated to Tiberias from Jaffa and Tel-Aviv. Among the celebrants were representatives of the Jewish community in Tiberias, rabbis from the religious courtyards, the migration committee, the schools' management, the Lower Galilee villages' union, representatives of the various political parties, teachers, and other members of the community. The chief rabbi recited the *Shehechiyanu*[1] blessing and other representatives spoke about the importance of unity at that time:

[1] *Shehechiyanu* is a Jewish blessing thanking God for enabling a new experience or on a special occasion.

E. Yankelevitch (✉)
University of Haifa, Haifa, Israel

© The Author(s) 2019
E. Madigan and G. Reuveni (eds.),
The Jewish Experience of the First World War,
https://doi.org/10.1057/978-1-137-54896-2_5

This is the first assembly that has gathered all the representatives of our people, and we should emphasize the unity of the Jewish community ... We declare our formal language Hebrew and we expect all orders to be translated into Hebrew. Now we must demand to be represented in accordance with our relative number in the population.[2]

It was a moment of real jubilation: the Galilee was free. A year had passed since the Balfour Declaration, and the local Zionist executive expected its members to continue organizing community life in the days ahead.

Four years of continuous anguish had come to an end. During the war, the Jewish community in Palestine had been under siege, facing ongoing difficulties, including ever-increasing food shortages, deteriorating health conditions, mistreatment at the hands of the Ottoman authorities, deportation of community leaders, the closing down of Jewish institutions, and the expulsion of non-Ottomans. The distress of the Jewish community in the region—the *Yishuv*[3]—peaked at the beginning of 1917, when the front-line extended to their doorstep and Ottoman repression became even more intense.[4] Ahmed Djemal Paşha, or Cemal Paşha, one of the most controversial figures in the Ottoman regime, served as Minister of the Navy and Commander of the Fourth Army on the Syrian front during the war and is still regarded, in Jewish historiography, as being primarily responsible for the hardships suffered by the Jewish population during the war.[5] The expulsion of the Jews of Jaffa and Tel-Aviv in the spring of 1917 resulted in an inevitable conflict between the expelled Jewish population and the local communities in the cities of Tiberias and Safed. More than 1100 deportees settled in

---

[2] Minutes of the joint meeting that took place after the occupation of Tiberias, Central Zionist Archives (hereafter CZA), L2/216-144, September 25, 1918.

[3] *Yishuv* is a general term designating the Jewish community in Ottoman and British-ruled Palestine prior to the establishment of the State of Israel. It was made up of individuals from various backgrounds.

[4] Nathan Efrati (1991), *The Jewish Community in Eretz-Israel During World War I (1914–1918)* (Jerusalem, Yad Ben-Zvi), 284–285 [in Hebrew].

[5] Cemal Paşha (1872–1922), was one of the leaders of the Committee of Union and Progress. See, Djemal Paşha (1973), *Memories of a Turkish Statesman, 1913–1919* (New York); M. Talhat Çiçek (2014), *War and State Formation in Syria: Cemal Paşha's Governorate During World War I, 1914–1917* (New York, Routledge).

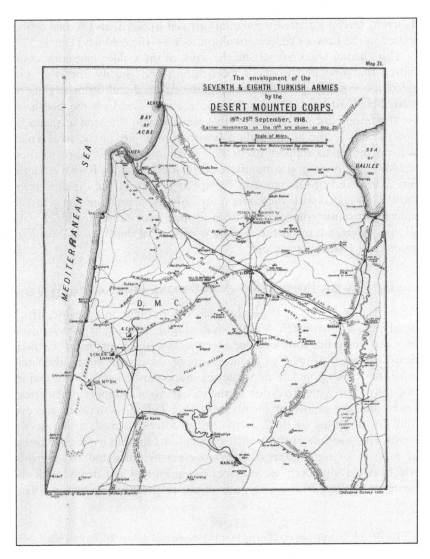

Fig. 1 Map showing the positions of the British and Turkish forces during the final phase of the war in Palestine, with the Sea of Galilee located in the north-east (*Source* Cyril Falls, *History of the Great War: Military Operations Egypt & Palestine, from June 1917 to the End of the War. Part II*, HMSO, London, 1928)

Tiberias, several hundred immigrants arrived in Safed, and several others settled in the Lower Galilee agricultural farms—the colonies (Fig. 1).[6]

This chapter seeks to evaluate the work of the Galilee migration committee that operated in the region during and shortly after the war, aided the exiled population in their time of need and ultimately alleviated their hardships. The migration committee cared on the one hand for the immigrant population, as that was its main aim, and at the same time, cared for the long-standing Jewish community in the area, which had no means to support itself. This involuntary melting pot, orchestrated by the migration committee, of the local religious Jewish community, composed of Oriental and European Jews, and the expelled Jews, mostly associated with the community composed predominantly of late nineteenth century immigrants from Europe who closely identified with Zionist ideals, advanced the awareness of Zionist and national ideology among the Jewish population.[7]

THE JEWISH POPULATION IN PALESTINE DURING THE WAR

When war broke out in 1914, the Jewish community in Palestine, which numbered approximately 85,000, was caught in the grip of a struggle between powerful, long-established empires and cut off from its traditional European sources of financial support. The war would ultimately leave the Jewish population in Palestine impoverished and diminished by one-third, but it survived due to the indispensable support of American Jewry and the ability of members of the *Yishuv* to network successfully. In the spring of 1917, as the British forces were advancing northwards, the position of the Jewish population came under serious threat as a result of the Ottoman order to evacuate Jaffa and its environs, which would ultimately see evacuees facing hunger and death. With the memory of the Armenian atrocities fresh in their minds, the members

---

[6]The Jewish population in Tiberias in 1914 numbered 5700. There were also about 2300 Moslems. In 1916, there were approximately 3000 Jews. In Safed in 1914, there were 7500 Jews out of a total of 13,500.

[7]The old *yishuv* refers to all the Jews living in Palestine before the Zionist immigration wave of 1882. This community lived mainly in Jerusalem, Safed, Tiberias, and Hebron, and was supported by the *haluka*, the traditional system of distribution charity within the Jewish community in Palestine, while the new *yishuv* were the newcomers ideologically related to the Zionist movement.

of the various Jewish communities feared the worst. From the political perspective, the intervention of Germany, an ally of the Ottoman Turks, prevented the danger that hovered over the Palestinian Jews in 1917.[8] The German representatives in the region feared that the evacuation would be regarded as a deliberate act of persecution, for which not only Turkey but also Germany would be held responsible. Ultimately, German intervention saved the Jews from an uncertain fate.

The Ottoman Empire would not formally enter the world war until the beginning of November 1914, but the *Yishuv* began organizing to confront the crisis and plan for economic survival under the new circumstances as soon as the conflict erupted in August. Efforts were made to find alternative export markets for the *Yishuv's* products in the United States and to tighten the connection with the American Jewish community. Later, the Ottoman government reacted to the situation by abolishing the 'capitulations', the privileges that foreign subjects enjoyed in the Ottoman Empire, which allowed them to reside and trade in Ottoman lands. Many became subjects of enemy powers, including about forty thousand Russian Jews and several thousand Jewish subjects of the French and British empires. Foreign post offices were closed, and foreigners living within the Ottoman Empire were made subject to Ottoman laws and courts. A wave of restrictions and new orders were thus imposed on the Jewish population which included a prohibition on carrying weapons, a night curfew, and a ban on writing letters in Hebrew or Yiddish. The Jewish community was also subjected to searches for political leaders and of political leaders' houses. Finally, schools, stores, and workshops belonging to 'enemy subjects' were closed, as were all branches of the Anglo-Palestine Company, along with many other restrictions.[9]

These measures were all prompted by the fact that the Ottoman regime suspected members of the *Yishuv*, and particularly newly arrived Zionists, of disloyalty to the Sublime Porte in Constantinople. On 17 December 1914, in one of the more extreme moves of the early months of the war, Baha al-Din, the governor of Jaffa, issued a general decree of deportation of all foreign subjects who had not yet become Ottoman.

[8] Isaiah Friedman (1971), 'German Intervention on Behalf of the Yishuv, 1917'. *Jewish Social Studies* 33:1, 23–43.

[9] Oded Neuman (1993), 'A Battle for Survival: The Struggle of the Jewish Yishuv for Existence during World War I, 1914–1918,' (PhD diss., University of California).

Panic spread throughout Jaffa, where foreign residents feared an all-out massacre. Deportations, draconian taxation, and abuse of Jewish residents across the region were carried out under the same policy of punitive and often violent repression that the Turkish regime imposed throughout its disintegrating empire.[10] Repressive measures, such as coercive enlistment, expropriation of food and property, mass deportations and starvation were used to threaten the existence of Palestine's Jews. The situation turned especially dire for the Jewish community when Palestine became a major base of operations for the Ottoman military forces planning an offensive against the British at the Suez Canal in Egypt. The big shift in the military arena began in January 1917, when the British army conquered Rafah, and intensified ten months later when it occupied Be'er Sheva and Gaza. In advance of the battles of Gaza, no fewer than 40,000 residents of the city were expelled from their homes.[11]

THE JEWISH COMMUNITY IN THE GALILEE ON THE EVE OF THE FIRST WORLD WAR

The Jewish settlement in the Galilee included two ancient cities, Tiberias, on the shores of Lake Galilee, and Safed in the Upper Galilee. These towns constituted two out of four holy cities, which throughout the exile period attracted local religious Jews and immigrants returning to the Holy Land for spiritual reasons. Tiberias and Safed had developed in a similar way until the interest of the new *yishuv* in land development that led to the purchase of land in the Upper Galilee, where the first *Moshavot* (colonies) were established in the 1880s. Eighteen years later, the Jewish Colonization Association (JCA) purchased land in the eastern Lower Galilee and developed the regional settlement by establishing a 'model farm' at *Sejera*, and seven *Moshavot*.[12] In 1911, another small agricultural settlement was founded on the outskirts of Tiberias.

[10]Friedman (1971), German Intervention, 29–30; Fruma Zachs (2012), 'A Transformation of Memory of a Tyranny in Syria: From Djemal Pasha to 'Id al-Shuhada', 1914–2000,' *Middle Eastern Studies* 48:1, 75–76.

[11]Neuman (1993), 'Battle for Survival', 91–135; Efrati (1991), *Jewish Community*, 16–33.

[12]Arieh Bitan (1982), *Changes of Settlement in the Eastern Lower Galilee (1800–1978)* (Jerusalem, Yad Ben Zvi), 81–96 [in Hebrew].

Soon afterward, the Zionist movement and its executive arm, the Jewish National Fund (JNF), purchased land in the Jordan Valley and initiated the Zionist settlement of the area. This enterprise changed the character of the region and presented new economic opportunities for the city. Dr. Arthur Ruppin, representative of the Zionist movement in Palestine and director of the Palestine Office of the Zionist movement,[13] proposed to develop the area as part of a Jewish autonomous region which was yet to come into existence. To this end, he suggested developing Tiberias as a trade centre, setting up hotels by the city's hot baths, and promoting light industry.[14] However, while the new settlements around Tiberias continued to develop, the city itself remained economically and socially disadvantaged. The new entrepreneurial population did not reach the city but settled in its agricultural periphery. Attempts to establish urban neighborhoods outside the walls of old city at the beginning of the twentieth century did neither materialize, nor did the Zionist establishment's efforts to improve the situation in the city.[15]

In ethnic terms, Tiberias was a 'mixed city' comprised of significant numbers of both Jews and Arabs. Toward the end of the nineteenth century, it became the first city in Palestine with a Jewish majority. At that time, the Jewish community in Palestine began organizing the local Jewish committees. Inter-Jewish relations in Tiberias suffered from complications resulting from the cultural encounter between the Zionist members of the new *yishuv* and the orthodox, usually non-Zionist Jews of the old *yishuv*. The old Jewish community of Tiberias, located in the old city, included two separate ethnic communities, the Sephardic and the Ashkenazi. The first attempts to organize the Jewish committee after the First World War failed due to internal conflicts between these

---

[13] In 1908 the Palestine Office (*Palaestinaamt*) was established, with its seat in Jaffa, by the executive of the Zionist Organization. Headed by Arthur Ruppin, it served under the Ottoman regime as the central agency for Zionist settlement activities, including land purchase and aiding immigration.

[14] Etan Bloom (2011), *Arthur Ruppin and the Production of Pre-Israeli Culture* (Leiden, Brill), 148–232.

[15] Yossei Kats (2009), *The Business of Settlement: Private Entrepreneurship in the Jewish Settlement of Palestine, 1900–1914* (Jerusalem and Ramat Gan, Magness Press and Bar-Ilan Press), 298–301.

communities.[16] Although many of the Sephardic townspeople were employed on the neighboring farms, they remained on the margins of the Galilee; they were not integrated in the cultural and educational activities of various political parties and workers associations and were not effective in promoting the city's improvement.

Safed, on the other hand, was more isolated and suffered from a lack of economic potential and an absence of efficient transportation. The veteran Jewish population was predominately orthodox, and the city was not a focal point for new *yishuv* settlement, with only three colonies in the vicinity. In 1911, just a few years before the outbreak of the Great War, Menachem Sheinkin, a Zionist activist, described the situation of the Jews of Safed who made their living primarily from the organized collection and distribution of charity funds collected in the Jewish diaspora for Jewish residents in Palestine (a system known as *haluka*), 'that generously came because of the importance of the place and is distributed more honestly than in other cities'.[17] There is no doubt about the central role of the *haluka* in the economy of Safed, but it seems that the economic well-being was not shared by all of the city's Jews. In his study of Safed, Zeev Perl describes the existence of a certain amount of prosperity since the late nineteenth century but argues that this all dissolved with the outbreak of war, indicating that any prosperity promoted by aid from the diaspora had not made deep roots in the city.[18]

The Expulsion of Jaffa-Tel Aviv

By March 1917, after two and a half years of war, the British forces had succeeded in pushing northward from Egypt and conquering the southern part of Palestine. Meanwhile, the Turks were fighting fierce rearguard actions. On 27 March 1917, following the British defeat at Gaza the previous day, Izzet Bey, Governor (or *Mutasarrif*) of the *Sanjak* of

---

[16] Estie Yankelevitch (2014), 'The Jewish Community in Tiberias, from the Jewish Committee to the Tiberias Hebrew Committee', in *Religion Nationalism: The Struggle for Modern Jewish Identity, Jewish Studies, an Interdisciplinary Annual*, Yossi Goldstein, ed. (Ariel, Ariel University), H18–H23 [in Hebrew].

[17] Menachem Sheinkin (1935), 'Galilee', in *Menachem Sheinkin Letters*, Aron Hermoni, ed. (University of Michigan), 21 [in Hebrew].

[18] Zeev Perel (1999), 'Crisis in Jewish Safed During World War I' (PhD diss., Bar Ilan University), 29–49 [in Hebrew].

Jerusalem, arrived unexpectedly in Jaffa. He summoned the notables of all denominations and notified them that, in the event of an enemy advance, a major evacuation of the civilian population of Jaffa and its environs would be put into effect. Only farmers would be allowed to remain until after the harvest. Apart from the *Sanjak* of Jerusalem and the coastal towns of Haifa, Acre, and Beirut, the evacuees would be free to go anywhere. Those without means would be transported to the Syrian hinterland and looked after by the Ottoman Government. The Moslem orange-grove owners contested the idea of leaving their property and while the *Mutasarrif* was apparently sympathetic, when their Jewish neighbors expressed similar concerns, they were threatened with immediate expulsion.[19] Thereafter, the cities of Gaza, and later Jaffa and Tel-Aviv were evacuated. The threat of British occupation of Palestine compelled Cemal Paşha to evacuate the southern coastal cities immediately after the first battle of Gaza.[20] Despite the fact that the battle ended in British defeat, Cemal Paşha considered the military situation a serious matter, and the evacuation was planned as a measure against possible naval action by the Entente powers.[21] He also decided to evacuate Jerusalem but did not carry out this plan due to diplomatic pressure. The order was understood as an act directed mainly against the Jews.[22] The Germans suspected that the Turks' aim was to annihilate the Jewish population in Palestine and the German representatives in Palestine confronted the Ottoman authorities, advising Cemal Paşha not to present the enemy with gratuitous propaganda and waived the privilege of exemption for gentile nationals. Brode, the German Consul, emphasized that discrimination on religious grounds would make a very bad impression. The military governor of Jaffa informed the German vice-consul in Jaffa, Baron Karel Freiherr von Schabinger, of the planned evacuation. However, Schabinger suspected that the deportation of the Jews was

---

[19] Friedman (1971), *German Intervention*, 23–43.

[20] Çiçek (2014), *War and State*, 86–89.

[21] Meir Dizengoff (1921), '*Eem Tel-Aviv Ba-golah*', [With Tel-Aviv in Exile] (Tel-Aviv), 50–51 [in Hebrew].

[22] CZA, L 6/2/I, Thon to Zionist Executive. 18 April 1917; Mordechai Ben Hillel Ha'Cohen (1929), *Milhemet Ha'amim* [War of the Nations] (Tel-Aviv, Yad Ben-Zvi), 124–125.

part of Cemal Paşha's plan to get rid of the Jews without distinction of nationality.[23]

On 2 April 1917, the Spanish diplomat Antonio Conde de Ballobar met with Cemal Paşha, and later wrote in his diary:

> He [Cemal Paşha] first received the German, whom he was in such a hurry to see that he sent his own car for him. The object of the conversation was a complaint by the Pasha about the conduct of Schabinger, the German consul in Jaffa, who seemed to have been a little exaggerated or violent in his language criticizing the evacuation of Jaffa.[24]

One cannot determine whether there was deliberate intent to annihilate the entire Jewish community in Palestine. What is clear is the fact that the information that leaked out and was published in leading newspapers in the Entente and neutral countries had its impact, but only Germany could influence Turkey to improve the deputies' conditions and prevent the total destruction of the Jewish population in Palestine.[25]

Yuval Ben-Bassat has analyzed encrypted wartime Ottoman telegrams located in the Istanbul archives dealing directly and indirectly with the Jewish population and argued that the Ottoman authorities' insistence on evacuating civilians was apparently inspired by the military need to let the army operate without the distraction of dealing with large numbers of non-combatants.[26] Zionist historiography has nonetheless accused Cemal Paşha of being driven by sheer hatred of the Zionist movement and the entire Jewish population. It should be noted, however, that, out of consideration for the Jewish Passover, the date of evacuation, originally set for 31 March, was postponed to 9 April. The farmers were also allowed to stay, and the evacuees were promised free transport facilities. Representatives of the Jewish community were told that the measure was not directed exclusively against their people, but rather applied to 'all the inhabitants' and was merely intended to ensure their safety. Cemal Paşha himself, accused of persecution of the Jews, claimed in private

[23] Friedman (1971), *German Intervention*, 25.

[24] Conde de Ballobar (2011), *Jerusalem in World War I*, Eduardo Manzano Moreno and Roberto Mazza, eds. (London, I.B. Tauris), 148.

[25] Friedman (1971), *German Intervention*, 28–29.

[26] Yuval Ben-Basat (2015), 'Enciphered Ottoman Telegrams from the First World War Concerning the Yishuv in Palestine', *Turcica* 46, 279–299.

engagements with Meir Dizengoff,[27] 'I am not an antisemite, I am only an anti-Zionist',[28] and insisted that had he acted otherwise he would have been guilty of dereliction of duty. Zionist sources indicate that a negative shift in Cemal Paşha's attitude toward Zionism and Zionist activity can be traced to early 1917. Ben-Bassat, however, assumes that Cemal Paşha opposed the political facets of Jewish activity in Palestine long before 1917.

In a thorough report published shortly after the war ended, Yacov Thon points out that the evacuation order excluded the Mikeve Yisrael Agricultural School and the winery at Rishon le-Zion, and suggests that, as these two Jewish institutions had good ongoing relations with Cemal Paşha, the decision to evacuate was not influenced by military expediency.[29] Thon saw the sole purpose of this act as part of the plan to limit the power of both the Jewish and Arab communities, fearing they would join forces with the enemy.[30] The Spanish Consul, Conde de Ballobar, accompanied by the German Consul, Dr. Johann Wilhelm Brode, and the Austrian Consul, Fredric Kraus, attempted to persuade Cemal Paşha to change his order. In response, he announced, 'I know the Jews are waiting for the enemy as a bride for her groom, but I shall prevent this joy, the lovers will not be reunited'. He added that, before the withdrawal, he would burn down all the flourishing Jewish settlements.[31]

A local public figure and journalist, Mordechai Ben-Hillel Ha-Cohen, described the evacuations in his diary as follows, 'The noise of wagons

[27] Meir Dizengoff (1861–1936), was among the founders of the Association of Builders of Jaffa. The association's objective was to build a new and modern Jewish neighborhood outside the walls of Jaffa. In 1911, Dizengoff was elected head of the committee, a role he held until he was elected first mayor of Tel-Aviv in 1921. During the 1917 Ottoman exile from Tel-Aviv, Dizengoff went to Haifa and later to Damascus, as head of the migration committee.

[28] Friedman (1971), *German Intervention*, 25–26; CZA, L 6/2/I, Thon to Zionist Executive. 18 April 1917; Dizengoff (1921), *Tel-Aviv*, 45–52; and Ha'Cohen (1929), *Milhemet*, 124–125.

[29] Yacov Thon, a native of Lwow, Poland, settled in Palestine in 1907 and served as deputy to Dr. Arthur Ruppin, head of the Zionist movement's Palestine Office. During the war, Thon replaced Ruppin who was expelled from the country, and later served as managing director of the Palestine Land Development Company.

[30] Yakov Thon (1919), *Eretz-Israel During the World War* [in Hebrew] (Jaffa, Typewritten Report), 194.

[31] Ibid.

on the paving stones was heard throughout the night in Tel Aviv... the tumult and the uproar of flight, the sound of the bell of exile'.[32] The Jewish expellees scattered to Tiberias, Safed, Kfar Saba, Petach Tikva, Zichron Yaakov, and Jerusalem. Approximately 10,000 Jews, out of a total population of 70,000–75,000, had to flee the coastline within 48 hours. The fact that the Jews were 'only' driven as far as the Galilee and later to Damascus is reasonable, as Cemal Paşha justified the act of deportation as merely wanting to protect the civilians from getting caught on the battlefield, for fear of the coast being shelled by British warships.

Not long afterward, in April 1917, the central Jewish migration committee was formed. The committee was originally formed by the Tel-Aviv City Board as a spontaneous response to the situation and oversaw the transfer of emigrants to new locations and looked after their well-being as much as possible. Only later was this committee officially appointed by Cemal Paşha as a formal board responsible for the welfare of all the deportees.[33] The members of the committee were public figures and in the early days, the committee acted within a local framework, as a voluntary and independent body organized to assist and ease the plight of the refugees. The committee's authority and ability to act was based on the personalities and status of its members.[34] The local migration branch of the Galilee, located in Tiberias, was in charge of organizing and absorbing the exiles that arrived in the region.

In one of the first circulars distributed by the committee to the wider Jewish community, Dizengoff emphasized the need of the hour. 'This is our opportunity, right now, to show our brothers in the diaspora that in times of trouble, when disaster has struck our communities, we know how and can help ourselves by ourselves. Furthermore, we can no longer depend on financial support from our generous people in America'.[35] And so, the communities that remained comparatively better off were expected to come to the aid of those who had been uprooted and displaced as a result of the evacuations.

As mentioned above, the majority of the Jewish community in Tiberias was poor and dependent on the *haluka*, and thus the migration

---

[32] Ibid.

[33] Ibid., 195.

[34] Efrati (1991), *Jewish Community*, 287–291, 295–297.

[35] CZA J90/142, The Migration Committee to the Jewish Communities, April 1917 [emphasis in original].

committee found itself caring for the local population as well. The fact that the committee members took it upon themselves to organize and care for the needy was in no way taken for granted and their actions appear to have provided a ray of hope for the impoverished and displaced members of the Palestinian Jewish community during this time of crisis.[36] Although the local communities welcomed the newcomers and offered help enthusiastically during the first days of exile, the honeymoon period quickly ended once the harsh daily reality set in.[37] The only grain of hope for assistance during this period was from the representatives of the Zionist Administration in Palestine: the *Eretz Israel* bureau and its manager at the time, Dr. Jacob Thon, and the Anglo-Palestine Bank and its manager, Eliezer Siegfried Hoofien.[38] They were expected to raise the funds required to support the Jewish community in Palestine from the Jewish diaspora through neutral countries and in Turkey's allies. In his report to the Joint Distribution Committee in New York, Hoofien described the situation as follows:

> The conditions of the evacuated during the months April-July, 1917 were bad enough, but during the months August-December, 1917, they became abominable. The poor people who had sought refuge in Petach-Tikvah and Kfar-Saba were continually driven hither and thither. Every day brought a new decree, a new order for evacuation. A fire destroyed a good number of the poor Kfar-Saba huts; in the rainy season, they became, of course, uninhabitable. Spotted fever broke out in several places, hundreds of "recruits" were arrested, and there was no end of suffering. The local Governors of Haifa, Safed, and Tiberias tried on several occasions not to admit refugees or to drive them away if they had settled.[39]

[36] Efrati (1991), *Jewish Community*, 291–295.

[37] CZA, J90/141, April (Passover) 1917, Dizengoff to the Migration Committee in Tiberias; Gur Alroey (2006), 'Exiles in Their Own Land? The Expelled from Tel Aviv and Jaffa in Lower Galilee 1917–1918' [in Hebrew], *Cathedra* 120, 135–160.

[38] Thon (1919), *Ertz Israel*, 197; CZA L2/553-253, Central migration committee to Thon and Hoofien, 19 September 1917. Eliezer Siegfried Hoofien (1991–1957), born in Utrecht, Holland immigrated to Palestine in 1912, after serving as director of the Cologne office of the Zionist Central Office. During the war, he was the manager of the Anglo-Palestine Bank. Nathan Efrati (1991), 'Eliezer S. Hoofien, Director of A.P.C Bank: His Role within the Yishuv during World War I and its Aftermath', in Mordechai Eliav, ed. *Siege and Distress* (Jerusalem, Yad Ben-Zvi), 84–96.

[39] Siegfried Hoofien (1917–1918), *Report to the Joint Distribution Committee of the American Funds for Jewish War Sufferers* (New York, American Jewish Committee), 19.

German and Austrian observers held Cemal Paşha particularly accountable for the situation the Jewish population encountered.[40] Cemal Paşha nominated Meir Dizengoff as head of the official migration committee and ordered the committee to be supplied with grain and a budget of 3000 Turkish pounds to finance the aid. Furthermore, two Jewish doctors were discharged from army service and assigned to open clinics, Arie Lieb Pachovski in Tiberias and Dr. Sherman in Haifa. Two months after this appointment, the committee was converted from a volunteer-based body to an officially legislated committee.[41]

In the Jaffa Tel-Aviv region, the evacuation decree was primarily directed at the Jewish population, whereas according to some reports the Arab population stayed or commuted daily between Jaffa and the Arab villages surrounding it.[42] Half of the exiles had no financial means and transportation was provided by the Lower Galilee colonies via wagons, horses, mules, and donkeys, which made their way to save the deportees from disaster. Still others made the journey by train to Samakh, an Arab village at the southern tip of Lake Tiberias and from there by boats to Migdal and Tiberias.[43] The picture of the fleeing Jews was pitiful: some 2500 of them, mainly the poor, wandered as far as the small northern farming communities, contending with the climate, hunger, poverty, and typhus. Sending the deportees to Tiberias was a convoluted and hazardous measure, as they were forced to join and live among the already-established poor local Jewish community that faced sporadic epidemic outbreaks every few years due to the inadequate sanitation conditions in the old city. They survived the first few months, but in the winter of 1917–1918, hundreds died of exposure, disease, and hunger. Most of the dead were buried hastily in unmarked graves dotted around the countryside.

The special committee for the relief of Jews in Palestine that was located in Cairo reported to Dr. Judah Magnes, head of *Kehilla*, the Jewish democratic movement in New York, that 'thousands were wandering

[40] Friedman (1971), *German Intervention*, 34.

[41] Efrati (1991), *Jewish Community*, 295–299.

[42] Ha'Cohen (1929), *Milhemet*, iv. 5, 30–33, 65, 76; Dizengoff (1921), Tel-Aviv, 76–80; CZA, L 6/211, Dizengoff (1917), 'Rapport sur les Emigres de Jaffa', 1 July 1917 (submitted to Djemal Paşha); Ibid., Thon to Ruppin, July 6, 9; and Thon to Hantke, July 11; K179122, Thon to Warburg, 4 July 1917.

[43] CZA, J90/141, 15 April 1917, Glikin to Erlich.

helplessly on the roads, starving, overcrowding colonies, increasing misery, disease ... Forcible evacuation of colonies imminent ... special local Committee gather funds for relief of Jewish population whose plight lamentable ...'.[44] The first report was issued by the 'Central Evacuation Committee from Jaffa' to the 'Evacuation Committee in Samaria and in the Upper and Lower Galilee' and signed by a certain Bezalel Jaffe.[45] The report began by reciting the order from Cemal Paşha, 'to bring all the population except the farmers and owners of orchards and vineyards to the Lud station centre tomorrow at sunrise'. The Evacuation Committee obtained permission to bring part of the population to Ras-el-ain station and to Kfar Saba. On arriving at these locations, however, it seemed there were no trains at the stations.

The people were thus left helpless, and in spite of possible objections, the committee believed that it was best to allow the migration of refugees into Galilee, although many of them might be 'swallowed up by the multitude Moslem poor class there'.[46] There were such crowds at the station that it was impossible to obtain detailed lists of the deportees and their destinations. The committee had hoped that they could distribute the refugees among the various villages, but eventually most of them were sent to Tiberias. The committee was strongly against the idea of so many crowding into the city, both for fear of epidemics and because the refugees would only be 'another beggar-mob that will be added to the Tiberias population ever accustomed to receiving charity'.[47] The migration committee wanted to distribute the refugees in the villages and requested that the farmers do their best to accommodate as many as possible. In an attempt to encourage the farming community to co-operate, the committee offered to refund farmers part of the expense of organizing agricultural enterprises for the employment of the refugees, as it

---

[44] The special committee for relief of Jews in Palestine to Judah Magnes, [no date] Central Archive for the History of the Jewish People, Jerusalem, Magnes Archive, P/1033. [Hereafter CAHJP MA]. The head of the committee was Jack Mosseri, a banker and a member of an affluent and influential Sephardic family in Egypt; the other members were representatives of the *yishuv* that were deported to Cairo shortly after the war broke out.

[45] Bezalel Jaffe was a Zionist pioneer in procurement of land for Tel-Aviv, industrialist and irrigation expert, and a leader in political organization of the Jewish community in Tel-Aviv.

[46] CAHJP MA, P/1033, Synopses of four circulars issued by the "Central Evacuation Committee in Judea", April 1917.

[47] Ibid.

desired that all workmen and artisans be distributed in the villages and towns, so that the American funds could be used only for relief purposes in Tiberias. The committee also obtained some of the most urgently needed medicines, which were distributed in the various refugee settlement centres in the Galilee. Finally, they prepared and circulated questionnaires, the replies to which they hoped would help to systematize the data for a detailed report to be submitted to the American Council.

Transporting the evacuees to the Galilee took about 5–6 days. Despite the degree of public goodwill toward them, many families remained at the railway stations in the heat during the day and in the cold at night, with no food or shelter. Finally, about 2700 refugees migrated to the Galilee. The reasons for transferring the Jews to this area were the relatively low cost of local grain and its sufficient quantities to feed the people, along with the opportunity for employment in the agricultural settlements. There were also adequate dwelling conditions in most of the colonies. The people that transferred to Tiberias were settled in the Orthodox Jewish college of Rabbi Meir Baal ha-Ness, but many of them soon fell sick with malaria, spotted fever, and especially bowel disease. Within the town itself, the situation was a little better, as most of the families were accommodated in apartments and some of them managed to earn a living. Even though the people of the settlements in the Galilee did their best to ease the plight of the deportees, in practice the situation deteriorated. The hot climate, having to sleep under the open sky, disease and epidemics, along with lack of employment and income all had their effect on the deportees and their hosts.

In October 1917, the Turks exposed the Nili underground,[48] a Jewish spy ring that had assisted British intelligence agents, and the capture of its members threatened to lead to fierce reprisals against the Jewish community of Palestine. A full siege was imposed on Atlit, Hadera and Zichron Yaakov, where some members of the spy group were active, with elderly people, women, and children arrested. The governor of the Haifa district and the military governor of Nazareth, both of whom had taken

---

[48] *Nili*, known as the Aaronsohn group, was a small but efficient spy-ring in Palestine. The group supplied information mostly on military matters. Aaron Aaronsohn, an agronomist, was working at the time for the British Military Intelligence in Egypt. NILI: acronym in Hebrew for the biblical expression "The Glory of Israel Does Not Deceive or Change" (1 Samuel 15:29).

part in massacres of Armenians earlier in the war, were given responsibility for arrests and interrogations after the exposure of the espionage ring. Detainees at the Nazareth and Haifa prisons were severely tortured. The governor of Jerusalem, Izzet Bey, accused the Jewish community of treason and pressed for its annihilation. Forty Jews were deported on foot to Jordan, while community leaders were jailed at the Kishle, the Turkish prison near the Jaffa Gate in Jerusalem.[49]

THE JEWISH MIGRATION COMMITTEE IN THE GALILEE

Shortly after these events, a local committee was appointed for the Galilee, which was chaired by Zalman Jacobson, with Eliyhu Yanovski appointed as the central committee's representative in Tiberias. After the initial period of turmoil, the committee proceeded to reorganize Jewish community life under the new circumstances. Each community was requested to forward relevant information regarding the number of deportees, those employed, the ones who were in need of an allowance, the cost of bread and so forth. In order to obtain control of and properly assess the situation, deportees were not allowed to change their location unless it was for medical reasons, and only on doctor's orders.[50]

Within a short while, Eliyhu Yanovski, as official in charge of the employment office, announced that all people capable of working would be expected to do so. One of his first initiatives was to send a few Yemenite Jews to work in the neighboring colony of Sejera, but difficulties quickly arose due to a lack of work and workers, as well as health-related issues.[51] One option suggested by the village secretary was to send some of the families to Safed, but that did not seem like a viable alternative since people were dying there from hunger and disease. Thus, the newcomers simply had to adjust to their new environment and make the most of the situation, consistent with the 'productivity' idea, which was identified with Zionist ideology and the new *yishuv*. Yanovski was also in charge of purchasing wheat and distributing it to the various communities, but

[49]Neuman (1993), 'Battle for Survival', 305–325; Efrati (1991), *Jewish Community*, 31–33.

[50]CZA, J90/116, Circular No. 7, Central Committee in the Galilee, 21 August 1917.

[51]CZA, J90/252, 26 June 1917, Sejera Secretary's Report to the Migration Committee.

the constant shortage of finances made his mission practically impossible and forced him constantly to pursue alternative sources of income.[52]

According to reports sent from the agricultural settlements, approximately 50% of the people who settled in the villages of the Lower Galilee were employed in trades, such as tree cutting, fruit picking, legume harvesting, and preparing charcoal, among other things. Yanovski organized the newcomers' employment according to their qualifications and skill-sets and tried to match them with proposals he received, such as road repairs and road building, building in Safed and the colonies, and agricultural tasks, including stone clearance in the fields. Women were partially employed in spinning, weaving, and needlework. However, the bigger dilemma was whether the deportees were capable of working under these harsh conditions. As mentioned, most of these people came from urban backgrounds and had difficulty adjusting to the physical labour required in agriculture and construction. They nonetheless had to support and occupy themselves since the duration of their exile was unknown and hard to anticipate. Local farmers financed part of the building inside the colonies, while the rest of the financing came from the committee's budget. The people who were listed as active workers were off the payroll of the committee, and once the committee was unable to raise the funds to finance the work, they were left with no income.

Deported teachers established their own board and took charge of organizing the children in study groups. Existing schools were expanded as much as possible and deported teachers were integrated into the system. In Tiberias and Safed, moreover, Mrs. Hoofien opened needlework schools to employ the young girls.[53] Additional challenges the committee had to tackle included the provision of medical aid, soup kitchens, and accommodation. The committee also had to distribute the deported families based on the surrounding communities' ability to absorb them. In this regard, Dizengoff urged the committee to avoid sending the deportees to Safed County, as the cost of living there was high while job prospects were low. Nonetheless, Moshe Glikin, director of the Migdal farm, received a special permit from the committee to send a cart of deportees to Safed. He was willing to help settle the capable workers,

---

[52] CZA, J90/162, 1917–1918, Letters sent by Yanovski in Tiberias to Thon, Yaffe and Dizengoff.

[53] CZA, J90/252, 6 August 1917, Dizengoff to the Migration Committee in Safed.

provided their salary was funded by the committee.[54] In the villages, a board nominated for this purpose placed people in vacant houses, rooms, or sheds. In private properties, rent was paid by the central committee.

By July 1917, Haim Margalit Kalvarisky, the Jewish Colonization Association (JCA) representative in the Upper Galilee, managed, with Dizengoff's assistance, to organize financial support from the JCA through their agent in Germany, James Simon. One hundred thousand Deutschmarks were transferred as a loan, which was calculated to finance labour and food supplies for three months. Dizengoff requested that the committee members in Tiberias not disclose the fact that aid had been received and that they continue organizing the purchase of wheat. By early August 1917, the Zionist Executive, the executive arm of the Zionist Organization, was assured that no further evacuation was expected in the foreseeable future.[55] Relief funds were subsequently permitted to be transferred without interference, and the evacuees showed enough ingenuity to overcome difficulties.[56] Periodically, with an eye on the press, Cemal Paşha continued to make gestures of goodwill, but on the question of repatriation, he was adamant.

Later that month (August 1917), Dizengoff presented a dismal report, which outlined the harsh conditions of the evacuees including detailed references to hunger, disease, and mortality, along with a demand to allow the people to return to their homes. Cemal Paşha accused Dizengoff of presenting a distorted and manipulative description, and of presenting the evacuation as unjustified. He went on to demand a modification of the report and offered a subsidy of 13,500 Turkish pounds for the evacuees and an equivalent sum in the form of loans. Cemal Paşha also promised to supply grain from army stores and to set aside a small budget to finance both the purchase of wheat and any additional tasks the committee had to perform in preparation for the

---

[54] CZA, J90/143, 29 June 1917, Glikin to the Galilee Central Committee.

[55] The Zionist Organization was founded by Theodor Herzl at the First Zionist Congress in Basle in 1897. Its goals were set forth in the Basle Program: "Zionism Seeks to Establish a Home for the Jewish People in Palestine, Secured Under Public Law." CZA, L 6/2/I Ruppin to Warburg, 9 August 1917 in Friedman (1971), *German Intervention*, 37.

[56] Ibid., A sum equivalent to 2,459,815 francs was contributed by the Jewish communities in Russia, Germany, and Holland. American Jewry contributed the equivalent of 1,359,946 francs.

coming winter.[57] Ultimately, however, the deportees who were living in buildings on the outskirts of Tiberias were forced to evacuate yet again as their accommodation was needed for the billeting of Turkish soldiers, and they were thus left without shelter in the autumn of 1917.[58]

Dizengoff was troubled with the attitude displayed toward the people who sought refuge and asked Zalman Jacobson, head of the Galilee committee, to gather accurate information concerning the well-being of the deportees. He also asked if this attitude was shown only to Jewish refugees or was a general policy toward all the migrants.[59] As the overall atmosphere was harsh, it was clear that the lack of funds made it impossible to manage things properly. Dizengoff turned to Jacobson suggesting that he share the work with the other committee members and that he should consider public opinion, even if that was difficult. He also proposed that sharing responsibility with the other members of the committee would help matters, as would conferring tasks to extensions of the committee.[60] Finally, Dizengoff pointed out that he was in need of accurate information concerning all matters in preparation for an upcoming meeting with Cemal Paşa.

Throughout this period, the sources tell us of the non-harmonious relations that existed between the Galilee committee members. This tense atmosphere led to the resignation of some members who later relented and rejoined, as there was no other alternative.[61] It should be understood that the committee members had gathered ad hoc, and came from very different backgrounds, some from the old *yishuv* and some from the new *yishuv*, and the disputes between them were frequent. The need to organize accommodation and clothing, to oversee the medical situation, as well as providing food, employment, education, homes for orphans, purchasing grain and its distribution, and caring for everyday life made for an extremely demanding mission. As funds were

[57] Ibid.; CZA A249/33, Dizengoff (in Damascus) to Jacobson 12 August 1917; Ibid., A249/36 Meir Moshaiof to Jacobson, 20 November 1917.

[58] Zeev Liebovitch (1943), Immigration and Building (Jerusalem, Reuven Mass), 118–119 [in Hebrew].

[59] CZA A249/33, Dizengoff to Jacobson, 31 August 1917.

[60] Ibid., Dizengoff to Jacobson, 3 August 1917.

[61] See for example, CZA, J90/135 Karniel's resignation, 2 September 1917; The Resignation of All the Committee's Members, 20 November 1917; and A249/25 Dr. Green's resignation, 13 April 1918.

scarce and the future was uncertain, Dizengoff insisted they keep within the approved budget. The Galilee committee felt it could no longer shoulder the burden of responsibility and demanded a visit from Thon or Hoofien. Cases of disease were increasing, the death toll rose every day, and the moral accountability for these poor conditions was theirs.[62] A few days later, Dr. Yehuda Leib Pochovski announced that he could no longer operate the hospital.[63]

A new stage in the committee's position emerged in October 1917, once the British army began moving north. By December 1917, Field Marshal Allenby had successfully taken Jerusalem and a new front-line between the Ottoman and British forces was established. The future of the Jewish population still under Ottoman rule remained uncertain. The changing military dynamics of the conflict had interfered with territorial continuity in the region, and the area became subject to the authority of the Governor of Beirut. The committee could no longer depend on the Zionist official representatives in Jerusalem. The central committee was transferred to Damascus, but the local community was left without funds and the situation became even gloomier. Two of the most pressing problems facing the committee were, first, whether the government in Beirut would continue to support and sponsor their activity, and second, how to continue dealing with the refugee crisis in light of the termination of the connection with *yishuv* institutions in Jerusalem and Petach Tikva.[64] The humanitarian burden of the migration committee had also widened. Up to this point, it had cared for the general welfare of the deportees, but, from now on, it also had to care for the indigent, who had previously been supported by the Joint Distribution Committee of the American Funds for Jewish War Sufferers, and maintain the farms and settlements that were under the custody of the JCA and the Palestine Office.

As time wore on, the challenges the committee faced continued to grow. Dr. Abraham Green, the Safed doctor and head of the local

[62] Ibid., J90/139, Galilee Committee to Thon, 11 October 1918.

[63] Dr. Yehuda Leib Pochovski (1869–1963) was born in Russia, immigrated to Palestine in 1906, and worked as a physician, first in Rehovoth and later in Jaffa. During the war he was recruited to the Ottoman army and served as an officer in army hospitals. Later he was released from active service and was sent to Tiberias to help out with the outbreak of the cholera epidemic.

[64] Efrati (1991), *Jewish Community*, 327.

committee, contracted spotted fever and passed away in April 1918; typhus, cholera, and malaria were widespread; more orphans required shelter; and medical conditions had become unbearable.[65] Eliezer Paper, the school principal, was appointed the new head of the local committee. Several matters that Green had taken care of, such as running the pharmacy, medication, and the orphanage, remained obscure. Most of the Safed population was needy. The distress that prevailed in Safed, and the sense of deprivation of townspeople compared with deportees, instigated a migration movement of families to Australia.

Once Cemal Paşha had left the region, all requests for help from the Ottoman authorities in Beirut or Damascus were ignored or postponed, sending the applicants to the army commanders or to the Governor at Damascus. No budget was provided to ease the hardships of the civilian population. As a result, sources of income received via American aid, along with additional loans from the Anglo-Palestine Bank, were organized under the auspices of the committee and were distributed according to the specific needs of each community. Dizengoff sent an appeal to all local committees in Hadera, Haifa, Tiberias, and Safed to do everything in their power to cut expenses and to integrate all those able to work on the farms.[66]

A key issue, which the central migration committee and the local committees in Safed and Tiberias struggled with, revolved around the status and support of the poor in these two cities. The central committee viewed its mission as supporting the expelled population, while the local committees claimed that their efforts should be aimed primarily at supporting the weak and vulnerable population in these cities, irrespective of where they had come from. This dispute reflected the ongoing tensions between the new *yishuv* and the old *yishuv*. Conversely, in the spring of 1918, as the local farmers began harvesting, they were requested by the committee to contribute provisions of wheat in exchange for reimbursement once the war ended. All efforts were subsequently devoted to food production, vegetables, and grain cultivation. In addition, new working groups were formed, which, for the first time, included youths from the

---

[65] Dr. Abraham Green sent his blood samples to be examined in Tiberias and a few days later, he passed away. Beit HaMerie Archive, Safed, A.11.03, 18 April 1918, Green to the Committee in Tiberias.

[66] CZA, J90/112, Dizengoff to the Local Committees, 7 May 1918.

orthodox old *yishuv*, who were recruited to participate in and facilitate food production.

THE DEPORTEES IN DAMASCUS

Another location to which the deportees were sent in the northern part of the country was Damascus. In October 1917, the first wave of expelled Jews arrived in the city and, within a few months, 2000 deportees had joined the already impoverished Jewish community there. Some of the deportees were deserters caught in the colonies; others were workers, watchmen, and craftsmen. Once the Nili underground organization had been exposed, many more were expelled together with American citizens and distinguished leaders of the Jerusalem community, who were deported after the USA had joined the war. Some of them were imprisoned in Damascus. After three years of war, the local community was in a poor social and economic situation and lacked the resources to absorb thousands of immigrants, who invariably arrived almost penniless. The elite section of the community was also accused of ignoring the severe distress of the newcomers.[67] This ancient oriental community lacked a sense of national spirit and struggled to embrace the expelled Jews who were mostly Ashkenazi and western, and did not grasp the oriental features and the traditional way of life of their community. Relations between the deportees and the Jewish community of Damascus was thus quite complex.[68]

As the Ottomans were withdrawing from the southern parts of the Empire and Palestine, the administration and Cemal Paşha's headquarters transferred to Damascus. This led to a greater threat to the deportees and the wider Jewish community. The central evacuation committee had also moved to Damascus, and it seemed as though the deportees might be able to run their own lives alongside the community, with no connections between the two. Before long, however, the poorer members of the community approached the committee for aid, and despite the committees' obligation to care for the deportees, they could not ignore the distress of their co-religionists. Due to these circumstances, Hoofien promised to reach out and raise money for the community too.

[67] CZA, A153/146/6, Yalin to Hoofien, Damascus, 3 October 1917.

[68] Yaron Harel (2015), *The Beginnings of Zionism in Damascus* (Jerusalem, Zalman Shazar Center), 91–97.

A soup kitchen was established, and the poor were allowed to eat there. The committee also established a local clinic for the deportees and the pre-existing community and financed medication.[69]

Within a short time, the deportees began organizing cultural and educational activities. The demand for Hebrew lessons grew and within a short while, seven classes were established, with the local population taking part in these activities alongside the deportees. The curriculum included Bible lessons, reading and writing in Hebrew, history and Hebrew literature, nature, mathematics, and the geography of Palestine, all of which strengthened the Zionist idea and a sense of national spirit. The Jewish community of Damascus, which chose at first to ignore the newcomers, began gradually to open up to the new ideas. Once they realized that the old order no longer existed, they sought a new way of life through which they could reshape their identity and their organizational structure. Ultimately, the Zionist ideology they encountered during the last stage of the war seemed to offer answers and open a path to a better life.

CONCLUSION

At the end of September 1918, the war in Palestine came to an end and the committee's final mission to oversee the safe return of the exiles to their homes began. Unfortunately, travel had to be delayed because Tiberias was under quarantine due to an untimely outbreak of cholera. Within a few months, however, life very gradually returned to normality. Once again, a call was sent to the farmers in the Jewish settlements, asking them to enlist, this time to help deportees return home.[70] In retrospect, it would seem that the contribution of the local migration committee, along with the efforts of several deportees that lived in Tiberias, Safed and Damascus during the same period, was undeniably positive. Indeed, in the course of these disastrous and unforeseen circumstances, the committee's actions saved the expelled Jews and helped them cope with seemingly insurmountable daily challenges. Furthermore, the encounter between the different communities advanced awareness of Zionist and nationalistic ideology and went some way toward

[69] Ibid., 101.

[70] CZA, A249/17, The Galilee Migration Committee's Call to the Farmers, 24 October 1918.

developing a sense of Zionist and national identity among the local Jewish population.

Some tensions clearly remained, and disputes continued to be a feature of life in the Jewish communities in Tiberias and Safed. Yet, by the time the British army marched into Tiberias, the infrastructure for a national and voluntarily organized community had been laid. The migration committee had transformed behavioural patterns, helped engender a sense of unity and common purpose, offered expanded employment opportunities, and laid the foundations for what later evolved into the town community board, which oversaw the needs of Jewish society. The impact of Cemal Paşha's acts against the Jewish population during the war can be deduced from the fact that the harsh steps he took ultimately reduced their number by a third when the bulk of this number were the Zionist leadership and those identified with Zionist ideology. This harsh wartime reality seems likely to have had an influence on the change of attitude of the Jewish population in Palestine, which tended to support the Central Powers in the early stages of the war but drifted toward the Entente as the years went by. Jewish battalions from Palestine joined the fighting alongside the British Army, and, as mentioned, even set up a small but efficient spy-ring in Palestine that assisted the British against the Ottomans. Ultimately, the British Empire had become the centre of Zionist activity and the British government of course offered a major boost to the Zionist movement, and to the Jewish population of Palestine, in the form of the Balfour Declaration in November 1917.

Towards a Consolidation of Zionist National Consciousness in Palestine During the First World War: A Local Urban Perspective

Anat Kidron

The First World War was both a moment of severe adversity and great opportunity for the population of Palestine. The conflict created a long-term humanitarian crisis, in which economic activity was almost completely frozen and most of the banks in the region were shut down. This led to a severe shortage of money, medicines, and basic necessities. Swarms of locusts that raided the country in 1915 destroyed the grain and exacerbated the food shortage. The military confiscation or requisition of goods and property, along with recruitment into the Ottoman army, further intensified the crisis. European Jews who had settled in the region in the years before the war suddenly became enemy aliens, and thus faced the threat of deportation. Large swathes of the country's population were exposed to starvation and disease, including a particularly

A. Kidron (✉)
Ohalo Academic College of Education and Sport,
Golan Heights, Israel

A. Kidron
Department of Israel Studies, University of Haifa, Haifa, Israel

lethal typhus epidemic. For the various Jewish communities, which relied heavily on European sources of capital and supply, the effect of isolation was devastating. The impact of the war on the people of the region is very clearly reflected in falling population figures. The overall population of the country is estimated to have shrunk from 800,000 on the eve of the conflict to about 700,000 in July 1919. Within this, the Jewish population, which was estimated at 85,000 before the war, shrank to 56,000.[1]

The crises of the war and the transition from Ottoman rule to British colonialism have become directly connected, in collective academic and popular memory, to the establishment of the Zionist movement in Palestine. A number of studies have adopted this perspective and focused mainly on the new *yishuv's* aid organizations during the war.[2] Abigail Jackobson's research, which explores the joint Jewish-Arab civil defence in Jerusalem during the war years, has made a particularly notable contribution to our understanding of the links between the experience of the war in Palestine and the rise of Zionism.[3] Historians who have explored the impact of the war on the Jewish communities in Palestine during the

---

[1] Uziel Schmaltz (1991), 'Hitma'atut Ukhlusiyat Erets-Israel Bemilḥemet Ha'olam Harishona', in Eliav Mordechai, ed. *Bamatsor Uvamatsok: Erets-Isarael Bemilḥemet Ha'olam Harishona* (Jerusalem), 17–47. For a general overview on the war in Palestine, see Eliav Mordechai, ed. (1991), *Bamatsor Uvamatsok: Erets-Isarael Bemilḥemet Ha'olam Harishona* (Jerusalem). Studies on the war's social and cultural context began to be published in the 1980s and in their wake, the idea emerged that the war may also be seen as a window of opportunity and as leverage for social processes. For a historiographical review, see Billie Melman (1998/1999), 'Lahafoch et Hamilḥama Lehistorya: Hamilḥama Hagdola, Historya Ve-Historyonim, 1914–1998', *Zmanim*, 65, 6–23. For updates in civilian historiography of the war, see Iris Rachamimov (2014), 'Hahistoryografia Haezraḥit shel Milḥemet Ha'olam Harishona—Hamilḥama Hagdola Baktiva Ha'akademit ha'akhshavit', *Historia* 33, 9–34.

[2] See Natan Efrati (1991), *Mimashber Letikva* (Jerusalem); Rachel Hart (2009), '*Yaḥaso Shel Hayishuv Hayehudi el Hayishuv Ha'aravi Be-Yafo Uve-Tel-Aviv, 1881–1930*' (PhD diss., University of Haifa), 139. Hart notes that during the crisis an alliance was formed between the Sephardi elite of Jaffa and Zionist circles and regards these two groups as Zionist. My article on Haifa has also reached the same conclusion, which is undermined, however, when taking a broader look at other mixed cities. Anat Kidron (2009), 'Va'ad Hakehila Vekinun Kehila 'Al-'Adatit Be-Haifa Bemilḥemet Ha'olam Harishona', *Iyunim Bitkumat Israel* 19, 401–421. Studies dealing with the 'old *yishuv*' also mention the war as a particularly low point in its decline in status. Menahem Friedman (1991), 'Hevra Bemashber Ligitimatsya: Hayishuv Haashkenazi Hayashan, 1900–1917', in Moshe Lissak, ed. *Toldot Hayishuv Hayehudi Be-Erets-Israel Meaz Ha'aliya Harishona* (The Ottoman Period, 2) (Jerusalem, Mossad Bialik), 116.

[3] Abigail Jacobson (2011), *From Empire to Empire: Jerusalem Between Ottoman and British Rule* (Syracuse, Syracuse University Press).

war have essentially taken the rise of Zionism during the war almost for granted and have tended to focus on explaining the mechanism that enabled it.

Given this traditional historiographical focus, it seems timely to consider whether the Zionist movement actually used the crisis of the war to consolidate its position within the Jewish community in Palestine. In order to do this with a degree of certainty, however, we must compare the situation before and after the war. This chapter will seek to do this by focusing on two currents of change; namely, the ideological one, which pertains to nationalist/Zionist ideas, and the political and organizational one, relating to the centrality or even dominance of the organizational and political model proposed by the Zionist movement. It should be remembered that during the period in question the Zionist movement sought primarily to construct a Jewish national community that would also regard itself as a political entity and have a unifying institutional organization for the purpose of self-rule. This was a multifaceted goal that involved changing consciousness in Jewish society from a religious and ethnic vision to a national one based on modern European social values, establishing an organizational and political system, and attaining dominance for both of them in Jewish public life. In the period before the outbreak of war in 1914, however, the Zionist movement was weak both in terms of organization and demographic support and the dream of a Jewish nation-state was still far from being realized.

Most of the immigrants who came to Palestine in the two decades before 1914 and joined the 'new yishuv' settled in urban areas, where members of older Jewish communities already lived alongside their Arab neighbours in mixed districts. The change in consciousness sought by Zionists, especially the blurring of ethnic differences within Jewish society and increasing segregation from the Arab population, was particularly difficult to achieve in these local urban areas.[4] Unlike the clear, chronological distinction between immigrants and old-timers, however, the actual social boundaries between the old-timers and the new settlers ('new yishuv'), and therefore between those who belonged to Zionist

---

[4] Jay Winter emphasizes the diversity of urban identities that are of local rather than national in wartime. Jay Winter (2007), 'The Practices of Metropolitan Life in Wartime', in Winter Jay and Jean-Louis Robert, ed. *Capital Cities at War: Paris, London, Berlin, 1914–1919*, vol. 2 (Cambridge, Cambridge University Press), 1–19.

circles and those who did not, were unclear both before and during the war years.[5]

In the sections that follow, I will argue that the crisis brought about by the advent of war was used by Zionists as an effective instrument to achieve a change in national consciousness and redefine social distinctions in accordance with a differentiated Zionist image and, importantly, to emphasize the new *yishuv*'s supremacy. It will be seen that these distinctions did not reflect any particular social reality but rather the effort to create new social awareness. Social reality in the mixed urban environments on the eve of the war was shaped by processes of change and modernization which were not necessarily connected to immigration or national consciousness. The term 'old *yishuv*' served Orthodox circles at that time for distinguishing between 'modernizers' and 'preservers' and related to processes of modernization and productivity. By contrast, those in Zionist circles embraced a distinction based on the modern national sentiment, while ignoring other criteria. For the purposes of this chapter, I use the term 'old *yishuv*' as it was used by the people at the time, to refer to the Ashkenazi Jewish Orthodoxy, and the term 'old-timers' in reference to the Jewish population prior to the first major wave of Zionist immigration to the region that began in the 1880 and is usually referred to as the first Aliyah. The term 'new *yishuv*' is used in its Zionist sense, referring to the immigrant population, which was largely modern and national in character and outlook, who had settled since the first Aliyah.

My study focuses on mixed urban societies in which members of the 'new *yishuv*' were largely concentrated. There were differences between cities regarding the nature and composition of their general populations and their elites. Scholars agree that the war was a catalyst for the rise in the relative strength of the new *yishuv* because its productive economic structure and organizational capabilities allowed economic dependence on its institutions to develop among the wider Jewish community.[6] The

---

[5] Anat Kidron (2017), Constructing the Boundaries of Social Consciousness Under Conditions of War: The Urban Jewish Society in Eretz Yisrael/Palestine During World War I, *Journal of Levantine Studies*, 7:2 (Winter) 9–34.

[6] See, for example, Natan Efrati (1991), *Mimashber Letikva* (Jerusalem, Yad Ben-Zvi); Menahem Friedman (1991), 'Hevra Bemashber Ligitimatsya: Hayishuv Haashkenazi Hayashan, 1900–1917', in Moshe Lissak, ed. *Toldot Hayishuv Hayehudi Be-Erets-Israel Meaz Ha'aliya Harishona* (The Ottoman Period, 2) (Jerusalem, Mossad Bialik), 116.

bank of the Anglo Palestine Company (APC), which was staffed and directed by members of the new yishuv, serves as a key example of this. It was the only bank allowed to operate in Palestine and it, therefore, coordinated most of the national and local aid during the war years. The end of the war and its aftermath heightened this dependence, even more, increasing the power of new *yishuv's* organizations, which resulted, for instance, in the almost total dependence of the entire Jewish community in the region on the Delegations Commission in the immediate aftermath of the war. There would thus seem to be little doubt that the dislocation engendered by wartime circumstances led to a significant rise in the influence of the Zionist immigrant population and, in turn, the rise of Zionism. And yet when one examines developments during the war years from a local comparative perspective, a number of intriguing questions arise, especially regarding the leading role of the new *yishuv* in social and national changes during the war. The evidence suggests that a significant gap developed between the actual supremacy of the new *yishuv* during the war and the supremacy of its image, and that this was a key factor in the ongoing social integrity and survival of Jewish society in the region.[7] I will attempt to demonstrate the different factors that worked to strengthen the image of the Zionist movement in Palestine during the war despite the gap between it and the experienced reality. It will be demonstrated that this image later allowed for the emergence of a distinct national social formation within Palestine and redefined the relationships between the social groups there.

My argument is based on the following methodological and intellectual assumptions. First, a local perspective highlights geographical diversity within cities and the different levels of interest taken by the new *yishuv's* leadership in them. Second, it is important to understand that the maintenance of good relations with the Ottoman authorities was one of the bases for the success of local relief operations. It is also important to remember that the Ottoman authorities tried to encourage local civil organizations but regarded any forms of non-Ottoman nationalism (whether Arab or Zionist) as treason. Third, the ongoing crisis of the war years necessitated exceptional social organization. It soon became clear that Jewish society in Palestine, old-timers and immigrants alike, would

---

[7]Winter emphasizes the gap between 'imagined reality' (national in our case) and the 'experienced reality' which provides a different picture. See Jay Winter (2007), 'The Practices of Metropolitan Life in Wartime'.

not have been able to get through the crisis without the extensive aid received from the diaspora, and especially from American Jewry. Finally, in order to examine the question of Zionist organizational dominance, one has to examine not only the aid mechanism, but also its character. Did they succeed in basing the aid principles on the national ideas on behalf of which they acted? In other words, we must examine extent to which the new *yishuv* managed not only to survive itself, but also to contribute to the survival of Jewish society as a whole, and whether it succeeded in laying the foundations of national, non-ethnic and modern thought, and in leading the change in consciousness in Jewish society that emerged in the aftermath of the war.

THE NEW *YISHUV* IN PALESTINE'S CITIES ON THE EVE OF THE WAR

According to the census of the Palestine Office in 1916, which was adopted by the Statistics Department of the Jewish Agency, there were approximately 85,000–90,000 Jews living in Palestine on the eve of the war. Approximately 85% of this Jewish population was urban,[8] and this chapter will focus on five cities with a substantial Jewish population: Jaffa, Haifa, Tiberias, Safed, and Jerusalem. Most of the Jewish population left Gaza shortly after the outbreak of hostilities and hence the city did not belong to this category during the war years.[9] Most of the urban Jewish population consisted of old-timers belonging to very long-standing communities, some of whom actively rejected nationalist ideas or simply did not wish to share them.

The figures for Jewish population growth, especially after the early 1880s, the first years of Zionist settlement, quite clearly indicate the demographic centres of the new *yishuv*.[10] The growth rate was highest in Jaffa and Haifa. Although the Jewish population of Jerusalem increased

---

[8]Shmaltz, who relied on Ottoman sources, presents different data regarding the general population and the Jewish population. Uziel Schmaltz (1991), 'Hitma'atut Ukhlusiyat Erets-Israel Bemilhemet Ha'olam Harishona', in Mordechai Eliav, ed. *Bamatsor Uvamatsok: Erets-Isarael Bemilhemet Ha'olam Harishona* (Jerusalem), 17–47.

[9]Dotan Halevi (2015), 'The Rear Side of the Front: Gaza and Its People in World War I', *Journal of Levantine Studies* 5:1, 35–57.

[10]Yehoshua Ben-Aryeh (1981), 'Shenem-'Asar Hayishuvim Hagdolim Be-Erets-Israel Bamea Ha-19', *Cathedra* 19, 83–143.

Table 1   The growth of Jewish urban population before the First World War[a]

	Jerusalem	Jaffa	Haifa	Safed	Tiberias	Hebron and other cities	Total
1880	18,000	1000	600	4300	2400	700	27,000
1900	35,000	3500	1500	6300	4000	900	51,200
1914	45,000	10,000	3600	7500	6000	1000	73,100

[a]Yehoshua Ben-Aryeh (1981), 'Shenem-'Asar Hayishuvim Hagdolim Be-Erets-Israel Bamea Ha-19', Cathedra 19, 83–143, 113. The figures in this table are approximate figures, for Haifa they are based on Carmel Alex (1990), 'Haifa Besof Hatkufa Ha'otomanit', in Naor Mordechai and Yossi Ben-Artzi, eds. *Haifa Behitpathuta, 1918–1948* (Jerusalem), 2–19; Ben-Artzi Yossi (1985), 'Kavey Yesod Betoldot Haifa Vehitpathuta Bazman Hahadas', in Schiller Elli, ed. *Haifa Veatareha, Ariel* 37–39, 13–23; and Schmaltz, 'Population of Palestine', 17–47. According to the Palestine Calendar, Schmaltz finds 4600 persons residing in Safed. In Tiberias, he notes 3200 Jews out of a population of 12,000 people, in Haifa he finds 2400 Jews. Dan Giladi and Shavit Ya'akov (1983), 'Galey Ha'aliya shel 1882–1914 Utrumatam Layishuv Hayehudi Ha'ironi', in Ben-Arieh Yehoshua and Yisrael Bartel, eds. *Hahistorya shel Erets-Israel Beshlhey Hatkufa Ha'otmanit* (Jerusalem), 292. Shor indicates that in the beginning of the twentieth century, there were 6000 people in Tiberias and on the eve of the war, the population grew to about 8000 out of which 6000 were Jews. Nathan Shor (1988), 'Nekudot Ikariyot Behitpatkhut Ukhlusiyat Tveria Batkufa Ha'otmanit', *Matov Tveria* 6, 9–14

and it became the leading city, its growth rate was lower and even declined since the beginning of the century. The population of Safed and Tiberias also grew, mostly due to migrant members of the old *yishuv* who moved there from Jerusalem (Table 1).[11]

The size of the new *yishuv* communities, their organization, and the extent to which they impacted on wider urban Jewish society differed from city to city. There were new institutions in every city, however, particularly branches of the APC Bank and Hebrew educational institutions that had a varying influence on the overall Jewish population.[12] However, not all of these new institutions were linked to community organizations that reflected the new nationally minded values. The demographic and organizational strength of the new *yishuv* in the decades before the war and the nature of the connections between the new *yishuv* and the old-timer *yishuv* in each city largely determined the

[11] Ibid.

[12] Rachel Alboim-Dror (1980), *Hahinukh Ha'ivri Berets-Israel* 2 (Jerusalem), 15–120; Rachel Alboim-Dror (1991), 'Hamilhama kehizdamnut lekibush hahegemonia bakhi', in Mordechai Eliav, ed. *Bamatsor Uvamatsok: Erets-Isarael Bemilhemet Ha'olam Harishona* (Jerusalem), 48–60.

former's ability to become active during the wartime crisis, lead social change, and consolidate the standing of the Zionists' image.

Jaffa and Haifa were developing coastal cities which attracted an immigrant population with a generally modern and entrepreneurial orientation. Jaffa was very much the Zionist organizational centre in the region and the Palestine Office was opened there in 1908. The city's Jewish Committee, which included Ashkenazi and Sephardi representatives, was established, on the initiative of the new *yishuv*, in 1891, out of a desire for shared ethnic representation rather than true partnership. The committee saw ups and downs in its activities and ceased operating before the war without reforming the divided political power structure of the city. Tel Aviv, which was founded in 1909 as a Hebrew quarter of Jaffa,[13] attracted affluent immigrants who established separate economic and neighbourhood organizations.

In the years before the war, Haifa witnessed the beginning of processes of geographical separation along national lines. Distinct Jewish neighbourhoods were established but never achieved full urban separation. The city's old-timer *yishuv*, both Sephardi and Ashkenazi, lacked significant leadership and new *yishuv* organizations had begun establishing roots in Jewish public life there before the war, with the Integrated City Committee being established in 1906. Although it fell apart shortly before the outbreak of the war, its activity indicates the increasing dominance of the new *yishuv* and the weakening of the old-timer Sephardi community during this period.[14]

As holy cities identified closely with the old *yishuv*, Tiberias, Safed, and Jerusalem had quite different experiences. The status of Jerusalem was different because of its central role and its symbolic significance, which influenced the social and organizational processes that occurred there. New *yishuv* communities in the city began their activities in the late nineteenth century, and, despite being small, they were able to bring about a degree of change, especially in the areas of education, health, trade, and services.[15] It should also be noted that Tiberias and Safed

---

[13] The term 'Hebrew' is used to distinguish it from the term 'Jewish' and to emphasize the Zionist national ambitions.

[14] 'The Jewish Community in Haifa, a General Overview of the Composition and the Activities of the Committee Since Its Founding', Haifa City Archive [henceforth: HCA], 208/4 (undated).

[15] Kobi Cohen-Hattab (1996), 'Me'oravut Va'ad Hakehila shel Yerushalaim Behitpathut Ha'ir, 1917–1948', *Cathedra* 82, 111–134.

experienced a decline in economic status, as the economic centre moved to coastal cities in the late nineteenth century.

The interest taken by the new *yishuv* in Tiberias and in particular the purchase of land in eastern Lower Galilee by the Jewish Colonization Association (JCA) changed this region and brought new economic opportunities for the city's residents.[16] However, the city itself did not attract significant numbers of immigrants and Tiberias remained characterized by 'density and congestion'.[17] Good relations were established between the new *yishuv* and the *Hakham Bashi* (Chief Rabbi) of Tiberias, Aharon Bechor Elhadif, and his successor Isachar Abulafia.[18] However, these relations actually exacerbated the rift within the city's Jewish community, especially among the Orthodox Ashkenazi minority, which was characterized by conservative radicalism and suffered from internal divisions.[19] In autumn 1913, the few members of the new *yishuv* in the city tried to create an organized community and established an executive committee. This served as the nucleus for civilian organization during the war, but its activity was limited and it did not succeed in gathering all Jewish residents under its administrative umbrella.[20] Safed, a relatively small city located north-west of the Galilee Mountains, lacked economic potential, had considerable transportation difficulties and most of its Jewish population was Orthodox and conservative. The city's main source of income was the *halukka* [charity distribution], and in the decades between the 1880s and 1914 no new community institutions were established in the city.

---

[16] Aharon Feldman and Hadani Ever (1955), *Hahityashvut Bagalil Hathton: Hamishim Shnot Koroteha* (Ramat Gan), 95–96; Arie Bitan (1987), *Temurot Yishuviyot Bagalil Hathton Hamizrahi 1800–1978* (Jerusalem 1982), 84.

[17] Ya'akov Bargaret (7 August 1914), 'Teveriya Veaklima', *Hapoel Hatzair*.

[18] David Sarid (1984), 'Hatmurot Bayishuv Hayehudi Be-Teveria Bitkufat Ha'aliya Harishona Vehashniya 1882–1914' (MA thesis, Bar-Ilan University), 30–56, 61; Oded Avishar (1973), *Tiberias* (Jerusalem, 1973), 208–212.

[19] Ibid., 163.

[20] Dr. Ya'akov Bargaret, Yahye Nizri, Yaakov Moshe Toledano, Aharon Segal and Leib Yaffe to Menachem Ussishkin [undated], Central Zionist Archive [henceforth: CZA] 61/24 A. 1916; Boord Matan (2011), 'Yahasam shel Halutsey Emek-Hayarden Leyehudey Hayishuv Hayashan Be-Teveria, 1908–1930' (MA thesis, University of Haifa), 71.

THE LEADERSHIP OF AID INITIATIVES
IN THE CITIES: IMAGE AND REALITY

Local organizing processes, based on the principles of mutual assistance, began in all the major cities in the region in August 1914, several months before the Ottoman Empire's formal entry into the war. Three different kinds of organizations can be identified: professional, class or ethnic-based organizations, Jewish communal organizations, and local civil organizations (which were concerned with both Jewish and Arab interests and affairs). From the autumn of 1915, once a supply of American aid was established, the local organizations in all the cities were mainly engaged in distributing aid sent from abroad rather than organizing their own resources.

At the beginning of the war, the organizing process among the old-timers as well as the new *yishuv* was mainly spontaneous and based on former local affiliation: aid organizations based on prior organizational affiliation, such as trade unions, especially among workers and craftsmen; members of the Bezalel art school in Jerusalem set up a mutual aid fund; and the Orthodox communities, which continued to maintain their charity community organizations. The first organizations were established in Jaffa, partly because it was the centre of the new *yishuv* and had many local and especially professional organizations before the war.[21] Merchants were the first to get organized in Jaffa and then in Jerusalem. Merchants committees were the first to assume broader public responsibility, trying to control food prices, which skyrocketed. In merchant committees, members of the new *yishuv* worked together, usually along class lines, with members of the old-timer community who held modern economic views and shared their ideas of public and economic responsibility but not their nationalist ideology.

Local general organizations such as city committees or local relief committees were also established. As already mentioned, their actions depended on the character and general make-up of the local Jewish community prior to the war. The General City Committee was established in Jaffa a few days after the outbreak of war and included representatives of old-timers and of the new *yishuv*, as well as the *Hakham Bashi* Rabbi Uziel, who was close to the new *yishuv*. The committee levied taxes on

---

[21] Hana Ram (1986), *Hayishuv Hayehudi Be-Yafo Ba'et Haḥadasha Mikehila Sefaradit Lemerkaz Tsiyoni 1839–1939* (Jerusalem), 274–290.

the Jewish residents based on their personal circumstances rather than affiliation (ethnic or otherwise) and a soup kitchen and subsidized store for basic goods were opened. Although the committee tried to organize all aid activity in the city, it had difficulties functioning due to numerous internal disputes. One such dispute related to the separate organization of the residents of Tel Aviv, which municipally and community-wise belonged to Jaffa, but operated independently. Tel Aviv residents complained, for example, about the difficulty of collecting taxes in Jaffa and blamed this on the lack of national awareness and public accountability among the residents there. In the debate, there was no reference to the fact that the Tel Aviv neighbourhood was more affluent than its counterparts elsewhere and its residents could more easily afford to contribute funds for public causes.

Eight days after the outbreak of the war, the Committee for Easing the Crisis was established, transferring the power centre of the aid activity to the new *yishuv*. The committee was established and chaired by Meir Dizengoff, head of the Tel Aviv Committee,[22] and started operating on two levels: local and national. In time, however, internal disagreements about its management, and its subordination to the Palestine Office reduced the committee's local activity in Jaffa while strengthening its activity in the areas of the new *yishuv* in Tel Aviv and in the settlements in Judea. The committee also had quite a narrow public mandate, since it mainly drew on the organizations of the new *yishuv*.[23] Indeed, its local subcommittees served almost exclusively the new *yishuv*. The Loan Committee, for example, employed productivity principles and provided loans for collaterals only to those who could prove a sound economic basis which got 'stuck' because of the war in Europe, and thus it also turned into a primarily sectorial body.

In Jerusalem, which did not have an integrated city committee before the war, an emergency meeting of some 70 members of the Jewish elite was organized on 10 September 1914. The elected Provisional Committee was composed entirely of people close to or belonging to Zionist circles, who formed a Sustenance Committee mainly to establish

---

[22] Ibid., 276–278.

[23] Such was the case in the Tel-Aviv Committee. In the Jaffa Committee, there were representatives from other social strata.

soup kitchens.[24] It was the first attempt to unite all activities in a single organization, but, in practice, this committee mainly focused on supporting the activities of the new *yishuv*. Contrary to the accepted image, Orthodox organizations, mainly led by educated Orthodox young people, were also based on general principles, and not on the traditional *halukka*.

In Safed, the new *yishuv* community had initially suffered from demographic and organizational weakness and was unable to coordinate a coherent aid operation, even along ethnic lines. At the beginning of the war, members of the new *yishuv*, especially Yehoshua Karniel, manager of the APC bank, tried to take advantage of the state of emergency and to develop a non-ethnic organizational and social infrastructure. Karniel attempted to establish the Relief Committee which was supposed to include all social sectors, including representatives of the various *Kolellim* or *Landsmannschaften* (i.e. local organizations, led by rabbis, of people of common origin within the Orthodox community) in the city. The first action of the committee was to establish a grocery store that sold goods at controlled prices, which remained open for about two months. This activity did not last partly because of disputes among the heads of the *Kolellim* about the manner of distribution, but also as a result of a general lack of Jewish communal solidarity in the city. A local General Relief Committee started operating following the arrival of American aid,[25] according to the requirements of the Central Relief Committee, but its activity was insufficient to give rise to a general Jewish organization in the city.

---

[24] Zevi Shiloni (1985), 'Changes in Jewish Leadership During World War I', *Cathedra* 35, 59–63 [Hebrew]; Abigail Jacobson (2009), 'A City Living Through Crisis: Jerusalem During World War I', *British Journal of Middle East Studies* 36:1, 73–92.

[25] The America relief committees which united under the American Jewish Joint Distribution Committee became the prominent Jewish aid agency during the war. The JDC was not a Zionist organization but the aid to Palestine was organized together (and separately) with the Provisional Executive Committee for General Zionist Affairs that was established at the outbreak of the war, and in cooperation with the Secretary of State and the American ambassadors and consuls. The JDC sent money and food (especially rice and wheat). The first aid transport arrived at Jaffa on August 2014 on the US cruiser *North Carolina* with $50,000 and food supplies. See Nina Lubovitz (2011), 'Hasiyu'a shel Yehude Artsot Habrit Lema'an Hayishuv Hayehudi Be-Erets-Israel Bemilhemet Ha'olam Harishona Veaharea, *1914–1921*' (MA thesis, University of Haifa).

The situation in Haifa differed from that of other cities in the region. Initially, the old-timer population of this coastal city lacked the wherewithal to help themselves and the local organization was led by the leaders of the Ashkenazi new *yishuv*. Before the war, the local Sephardi community suffered from dwindling community taxes and external contributions and could not lead or even be an equal partner in leading the city's Jewish society.[26] The New Ashkenazi Committee, as it was called, took on the entire organization of the aid operation. It operated within a political framework, taking care of welfare, social aid, and health issues. As for religious issues, the ethnic distinctions remained intact and became even more pronounced. During the war, a separate Ashkenazi *Hevra Kadishah* (Jewish burial society) was established in the city, an indicator of the weakness of the Sephardi committee in the city, but also to the ethnic cleavage.[27]

It should be noted that the arrival of American aid and the inability of Jewish communities in the region to help themselves did not actually change the local picture a great deal. Despite Zionist control of key positions in the American aid mechanism, especially those held by Arthur Ruppin and the Palestine Office officials, the local balance of power in each city did not change. Aid mechanisms reflected the social structure on the eve of the war and empowered it but did not change it to a great degree.

---

[26] Since the archive of the Sephardi community in the city burned down, we do not have documentation regarding the activity of the committee; however, the fact of its existence is indisputable. Information about its activity can be found in the archive of the Ashkenazi Community Committee (HCA, 220/10) and from external publications such as *Bein Hazmanim*, which was published in Safed and represented the opinion of the new *yishuv*. The editor Waldstein rebuked the Sephardi community in Haifa for doing nothing to alleviate the situation despite the hardships of its members. Yanait Rachel and A.S. Waldstein (1916), *Bein Hazmanim* (Safed), 69. It is clear that this rebuke ignored the limited economic and organizational ability of the Sephardi committee in the city.

[27] From the beginning of the twentieth century and until the war, Sephardi Jews used the services of the Sephardi *Hevra Kadishah*. 'Full Minutes of the Council, 26 March 1919', HCA 220/08.

ZIONIST LEADERSHIP AND THE EVOLUTION OF NATIONAL CONSCIOUSNESS DURING THE WAR

Among other aspirations, Zionists generally sought to build a society based on productive principles and a non-ethnic vision. An examination of the aid operation in light of these principles during the war shows that in those places where they were upheld, it was not only because of Zionist leadership, but also due to a combination of domestic and external forces operating in the field of aid. The attempt to advance a national, non-ethnic perspective had already failed in the first months of the war. As mentioned above, none of the cities had common institutions or joint city committees with a non-ethnic vision. The entire aid operation of the American Relief Committee was thus managed by ethnic committees. The Committee for Easing the Crisis, an organization founded and directed by members of the new *yishuv*, also acted from the outset through local ethnic committees and did not try to lead any change in this area.

An examination of Zionist leadership in advancing productivity and avoidance of charity is more complex: attempts to make Jewish society productive were central to the worldview of the new *yishuv*, but also to that of many young educated Orthodox leaders and of some Jewish philanthropic bodies.[28] *Halukka* was the main cause of the non-productive base of the Ashkenazi Orthodox society, but large-scale distribution to various communities of origin (*Landsmannschaften*) was already declining before the war as a result of internal processes in Orthodox society in Europe and the United States. The productive base kept expanding in old-timer communities, especially among the Sephardi. Donations were still accepted in Zionist communities, by contrast, except among workers' organizations, though there was a discussion about how they should be most appropriately used. Jewish charity and bourgeois philanthropy remained essential social values, but they were not really welcome as an economic basis for society and they were generally intended to be used to precipitate investment to create or maintain productive works. During the first year of the war, in lieu of conventional charity, both Orthodox and Zionist leaders tried to provide the sort of financial support that could contribute to the survival of the economy in the long

---

[28] Menachem Friedman (1978), *Hevra Vedat, Haortodoksia Ha-lo Tsiyonit Be-Erets-Israel 1918–1936* (Jerusalem), 16–17.

run—as exemplified in activities of the merchant associations in Jaffa and Jerusalem, or in the establishment of *kupot milveh* (loan funds). Since the first arrival of American aid, the guidelines for aid were compatible with the principles of the American institutions.[29] The distribution of American aid was influenced by a desire to support ongoing self-reliance, rather than dependence on charity. The American aid workers thus chose to work with the new *yishuv* bodies in Palestine, not out of loyalty to national values but due to organizational considerations: the new *yishuv* was better organized, had established a system of institutions and shared the productive worldview of the American institutions. Despite those shared interests, pressure from Orthodox circles in Jerusalem and the United States meant that it was ultimately decided that approximately half of the American aid would be provided through direct charity support rather than on the basis of productivity.

The problematic nature of these principles became apparent from the earliest days of the war. First, financial support to promote longer-term self-reliance was only appropriate for an economy based on productivity and thus excluded those who lacked this ability prior to the crisis. This applied especially to the Ashkenazi Orthodox, but also to others on the margins of society who lacked earning capacity. During the war years, these divisions did not reflect a struggle over principles and ways of life, as it did not allow for the changing lifestyles of the traditional Orthodoxy, but simply excluded them.

The ideological struggle over the manner of allocating aid funds crossed the narrow delineations of 'new *yishuv*' or 'old-timers' and was intertwined with the struggles for leadership in the old-timer *yishuv* among educated young people and the heads of Orthodox *Kolellim*, both Sephardi and Ashkenazi. The modern principle of providing charitable support in the form of food and essential commodities instead of money, and by personal distribution according to lists of the poor, was designed to bypass the traditional *halukka* method and its leadership. In places where the *halukka* method had not been employed, namely Jaffa and Haifa, charity activity (by ethnic committees) was based on 'poor lists'. By contrast, in the holy cities, 'modernizers' from the Orthodox *yishuv* rather than new *yishuv* leaders attained the leading positions in the

[29] Nina Lubovitz (2011), 'Hasiyu'a shel Yehude Artsot Habrit Lema'an Hayishuv Hayehudi Be-Erets-Israel Bemilhemet Ha'olam Harishona Veaharea, 1914–1921' (MA thesis, University of Haifa).

general distribution of charity support. Thus, Ephraim Cohen Reiss, who belonged to the modern Orthodox elite and was considered anti-Zionist, led the distribution of American aid in Jerusalem. Reiss supported the idea of productivity, and although he insisted on allocating part of the aid funds to charity, he ensured the existence of the 'poor list' and a distribution that by-passed the leadership of *Kolellim*, for which he had to face a hard internal struggle and opposition from the Orthodox in the Relief Committee that eventually led to their leaving the committee.[30]

In Safed, where the winds of innovation within Orthodox society were weaker, initiatives to organize relief on a general basis met with stiff local opposition and failed to bring about change. The local Relief Committee, chaired by Joshua Karniel, included twelve representatives of the Jewish groups in the city. The relief principles that Karniel attempted to dictate met the requirements of the Americans guidelines: establishing a subsidized grocery store, providing loans to workshop owners and workers, and only providing support to families of army recruits, while allocating 40% of the funds to purchasing food products and essential goods, and the remaining 60% to loans. But these principles did not stand the test of reality and the local Relief Committee ignored the guidelines.[31] Ultimately, more than 75% of the funds were granted as charity support and the poor lists were compiled by the heads of the *Kolellim*, a move that effectively perpetuated the old *halukka* system.[32] Efforts by officials in the Palestine Office, which conducted its own 'census of the poor' in August 1915 in order to overcome the problem, failed.[33] Repeated attempts to base aid and aid distribution on modern principles also failed and the old patterns generally remained intact.[34]

Charitable support arrived later in Tel Aviv, which was a neighbourhood of 'homeowners' with a more solid economic base. The Zionist workers who lived in the neighbourhood depended on those homeowners to earn their livelihood and without them, they would struggle

---

[30] Natan Efrati (1991), *Mimashber Letikva*, 9–64.

[31] From Aharonson to Karniel, without date, CZA, J90/99.

[32] Zeev Perel (1999), *Hamashber be-Zefat hayehudit be-milhemet haolam harishona* (Thesis, Bar Ilan University), 115.

[33] The assessment conducted by Ruppin defined 5000 out of 7000 Jewish residents of Safed as poor. Ibid., 56.

[34] See for example the correspondence between Karniel and Kalvarisky, dated 15 January 1916, CZA, J15/6447.

Table 2   The main relief funds[a]

	Loan percentage	Support percentage
Haifa	69.30	30.45
Jaffa	59.33	39.42
Tiberias	58.80	38.55
Safed	30.99	61.96
Jerusalem	36.06	61.44
Lower Galilee	63.89	36.11
Upper Galilee	80.25	17.35
Judea Colonies	82.06	16.48

[a]According to the 'distribution report of the "First Fund" of the Relief Committee', without date, CZA L2/610. The percentages do not always add up to 100% but this is how it appears in the original document.

to survive the war crisis. The Committee for Easing the Crisis ceased to exist in its local form with the arrival of American funds and became the executive arm of the American Aid Committee. Ruppin replaced Dizengoff as chair, and the name of the committee was changed to the Provisional Committee for American Aid. The committee's work principles were dictated by the balance of political power inside the American relief bodies and by Ruppin's ambitions, which faced strong local Jewish opposition. In Haifa, the organizations of the new *yishuv* succeeded in coordinating most of the relief activity. They did not manage to base the activities on productivity alone or to avoid charity support but the percentage of charitable support was lower than in the other cities, which shows the stronger influence of the new-*yishuv* organizations in the city.[35]

Local differences, as well as the inability of the American relief organization and of the Zionist leadership to maintain a unified policy, were reflected in the first distribution report of the Relief Committee in the autumn of 1915. The report was more a reflection of the ideological desire of the various relief bodies than the necessity created by the continuation of the war (Table 2).

[35]'Minutes of the Support Committee', 13 September 1914, HCA 220/9. Regarding attempts to increase the scope of the support, see for example, a letter from Aharonson to Ruppin, 20 June 1915, in Livne Eliezre (1969), *Aharon Aharonson: Haish vezmano* (Jerusalem), 190.

DEFINING SOCIAL BOUNDARIES

Constructing the consciousness of distinctness or separateness from others is central to establishing a collective national identity, both in relation to other nationalities and with respect to non-national groups in society. The creation of dichotomous definitions served the image of a coherent Zionist new *yishuv* and blurred the profound differences between the various groups within each category while ignoring the areas where the categories overlapped. A good example of the ways in which a constructed image can influence perceptions of reality is the wartime support for educational institutions in Palestine, which reflects a struggle to preserve a way of life rather than a struggle for survival. One of the documented consequences of the war among the Jewish communities in the region was the collapse of the *Haredi* education system and the growing power of the Hebrew education system due to the organizational abilities and the adopted values of the leaders of the Zionist movement.[36] An examination of the causes of this state of affairs shows, however, that here again both the new *yishuv* bodies and the non-Zionist American aid bodies opposed supporting the Orthodox schools, with the aim of bringing about change and productivity. For the Orthodox, the community's responsibility to maintain Torah students culture in the Holy Land was an essential principle and the public's duty. The local Orthodox society supported this learning culture for as long as it was possible. In Jerusalem, Jaffa and in some new *yishuv* settlements, they undertook to pay monthly expenses 'For a full position of a *melamed* [religious teacher] or half of it', in order to prevent the closing of yeshivas.[37] The support received from some agricultural settlements illustrates the importance attached to *hevrat lomdim* by some members with Zionist/Orthodox views. Members of the new *yishuv* also fought for the survival of their educational institutions, even in the darkest hours of the war. The new *yishuv's* fight to protect its educational institutions was essentially identical to the Orthodox one and inconsistent with the struggle against the leadership of the old *yishuv*, pursued in order to give preference to productivity. The distinction between the ethical and necessary support for the Hebrew education system and the lack of support

---

[36] Alboim-Dror (1990), 'Hamilḥama kehizdamnut', 48–60.

[37] Menahem Sheinkin (1935), 'Erets-Israel Bymot Hamilḥama', in *Katavim*, 1, Aharon Hermony, ed. (Jerusalem), 43.

for other education systems due to their lack of productivity reveals the struggle for the future way of life in Palestine, which was both organizational and mental.

Another example is the use of the term 'old *yishuv*' to define Orthodox communities, mainly Ashkenazi, who opposed modern reforms in various areas of life and who mostly relied on *halukka* funds. In distinguishing between 'old' and 'new', this definition implied a closeness between the national new *yishuv* and parts of the non-conservative but not necessarily nationalist old-timer community and distinguished between these two and the traditional Orthodox leadership. This proximity created fertile ground for cooperation during the war, which was perceived as an opportunity for Zionist activity. For example, the cooperation with part of the Sephardi elite, especially in Jaffa and Jerusalem, was described as a process of national revival stemming from the organizational superiority of the new *yishuv*. Yet the cooperation with the Sephardi leaders was also influenced by relationships that existed prior to the war, which included trends of national revival in conjunction with frictions caused by the European nature of the Zionist movement.[38] This was particularly evident in Jaffa and Jerusalem, where most of the Sephardi elite resided. People such as Albert Antebi, who was the representative of the Jewish Colonization Association (JCA) in Jerusalem, a merchant and a public figure, close to the circles of both the new *yishuv* and the old-timer *yishuv*, were key figures in managing the relations between the Zionists, the old-timers, and the Ottoman rulers.[39] Antebi did not see himself as a Zionist, but he shared their interest in national revival and modernization. The Sephardi elite in Jaffa, Haifa, and Jerusalem and the urban Zionist leaders also shared class similarities. The collaboration, as well as the assistance extended by the Sephardi elite to Zionists leaders, stemmed from the dominance of the old-timer Sephardi leadership rather than that of the new *yishuv*; the Sephardi elite had the advantage of having ties to the Ottoman authorities, knowledge of the local language and customs, and connections with the local Arab communities. One of the highlights of Sephardi assistance was Antebi's success in cancelling the deportation order, issued by Cemal Paşha, in May

---

[38] Yzak Bezalel (2007), *Noladetem Tsiyonim: Ha-Sefaradim be-Erets-Israel Batsiyonut Uvaṯẖiya Ha'ivrit Batkufa Ha'otmanit* (Jerusalem), 162–208.

[39] Ibid., 173–174.

1915, for 49 prominent activists who were considered traitors. Most of these were Zionist activists.[40]

The deportation of Jews from Jaffa and Tel Aviv in March 1917 may serve as another example. During the first twenty days of deportation, 9000 people left Jaffa; at least 6500 of them belonging to the poor, marginalized section of the community.[41] The events are ingrained in collective memory as an example of the organizational capability of the new *yishuv*, since the Migration Committee took care of the exiled population.[42] The committee, headed by Dizengoff, became an official body, recognized by the authorities and placed under the direct orders of Cemal Paşha. The central focus on those exiled from Tel Aviv (rather than Jaffa) symbolized the organized Zionist *yishuv* in the contemporary account and strengthened the dichotomous image of the 'new' and the 'old' *yishuv*. However, this picture obscures several crucial points.

To begin with, many of the deportees, certainly the disadvantaged ones, who needed the assistance of the Migration Committee, were old-timers from Jaffa. The Migration Committee, which was considered a new *yishuv* body, was actually a local initiative established by the Jaffa and Tel Aviv committees, which represented cooperation between the new *yishuv* and the predominantly Sephardi elite. The committee was headed by Dizengoff *and* by the *Hakham Bashi* of Jaffa, the Orthodox Sephardi Rabbi Uziel. It should also be remembered that the Migration Committee operated under the auspices and with the assistance of Cemal Paşha, and most of its money came from American aid funds. The committee's organizational success was due to these factors and to Dizengoff's political and organizational ability. Ascribing the committee's operation to the new *yishuv* alone ignores those factors.

In addition, the Migration Committee encountered numerous manifestations of a lack of solidarity on part of the new *yishuv*. At the local level, most sectorial organizations and especially trade unions and professional associations took care of their members separately. The deported, even workers who were not organized but sought to become union members, were summarily rejected.[43] Some people from settlements in

[40] Yosef Eliyahu Chelouche (1931), *Parashat Hayay 1870–1930* (Tel Aviv), 230–239.

[41] Natan Efrati (1991), *Mimashber Letikva*, 284–291.

[42] Gur Alroey (2006), 'Golim be-artsam: Parashat megorashey Tel-Aviv Yafo bagalil hatahton, 1917–1918', *Cathedra* 120, 138–143.

[43] Ibid., 140.

Judea, for example, charged exorbitant prices for transporting the deportees.[44] Apart from instances of assistance and mutual aid, there were also many cases of exclusion and unwillingness to help in the absorption of deportees.[45] The latter stemmed from the perception of the deportees' distress as the distress of a local group (the residents of Jaffa and Tel Aviv) rather than a collective distress of the new *yishuv* persecuted because of its nationalism.[46] Finally, the ill-feeling rising between the local old-timers and the Migration Committee was the factor that perhaps contributed the most to the strengthening of the image that this was an affair of the new *yishuv* and that the Migration Committee was an expression of a Zionist takeover of relief funds from abroad. It seems that despite the directives of the American Relief Committee to distribute the relief funds among the deported and the local poor, the distribution of the funds was actually subject to local interpretation and was subject to change according to the power relations on the ground. This issue was most prominent in Safed, where 900 deportees arrived.[47] Severe tensions characterized the interrelations between the relief institutions of the new *yishuv* and the local population, which also found expression in the absorption of the deportees, especially in light of the fact that the funds transferred by the Migration Committee were insufficient to support the refugee population. Jacobson, a representative of the Migration Committee who did not reside in Safed, based the committee's activity on the assumption that the *Kolellim* maintained an independent support system and therefore did not need additional aid. The assumption was based on the fact that at the beginning of the war, the heads of the *Kolellim* had American support funds at their disposal and

---

[44]In March 1917 Hillel Yaffe rebuked the people of Zichron Yaakov for the profits they made from transporting deportees from Jaffa. Hillel Yaffe (1971), *Dor hama'apilim* (Jerusalem), 384–385; also in Shimon Rubinstein (1985), *Hanosaḥ hamale shel haḥe'arot shkatav Shimon Rubinstein le- vol. 2 shel hasefer: Mordechai Ben Hillel Hacohen, Milḥemet Ha'amim*, 2nd ed. (Jerusalem), 40.

[45]Abraham Almaliah (1929), *Erez Israel ve- Syria Bemilḥemet Ha'olam Harishona* (Jerusalem), 105.

[46]Ibid., 105. The large majority of the population (in Galilee and Jerusalem) was indifferent to these events.

[47]Perel states that the first wave included 193 people who arrived directly from Jaffa. Perel (1999), 'Hamashber be-Zefat hayehudit', 75. Later another 724 were transferred from Tiberias due to illnesses. According to the data of the Migration Committee, in Alroey (2006), 'Golim be-artsam', 143.

prevented Karniel's attempts to use a poverty index as basis for support. But in spring 1917, these funds ran out and the situation of the Jewish population in Safed became desperate.[48] A local new *yishuv* leader, Haim Kalvarisky, who was the JCA representative in Rosh Pina, tried to address the problem and demanded to spend part of the Migration Committee funds in Safed on the care of the local poor. Jacobson refused on the grounds of irregularities in the management of the local committee. In summer 1917, as the deportees' situation deteriorated, Jacobson decided also to stop the already limited sales of wheat from the Migration Committee warehouses to the city's residents, which deepened the rift.[49]

CONCLUSION

When considering the organization of Jewish society during the war in terms of constructing Zionist consciousness, several important trends can be observed. First, there was a gap between the national activities of the new *yishuv* and the activities of the local leadership in the cities. Both struggled for survival and were guided by the modern principles of productivity, which they tried to implement, at least initially. The national Zionist leadership emphasized the sense of distinctness, stressing the supremacy of the national '*yishuv*', its values, and its leadership. This was reflected in the relations to the entire Orthodox community in the region, which was defined as 'old', and in relation to the modernizing trends inside Orthodox circles, to the old local Sephardi and Mizrahi society, and to attempts at organizing common Jewish–Arab civil defence. Second, the distinction of 'new *yishuv*' and 'old-timers' was a consciousness constructing distinction that sought to draw social boundaries of national consciousness. In both societies, there were first and foremost local professional or ethnic group's survival attempts, which were based on economic and class similarity rather than on shared

---

[48] 'Meeting of the Migration Committee in Safed', 25 August 1917. Shimon Rubinstein (1985), *Hanosaḥ hamale shel hahe'arot*, 201. Efrati defines Jacobson's assumption as a 'local error' which prevented the distribution of money to the local population. Efrati (1991), *Mimashber Letikva*, 302–303. But it seems that dismissing this matter as an 'error' ignores the previous complicated relations in the city.

[49] Meeting of the Migration Committee in Safed, 25 August 1917, Rubinstein (1985), *Hanosaḥ hamale shel hahe'arot*, 201. In Haifa, for instance, the deportees were integrated in the community and its organization was remembered and described as the finest hour of the community. Anat Kidron (2009), 'Va'ad Hakehila Vekinun Kehila 'Al-'Adatit Be-Haifa Bemilḥemet Ha'olam Harishona', *Iyunim Bitkumat Israel* 19, 401–421, 417–419.

national ideas. The efforts of local organizations, such as merchant associations, or collaboration with Sephardi leaders crossed national divisions and represented attempts at organizing civil defence based on the pooling of resources in the face of distress.

Third, and importantly, the new *yishuv* organizations, along with the American relief organizations and modern Orthodoxy, attempted to take advantage of the crisis brought about by the war to effect long-term social change. These common interests were a key factor in allowing new *yishuv* leaders to take control of general relief activities, but the influence of these leaders did not suffice to change social reality in local urban settings. The Zionist leadership was unable during the war to improve its standing in urban societies and its local conduct largely reflected the reality prior to the war. Lastly, the new *yishuv*'s success in leading change closely corresponded to the degree of interest it had in different cities before the war. In the coastal cities, Tel Aviv residents' consciousness of their distinctness from Jaffa grew stronger, and in Haifa the new *yishuv* managed to establish itself and to create a social infrastructure. But in Tiberias and Safed, where the new *yishuv* had been demographically and organizationally weak before 1914, it did not succeed in leading an efficient civil organization during the war years. Jerusalem, where local Orthodox and new *yishuv* relief organizations operated side by side, illustrated more than anywhere else the cultural or ideological struggle over a way of life. In the presence of a significant Orthodox society, the activities of the new *yishuv* actually led to wider gaps between the two societies.

The end of the war and the ensuing geopolitical changes fundamentally transformed the situation on the ground in Palestine. The Zionist movement played a significant political role in achieving the Balfour declaration and the presence of members of the new *yishuv* in key positions in the general relief organizations and the Zionist dominance in the Delegation Commission immediately after the war became a symbol of Zionist dominance in Palestine. The 'window of opportunity' which established the prominent position of the Zionist movement in Palestine appeared at the end of the First World War rather than during it. Nevertheless, the leadership of the new *yishuv* had succeeded in using the war crisis to consolidate Zionist national consciousness within the Jewish community in Palestine and, importantly, in the mindset of future British officials. This active position of constructive consciousness would go on to play a key role in the Zionist dominance in Palestine during the period of the British mandate.

PART II

Western Fronts

A Mixed Bag of Loyalties:
Jewish Soldiers, Ethnic Minorities, and State-Based Contingents in the German Army, 1914–1918

Gavin Wiens

On 21 March 1918, General Erich Ludendorff, the First Quartermaster General of the German Supreme Command, launched the first of a series of offensives against the British and French armies on the Western Front. Over the preceding months, thousands of German soldiers had been

An early version of this paper was presented at the conference 'Contesting Jewish Loyalties: The First World War and Beyond' which took place at the Jewish Museum Berlin in December 2016. I am grateful to the Anne Tanenbaum Centre for Jewish Studies and the Central European History Society for supporting this research and to Doris Bergen, Roger Chickering, and James Retallack for providing thoughtful comments on drafts of this essay. I am equally indebted to Nisrine Rahal for ordering scans of several documents from the Geheimes Staatsarchiv Preußischer Kulturbesitz in Berlin-Dahlem.

G. Wiens (✉)
Department of History, University of Toronto, Toronto, ON, Canada
e-mail: gavin.wiens@mail.utoronto.ca

© The Author(s) 2019
E. Madigan and G. Reuveni (eds.),
The Jewish Experience of the First World War,
https://doi.org/10.1057/978-1-137-54896-2_7

transferred to Belgium and France from Eastern Europe, munitions and supplies had been stockpiled in the rear areas, and units had been trained in new tactics designed to break the deadlock of trench warfare. At the same time, the Supreme Command sought to ensure the reliability of the army. Responding to demands for peace from the *Reichstag* and signs of exhaustion among the troops, official propaganda was intensified in the summer of 1917. Mass-produced brochures and regular lectures emphasized that the current hardships were temporary and that unity would guarantee a victorious conclusion to the war.[1] Despite these preparations, the spring offensives ended in failure. Although the first few weeks witnessed spectacular advances, between the end of March and mid-July, the German armies in the West suffered approximately one million casualties. These horrific losses and a general refusal to risk life and limb for post-war annexations encouraged, in the words of Wilhelm Deist, a 'covert military strike' throughout the army. In the final months of the war, 'shirking' became a mass movement. A huge number of German soldiers—perhaps as many as 750,000 to one million—lingered in field hospitals or supply depots, separated themselves from their units, or simply wandered about in the rear areas.[2] By the late summer of 1918, morale had deteriorated to the point that the Supreme Command could no longer count on the loyalty of a majority of its fighting men.

The failure of Ludendorff's 'last throw of the dice' before the vast manpower and material resources of the United States tipped the scales in favour of the Entente precipitated the collapse of the German army. This chapter nevertheless argues that, long before the summer of 1918,

[1] 'Leitsätze für die Aufklärungstätigkeit unter den Truppen', July 29, 1917, in Wilhelm Deist, ed. (1970), *Militär und Innenpolitik im Weltkrieg 1914–1918* (Düsseldorf, Droste Verlag), 841–846. For the military planning and preparations, see Holger H. Herwig (1997), *The First World War: Germany and Austria-Hungary, 1914–1918* (London, Arnold), 392–402. In his memoirs, Ludendorff admitted that already in the autumn of 1917 large numbers of men left the trenches during periods of fighting only to reappear after their units had been withdrawn to the rear areas. Erich Ludendorff (1920), *Meine Kriegserinnerungen 1914–1918* (Berlin, E.S. Mittler), 434.

[2] Wilhelm Deist (1986), 'Der militärische Zusammenbruch des Kaiserreichs. Zur Realität der 'Dolchstoßlegende'', in Ursula Büttner, ed. *Das Unrechtsregime. Internationale Forschung über den Nationalsozialismus* (Hamburg, Hans Christians Verlag), 101–129. Alexander Watson disputes Deist's claim of a 'covert military strike' and instead argues that from mid-1918 onwards German soldiers often took part in 'ordered surrenders' in which demoralized junior officers arranged for their passage into Allied captivity. Alexander Watson (2008), *Enduring the Great War: Combat, Morale and Collapse in the German and British Armies, 1914–1918* (Cambridge, Cambridge University Press), 184–231.

the military authorities harboured doubts about the loyalty and reliability of many of the soldiers under their command. The German army that fought the First World War was composed of a number of minorities. The largest of these were the Bavarians, Saxons, and Württembergers who served in self-contained contingents and swore oaths to their own monarchs as well as the Kaiser. Alongside these state-based groups were the Alsatians, Danes, and Poles of the Prussian army. If it was at least some comfort that the Kaiser shared the loyalties of Bavarians, Saxons, and Württembergers only with the empire's lesser kings, the national allegiances of these ethnic groups were perceived as a far greater danger. Finally, there were the Jews. Although these men served throughout the army in large numbers, their culture and religion ensured that they were never completely trusted. Indeed, in the eyes of many, a Jew could never be a loyal servant to either Kaiser or king.

Concerns about these minorities only increased as the war progressed. Already in the first weeks after mobilization, the Prussian ministry of war and the Supreme Command introduced a torrent of administrative and organizational measures. These early measures were intended to keep in line those who were perceived to represent the greatest threat to the cohesion of the army: the Alsatians. By the autumn of 1916, however, the situation had changed. In the wake of massive losses during the 'battles of material' at Verdun and along the Somme, it appeared necessary to ensure that the empire's manpower was exploited to the fullest possible extent. Going hand-in-hand with these efforts was a renewed interest in the army's minorities. New measures were introduced to prevent desertion among non-Germans and fortify the morale of Bavarians, Saxons, and Württembergers. Moreover, in the increasingly desperate final years of the war, census takers attempted to quantify the presence of specific groups at the front.

It is within this context that the German-Jewish experience of the First World War should be understood. The discrimination against Jewish soldiers was undoubtedly motivated by a well-established tradition of antisemitism in the army and society. At the same time, the treatment of Jews in the officer corps and the doubts raised about the Jewish contribution to the war effort were also symptomatic of the military authorities' discomfort with the broader patchwork of loyalties within the army. This is not to suggest that Bavarians, Jews, and Poles were treated in identical or even similar ways. Some groups were forced to endure censorship, the refusal of home leave, or transfer away from their units, others were excluded from performing certain functions or subjected to humiliating decrees, and still others enjoyed the support of institutions that ensured their preferential treatment. In the eyes of the military authorities, these groups were nevertheless seen as different sides of the same coin. Taken together, the measures which were introduced against them highlight the extent to which dual loyalties were considered a threat to the army between 1914 and 1918.

Perhaps unsurprisingly, the ethnic fault lines running through the Austro-Hungarian army have received considerable attention from scholars. Even before the revolutionary shock of 1848–1849, the military authorities in Vienna had sought to remove regiments from potentially dangerous influences in their home districts. This deployment policy was modified in the early 1880s; although men were stationed within their own recruitment areas, a system of rotation meant that units often spent only a few years in a particular garrison. At the same time, a combination of factors—the introduction of universal military service in 1868, the creation of a Hungarian territorial force, the *Honvéd*, and rising levels of education across the empire—eroded the German character of the army.[3] Despite concerns about these developments and to the astonishment of many observers, mobilization did not lead to a Habsburg collapse in 1914. Although there were isolated incidents, an overwhelming majority of the empire's subjects responded to their call-up orders. It was only when defeats mounted, casualty lists lengthened, and food shortages became acute that national antagonisms threatened to boil over. The mass desertions from Czech regiments in the spring of 1915 were the first serious warning signs. In response, the military authorities frequently mixed Czechs, Italians, Poles, Serbs, Romanians, and Ukrainians with more reliable Bosnians, Germans, and Hungarians or otherwise assigned the former to less important roles. Even so, when Kaiser Karl requested an armistice in October 1918, a large part of the Habsburg army was not in the trenches but suppressing strikes and mutinies or searching for deserters in the interior of the empire.[4]

---

[3] Rudolf Kiszling (1959), 'Das Nationalitätenproblem in Habsburgs Wehrmacht 1848–1918', *Der Donauraum. Zeitschrift des Instituts für den Donauraum und Mitteleuropa* 4, 82–88; Gunther E. Rothenberg (1967), 'The Habsburg Army and the Nationality Problem in the Nineteenth Century, 1815–1914', *Austrian History Yearbook* 3, 70–87; and Lawrence Sondhaus (1990), *In the Service of the Emperor: Italians in the Austrian Armed Forces, 1814–1918* (Boulder, CO, East European Monographs), especially 96–103.

[4] István Deák (1985), 'The Habsburg Army in the First and Last Days of World War I: A Comparative Analysis', in Béla K. Király and Nándor F. Dreisziger, eds. *East Central*

The Russian army has likewise been the subject of extensive research. In 1874, Minister of War D. A. Miliutin introduced conscription to the empire. Building on the Emancipation edict of 1861, this measure was intended to spread the burden of military service evenly across the entire population. In practice, numerous exemptions instead demonstrated, in the words of one historian, the empire's 'limits of reform'. For example, the Muslim populations of the Caucasus and Central Asia were excluded from the conscription measures. Generally considered unsuited for military service, some high-ranking officers even feared that equipping these groups with modern weapons and training them in their use could have disastrous consequences for the Tsarist regime.[5] These fears did not disappear following the outbreak of war in 1914. As a rule, the military authorities sought to maintain a majority of 'Great Russians'—including Belarusians and Ukrainians—in most units. Circumstances nevertheless forced the army to adopt a more flexible approach. Czechs, Poles, and Slovaks were recruited from among prisoners of war in an attempt to undermine Habsburg authority over these groups and, in the months following the February Revolution, the Provisional Government attempted to retain its control through the formation of ethnically-homogenous Ukrainian units. As the war progressed, and in order to replace the growing number of casualties, the military authorities also became increasingly eager to exploit previously untapped manpower resources. In the summer of 1916, conscription was introduced in Turkestan. However, the result—an uprising that diverted large numbers of men and resources from

European Society in World War I (New York, Columbia University Press), 301–312; Kiszling (1959), 'Das Nationalitätenproblem', 88–91. For the impact of the war on the civilian population of the empire, see Maureen Healy (2004), *Vienna and the Fall of the Habsburg Empire: Total War and Everyday Life in World War I* (Cambridge, Cambridge University Press), especially 122–159.

[5] Robert F. Baumann (1987), 'Subject Nationalities in the Military Service of Imperial Russia: The Case of the Bashkirs', *Slavic Review* 46, 489–502; Mark von Hagen (2004), 'The Limits of Reform: The Multiethnic Imperial Army Confronts Nationalism, 1874–1917', in David Schimmelpennick von der Oye and Bruce W. Menning, eds. *Reforming the Tsar's Army: Military Innovation in Imperial Russia from Peter the Great to the Revolution*, (Cambridge, Cambridge University Press), 34–46.

the front—only highlighted the dangers of mobilizing ethnicity in the Russian empire.[6]

Although historians have long recognized that German unification was far from complete in 1871, the presence of subnational loyalties within the German army has largely been overlooked. With a few notable exceptions, the Kaiser's armies have been portrayed as culturally and ethnically homogeneous.[7] Moreover, and in contrast to research on the Russian army, the experience of German Jews in both the officer corps and the ranks has often been considered in isolation.[8] This chapter seeks to address these shortcomings by placing official attitudes toward Jewish soldiers, ethnic minorities, and the state-based contingents in the German army alongside one another. Before 1914, high-ranking officers possessed views of these groups that were informed by a diverse set of prejudices, ranging from intense antisemitism to a simple dislike of South German peculiarities. During the First World War, these views coalesced into an obsession with dual loyalties, a concept which, in the eyes of many in the Prussian ministry of war and the Supreme Command, threatened to tear the German army apart from within.

[6] Mark von Hagen (1998), 'The Great War and the Mobilization of Ethnicity in the Russian Empire', in Barnett R. Rubin and Jack Snyder, eds. *Post-soviet Political Order: Conflict and State Building* (London, Routledge), 34–57; Allan K. Wildman (1980), *The End of the Russian Imperial Army: The Old Army and the Soldiers' Revolt (March–April 1917)* (Princeton, NJ, Princeton University Press), 103–104. For the uprising in Turkestan, see Daniel Brower (2003), *Turkestan and the Fate of the Russian Empire* (London, Routledge), 152–175.

[7] The German army has consistently been overlooked in the research on multiethnic armies. For example, see the essays in N.F. Dreisziger, ed. (1990), *Ethnic Armies: Polyethnic Armed Forces from the Time of the Habsburgs to the Age of the Superpowers* (Waterloo, ON, Wilfrid Laurier University Press). The German army is also omitted from the comparative framework in Alfred J. Rieber (2015), 'Nationalizing Imperial Armies: A Comparative and Transnational Study of Three Empires', in Stefan Berger and Alexei Miller, eds. *Nationalizing Empires* (Budapest, Central European University Press), 593–628.

[8] For example, see Robert F. Baumann (1986), 'Universal Service Reform and Russia's Imperial Dilemma', *War and Society* 4, 31–49; Franziska Davies (2013), 'Eine imperiale Armee – Juden und Muslime im Dienste des Zaren', *Jahrbuch des Simon-Dubnow-Instituts* 12, 151–172.

ETHNIC, RELIGIOUS, AND STATE-BASED GROUPS
IN THE PRE-WAR GERMAN ARMY

The minorities in the German army which have received the least attention from historians are the Bavarians, Saxons, and Württembergers. Like the Badenese, Hessians, and Mecklenburgers, these groups were ethnically German. Yet, the structure of the army nevertheless ensured that they were perceived differently by the military authorities. For the entire existence of the empire, the army remained a collection of state-based contingents. This system had emerged during the Wars of Unification (1864–1871) and as a result of the unwillingness of the monarchs of Bavaria, Saxony, and Württemberg to completely surrender their military rights to Prussia. The result was a series of overlapping agreements.[9] On the one hand, the imperial constitution placed 'the entire land power of the empire' under the command of the Kaiser, who was also the King of Prussia, 'in war and peace'. In time of war, it was accepted that the Prussian general staff would assume operational control over the entire army. In peacetime, the Kaiser also possessed 'the duty and the right' to ensure uniformity in equipment and training through inspections of non-Prussian units.[10] On the other hand, military agreements with Saxony in 1867 and Bavaria and Württemberg in 1870 superseded some of these provisions. These agreements recognized the monarchs of Bavaria, Saxony, and Württemberg as *Kontingentsherren*, or commanders of their own contingents, and safeguarded their control over personnel appointments, the deployment of units, and even the design of insignia and uniforms. Bavaria enjoyed the most independence within this system, the Bavarian army being recognized as 'a self-contained component of the federal army' and as being 'under the military command of His Majesty the King of Bavaria' in peacetime.[11]

---

[9] For the negotiations between Prussia and the smaller German states before 1871, see Otto Pflanze (1963), *Bismarck and the Development of Germany: The Period of Unification, 1815–1871* (Princeton, NJ, Princeton University Press), 348–354, 480–490.

[10] 'Gesetz betreffend die Verfassung des Deutschen Reiches', in *Die Stenographischen Berichte über die Verhandlungen des Reichstages, Anlagen* (Berlin, 1871), 8–9.

[11] 'Militär-Konvention zwischen dem Norddeutschen Bund und dem Königreich Sachsen vom 7. Februar 1867', 'Der Bundesvertrag betreffend den Beitritt Bayerns zur Verfassung des Deutschen Bundes vom 23. November 1870', and 'Militärkonvention zwischen dem Norddeutschen Bunde und Württemberg vom 21./25. November 1870', in Ernst Rudolf Huber, ed. (1986), *Dokumente zur Deutschen Verfassungsgeschichte* (Stuttgart, Verlag W. Kohlhammer), 292–294, 329–333, 339–342.

The administration of the military was equally complex. Ministries of war in Dresden, Munich, and Stuttgart oversaw the arming, clothing, feeding, housing, and training of Bavarians, Saxons, and Württembergers and cadet schools and war colleges continued to exist in some of the non-Prussian kingdoms.[12] Making matters worse, many Prussian officers had emerged from the Wars of Unification with a low opinion of their comrades-in-arms. In October 1872, the Prussian military attaché in Munich reported that, despite having adopted Prussian service regulations, what was most lacking in the Bavarian officer corps was adequate education and leadership. It was thus necessary, he argued, to transfer Bavarian officers to Prussia for extended periods of training.[13] Beginning in the mid-1870s, a small number of Bavarian staff officers did indeed serve with the Prussian general staff in Berlin.[14] Concerns about the suitability of non-Prussians for command appointments therefore diminished in the decades after 1871. Even so, the Kaiser, often under pressure from his advisors, continued to exploit the military agreements with the non-Prussian kingdoms in order to ensure that Prussia retained its influence throughout the army. Only two native Württembergers rose to command of their kingdom's XIII Army Corps before 1914, and the responsibility for inspecting the Bavarian army was not transferred to a Bavarian general until 1892 and only after a lengthy debate in Prussian government and military circles.[15]

---

[12] Because an imperial ministry of war was never created, the Prussian minister of war presented the army's budget to the Reichstag and defended the Kaiser's power of command, or *Kommandogewalt*, from civilian interference. See Gordon A. Craig (1955), *The Politics of the Prussian Army, 1640–1945* (Oxford, Oxford University Press), 219–232.

[13] Report of Major Hermann von Stülpnagel, October 16, 1872, Politisches Archiv des Auswärtigen Amtes [PA AA] Berlin, R 2704. Only a few months later, Stülpnagel complained that the Bavarian minister of war opposed the transfers of Bavarian officers to Prussia for 'particularistic purposes'. Stülpnagel's report, February 8, 1873, PA AA Berlin, R 2708.

[14] Othmar Hackl (1999), *Der bayerische Generalstab (1792–1919)* (Munich, C.H. Beck), 277–279, 292–296, 326–347.

[15] Personnel appointments consistently created tension between Prussia and the smaller kingdoms. See Harald Rüddenklau (1972), 'Studien zur Bayerischen Militärpolitik 1871 bis 1914' (PhD diss., Universität Regensburg); Robert T. Walker (1974), 'Prusso-Württembergian Military Relations in the German Empire, 1870–1918' (PhD diss., The Ohio State University).

In contrast to the state-based contingents, the army's ethnic minorities seemed to represent a far greater threat. Foremost among them were the Alsace-Lorrainers. Following the Franco-Prussian War (1870–1871), Alsace and part of Lorraine had been annexed to the German empire. Whereas the majority of the population of Alsace spoke German, one-third of the inhabitants of Lorraine were French-speaking. Despite an influx of so-called *Altdeutschen* and the emigration of French speakers abroad, French culture and language remained a defining feature for many in the *Reichsland*.[16] The introduction of conscription in the region in the autumn of 1872 was thus thought by some to be a potentially risky measure. Robert Morier, the British envoy to Bavaria, certainly thought it was unwise. The population, he wrote, could not be integrated into the empire in the same way that Northern and Western Germans had been absorbed into Prussia after 1866. 'Scratch the surface of the Hanoverian or the Holsteiner and you get at the German beneath,' he claimed, but 'employ the same process with an Alsace-Lorrainer and it will be a long time before you get at anything but an Alsace-Lorrainer, but what you do get to at last is French and not German'.[17] The military authorities appear to have agreed and Alsace-Lorrainers rarely served in their home districts, but were transferred across the Rhine to Prussian garrisons. In 1912, less than half of the 14,000 Alsace-Lorrainers in the army were serving in the *Reichsland*.[18] For their part, these men were never enthusiastic recruits. Although the numbers decreased after 1871, they remained more likely to avoid military service than ethnic Germans. When the war broke out in the

---

[16]Eva Rimmele (1996), *Sprachenpolitik im Deutschen Kaiserreich vor 1914. Regierungspolitik und veröffentlichte Meinung in Elsaß-Lothringen und den östlichen Provinzen Preußens* (Frankfurt am Main, Peter Lang), 17–22.

[17]Robert Morier, British envoy to Bavaria, to the Foreign Office, October 21, 1872, The National Archives [TNA] Kew, FO 9/216. Before writing this report, Morier had traveled extensively throughout Alsace-Lorraine and spoken with numerous government authorities and local notables about the attitude of the region's population.

[18]Dan P. Silverman (1972), *Reluctant Union: Alsace-Lorraine and Imperial Germany, 1871–1918* (University Park, PA, Pennsylvania State University Press), 70–74. For the relationship between Alsace-Lorraine and the empire, see Hans-Ulrich Wehler (1970), 'Unfähig zur Verfassungsreform. Das 'Reichsland' Elsaß-Lothringen von 1870 bis 1918', in *Krisenherde des Kaiserreichs 1871–1918. Studien zur deutschen Sozial- und Verfassungsgeschichte* (Göttingen, Vandenhoeck & Ruprecht), 17–63.

summer of 1914, around 7000 Alsace-Lorrainers were under investigation for desertion.[19]

The Polish population of the eastern borderlands posed an equally pressing problem for the military authorities. Since the partitions of Poland in the late eighteenth century, Prussia had been home to a large Polish-speaking minority—ten per cent of the kingdom's population—which was concentrated mainly in the provinces of West Prussia, Posen, and Silesia. Beginning in the 1880s and responding to concerns about Polish population growth, the Prussian government sought to 'germanize' this minority. The German language was made compulsory in schools, property was transferred from Poles to Germans, and foreign seasonal workers, mainly Russian Poles, were expelled from Prussia.[20] The army nevertheless refrained from adopting an official anti-Polish attitude. In fact, although the military authorities limited the number of Polish-speaking soldiers in each garrison, transfers were conducted within army corps districts. As late as 1886, 12% of the recruits stationed in Posen were still Poles. It was not until 1894 that the Prussian ministry of war, under pressure from the government and conservative-nationalist political parties, agreed to limit the proportion of Poles in regiments that were garrisoned in Polish-speaking areas to 5%. In the decades before the First World War, thousands of Poles completed their military service in Brandenburg and the Rhineland, while a corresponding number of ethnic German recruits were transferred eastwards. The objective of this unofficial policy—it was never incorporated into the military service law—was simply to expose Poles to German language and culture and remove them from the perceived dangers of their home districts.[21]

---

[19] Christoph Jahr (1998), *Gewöhnliche Soldaten. Desertion und Deserteure im deutschen und britischen Heer 1914–1918* (Göttingen, Vandenhoeck & Ruprecht), 254; Alan Kramer (1997), 'Wackes at War: Alsace-Lorraine and the Failure of German National Mobilization, 1914–1918', in John Horne, ed. *State, Society and Mobilization in Europe During the First World War* (Cambridge, Cambridge University Press), 110–111.

[20] Richard Blanke (1981), *Prussian Poland in the German Empire (1871–1900)* (Boulder, CO, East European Monographs), especially 39–86. For the percentage of Poles in Prussia's eastern provinces, see Rimmele, *Sprachenpolitik*, 32–47.

[21] Jens Boysen (2008), *Preußische Armee und polnische Minderheit. Royalistische Streitkräfte im Kontext der Nationalitätenfrage des 19. Jahrhunderts (1815–1914)* (Marburg, Verlag Herder-Institut), 29–46.

Unlike the state-based and ethnic minorities of the empire, the Jews were not considered a threat because of competing monarchical or national loyalties. Instead, an aversion to middle-class culture and a shared belief that a high percentage of German Jews were members of the political opposition, especially the Social Democratic Party, ensured, according to one observer, that many in the officer corps saw red whenever it was suggested that a Jew could join their ranks.[22] Although repeatedly denied by the army, the exclusion of Jews from the officer corps was all but confirmed by Kaiser Wilhelm II in 1890. In an oft-cited cabinet order, the Kaiser acknowledged that the Prussian aristocracy was no longer capable of providing a sufficient number of officer candidates and therefore consented to a widening 'of the circles which come into consideration for the replenishment of the officer corps'. Not everyone would be accepted, however, but rather only 'the sons of such respectable middle-class houses in which the love of king and Fatherland, a warm heart for the soldiering class, and Christian modes of behaviour are cultivated and instilled'.[23] The numbers reveal the extent to which these criteria were taken seriously even before 1890. Whereas over one hundred Jews had received field promotions during the Franco-Prussian War, only a small number were permitted to enter active service in the Prussian army after 1871. Those who did came from wealthy and influential families and, crucially, by 1878, all of them had converted to Christianity in order to improve their career prospects. Similarly, although a limited number of Jews were allowed to enter the reserve officer corps in Prussia during the 1870s, none were admitted after 1885.[24]

[22] Diary entry for January 18, 1908, in Robert Zedlitz-Trützschler (1924), *Twelve Years at the Imperial German Court* (London, Nisbet), 214–218. In the spring of 1890, the Prussian envoy in Dresden was surprised to learn that the son of a wealthy Jewish banker who had recently converted to Christianity had been rejected by a Saxon cavalry regiment because of concerns that the candidate would adversely affect the behaviour and morals of the other officers. Carl von Dönhoff to the Foreign Office, April 11, 1890, PA AA Berlin, R 3236.

[23] 'Eine Kaiserliche Kabinettsordre über den Offizierstand', March 29, 1890, in Gerhard A. Ritter (1992), *Das Deutsche Kaiserreich 1871–1914. Ein historisches Lesebuch* (Göttingen, Vandenhöck & Ruprecht), 95–97. For the ever increasing shortage of officer candidates from aristocratic families, see Craig, *The Politics of the Prussian Army*, 232–238.

[24] Martin Kitchen (1968), *The German Officer Corps, 1890–1914* (Oxford, Oxford Univesity Press), 37–43; Manfred Messerschmidt (1984), 'Juden im preußisch-deutschen Heer', in Militärgeschichtliches Forschungsamt, ed. *Deutsche Jüdische Soldaten 1914–1945. Katalog zur Wanderausstellung des Militärgeschichtlichen Forschungsamtes* (Bonn, E.S. Mittler), 116–117; Derek J. Penslar (2013), *Jews and the Military: A History* (Princeton, NJ, Princeton University Press), 88–91.

The situation was slightly better in Bavaria. Unlike in Saxony and Württemberg, where the Kaiser could more easily influence personnel appointments, the King of Bavaria retained exclusive control over the composition of 'his' officer corps. As a result, a small number of Jews were granted commissions as active and reserve officers in the Bavarian army after 1871. Antisemitism nevertheless steadily gained ground in southern Germany. Although six unconverted Jews received commissions in active Bavarian regiments between the Wars of Liberation (1813–1815) and the outbreak of the First World War, the last was appointed in 1885. Two decades later, only four of twenty-five Jewish candidates (1.6%) who had fulfilled the educational and service requirements were commissioned as reserve officers. In stark contrast, no fewer than 44% of Christian candidates reached this socially-prestigious rank.[25] That negative perceptions of Jews had become common in the army in the years before the First World War is suggested by a conversation that took place in the winter of 1907 between the Bavarian military plenipotentiary in Berlin and the Prussian minister of war, General Karl von Einem. Disturbed by reports that North German Jews were travelling to Bavaria in search of better career prospects in the army, Einem conceded that a Jew 'could, on occasion, be a good and even outstanding officer'. He nonetheless considered it to be an irrefutable fact that 'the entire Jewish character, the entire mentality, and behaviour of the individual and of their tribe, is so entirely different from the kind of spirit which fortunately runs through the German officer corps that an infiltration of Jewish elements into the active officer corps would be considered not only harmful, but downright ruinous'. The Bavarian officer wholeheartedly agreed.[26]

[25] Wolfgang Schmidt (1996), 'Die Juden in der Bayerischen Armee', in Frank Nägler, ed. *Deutsche Jüdische Soldaten. Von der Epoche der Emanzipation bis zum Zeitalter der Weltkriege* (Hamburg, E.S. Mittler), 71–79. For the tension between popular and official attitudes towards Jews in Bavaria, see James Harris (1994), *The People Speak! Anti-semitism and Emancipation in Nineteenth-Century Bavaria* (Ann Arbor, MI, University of Michigan Press).

[26] Colonel Ludwig von Gebsattel to the Bavarian ministry of war, January 14, 1907, Bayerisches Hauptstaatsarchiv [BayHStA] Munich, Abteilung IV Kriegsarchiv [IV KA], MKr 43.

DUAL LOYALTIES IN THE GERMAN ARMY
DURING THE FIRST WORLD WAR

Because many German Jews considered themselves to be German first and Jews second, the army's antisemitic attitude received intense criticism in the liberal and socialist press and provided grounds for periodic interpellations of the Prussian minister of war in the Reichstag.[27] The outbreak of war in 1914 was therefore at first greeted as an opportunity to complete the process of emancipation. In the minds of many, military service would demonstrate that a Jew could also be a loyal German. At least initially, these hopes seemed to be validated. After the proclamation of the *Burgfrieden*, or civil truce, by the Kaiser in early August, the military authorities ratcheted up their censorship of the press.[28] In November, the Prussian ministry of war issued a circular that reminded censors that any expression of doubt about the 'national spirit and resolve of any German, party, or newspaper' had the potential to undermine the war effort. What this meant for the status of Jewish soldiers was clarified a few months later. Printed materials which threatened to deepen religious or political antagonisms and thereby damage the 'feeling of unity in the population' were banned.[29] During the first two years of the war, the military authorities took their censorship responsibilities seriously. For example, in the spring of 1915, the *Verband der deutschen Juden* (VddJ) complained that leaflets which advocated the conversion of Jews to Christianity had been found in military barracks. At a time when so many German Jews were at the front, the executive committee

---

[27] Werner T. Angress (1972), 'Prussia's Army and the Jewish Reserve Officer Controversy Before World War I', *Leo Baeck Institute Year Book* 17, 19–42. For Jewish attempts at greater integration and the Christian response more generally, see Uriel Tal (1975), *Christians and Jews in Germany: Religion, Politics, and Ideology in the Second Reich, 1870–1914* (Ithaca, NY, Cornell University Press).

[28] David Engel (1986), 'Patriotism as a Shield: The Liberal Jewish Defence Against Antisemitism in Germany During the First World War', *Leo Baeck Institute Year Book* 31, 152–153; Christhard Hoffmann (1997), 'Between Integration and Rejection: The Jewish Community in Germany, 1914–1918', in John Horne, ed. *State, Society and Mobilization*, 92–95.

[29] Circular of the Prussian ministry of war, November 9, 1914, and the memorandum of the staff of the VII Army Corps district, June 1915, in Deist, *Militär und Innenpolitik*, 1:81–83, 95–98. For the declaration of the *Burgfrieden*, see Wilhelm II's speech from the throne, August 4, 1914, in *Stenographische Berichte* (Berlin, 1916), 1–2.

feared that these leaflets might impact Jewish soldiers' willingness to sacrifice their lives for Kaiser and Fatherland. An investigation was launched shortly thereafter and the VddJ was assured that no such leaflets had been distributed to the troops.[30]

There were nevertheless already warning signs that the army did not entirely trust some of its soldiers. In particular, the cultural and linguistic connections to France and the fact that the *Reichsland* remained one of the staging areas for the Western Front throughout the war meant that Alsace-Lorrainers were singled out for particularly harsh treatment. The outbreak of war had prompted many of these men to flee to Switzerland to avoid military service. Moreover, reports of mass desertions to the French and hostility from the population only confirmed the military authorities' worst fears about the loyalty of the Alsace-Lorrainers.[31] As a result, from the first weeks of the war, they introduced a series of discriminatory measures. In the winter of 1914–1915, restrictions were placed on leave so as not to expose soldiers to harmful sentiments at home. From February 1915 onwards, the letters of Alsace-Lorrainers were heavily censored. Also, and importantly, the Prussian ministry of war decided in early 1915 to remove those soldiers who appeared particularly unreliable from the West and transfer them to units on the Eastern Front. In the months that followed, even *Altdeutschen* who had business or familial connections to France before the war were swept up by this decree and, in January 1916, the minister of war was forced to issue a clarification: only those in the military administration or who were serving as orderlies to high-ranking officers were to be transferred. These men might otherwise gain access to sensitive information.[32] In contrast, Poles were treated much less harshly at the outset of the war. Although individual officers prohibited soldiers from writing home in Polish and rates of desertion were high in some units, especially those

---

[30] Executive committee of the VddJ to the deputy command of the Prussian Guard Corps, June 17, 1915, and the deputy command's reply, July 20, 1915, Bundesarchiv Militärarchiv [BA MA] Freiburg, PH 7, file 27.

[31] Jahr, *Gewöhnliche Soldaten*, 255–260; Kramer, 'Wackes at War', 108–111.

[32] Decree of the Prussian ministry of war, January 11, 1916, and a second clarification to the deputy command of the XV Army Corps, February 2, 1916, BA MA Freiburg, PH 1, file 8. For the earlier measures against the Alsatians, see Jahr (1998), *Gewöhnliche Soldaten*, 260–263; Benjamin Ziemann (1996), 'Fahnenflucht im deutschen Heer 1914–1918', *Militärgeschichtliche Mitteilungen* 55, 122.

from Posen, the transfer of Poles to ethnically-German units ceased in 1914. Ultimately, most Poles went to the front surrounded by men from their home districts.[33]

German soldiers endured some of the most costly and prolonged fighting of the war in 1916. In February, the assault on the fortress of Verdun began and continued until the late autumn. Even before the 'mill on the Meuse' stopped grinding, the British launched an offensive on the Somme that compelled the chief of the general staff, General Erich von Falkenhayn, to transfer large numbers of troops to the threatened sector. Despite this enormous pressure, the German front held, but at an extraordinary cost. At the end of 1916, the Supreme Command estimated that the army had suffered almost two million casualties, including 350,000 killed, over the preceding twelve months. During the most intense fighting between July and October, the formations in the West lost 800,000 men killed, wounded or missing. Worse still, Romania's declaration of war on the Central Powers in August increased the empire's enemies. As a result, Falkenhayn's successor, Field Marshal Paul von Hindenburg, and Ludendorff, the newly appointed First Quartermaster General, endeavoured to more fully mobilize both manpower and resources. Only days after their appointment in August 1916, orders for an increase in the production of equipment and munitions were issued. At the beginning of December, the Reichstag passed the Auxiliary Service Law which conscripted all male Germans between the ages of seventeen and sixty for labour on farms or in factories. In addition to ensuring that the agricultural and industrial sectors received sufficient manpower, Hindenburg and Ludendorff worked to put as many Germans into uniform as possible. During the winter of 1916–1917, those men who had previously been designated fit for duty only in the rear areas and those who had recovered from their wounds were formed into new divisions. Together with the recruiting class of 1898, which was called up three months early, the Supreme Command managed to cobble together over one million additional men by the spring of 1917.[34]

[33] Alexander Watson (2010), 'Fighting for Another Fatherland: The Polish Minority in the German Army, 1914–1918', *English Historical Review* 126, 1144–1151; Ziemann, 'Fahnenflucht', 124.

[34] Gerald D. Feldman (1996), *Army, Industry and Labor in Germany, 1914–1918* (Princeton, NJ, Princeton University Press), 149–249; Herwig, *The First World War*, 244–266.

At least one historian has observed that 'total war' disproportionately impacts ethnic and racial minorities, often worsening their situation. As society mobilizes, people and resources are placed under more stringent control. More ominously, fear and suspicion of traditional outgroups increase, particularly in the wake of defeats on the battlefield.[35] This was especially the case for the German Jews. The *Burgfrieden* had ensured that openly antisemitic newspaper articles and pamphlets were muted if not silenced by the censors. Nevertheless, rising prices and severe food shortages at home and the seemingly endless casualty lists from the front produced an upsurge in antisemitism as the war progressed. The army was not immune to these changes. The Kaiser's military cabinet— largely responsible for personnel matters—had been faced with little choice but to commission educated, middle-class Jews following the massive losses of the first months of the war. Even so, the officer corps never shed antisemitism as one of its defining characteristics. Officers increasingly described Jews under their command as shirkers and some regimental messes became centres of antisemitic agitation.[36] Their complaints quickly reached the military authorities. Having been flooded with letters and petitions claiming that Jews were unfairly profiting from the war and not serving in sufficient numbers at the front, the Prussian minister of war, General Adolf Wild von Hohenborn, initiated a census of German-Jewish soldiers in October 1916. The stated goal was to assess the contribution of Jews to the empire's war effort. This decision was undoubtedly motivated by a resurgence of antisemitism, but, as Werner Angress points out, the context in which the *Judenzählung* was conducted is significant. After the fighting at Verdun and the Somme, the army was confronted with an acute manpower shortage and

[35] Panikos Panayi (1993), 'Dominant Societies and Minorities in the Two World Wars', in Panikos Panayi, ed. *Minorities in Wartime: National and Racial Groupings in Europe, North America and Australia During the Two World War* (Providence, RI, Berg), 3–23.

[36] See the essays by Saul Friedländer, 'Die politischen Veränderungen der Kriegszeit und ihre Auswirkungen auf die Judenfrage', and Werner Jochmann, 'Die Ausbreitung des Antisemitismus', in Werner E. Mosse (1971), *Deutsches Judentum in Krieg und Revolution 1916–1923* (Tübingen, Mohr Siebeck), 27–65, 409–510. For the revival of antisemitism in the officer corps during the war, see Messerschmidt, 'Juden im preußisch-deutschen Heer', 119–120.

Hohenborn's census order was likely also influenced by the Supreme Command's desire to put every available man into uniform.[37]

The census of Jewish soldiers in the autumn of 1916 has frequently been interpreted as a turning point in German-Jewish relations. If one considers this measure in isolation and with the benefit of hindsight and knowledge of the crimes of the National Socialist regime, this is certainly true. However, the *Judenzählung* was also one of many measures introduced in the second half of the war in response to concerns about the cohesion of the army. Already in the spring of 1916, several units had initiated censuses of the Alsace-Lorrainers under their command. This measure was meant to weed out any men who might desert to the French and, as in the first years of the war, transfer them to the Eastern Front.[38] During the winter of 1916–1917, at least one Bavarian division also collected reports on the performance of soldiers from the Palatinate, an exclave of the kingdom of Bavaria in the Rhineland. These men were thought to possess a whole range of unsoldierly characteristics and their frequent appearances in front of courts martial had become a particular concern for their superiors.[39] The transformation of the army's attitude towards the Poles occurred even before the assault on Verdun began. Because desertions had increased in units from Posen and West Prussia, the Prussian ministry of war introduced a new deployment policy in November 1915. Unlike the Alsatians who were increasingly sent to the East, Poles were to be scattered throughout the army. In a measure that resembled its peacetime predecessors, Poles were trained in army corps districts in Prussia's western provinces and assigned to units containing a majority of ethnic Germans. There were exceptions. Because they could

---

[37] Werner T. Angress (1978), 'The German Army's 'Judenzählung' of 1916: Genesis—Consequences—Significance', *Leo Baeck Institute Year Book* 23, 121–125. For the census instructions, see the copy of the order of the Prussian ministry of war, October 11, 1916, BayHStA Munich, IV KA, MKr 10791.

[38] For example, Armeeoberkommando A to the Prussian ministry of war, April 28, 1917, Landesarchiv Baden-Württemberg, Hauptstaatsarchiv [HStA] Stuttgart, M 30/1, file 107. For a similar census initiated by the 8th Bavarian Reserve Division in April 1916, see Ziemann, 'Fahnenflucht im deutschen Heer 1914–1918', 122–123.

[39] For example, see the report of the 8th Bavarian Infantry Brigade to the 14th Bavarian Infantry Division, February 21, 1917, and the brigade's subsequent statistical compilation of military justice cases dated March 15, 1917, BayHStA Munich, IV KA, Infanterie-Divisionen (WK) 5932.

boast lower desertion rates, Upper Silesian Poles were excluded from the new measure in the spring of 1916.[40]

The collapse of Russia convinced Ludendorff in December 1917 to limit the transfer of supposedly unreliable soldiers from the West. In his view, the preparations for the spring offensives and the cessation of hostilities on the Eastern Front meant that disloyalty and unreliability might be seen as being rewarded. This could have disastrous consequences for the morale of ethnic Germans.[41] Even before the winter of 1917–1918, Ludendorff had also become concerned about the loyalties of the state-based contingents. In the summer and autumn of 1916, the Prussian envoy in Munich submitted a series of reports on the situation in Bavaria. Although they had entered the war with the same enthusiasm as their Prussian, Saxon, and Württemberg comrades, food shortages and war weariness had ensured that disillusionment and resentment were becoming more and more evident among Bavarian soldiers. Rumours circulated that Prussians habitually ordered Bavarian units to attack well-entrenched positions and, if they were successful, took the credit from their southern comrades.[42] Reports from the front also indicated that friction between the state-based contingents had become a serious issue. The Bavarian military plenipotentiary attached to General Headquarters reported in August 1916 that an entire company of Bavarians had been wiped out when a Saxon unit withdrew prematurely from their trenches. When the Bavarians arrived to relieve their comrades, they found only French troops. The friction that developed within the 14th Bavarian Infantry Division—a formation consisting of both Bavarian and Prussian units—during the fighting around Verdun

---

[40] Prussian ministry of war to the Prussian ministry of the interior, November 1915, Geheimes Staatsarchiv Preußischer Kulturbesitz [GStA PK] Berlin-Dahlem, I. Hauptabteilung [HA], Rep. 90A, file 3748. For the increasing concerns about the reliability of Polish soldiers in units from Posen and West Prussia, see the report of the 155th Infantry Regiment to the 77th Infantry Brigade, September 11, 1915, GStA PK Berlin-Dahlem, I. HA, Rep. 90A, file 3748. See also Watson, 'Fighting for Another Fatherland', 1156–1158; Ziemann (1998), 'Fahnenflucht', 124–125.

[41] Order of the Supreme Command, December 2, 1917, HStA Stuttgart, M 30/1, file 107.

[42] Reports of Carl-Georg von Treutler, Prussian envoy in Munich, to the Foreign Office, June 23, 1916 and November 2, 1916, PA AA Berlin, R 2736.

was considered grounds by the Bavarian ministry of war for the transfer of the Prussians elsewhere in the late summer.[43]

It was above all these 'mixed' formations which had caught the eye of Ludendorff by the autumn of 1916. Almost immediately after the outbreak of war, the barriers between the contingents had begun to break down. On the one hand, army corps suffered casualties at different rates and some districts possessed more trained recruits than others. Following mobilization, replacements were therefore assigned from wherever they were available to wherever they were most urgently needed. On the other hand, the need to respond to rapidly changing circumstances on a number of geographically distant fronts led the Supreme Command to transfer both entire units and individual personnel between the contingents.[44] The result was the emergence of a number of mixed divisions containing various combinations of Prussians and non-Prussians. Concerns for the combat effectiveness of these formations dovetailed with pressure from the empire's ministries of war. Under instructions from their superiors in Dresden, Munich, and Stuttgart, the Saxon, Bavarian, and Württemberg representatives in General Headquarters bombarded the Supreme Command with complaints in the summer and fall of 1916. At the beginning of October, Württemberg's military plenipotentiary, General Friedrich von Graevenitz, directly confronted Ludendorff in a tense conversation. In addition to condemning the lack of sensitivity for the wishes of the non-Prussian monarchs, Graevenitz—using a series of examples—pointed out how easily several mixed divisions could be transformed into

[43] General Karl von Nagel zu Aichberg, Bavarian military plenipotentiary in General Headquarters, to the Bavarian minister of war, August 25, 1916, BayHStA Munich, IV KA, MKr 1830. For the incident in the 14th Bavarian Infantry Division, see the order of the Bavarian ministry of war, October 12, 1916, BayHStA Munich, IV KA, MilBev Berlin 93.

[44] Tony Cowan (2014), 'A Picture of German Unity? Federal Contingents in the German Army, 1916–17', in Jonathan Krause, ed. *The Greater War: Other Combatants and Other Fronts, 1914–1918* (Basingstoke, Palgrave Macmillan), 147–148. In September 1914, the Bavarian minister of war angrily observed that no one had even notified him that Bavarian officers had been transferred to non-Bavarian units. General Otto Kreß von Kressenstein to the Bavarian military plenipotentiary in General Headquarters, September 24, 1914, BayHStA Munich, IV KA, MilBev Berlin 89.

homogenous Saxon or Württemberg formations.[45] Graevenitz's efforts had the desired result. Less than one week later, the Supreme Command issued a circular admitting the shortcomings of its personnel policy and promising to respect the federal structure of the army. Over the winter of 1916–1917, most of the mixed divisions were broken up.[46]

CONCLUSION

How necessary were these measures? Some evidence suggests that the presence of subnational loyalties within its ranks did not significantly impact the army's cohesion. Although Alsace-Lorrainers and Poles deserted in greater numbers during the second half of the war, thousands remained with the colours until hostilities ended. Jews, who had largely abandoned their hopes that military service would result in complete emancipation, continued to serve Kaiser and king, often with distinction. Some groups even escaped the military authorities' gaze altogether. The loyalty of units composed primarily of the 'Polish-speaking Germans' of Masuria seems never to have been questioned and, even though their superiors occasionally voiced concerns about their reliability, no systematic transfer policy was ever introduced for the Danish-speaking soldiers from Schleswig.[47] It can also be convincingly argued that the personnel policies both positively and negatively impacted the army's performance. The combat effectiveness of Württemberg units appears to have increased following their homogenization. Shortly before the end of the war, one officer complained that the Supreme Command relied too heavily on the Württembergers to stabilize the constantly disintegrating

---

[45] Reports of General Traugott Leuckart von Weißdorf, Saxon military plenipotentiary in General Headquarters, to the Saxon minister of war, August 25, 1916 and September 10, 1916, Sächsisches Hauptstaatsarchiv [SHStA] Dresden, Bestand 11250, file 54; General Friedrich von Graevenitz, Württemberg's military plenipotentiary, to the Württemberg minister of war, October 1, 1916, HStA Stuttgart, M 1/2, file 114.

[46] Order of the Supreme Command, October 6, 1916, HStA Stuttgart, M 1/11, file 351. See also Cowan, 'A Picture of German Unity?' 148.

[47] Claus Bundgård Christensen (2012), 'Fighting for the Kaiser: The Danish Minority in the German Army, 1914–18', in Claes Ahlund, ed. *Scandinavia in the First World War: Studies in the War Experience of the Northern Neutrals* (Lund, Nordic Academic Press), 267–282. For the perceived loyalty of the Masurians, see Watson, 'Fighting for Another Fatherland', 1150–1151.

front line. In his view, their units risked being burnt out.[48] Conversely, some high-ranking officers clearly thought that the army's ethnic minorities had contributed to the rumoured 'covert military strike'. In the final weeks of the war, General Wilhelm Groener, who succeeded Ludendorff as First Quartermaster General, lamented the fact that a division which had been transferred from the Eastern Front had refused to take up its positions in the West. This division, Groener noted, was composed mainly of Alsace-Lorrainers and Poles.[49]

The impact of the First World War on the army's relations with its minorities is much easier to assess. That the conflict represented a turning point in this respect is especially clear in the case of the German Jews. The unwillingness of the military authorities to publish the statistics collected during the *Judenzählung* created a vacuum in which conservative and extreme nationalist organizations, such as the *Reichshammerbund*, were able to make biased claims about the number of Jewish soldiers at the front, while high-ranking officers were able to push the blame for their own failures onto those groups that had supposedly undermined the German war effort from behind the lines. The *Dolchstoßlegende*, or 'stab-in-the-back myth', therefore emerged in the interwar years as a popular explanation for Germany's sudden military collapse. It would also form a central element in National Socialist propaganda.[50] It is nevertheless important to remember that Jews provided a convenient scapegoat in part because the empire was stripped of many of its minorities after 1918. Large populations of Alsatians, Danes, and Poles no longer

---

[48] Postwar report of Colonel Max Holland, April 6, 1919, HStA Stuttgart, M 1/2, file 245. In his memoirs, Ludendorff praised the Württembergers, whose units, in his opinion, were consistently some of the best in the entire army. Ludendorff, *Meine Kriegserinnerungen*, 204.

[49] Wilhelm Groener (1972), *Lebenserinnerungen. Jugend, Generalstab, Weltkrieg* (Osnabrück, Biblio Verlag), 442–443. Although he implied that the Alsatians and Poles in the division were responsible for this incident, Groener conceded that the 'influences of the *Heimat*' were more generally to blame for the army's deteriorating morale.

[50] The statistics collected by the Prussian ministry of war in the autumn of 1916, together with most of the documentary material relating to the 'Jewish census', were destroyed in the spring of 1945 when an Allied bombing raid struck the *Heeresarchiv* in Potsdam. Angress, 'The German Army's *Judenzählung*' of 1916', 124–125. For the postwar evolution of the 'stab-in-the-back myth', see Boris Barth (2003), *Dolchstoßlegenden und politische Desintegration. Das Trauma der deutschen Niederlage im Ersten Weltkrieg 1914–1933* (Düsseldorf, Droste Verlag).

lived within Germany's borders, and the dismantling of the federal character of the army meant that the distinctions between Bavarians, Prussians, Saxons, and Württembergers ceased to hold the same importance as before or during the war. Seen from this perspective, placing the treatment of ethnic, religious, and state-based minorities alongside one another does not diminish the importance of the First World War for German-Jewish relations. On the contrary, it reveals that not only were the army's dual loyalties a constant source of concern following the outbreak of war in 1914, but that the Prussian ministry of war and Supreme Command had, by the autumn of 1918, learned to disaggregate the soldiers under their command into two groups, one 'reliable' and the other not.[51]

---

[51] Peter Holquist argues that Russian civilian and military authorities had engaged in 'population politics' from the late nineteenth century onwards. See Holquist (2001), 'To Count, To Extract, To Exterminate: Population Statistics and Population Politics in Late Imperial and Soviet Russia', in Ronald Grigor Suny and Terry Martin, eds. *A State of Nations: Empire and Nation-Making in the Age of Lenin and Stalin* (Oxford, Oxford University Press), 111–144.

Between Inclusion and Exclusion: The Experiences of Jewish Soldiers in Europe and the USA, 1914–1918

Sarah Panter

When the armistice was signed in November 1918, the larger and longer-term impacts of the First World War were widely and intensely discussed within the societies that had, up to that point, been completely mobilised for the war effort of their respective nations and empires. Jews, like other groups with transnational bonds, had served in the armed forces of all of the belligerent states. The conflagration of the war had thus led many Jews in Europe and the United States to face a dilemma between their civic loyalties and their transnational bonds of Jewish identity and solidarity.[1] With the war coming to an official end in 1918, the

[1] For an in-depth analysis regarding this dilemma, see Sarah Panter (2014), *Jüdische Erfahrungen und Loyalitätskonflikte im Ersten Weltkrieg* (Göttingen, Vandenhoeck & Ruprecht). On the more general impact of the war analysed against the background of its global entanglements, see Jörn Leonhard (2014), *Die Büchse der Pandora. Geschichte des Ersten Weltkriegs* (Munich, C.H. Beck).

S. Panter (✉)
Leibniz Institute of European History, Mainz, Germany
e-mail: panter@ieg-mainz.de

© The Author(s) 2019
E. Madigan and G. Reuveni (eds.),
The Jewish Experience of the First World War,
https://doi.org/10.1057/978-1-137-54896-2_8

warring powers—along with their Jewish citizens—were divided into 'winners' and 'losers', enjoying either the fruits of victory or suffering the consequences of defeat. Jewish interpretations of the war, however, were more ambiguous and did not always follow these dichotomous categorisations.

Despite the centenary of the outbreak of the conflict in 2014 triggering renewed interest in the First World War,[2] the war's impact on the ways in which religious, ethnic and national minorities negotiated 'difference' remains a surprisingly under-researched topic.[3] This research gap is evident, moreover, not only in First World War studies, but also in Jewish history. Overshadowed by other watershed events in the twentieth century, and in particular the history of the Shoa, the years between 1914 and 1918 have generally been viewed not as momentous in their own right but rather as an inevitable prelude to the Second World War.[4] Yet it was precisely during the years of the 'war to end all wars' that negotiating Jewish 'difference' became a decisive issue at a transnational level and, importantly, on an entirely unprecedented scale. Between 1914 and 1918, Jews in Europe and the US were emotionally torn between raised hopes of integration and fears of discrimination that had their roots in the past, but whose situative dynamics changed during the war.

This dilemma, which was contingent on a mixture of structural as well as situative factors, appears in particular in debates about experiences of 'inclusion' and 'exclusion' among Jewish soldiers. The terms 'inclusion' and 'exclusion', as they will be used in this chapter, are dynamic

---

[2] For recent research surveys on the vast literature published during the centenary, see Stig Förster (2015), 'Hundert Jahre danach. Neue Literatur zum Ersten Weltkrieg', *Neue Politische Literatur* 60, 5–25; Alan Kramer (2014), 'Recent Historiography of the First World War, Part I', *Journal of Modern European History* 12:1, 5–28; and idem (2014), 'Recent Historiography of the First World War, Part II', *Journal of Modern European History* 12:2, 155–174.

[3] On attempts to change this, see Hannah Ewence and Tim Grady, eds. (2017), *Minorities During the First World War: From War to Peace* (Basingstoke, Palgrave Macmillan); Panikos Panayi, ed. (2014), *Germans as Minorities During the First World War: A Global Comparative Perspective* (Ashgate, Farnham).

[4] See David Rechter (2001), *The Jews of Vienna and the First World War* (Oxford, Littman Library), 2–3.

concepts, following multiple logics within the two analytical frames of Jewish/non-Jewish *and* inter-Jewish relations. The dynamics of 'inclusion' concerning the first frame include, for example, the question of upward mobility among Jews in the military based on merit and valour, but also the institutionalisation of a Jewish chaplaincy as a symbol of religious and civic equality. In the second frame, by contrast, the question of Judaism's importance in the lives of soldiers on active service and the role of chaplains as mediators between home front and fighting front features more prominently. Given the interconnectedness of 'inclusion' and 'exclusion', one also needs to keep the counterparts of integration, and hence the 'exclusionary' dynamics of the war, in mind. This pertains, for example, to encounters with antisemitism in the trenches but also to the dynamics of dissimilation caused by the uprooting of Jewish soldiers from their homes and social surroundings. In this context, then, the ambiguity of the Jewish experiences of the war becomes visible at the interfaces of both frames. For they could either trigger a sense of alienation from the Jewish soldier's Jewishness, serve as a watershed point to re-define and strengthen Jewish identity or simply have no impact at all on the soldier's sense of Jewishness. Though the third potential response is more difficult to identify within a historical analysis, as it usually manifested itself as silence on the issue of 'Jewishness', a combination of these three responses to the experience of the war among Jewish soldiers was very common.

This chapter seeks therefore to contribute to the overall research agenda of this volume by analysing the dynamics of 'inclusion' and 'exclusion' as part of the Jewish soldiers' war experiences in the German, Austrian, British and US armies.[5] Since I employ a broad understanding of 'war experiences' that brings its physical and emotional aspects

---

[5] There are thus far no consistent and exact numbers on Jewish participation during the war. Jacob Rosenthal, who gives numbers for all four countries analysed here, for instance, uses multiple sources, one of which is a publication of US Veterans from 1941 that offers the following numbers: Germany (100,000), Austria-Hungary (320,000), Britain (50,000) and the US (250,000). Jacob Rosenthal (2007), *'Die Ehre des jüdischen Soldaten.' Die Judenzählung im Ersten Weltkrieg* (Frankfurt, Campus Verlag), 204. Depending on the different recruiting schemes, numbers of Jewish soldiers and points of entry into the war, there were approx. 30 Jewish chaplains serving with the German, 76 with the Habsburg, 18 with the British and 23 appointed ones for the American forces (only 10 of which would arrive in France before November 1918). See Arnold Vogt (1984), *Religion im Militär. Seelsorge zwischen Kriegsverherrlichung und Humanität* (Frankfurt a.M., Peter Lang Verlag), 607; Erwin Schmidl (1989), *Juden in der K.(u.)K. Armee, 1788–1918* (Eisenstadt, Jewish

together with Jewish interpretations about their larger implications, the analysis includes not only the voices of Jewish soldiers and chaplains, but also of those members of the Jewish communities who stayed on the home front. Firstly, I will demonstrate how broader structural trajectories within the four wartime societies emerge when exploring aspects of 'inclusion' and 'exclusion' experienced by Jewish soldiers. Secondly—and closely related to this—I will outline the ambiguity of Jewish integration, concluding this sub-chapter with some comparative remarks on the infamous *Judenzählung* or 'Jew count' that was carried out in Germany in October 1916. Finally, I will turn my attention to a more specifically Jewish sphere and discuss the war's impact on the soldiers' Jewish consciousness, for they often had to consider their relationship both with the state and wider society as well as with the different Jewish communities at home and abroad. Over the course of the examination of these three salient themes, I will demonstrate how my comparative and transnational case studies enrich our understanding of negotiating Jewish 'difference' at the historical juncture of the First World War that connected the 'age of empire' with the 'age of extremes'.[6]

JEWISH 'INCLUSION' AND 'EXCLUSION' UNDER A MAGNIFYING GLASS

The relationship between 'inclusion' and 'exclusion' during the war was intensely debated in all four of the Jewish communities under review. Against this background, two interpretative patterns that show a remarkable interconnectedness emerge. First, all public voices and spokesmen of the Jewish communities were determined to highlight the patriotic contributions of Jewish soldiers, citizens—and sometimes, as in the British case, future citizens—to the general war effort of the societies to which

---

Museum Vienna), 80–81; Michael Snape (2008), *The Royal Army Chaplains' Department, 1796–1953: Clergy Under Fire* (Woodbridge, Boydell), 202; Lee Levinger (1921), *A Jewish Chaplain in France* (New York, The Macmillan Company), 86–87; and Albert Isaac Slomovitz (1999), *The Fighting Rabbis: Jewish Military Chaplains and American History* (New York, New York University Press).

[6]Eric Hobsbawm (1987), *The Age of Empire, 1875–1914* (London, Weidenfeld & Nicolson); idem (1994), *The Age of Extremes: The Short Twentieth Century, 1914–1991* (London, Michael Joseph).

they belonged. Second, the image of heroic and masculine Jewish fighters was likewise communicated in the public sphere in order to counter long-existing stereotypes of Jews as unmanly 'shirkers' or 'slackers'[7] and to claim a full-fledged acceptance and integration of Jews into society at large.

Although at first glance these interpretative patterns seem to have been a common denominator among Jews in the German-and English-speaking worlds, their persistency and persuasiveness on the Jewish home fronts in particular and the corresponding societies in general were quite different. In order to explain these similarities and differences, which are clearly identifiable from a properly comparative and transnational perspective, one needs to take more general factors into account. It is thus worth considering the structural dynamics and traditions of the four armies that set the larger framework for the agency of Jewish soldiers during their service. Among these are, for example, the systems of recruitment or the promotion criteria within the military—and hence the institution's aristocratic or civic character.[8]

The armies of the Central Powers, for instance, had relied on universal conscription to ensure recruitment since the mid-nineteenth century. However, the various armies of the German and Austro-Hungarian empires were characterised by marked differences with regard to their levels of Jewish integration. The multi-ethnic setting and, to a certain extent, the fact that Jews were not recognised officially as a nationality in the Habsburg Empire must be considered when trying to explain why attempts at exclusion in the Emperor's Army during the war were not primarily aimed at Jews. Paralleling larger trends within the Habsburg Empire, such exclusionary sentiments tended to focus on Czechs and Poles, and thereby groups that were largely characterised as 'unreliable'

---

[7]Lewis P. Brown (1918), 'The Jew is Not a Slacker', *The North American Review* 207, 857–862. 'Slacker' was less frequently used however than 'shirker', in particular in the British context. In German-speaking countries, a person accused of shirking from military service was called 'Drückeberger'.

[8]On the divergent logics of recruiting systems during the war, see Alexander Watson (2011), 'Voluntary Enlistment in the Great War: A European Phenomenon?', in Christine G. Krüger and Sonja Levsen, eds. *War Volunteering in Modern Times: From the French Revolution to the Second World War* (Basingstoke, Palgrave Macmillan), 163–188. For an excellent transnational historical survey of the relationship between Jews and the military, see Derek Penslar (2013), *Jews and the Military: A History* (Princeton: Princeton University Press).

nationalities because they strove for national self-determination and independence within and beyond the borders of the empire.[9] This changed only in 1917 when increased attempts were made to call for the introduction of 'exclusionary' measures against Jews.[10] Furthermore, in a practice that pre-dated the war and unlike their counterparts in Germany, Austrian Jews had a real chance of being promoted into the officer corps without officially renouncing their Jewishness by conversion to Christianity. Another symbolic manifestation of this divergent starting position was that, in a tradition that dated back to the Austro-Prussian War of 1866, the Austrian army had a pre-war Jewish chaplaincy.[11]

In contrast to the situation in the German-speaking lands, the debates about the war experiences of Jews in the military in Britain, and, from 1917, in the United States, focused mainly on both societies' self-proclaimed mission to make English-speaking citizens out of the vast number of soldiers from immigrant backgrounds.[12] Those Jewish soldiers in the British and US armies at which this policy was aimed came from completely different social, cultural and economic backgrounds when compared with, for example, the middle-class German-Jewish or Viennese-Jewish soldiers, whose parents and grandparents regarded themselves as intrinsically rooted in German culture. The everyday language of many Jewish immigrant soldiers resident in Britain or America but with family roots in Eastern Europe was Yiddish, and they were

[9] On the categorisation of different ethnic groups within the Habsburg military as 'reliable' or 'unreliable', see Mark Cornwall (2004), 'Auflösung und Niederlage. Die österreichisch-ungarische Revolution', in Mark Cornwall, ed. *Die letzten Jahre der Donaumonarchie: Der erste Vielvölkerstaat im Europa des frühen 20. Jahrhunderts* (Essen, Klartext), 174–201, here 181.

[10] 'Die militär. Reservatbefehle', *Jüdische Volksstimme* (10 August 1917), 1–2.

[11] For a historical overview of the German-speaking context, see Rosenthal (2007), '*Ehre*'; István Deák (1990), *Jewish Soldiers in Austro-Hungarian Society* (New York, Leo Baeck Institute); and Erwin A. Schmidl (2014), *Habsburger Jüdische Soldaten, 1788–1918* (Vienna, Böhlau).

[12] On the larger issue of turning immigrant soldiers into American citizens, see Christopher M. Sterba (2003), *Good Americans: Italian and Jewish Immigrants During the First World War* (Oxford, Oxford University Press); Nancy G. Ford (2001), *Americans All! Foreign-Born Soldiers in World War I* (College Station, Texas A&M University Press); and Christopher Capozzola (2008), *Uncle Sam Wants You: World War I and the Making of the Modern American Citizen* (New York, Oxford University Press).

usually brought up in predominantly Jewish immigrant neighbour-hoods—whether it was London's East End or New York's Lower East Side. Uprooted from their Jewish homes and customs in a state of national emergency and international crisis they often felt alienated in the military training camps and later on during their wartime service.

David de Sola Pool, for example, who served as field secretary of the Jewish Welfare Board for the United States Army and Navy (JWB),[13] wrote in one of his many reports about such cases that were brought to his attention when visiting the military training camp in Kelly Fields, Texas in the spring of 1918. There, a Yiddish-speaking soldier who had been recruited eight months previously expressed his sense of discomfort quite openly when complaining that he had to live 'among strangers who did not understand him and whom he did not understand'.[14] Although the Jewish soldiers serving in the Anglophone Allied forces and those who fought for the German-speaking Central Powers were therefore both confronted with the challenge of how to handle experiences of 'inclusion' or 'exclusion', they took on specific shapes that were often closely linked to concrete Jewish localities. This was due, among other things, not only to the fact that the Jewish communities in question were part of four different political communities and societies but also to the differences in size, internal power hierarchies and ratios between 'natives' and 'foreigners' within these respective communities.

[13] The JWB had been established in April 1917 as an officially recognised umbrella organisation for the welfare work among Jewish soldiers and still exists today. See JWB to Woodrow Wilson, 7 September 1917, 1, American Jewish Archives [AJA], MS-457, Box 174, Folder 2. During the war, it had four field secretaries (David de Sola Pool, Leon Goldrich, L.B. Bernstein, and Horace J. Wolf) who visited over 100 military training camps across the US. See Report of the Field Secretaries to the JWB Executive Committee, 3 June 1918, Center for Jewish History [CJH], American Jewish Historical Society [AJHS], I-337, Box 162, Folder 7. On the role of the JWB that has not received much scholarly attention regarding its origins during the First World War yet, see also Jessica Cooperman (2014), 'The Jewish Welfare Board and Religious Pluralism in the American Military of World War I', *American Jewish History* 98:4, 237–261.

[14] Report No. 23 by David de Sola Pool from Kelly Fields (visited on 5 April 1918), 3, CJH, AJHS, I-180, Box 338, Folder 1.

The Ambiguous Character of Jewish Integration During the War

Works by a younger generation of historians have tended to avoid exaggerating the collective impact of 'exclusionary' incidents experienced by Jewish soldiers during the war, and particularly those that were of an antisemitic nature. In this context, the case of German-Jewish soldiers has seen the most intense research.[15] Yet, at the same time, a different group of revisionist scholars, in turn, overemphasises a one-sided narrative of successful Jewish integration during the war, which, if taken too far, is equally problematic because it leads to a blind spot with regard to the dilemma potential military service could indeed present for Jews.[16] In order to avoid the pitfalls of such biased narratives, we should ideally focus instead on the ambiguity of 'inclusion' and 'exclusion' and their interconnectedness with the larger question of how societies negotiate 'difference' and manage diversity in times of national crisis.

Whether one subscribes to a lachrymose or a heroic narrative of Jewish war experiences, it is clear that in Germany, even before the 'Jew count' of October 1916, which involved a census of all 'conscripted members of the mosaic faith',[17] incidents of antisemitism took place on an individual and local level. In a letter from 1915, which was anonymously forwarded by the soldier's father to the *Central Association of German Citizens of Jewish Faith*, a young Jew named Karl complained that he was:

---

[15] See Tim Grady (2011), *The German-Jewish Soldiers of the First World War in History and Memory* (Liverpool, Liverpool University Press); Greg Caplan (2008), *Wicked Sons, German Heroes. Jewish Soldiers, Veterans, and Memories of World War I in Germany* (Saarbrücken, VdM); and Derek Penslar (2011), 'The German-Jewish Soldier: From Participant to Victim', *German History* 29, 423–444.

[16] See, for such blind spots, in particular, David Fine (2012), *Jewish Integration in German Army in the First World War* (Berlin, De Gruyter); Peter Appelbaum (2014), *Loyalty Betrayed: Jewish Chaplains in the German Army During the First World War* (London, Vallentine Mitchell).

[17] Kriegsministerium. An das Kaiserliche Generalgouvernement Warschau, 11 October 1916, No. 247/8. 16 C 1 b, PH 30/II/19, 28, Bundesarchiv-Militärarchiv [BArchiv-MA] Freiburg. Translation by the author. Here, as in the following, I have translated German quotes into English.

... the only Jew in the company. 'Damned Jew-boy' I have to hear myself being called by my superiors. My comrades call me the same names as well and I'm not even allowed to protest, and if I try to do so they say, I will punch you in the face, I will beat you to death ...[18]

What had changed in the autumn of 1916 was therefore the official, state-driven character of 'exclusion' and hence its overall impact on the collective self-identification of German Jewry. A point that is often neglected is that this transformation took place at almost the same time that the so-called 'Eastern Jewish question'[19] was making deep inroads into debates among extremist right-wing, or *völkisch*, groups on the German home front. Fears about future Jewish immigration from Eastern Europe seem to have caused some commentators to question the loyalty of German Jews and to call for them to be pushed to the margins of society.[20] Yet the impact of the 'Jew count' on the individual experiences of Jewish soldiers depended not only on situative factors and war-related social dynamics but also on larger sociopsychological aspects, such as one's own personal sense of identity prior to the outbreak of war in 1914.

In Austria, by contrast, the experiences of Jewish soldiers were shaped quite differently. On the one hand, the aforementioned supranational composition of the Habsburg Army with its emphasis on dynastic loyalty had historically eased integration in the military for Austrian Jews. On the other hand, as early as August 1914 debates about the Jewish experiences of the war were eclipsed by the 'refugee question' on the Austrian home front.[21] Hence, it was the encounter—and sometimes confrontation—with Jewish 'refugees' from Galicia and the Bukovina as Austrian citizens who had fled westwards in the face of Russian advances, especially to Vienna, Prague or Budapest that emerged as the central space in which Jewish 'difference' was discussed. Yet since many Jewish

[18]Anonym, ohne Datum, 28, B. 3/52-I/3, Aus WK 3/2, Zentralarchiv zur Erforschung der Geschichte der Juden in Deutschland, Heidelberg. The letter does not contain a concrete date, but it is filed under a folder containing correspondences from 1915/16; hence it was written before the 'Jew count'.

[19]On the importance of the image of the 'Ostjude', see Steven E. Aschheim (1982), *Brothers and Strangers: The East European Jew in German and German Jewish Consciousness, 1800–1923* (Madison: University of Wisconsin Press).

[20]See M.R. (1916), 'Die Ostjudenfrage I', *Ost und West*, 73–112, here 79.

[21]Panter (2014), *Jüdische Erfahrungen*, 120–130 and 288–295.

soldiers came from exactly those regions in Austria's Eastern territories, their socioeconomic and cultural profile frequently overlapped with that of the refugees.

Shifting our focus to the Anglo-American context, the recruitment campaigns provide one striking factor that influenced the different framework under which the relationship between Jewish soldiers and the military took shape during the war. Britain, the world's pre-eminent naval power, had traditionally relied on volunteerism to raise armies in times of war and, alone among the major belligerent states of 1914, had no system of military conscription in place when war broke out. This changed in 1916, when Parliament passed the *Military Service Act* and conscription was introduced for all British (male) subjects between the ages of 18 and 41.[22] The introduction of (universal) conscription also catalysed claims by public opinion that 'Russian' Jews living in Britain should voluntarily enlist and fight for the cause of king and country. If one puts this in numbers, it becomes clear how sensitive the issue was: The *Jewish Chronicle* estimated the number of 'Russian-born Jews' who were of recruiting age in late June 1916 at between 10 and 12,000. One month later a report of the Aliens Enlistment Committee even estimated that there were still about 30,000 foreigners from Russia, mainly from Jewish backgrounds, who could be recruited.[23]

Although, strictly speaking, only Jews that had recently immigrated to Britain and were as yet unnaturalised in terms of citizenship status should have been the subject of this debate, the boundaries were blurred between Jews born in Britain, recently naturalised Jewish citizens with an Eastern European background and Jewish 'friendly' aliens who originated in states allied to Britain. This conflation of highly distinctive sections of the broader Jewish community served to ethnicise questions of political loyalty and manifested itself in the imprecise and, from the Jewish

---

[22] On this issue, see also Anne Lloyd (2012), 'War, Conflict and the Nation: Between Integration and Separation—Jews and Military Service in World War I Britain', in Hannah Ewence and Tony Kushner, eds. *Whatever Happened to British Jewish Studies?* (London, Vallentine Mitchell), 43–63. At first, conscription applied only to unmarried men but was shortly afterwards extended to married ones as well.

[23] 'Russian-Born Jews and Enlistment', *Jewish Chronicle* (23 June 1916), 7; Report of the Aliens Enlistment Committee, 26 July 1916, 3, The National Archives Kew, Public Record Office, HO 45/10818/318095.

perspective, unhelpful notion of 'Russian Jews'.[24] Furthermore, and to the consternation of 'native' Jews who sought to highlight the difference between themselves and these newcomers, this terminological confusion had a negative impact on the status of *all* Jews in British society. The tendency to lump all Jews together, irrespective of their social or cultural backgrounds, bore additional potential for social conflict between Jews and non-Jews at a local level, especially in the East End of London and in Leeds, the third largest Jewish settlement in the UK that included many working-class Jewish immigrants as well. The military service question was therefore not only an issue of ethnicity but also one of class.[25]

Hence, the conflict about the military service of Jewish 'friendly' aliens on the home front marginalised the public debates over the experiences of Jewish soldiers already serving in the British army before and after conscription had been introduced. This becomes particularly clear when looking at the account of rabbi and senior chaplain Michael Adler, who was sent to the Western Front in January 1915. In his wartime writing, a completely different narrative, at least regarding the 'exclusionary' side of the Anglo-Jewish war experience, emerges:

> I have frequently been asked whether there were any signs of anti-Semitism in the life of the great British Army, and I say, without the slightest hesitation, that whatever indication of ill-feeling there was towards the Jew was so small as to be entirely negligible. The Christian soldier was warmly attached to his Jewish 'pal,' and the relations between the soldiers of all denominations were remarkably cordial.[26]

While it is certainly true that not all Jewish soldiers in the British army experienced instances of exclusion, Adler's interpretation itself refers only to possible 'differences' between Jewish and non-Jewish soldiers on

---

[24] See also Sascha Auerbach (2007), 'Negotiating Nationalism: Jewish Conscription and Russian Repatriation in London's East End, 1916–1918', *Journal of British Studies* 46, 594–620.

[25] See for example 'In the Communal Armchair: The Trouble at Leeds, and Other Places', *Jewish Chronicle* (22 June 1917), 8. In 1914, over two thirds of Jews in Britain lived in three major settlements: London (180,000), Manchester (30,000) and Leeds (20,000). See Todd Endelman (2002), *The Jews of Britain, 1656 to 2000* (Berkeley, University of California Press), 130.

[26] Michael Adler (1920), *A Jewish Chaplain on the Western Front, 1915–1918* (Lewes, Lewes Press) [Reprinted from the *Jewish Guardian*], 16.

account of religion, although he terms such a suspected sentiment antise-mitic. Looking at the sources of the 'native' Anglo-Jewish elite therefore partly conceals an important aspect: that the struggle about Jewish 'dif-ference' in Britain, and in particular its potential for social conflict was first and foremost tied to aspects of 'ethnicity', 'nation' and 'class' even in instances when religious issues were discussed.[27] From this perspec-tive, questions about keeping kosher, providing kosher food for Jewish soldiers or seeking leave for soldiers on Jewish holidays—to name only a few of the Jewish chaplain's tasks—not only opened up a discursive bat-tlefield for what Jewishness or the practising of Judaism were supposed to mean in a state of emergency, but also encompassed the question of what rights and forms of cultural self-assertion Jewish soldiers could attain as *Jews* at the front as well as at home.

In the case of the United States, one might assume, at least at first glance, that the presence of an even larger number of Eastern European Jewish immigrants would have created similar potential regarding claims for military service of non-naturalised Jews. That this turned out not to be the case was due to three major dynamics: the late entrance of the US into the war in April 1917, the withdrawal of revolutionary Russia from the conflict in March 1918, and the selective nature of the draft in May 1917. As a result of conscription, already 18% of all soldiers serv-ing with the American forces during the war had been born outside the territory of the United States.[28] Additionally, friendly 'alien' Jews, many of whom hailed from the territories of the Russian Empire, who had not applied for the process of naturalisation yet were not drafted into the army, partly because the legislators behind the *Selective Service Act* were well aware of the trouble the question of conscripting friendly aliens for military service had caused in Britain.[29] Given the large number of

---

[27] For an early attempt to problematise the 'exclusionary' aspects of the Jewish experience of the war in Britain, see David Cesarani (1989), 'An Embattled Minority: The Jews in Britain During the First World War', *Immigrants & Minorities* 8, 61–81.

[28] Ford (2001), *Americans All!*, 3.

[29] 'Conscripting Friendly Aliens', *American Israelite* (27 September 1917), 4; 'Aliens for War Service', *American Hebrew* (10 August 1917), 353; 'Urge Congress to Draft Aliens', *American Hebrew* (30 August 1917), 419. On practical difficulties when implementing the Selective Service Act regarding 'declarant', 'non-declarant' and 'enemy' aliens, see Nancy G. Ford (1997), "Mindful of the Traditions of his Race': Dual Identity and Foreign-born Soldiers in the First World War American Army', *Journal of American Ethnic History* 16:2, 35–57, here 36.

naturalised Jewish immigrants or soldiers who were second generation among the total of 250,000 Jewish-American soldiers, debates about 'inclusion' and 'exclusion' arose there as well and focused, at first, very much on the situation of the many Yiddish-speaking, working-class Eastern European Jewish recruits in the military training camps. It was in these transitional contact zones between home and front that draftees were transformed into American soldiers and thus turned into 'real', unhyphenated American citizens.

EXCLUSION OF A DIFFERENT KIND? THE 'JEW COUNT' FROM A COMPARATIVE PERSPECTIVE

As outlined above, the debates about the war experiences of Jewish soldiers in Europe and the United States were often characterised by the challenge of actual or potential 'exclusion' due to their Jewishness. This was equally true whether Jews served as a consequence of choice (volunteering) or of compulsion (conscription). At this point, however, it seems necessary to ask the question why, although attempts at exclusion occurred on all four home fronts, only the German authorities went to the extreme of organizing a census of its Jewish citizen soldiers. For, given Jewish self-identifications in Germany, the so-called *Judenzählung*, an act of discrimination legitimised by the state against its own Jewish citizens, born and bred in those regions that made up the German Empire since 1871, should indeed be considered extreme.

In order to answer this question, the collecting of statistics on Jewish participation in the national war effort seems to be a good point of departure, as Jewish leaders regarded this as a crucial issue not only in Germany but also in Austria, Britain and the US. Consequently, special committees conducting statistical efforts, such as, for instance, the Office of War Records of the American Jewish Committee, were set up.[30] The efforts made to collect statistics on Jewish soldiers point therefore to an important factor: that Jewish representatives on all four home fronts anticipated that it would be necessary to counter attempts to exclude Jews from the wartime national community. In this sense, the compiled

---

[30] On its activities, see American Jewish Committee (1919), *The War Record of American Jews: First Report of the Office of War Records* (New York, American Jewish Committee); Julian Leavitt (1918), *The Collection of Jewish War Statistics* (Philadelphia, Jewish Publication Society of America).

statistics were a preventive weapon designed to counter possible allegations that Jews were shunning their country's call. Furthermore, the collecting of statistics on Jewish soldiers also served a more specific purpose during the war: to positively identify Jewish soldiers in order to provide a specifically Jewish form of welfare to them; hence, efforts to compile statistics were made by different actors and according to competing agendas within and outside the Jewish sphere.

If these statistical inquiries were undertaken outside the Jewish sphere, as the case of the 'Jew count' demonstrates, their impact was most likely to be exclusionary. As we know today, actual Jewish wartime participation in Europe and the US showed that Jews on both sides of the conflict were more than willing to fight and die for their respective fatherlands.[31] Since 'native' citizenship status and patriotic self-identification could not protect Jews in Germany from being singled out as 'Jews' and 'shirkers', the 'Jew count' should also be seen as a symbolic watershed regarding the ethnicisation of German citizenship. To be sure, the tendency to discriminate against Jewish soldiers on the grounds of ethnicity or antisemitic predispositions also existed in Austria, Britain and the US, but they never took on a similar systematic form and state-sponsored character. In Austria, for example, Jewish members of the House of Deputies of the Imperial Council went so far to *ask* for a 'Jew count', but the Austrian Minister of Defence, Czapp von Birkenstetten, ultimately denied this. In his view, Jewish soldiers should not be singled out collectively because the implementation of such a measure would contradict the supranational dynamics of the Austrian state. In doing so, he did not differentiate whether such claims were portrayed as an 'inclusionary' measure (as the Jewish deputy from Galicia, Heinrich Reizes, intended it) or an 'exclusionary' one, aimed at discriminating against Jews (as suggested in responses from Polish deputies).[32] Hence, the 'Jew count' and its seismographic function point not only to the exclusionary character of German citizenship but also to the

---

[31] On the numbers, see for instance the compilation by Rosenthal (2007), '*Ehre*', 204–205.

[32] See ibid., 94. On Reizes parliamentary question, see Stenographisches Protokoll. Haus der Abgeordneten, 7. Sitzung (15 June 1917), 316–317. URL http://alex.onb.ac.at/cgi-content/alex?aid=spa&datum=0022&size=54&page=1276 (accessed on 13 September 2015). For the counter-initiative of the Polish deputies Witos, Kubik and Potoczek, see 'Offener Brief', *Dr. Bloch's Österreichische Wochenschrift* (23 November 1917), 783–784.

increased pervasiveness of antisemitism in the German military in particular and German society in general.

The Impact of the War on the 'Jewishness' of the Jewish Soldier

In order to measure the war's impact regarding what 'being Jewish' might have meant in the trenches, it is necessary to connect Jewish experiences of the war to the structural profiles of the analysed Jewish communities and their specific wartime challenges. In doing so, it becomes clear that there were not only multiple, and sometimes conflicting, concepts of what 'being Jewish' was supposed to mean in the microcosm of the military but also different understandings of *what* cultural and religious practices were regarded as 'exclusionary' or 'inclusionary'.

Jacob Sonderling, for example, who served as a Jewish chaplain with the German army on the Eastern Front, interpreted the war as a watershed because it not only resolved his personal struggle with the question of 'what are we, a people or religion?' but also because the 'four years in Russia had made' him 'a Jew'.[33] Like Sonderling, who would emigrate to the U.S. in 1923, many other German Jews who served as soldiers in Eastern Europe during the war—and hence in a densely populated Jewish area—had become quite aware of the region's peculiar but heterogenous understanding of 'Jewishness'. As a supplement to the *Ostgalizische Feldzeitung*, a German army newspaper whose editorial staff was made up of a number of Jewish intellectuals, wrote in the summer of 1917: 'The Jewish soldier in uniform who calls himself a German Jew is smiled at and told bluntly [by the Eastern European Jew], that he might be a German but not a Jew—or the reverse.'[34]

Compared to the situation of German-Jewish soldiers, Austria's army was characterised by a different Jewish social structure, for it included in its ranks many sons of more traditional Jewish families from the geographical but by no means cultural periphery of the empire, Galicia and the Bukovina. As a consequence, many Jewish soldiers in Austria,

---

[33] This is my Life. Jacob Sonderling, 3, 5, AJA, MS-582, Box 1, Folder 7. He wrote his autobiographical memoirs that are based in part on his diary from the First World War in Los Angeles in the 1960s where he died in 1964.

[34] 'Die jüdische Nation', *Beilage zur Ostgalizischen Feldzeitung* (14 July 1917), 3, BArchiv-MA, PHD 23/68.

especially those serving in regiments composed on a regional basis, spoke Yiddish. In addition, they practised more traditional forms of Judaism, combined sometimes with a strong Jewish-nationalist sentiment. Keeping kosher during their war service, an issue that was of almost no concern to German Jews, was a sensitive issue for Austrian-Jewish soldiers. Their situation was thus more similar, as we will see, to that of Jewish soldiers serving with the British and the American forces.

Although we should avoid taking the self-portrayed piety of Jews in the field at face value, the sources reveal few, if any, statements by Austrian-Jewish soldiers, and especially by Jewish soldiers from Galicia, whom chaplain Majer Tauber described as 'bearded reserve fighters',[35] that contradict the importance of the soldier's Jewishness during the war. This importance of Jewish religious identity is reflected, moreover, in complaints from individual soldiers to Jewish chaplains about not being able to live according to Jewish religious laws when on active service. In November 1916, for example, chaplain Samuel Lemberger issued an unmistakable warning to rabbi Max Grunwald in Vienna about the possible consequences of denying Jewish soldiers the opportunity to be religiously observant:

> Very often soldiers approach me crying and asking why no one at home ensured that they could buy kosher dishes, like canned soup, with their own money and why Jewry did not come to the help of its most loyal followers?[36]

Lemberger's account portrayed a disturbing scenario because it hinted at the possibility that non-observance of Jewish customs and religious rites due to military circumstances could be made a habit by Jewish soldiers after returning to civilian life. One of his British counterparts, Arthur Barnett, who still feared in 1919 that 'army life' had caused 'a sort of Jewish anaesthesia', especially among British orthodox Jewish veterans, equally shared his concerns.[37]

---

[35] 'Feldpostbrief eines jüdischen Militärseelsorgers', *Dr. Bloch's Österreichische Wochenschrift* (16 April 1915), 289–291, here 289.

[36] Samuel Lemberger to Max Grunwald, 19 November 1916, Central Archives for the History of the Jewish People, Jerusalem, A/W 357, 3. Underlining in the original.

[37] Arthur Barnett (1919), 'The Bacon Tasted Good', *Jewish Chronicle* (28 February); also reprinted in David Englander, ed. (1994), *A Documentary History of Jewish Immigrants in Britain, 1840–1920* (Leicester, Leicester University Press), 351.

More often than not, however, the reality lay somewhere in between the extremes of devotion and indifference. In this context, organised Jewry, especially Jewish chaplains and welfare workers, played an important role in shaping the Jewish soldier's war experiences and the way in which they were channelled. They catered to the religious needs of the soldiers, for example, by organising religious services, distributing prayer books or ensuring that leave would be granted on Jewish holidays by the authorities. They also functioned as mediators between the experiences of soldiers at the front and the expectations raised by the Jewish communities on the home fronts.

Many Jewish chaplains accordingly mentioned in their letters and the reports they sent home that their presence was a comforting factor, not only on a symbolic but also on a personal level.[38] Though these reports sometimes had their own political agenda, chaplains do appear to have fostered a sense of Jewish community (*Gemeinschaftsgefühl*) among soldiers on active service who were striving for normalisation during this moment of crisis. Gabriel Schwarz, an Austrian-Jewish chaplain stationed in Zagreb, described this process of normalisation by pointing out, that 'over time, as in times of peace, the chaplain becomes the rabbi of a community of Jewish soldiers'.[39] Moreover, this heightened sense of Jewish community at the front was supposed to be transplanted back home after the war was over and was thus interpreted as having the potential to create a positive legacy for the Jewish future. Against this background, German-Jewish chaplain Paul Lazarus, for example, combined his critique on the present state of Jewish knowledge with expectations for the future:

> Maybe out there [at the front] a time will come when it will no longer be necessary to be told by a Jewish soldier over and over again with an apologetic voice that he knows almost nothing about Jewish history or our holy language. Very often I have experienced that only a handful of our soldiers who were asked to give the blessing of the Torah were able to do so and

---

[38] See for instance the detailed reports of Leo Baeck (1914), 'Berichte des Feldgeistlichen Rabbiner Dr. Baeck an den Vorstand der jüdischen Gemeinde', *Allgemeine Zeitung des Judentums* (27 November), 569–571.

[39] 'Ein österreichischer Feldprediger', *Allgemeine Zeitung des Judentums* (12 February 1915), 76–78, here 77.

that imprisoned brothers-in-faith [Jewish prisoners of war] had to act as their substitutes instead.[40]

In Austria, Britain and the United States, by contrast, complaints about a lack of Jewish knowledge were made more often from the soldier's perspective. Cultural differences were thus not restricted to the sphere of Jewish/non-Jewish relations, where their existence seems not at all surprising, but could be an equally important issue in a more specifically Jewish sphere. Sometimes this triggered paradoxical situations, such as the one heavily criticised in a JWB report from Camp Doniphan in Oklahoma, regarding how the local rabbi conducted a religious service for mainly Yiddish-speaking, orthodox Jewish soldiers:

> At the Friday evening service that I attended, [Rabbi Blatt] was the only one present who was bareheaded. The service was so thoroughly Americanized, that no one of the boys could join in with the Kaddish even when the Kaddish was announced. They did not recognize that the opportunity for saying Kaddish had arrived.[41]

In the Austrian army, an even more disappointed chaplain, Rabbi Faerber, expressed similar dismay, and criticised some of his colleagues, asking how orthodox Jewish soldiers from East Galicia should react in a situation in which the Jewish chaplain responsible for their spiritual welfare was eating non-kosher meals at the officer's mess and regularly violating the Sabbath.[42]

While criticism of this sort did not always reach the public sphere, or did so only in a belated fashion, there were instances when the issue became so pressing on the home front that it was discussed quite openly. At the beginning of 1917, for example, the leading Anglo-Jewish newspaper, the *Jewish Chronicle*, published a statement by chaplain Vivian Simmons in which he claimed that orthodox Judaism had suffered a collapse at the front. His account triggered a response from many

---

[40] Paul Lazarus to Verband der Deutschen Juden, 30 September 1917, 1–2, Centrum Judaicum Berlin, 1, 75 C Ve 1, Nr. 388 (13011).

[41] Report No. 7B from Camp Doniphan by David de Sola Pool, 21–23 March 1918, 2, CJH, AJHS, I-180, Box 338, Folder 1. 750 Jewish recruits, mainly from St. Louis and Kansas City, were stationed there.

[42] See R. Faerber (1917–1918), 'Unsere israelitische Militärseelsorge', *Hickls jüdischer Volkskalender für das Jahr 5678*, 46–47, here 46.

Jewish soldiers. Though they did not deny that there was a lot of truth in his statement, they nevertheless regarded the chaplains as being at least partly responsible for this condition among Jewish soldiers at the front. One anonymous letter to the editor pointed to the gap between the ideals shaped on the home front or communicated by chaplains and the every-day exigencies and pressures of soldiers on the Western Front. For the 'average soldier', the author of the letter claimed, there were only three priorities when on active service: 'pay, rations, and leave'.[43] Another soldier voiced his criticism from an almost contrary perspective, not so much denying the importance of religion for soldiers but criticising the external influence on the practice of Judaism by representatives of organised Jewry. He did so in particular by accusing chaplain Simmons of trying to exploit the state of emergency at the front in order to introduce religious reforms among Jewish soldiers with an orthodox leaning:

> I have no qualms in saying that orthodox Judaism ... has been grossly betrayed. [Mr. Simmons] had before him a congregation most of whom, he says, were orthodox. To this congregation he reads a form of service largely in English [instead of Hebrew], and then triumphantly declares, as if it were a vindication of his action, that there was no protest ... Mr. Simmons claims to have some sort of mandate from Jews at the Front to introduce certain reforms, and it is in the capacity of a Jew at the Front that I wish to protest.[44]

On many other occasions, however, chaplains conscientiously strived to find a middle ground between the needs of the soldiers, their own goals as Jewish clergymen, and the expectations of their co-religionists at home. More than once during this process the chaplains had to question each other's expectations and adapt their work to the circumstances that confronted them when on active service. The reports of the JWB, for instance, clearly show how its representatives in the military training camps across the US backed the Jewish recruits' demand to establish a distinctly Jewish infrastructure, instead of relying on the facilities of the Young Men's Christian Association (YMCA). In doing so, welfare

---

[43] 'In the Communal Armchair, 'The Jewish Soldier's Religion:' What a Jewish Soldier Says', *Jewish Chronicle* (5 January 1917), 9–10, here 9.

[44] "'The Jewish Soldier's Religion:' 'Khaki' Reforms: A Protest', *Jewish Chronicle* (26 January 1917), 17.

workers of the JWB gave voice to the sentiment among Jewish recruits in the camps, who, despite all good intentions and interdenominational cooperation, nonetheless felt like 'step children' when using the facilities of the YMCA.[45] While those in charge at the JWB headquarters feared from a distance that non-Jewish soldiers and representatives could consider the establishment of independent Jewish huts an act of 'separatism', in the end, its four field secretaries, who had toured all of the 100 training camps across the country, managed to convince them that this was not the case.

At camps such as Upton or Yaphank, where many Jews from the Lower East Side were stationed, representatives of the JWB quickly realised the need to create a familiar atmosphere. If nothing else, because they did not want Jewish soldiers to have to radically change their life-styles, fearing that otherwise those recruits would abandon their Jewishness when they returned home to their families. At the same time, part of the mission of the JWB was to awaken a Jewish spiritual interest among those soldiers who had lived a life estranged from Jewish culture and religion prior to enlistment. Yet, it was not always an easy undertaking to entice Jewish recruits in the camps to participate in Jewish activities. The effort and commitment that was necessary in order to make Jewish soldiers receptive to the work of the JWB was vividly accentuated by David de Sola Pool in April 1918:

> All over the country, the [JWB's local] branches have to learn that if you put a few chairs into a room, and give the room a Jewish name, it does not make those chairs especially attractive. There is no such thing as a Jewish chair, or a Jewish table, and we cannot expect to attract men to our rooms, just because we give the rooms a Jewish name.[46]

In contrast to the situation in the European armies, the Jewish-American discourse remained therefore largely focused on the situation of Jewish recruits in the military training camps 'at home' and not so much on

---

[45] Morris D. Waldman to Jacob Billikopf, 26 October 1917, 4, AJA, MS-457, Box 172, Folder 6. On similar feedback, see also Report of field secretary Goldrich (submitted on 1 December 1917), 4, CJH, AJHS, I-180, Box 337, Folder 4; Report of Joseph C. Hyman regarding the conditions in Camp Upton, 26 October 1917, 1, CJH, AJHS, I-180, Folder 337, Box 1.

[46] Report No. 33. San Francisco (Northern California Branch). D. de Sola Pool, 19–25 April 1918, 4, CJH, AJHS, I-180, Box 338, Folder 1.

their situation as soldiers 'over there'. One reason for this was the late US entry into the war. Besides the time-lag factor, the geographical distance to the Western Front was equally decisive. By the time the JWB had finally arranged for the first Jewish chaplains to be posted to France the war was almost over. Yet, up to this point, the welfare of Jewish-American soldiers had not been entirely neglected at the front. Between 1917 and 1918, for instance, the aforementioned British chaplain, Michael Adler, and his colleagues had ministered, whenever possible, to Jewish-American soldiers in France.[47] They did so not only by virtue of sharing a common faith, but also a common language (English), which allowed them to distribute, for example, the prayer book that Chief Rabbi Joseph Hertz had compiled for Jewish soldiers in the British army to their American brethren. In this context, the JWB based its decision to cooperate with Anglo-Jewry's chaplains interestingly enough on the lack of English language skills among French civilian rabbis and Jewish chaplains, though the 'universal' languages of Jews, Hebrew and Yiddish, were usually read and spoken by them as well.[48]

CONCLUSION

As has been shown in the case of Jewish soldiers in Europe and the United States, the First World War left no Jewish community unaffected and placed the question of Jewish loyalty at a time of national emergency and international crisis on the agenda in a way that had simply never occurred before. Perhaps no one else described the emotional aspects of the war's inter-Jewish dilemma as pointedly as the Russian-Jewish writer Ansky did in his wartime memoirs, first published in Yiddish as *Khurbn Galitsye* (The Destruction of Galicia) in 1920:

> Jews on both sides fought each other, brother against brother. From the start, the Jews were gripped by this horror, and represented it in a legend of two [Jewish] soldiers meeting in battle ... In St. Petersburg I was told about a Jewish patient in a military hospital. During an attack, he had

[47] For more details on this cooperation, see Panter (2014), *Jüdische Erfahrungen*, 255–259.

[48] On this decision, see in more detail Moise Engelmann to August Goldsmith, 17 March 1918, AJA, MS-457, Folder 178, Box 17; Report of the Overseas Commission from Paris, 23 August 1918, 161.

bayoneted an Austrian soldier, and the victim had cried out, 'Hear, oh Israel ...!' The patient had instantly lost his mind.[49]

In this story, the Jewish tragedy underlying the encounter of two soldiers only becomes clear in the moment of death when the Austrian soldier reveals his Jewishness through his Hebrew prayer. Beyond the legend's mere symbolic implications, the multiple fronts at home and abroad appear not as separated, but highly interconnected zones of encounter, at the intersections of which Jewish soldiers, chaplains and civilians negotiated the meaning of Jewishness between 1914 and 1918. As such, the war interconnected Jewish hopes and challenges of the past, such as their full civic equality (Germany, Austria) or the integration of large numbers of Jewish immigrants into the respective societies (Britain, United States), with the quest for re-shaping the agency of Jewish communities across the globe in order to prepare for the future.

During the war, 'inclusion' and 'exclusion' were marked by ambiguity and we should thus avoid oversimplified generalisations. Whereas these concepts as such mirror aspects of the competing notions of 'citizenship' and 'nation' in Europe and the United States, it seems remarkable that the negotiation of Jewish 'difference' within a specifically Jewish sphere points to many similarities in terms of a pluralist understanding of how Jewish soldiers could remain 'Jews' and 'citizens' alike. In Germany such an ethnicisation of citizenship, as manifested in the 'Jew count', found its outlet primarily in discussions about the war participation of 'native' German Jews. Its counterpart in Britain and the United States, by contrast, was much more related to the question of how to handle the 'difference' of Jewish immigrants from Eastern Europe. In Austria, the situation was even more complex due to the multi-ethnic setting of the Habsburg Empire. The majority of Jews under Habsburg rule lived in Galicia and Bukovina, and not in Vienna or Prague. Hence, although 'native' in terms of their citizenship status, they were also deeply rooted in Eastern European Jewish culture.

Returning home after the war, many Jewish soldiers became active in Jewish communal politics, organising themselves, for example, in veterans' organisations. Through activism that transcended national borders,

---

[49] S. Ansky (2002), *The Enemy at His Pleasure. A Journey Through the Jewish Pale of Settlement During World War I*, ed. and trans. by Joachim Neugroschel (New York, Metropolitan Books), 23. The first English translation was published in 1925.

they not only ensured that the image of Jewish soldiers as manly heroes and patriots was disseminated in the post-war world, often amidst a heightened atmosphere of anti-alienism or antisemitism.[50] By formally organising themselves as the collective voice of Jewish ex-servicemen, they also strove to secure two broader achievements. Firstly, to keep alive the memory of their fallen comrades; and secondly, to conserve a lasting sense of Jewish community (*jüdisches Gemeinschaftsgefühl*) among those who now—often in stark contrast to public perceptions—returned home as shattered personalities, neither able to enjoy victory (Britain, US) nor to recognise and accept defeat (Germany, Austria). The war, and its catalyst effect, therefore, left multiple legacies for Jews around the globe and despite some disillusionment along the way it triggered new courses of Jewish actions and thought. One practical result of the Jewish experience of the war was a more pluralist conception of 'Jewishness' and a heightened sensitivity to the need to bridge the dichotomy of 'religion' and 'nation'. Given the rise of Jewish nationalism during the war, this pertained in particular to the necessity of re-thinking the relationship between modern–secular and traditional–religious notions of Jewishness—and hence the shifting logics of universalism and particularism. A comparative and transnational approach to the experiences of Jewish soldiers in Europe and the US during the war thus not only makes us aware of the diverse dynamics of 'inclusion' and 'exclusion', but also reveals what was a distinctive feature of one warring society and what represented a more general, transnational historical trend.

[50] On the role of internationalism and transnationalism in veterans' organisations, see Derek Penslar (2008), 'An Unlikely Internationalism: Jews at War in Modern Western Europe', *Journal of Modern Jewish Studies* 7:3, 309–323.

Between Faith and Nation:
Italian Jewish Soldiers in the Great War

Vanda Wilcox

In 2011, when Italy celebrated its 150th anniversary, Defence Minister Ignazio La Russa participated in a commemorative event to honour the 75 Roman Jews who died in the Great War. Laying a wreath at the memorial plaque attached to the outside of the Synagogue of Rome, he noted that the ceremony testified to 'the indissoluble link between this community, Rome and the fatherland'.[1] This was not the first time that the national government had participated in the local commemoration of Jewish soldiers—in fact, when the monument was first unveiled both King Vittorio Emanuele III and the war-winning army chief Armando

---

[1] Reported on the Ministry of Defence official website (accessed 27 August 2015). All translations author's own http://www.difesa.it/Primo_Piano/Pagine/Omaggioai CadutiallaSinagogadiRoma.aspx.

V. Wilcox (✉)
John Cabot University, Rome, Italy

© The Author(s) 2019
E. Madigan and G. Reuveni (eds.),
The Jewish Experience of the First World War,
https://doi.org/10.1057/978-1-137-54896-2_9

Diaz were in attendance.[2] Sounding a strongly patriotic note, such events present these fallen soldiers as primarily Italian, rather than primarily Jewish, even though the context and setting for commemoration is specifically religious, the community in Rome having chosen not just to erect a monument within the Ghetto neighbourhood but to affix it to the Synagogue itself.[3] From the moment of Italy's entry to the war in May 1915, the question of these two identities—national and religious—lay at the heart of debates over the nature of the Jewish war experience. This chapter will consider the questions of how these two identities were managed within the framework of Italy's deliberate choice for war, and what the war meant specifically for Italian Jews.

With a population of approximately 43,000 in 1900, and minimal immigration of Jews from other parts of Europe, the Jewish community in Italy is generally accepted to have been one of the most assimilated in Europe in the late nineteenth century. However, this truism conceals a major historical debate over the nature and effects of Italian-Jewish assimilation and its relationship to the much more flexible and inclusive concept of integration.[4] Contemporaries were much exercised by concerns about the relationship between Jewish culture in Italy and the newly established kingdom. Unification in 1861, along with the seizure of the capital in 1870, had brought emancipation from frequently repressive political, legal, social and economic structures in several parts of the peninsula. Moreover, many Jews had been active participants in the Risorgimento, seeing themselves as co-founders of the new Italian state.[5] Patriotism was thus a highly desirable quality for this generation, and Jewish children born in the closing decades of the century were often given names such as 'Italo' or 'Dante', or even 'Vittorio Emanuele' after the king, rather than more traditional first names.

---

[2] Stefano Caviglia (1996), *L'identità salvata: gli ebrei di Roma tra fede e nazione: 1870–1938* (Bari, Laterza), 168–169.

[3] This link between faith community and commemoration was relatively unusual in Italy: very few war memorials were erected in Catholic churches in Italy (owing to the Church's complex relationship with the Italian state and the war itself).

[4] For a thorough introduction to this debate, see Cristina Bettin (2010), *Italian Jews from Emancipation to the Racial Laws* (New York, Palgrave Macmillan).

[5] Dan Segre (1995), 'The Emancipation of the Jews in Italy', in Pierre Birnbaum and Ira Katznelson, eds. *Paths of Emancipation: Jews, States, and Citizenship* (Princeton, NJ, Princeton University Press), 206–237.

In the early years of the twentieth century, however, youth movements began to reject the assimilationist attitude of their parents and grandparents, and to search for a new, more clearly Jewish identity, in Italy as in some other parts of Europe.[6] There was considerable anxiety in religious circles about how few children were enrolled in Jewish schools—only about 4% in 1911—and about the general decline of Jewish culture. In response to this, the early twentieth century saw a boom of intellectual output, new periodicals exploring Jewish religious, political and cultural issues, youth congresses and activism, along with the beginnings of a distinctively Italian form of Zionism which emphasised the global elements of Judaism.[7] This intellectual and cultural movement was based primarily in Florence, and was exactly contemporaneous with Futurism, which was also centred in the Tuscan capital, so, unsurprisingly, there were certain links and similarities. In particular, both movements shared ideas about the close link between the aesthetic and the moral. The pre-war era witnessed the birth of a distinct vision of Italian Zionism, led by the charismatic Florentine lawyer Alfonso Pacifici. Along with other influential figures, such as the Galician rabbi Shmuel Zvi Margulies, Pacifici aimed to unify Jewish faith with the idea of Jewish nationality in a spiritual, ethical way to create an 'integrated Judaism'—a mystical vision which was inspired neither by a rational political choice nor a purely religious practice but 'a complete return to Judaism', a complex set of ideas which incorporated both ethical and aesthetic elements and which regarded Zionism and Italian patriotism as fully compatible.[8] Italian Zionism was not to be solely, or even primarily, a political movement but rather was a revivalist movement in the broadest sense. In the years before the war, however, it was very much a minority movement that attracted only young and highly educated individuals, and not many of them. By contrast, according to Mario Toscano's analysis of wartime

[6] On the 'Jewish renaissance' elsewhere see Michael Brenner (1996), *The Renaissance of Jewish Culture in Weimar Germany* (New Haven, Yale University Press); Inka Bertz (1999), 'Jewish Renaissance—Jewish Modernism', in Emily D. Bilski, ed. *Berlin Metropolis: Jews and the New Culture, 1890–1918* (Berkeley, University of California Press), 164–187.

[7] Cristina Bettin (2005), 'Identity and Identification: Jewish Youth in Italy 1870–1938', *Journal of Modern Jewish Studies* 4:3, 323–345.

[8] Simonetta Della Seta Torrefranca (1993), 'Identità religiosa e identità nazionale nell'ebraismo italiano del Novecento', in *Italia judaica: gli ebrei nell'Italia unita, 1870–1945: atti del IV convegno internazionale, Siena 12–16 giugno 1989* (Rome, Ministero per i beni culturali e ambientali, Ufficio centrale per i beni archivistici), 265–272, 272.

Judaism, most felt that 'traditional Jewish culture was less important than their Italian national identity', a sentiment which enabled 'a continual and growing decline of Jewish life'.[9] This assimilation has been identified in phenomena such as the growing geographical dispersal of Jewish families across Italy, as people chose to move away from the old ghettos and into new areas with new business, social or educational opportunities, as well as a dramatic rise in the rates of mixed marriages and of conversions to Catholicism in the late nineteenth and early twentieth centuries.[10] The perceived decline of Italian Judaism was a cause for concern among some older traditionalists, religious authorities and the rabbinical schools as well as to the young Zionists, but the solutions they proposed—straightforward religious revivalism as opposed to a broad regeneration of Italian Jewish life—were very different to those posited by Pacifici and others, and appeared to bear equally little fruit. It is nonetheless clear that there was no consensus on achieving a balance between national and religious identity in the pre-war years, and the very liveliness of the reaction *against* assimilation shows that the community was by no means monolithic in its views or practices.

THE JEWISH COMMUNITY AND THE WAR

When Italy declared war on its former ally Austria-Hungary in May 1915, the majority of the community committed itself firmly to patriotic support of the war effort, often drawing heavily on rhetorical appeals to the Risorgimento.[11] The leading Jewish periodical, *Il Vessillo Israelitico* (The Jewish Banner), nailed its colours to the mast in no uncertain terms, with articles in May and June 1915 positing direct continuity between the First World War and the wars of independence which had brought about emancipation; the Jewish contribution to the Italian

---

[9] Mario Toscano (1993), 'Gli ebrei italiani e la prima guerra mondiale (1915–1918): tra crisi religiosa e fremiti patriotici', in *Italia judaica: gli ebrei nell'Italia unita, 1870–1945: atti del IV convegno internazionale, Siena 12–16 giugno 1989* (Rome, Ministero per i beni culturali e ambientali, Ufficio centrale per i beni archivistici), 285–302, 286–287.

[10] Renzo De Felice (2001), *The Jews in Fascist Italy: A History* (New York, Enigma Books), 8–11.

[11] Ilaria Pavan (2006), 'Cingi al fianco, o prode, la spada'. I rabbini italiani di fronte alla Grande Guerra', *Rivista di storia del Cristianesimo* 2, 335–358.

conquest of Libya in 1911–1912 was also celebrated.[12] Most mainstream Jewish thought thus embraced the war, presenting wartime service as part of an ongoing Italian-Jewish tradition, which in most cases tended to further a process of integration and acculturation.[13] The 1921 memorial plaque on the Synagogue in Rome subsequently endorsed this view; dedicated to all those who died 'fighting for Italian independence', it incorporated the war dead of the nineteenth-century wars of independence as well as the Italo-Turkish war, showing a clear commitment to a Risorgimento-inspired vision of the Great War. But even the minority Zionist and revivalist movements responded to the outbreak war along patriotic lines, though for different reasons. For Zionists, there was a clear parallel between the nature of Jewish exile and the suffering of the 'unredeemed' Italians under Austro-Hungarian oppression. The large Jewish community of Trieste was particularly important to this understanding of the war, and served to symbolically unite both forms of hardship—fellow Jews and fellow Italians to be liberated from the enemy and brought into the welcome emancipation of the kingdom of Italy. Thus, while fears about the dangers of assimilation continued, these were not seen as a reason to avoid active support for and participation in the war, but rather motivated certain Jewish commentators to find a *Jewish* way to participate. The two identities would, it was hoped, intersect rather than conflict, and promote integration rather than assimilation.

Participation in the war effort took many forms, but military service was the most important in both practical and symbolic terms. Before addressing the extent to which the experience of Jews in the Italian armed forces was distinctive, and how it affected these ongoing debates about religious and national identity, it is worth exploring how many Jews served in the armed forces, and in what ways. The Italian army that went to war in 1915 was a mass conscript force, based on two years of compulsory military service for all at age 18, led by a small professional officer corps. The armed forces of the Italian kingdom were explicitly secular; in fact, even the institution of military chaplaincy had been abolished shortly after unification and chaplains were only reintroduced, at the express behest of Supreme Command,

---

[12] *Il Vessillo Israelitico*, 1915.

[13] Toscano (1993), 'Gli ebrei italiani e la prima guerra mondiale', 288.

in 1911 during the Italo-Turkish war.[14] This secular ethos meant that the army did not seek to keep records of the religious faith of officers or men, and tracing religious identity within the armed forces thus takes a lot of detective work. However, the rigorously secular character of the new state also helps explain the propensity among Italian Jews for military careers in post-Risorgimento Italy. A strong sense of national loyalty rooted in emancipation, combined with significantly above-average levels of literacy and education meant that Jews were well represented within the regular professional ranks of the army (serving both as officers and NCOs). Indeed, in the view of eminent military historian Giorgio Rochat, Italy almost certainly offered more opportunities for Jews to pursue a career in the armed forces than any other European nation in the late nineteenth century.[15] The relatively high socio-economic status of many Italian Jews played an important part in facilitating careers as regular army officers: an interesting comparison is provided by the small Protestant Waldensian community from the north-west, which shared a similar outlook and strong patriotic loyalty (having also benefitted from emancipation by the Liberal state), but owing to their socio-economic profile—most were peasant farmers—they served primarily as NCOs in the specialist mountain *Alpini* units, or as military police, rather than as officers. By contrast, Jewish Italians were over-represented in the officer corps and at senior levels in the army, including the general staff, from the 1890s onwards.[16]

Yet to what extent was the Jewish experience of military service different from that of other Italian soldiers? This question is not easy to answer—not least since it is not possible even to state with complete certainty how many Italian Jews served in the war. The most comprehensive study, published in 2009 by Pierluigi Briganti, highlights the extreme difficulty of establishing accurate data given the army's failure to reliably record religious faith. Briganti has traced the records of 3751 Jews who served in the First World War, of which 2409 were officers and 1182 enlisted men. This is certainly not the full story, as he makes very

---

[14]Roberto Morozzo della Rocca (1980), *La Fede e la Guerra: cappellani militari e preti-soldati (1915–1919)* (Rome, Edizioni Studium), 8–9.

[15]'Nota tecnica' by Giorgio Rochat, 15–16, in Pierluigi Briganti (2009), *Il contributo militare degli ebrei italiani alla Grande Guerra, 1915-1918* (Turin, S. Zamorani).

[16]Alberto Rovighi (1999), *I militari di origine ebraica nel primo secolo di vita dello stato italiano* (Rome, Stato maggiore dell'esercito, Ufficio storico), 8–9.

Table 1   Estimated figures for total Jewish military contribution, 1915–1919

	Italian Jews			Total Italian population		
	Number	% total Jewish pop.	% mobilised Jewish pop.	Number	% total pop.	% mobilised pop.
Population 1914	35,000			37,900,000		
Population 1919ᵃ	42,000					
Mobilised men (excl. overseas/*irredenti*)	4800	13.7		5,200,000	13.7	
Mobilised men (incl. Overseas/*irredenti*)	5500	13.1				
Officers (total)	2750	6.5	50	210,000	0.6	4
Decorated (total)	700	1.7	12.7	110,000	0.3	2.1
Fatalities (total)	450	1.1	8.2	650,000	1.7	12.5
Fatalities (officers only)	240	0.6	4.4	20,000	0.1	0.4
% fatalities: officers		53.3			3.1	

ᵃIncluding the newly incorporated *terre irredente* i.e. Trento and Trieste—the latter had a significant Jewish population, as did Zara and Bolzano. Data drawn from Briganti, pp. 33–34

clear, but without doubt his are the best, most reliable figures currently available. Using a variety of sources, he estimates that there were a total of around 5500 Jewish Italians mobilised during the war, of whom as many as 50% were commissioned officers.[17] Nearly 40 attained the rank of general during the war, including Italy's most decorated general of the conflict, Emanuele Pugliese, the noted artillery commander, Roberto Segre (who participated in the Italian military mission to Vienna after the Armistice), and the president of the Supreme Military Tribunal, Angelo Modena.[18] These experienced and high-ranking professional soldiers clearly found their religion no obstacle to attaining prestigious positions.

Notably, the number of Jews as a proportion of the wider Jewish community who served in the armed forces was almost identical to the proportion of men who served across the general Italian population.

[17] Briganti (2009), *Il contributo militare degli ebrei italiani*, 33–34. At least 118 of these officers would go on to be killed in action or after capture while fighting as partisans with the Italian Resistance in 1943–1945. Rovighi (1999), *I militari di origine ebraica* passim.

[18] Rovighi (1999), *I militari di origine ebraica*, 17–18.

As shown in Table 1, however, they were about ten times more likely to hold a commissioned rank (and possibly to achieve a non-commissioned position too) and significantly more likely to receive a military honour than the national norm. Though complete accuracy is impossible, Briganti has identified 399 confirmed Jewish fatalities during the war, of whom over 50% were officers, the youngest aged just 17 years and 7 months and the oldest 61; from this basis he has extrapolated an estimated total of around 450.[19] He has also traced the honours awarded to Jewish servicemen, identifying 549 documented recipients of a total of 719 medals or decorations awarded. Fifteen individuals were granted the Order of Savoy, which was designed to honour distinguished service in wartime and commonly reserved for senior officers, especially on the staff, while five received Italy's highest combat honour, the Gold Medal for Military Valour (four of these awards were posthumous while the last was issued to a blinded and disabled junior officer). A further 267 Silver and 305 Bronze awards for Valour were made along with 127 awards of the somewhat less prestigious War Cross for Valour. 92% of these medals were granted to officers, reflecting not only the very high proportion of officers among the total population of Jewish servicemen but also the tendency of the Italian military to disproportionately award honours to commissioned officers rather than rankers.[20] Consequently, this high rate of military awards is not necessarily indicative of individuals' greater than average combat performance, but rather is typical of Italian army practice, and suggests that in selecting recipients for honours, Jewishness was not a factor which affected the decisions of army authorities. A major commemorative volume, published in 1921, explored the personal histories and service records not only of many of these medal winners but also of the Jewish war dead, though despite its claims to comprehensiveness the list of men included is clearly incomplete.[21]

Just as significant as the very high rate of Jewish commissioned officers is the unusual deployment of Jewish manpower between branches of service. Briganti's figures offer little information on this issue

[19] Briganti (2009), *Il contributo militare degli ebrei italiani*, 154–155, 159, 249–251.

[20] Full data for comparison in Italia. Ministero della Guerra. Ufficio Statistico (1927), *L'ordine militare di Savoia durante la guerra 1915–1918* (Rome, Provveditorato Generale dello Stato).

[21] Felice Tedeschi (1921), *Gli Israeliti italiani nella guerra 1915–1918* (Turin, Ferruccio Servi).

but an alternative source of data is to be found in a list compiled at the request of Angelo Sacerdoti, Chief Rabbi of Rome during the war, who was appointed director of the Military Rabbinate by the Ministry of War in May 1915, and which is now preserved in the archive of the Union of Italian Jewish Communities (UCEI).[22] Sacerdoti requested that local organisations across the country send him complete lists of all serving Jewish men from their community, which were gradually compiled into a single directory by January 1916 under the supervision of Arturo Orvieto, the Chief Rabbi of Bologna. Only 1158 names appear in this collection, less than 25% of the figure which Briganti proposes for servicemen originating within Italy. Some reasons for this disparity are to be found in the date of compilation; young men who had not yet attained their 18th birthday by the end of 1915 were obviously not included, nor older men whose classes were yet to be called up by this date. Other problems lie in the collection of the data itself, since not all communities completed the task scrupulously; nor were all Jews necessarily known to the community groups responsible for producing the lists, indeed there was no guarantee that all Jewish families lived within areas which possessed these formal community structures. Nonetheless, the data gathered by the Chief Rabbi, though patchy, is richly informative and merits further attention. In particular, Orvieto's list reveals valuable information about the types of service performed, the geographical origins of Italian Jewish servicemen, and, in some cases, their civilian backgrounds.

Jewish servicemen were significantly more likely than others to serve in specialised branches of the army, such as the artillery or engineers, which required greater technical skills and literacy than standard infantry service, reflecting higher average educational standards than among the population at large. Qualified medical personnel usually served as military doctors while rabbinical students often obtained positions working with the Red Cross, and enlisted men often served as telegraph operators, drivers, electricians etc., rather than holding combat roles. Just 46% served as ordinary infantrymen, whereas, across the wider population,

---

[22] Unione delle Comunità Ebraiche Italiane (UCEI), Centro Bibliografico, Archivio Consorzio (AC), b.27 f.150; b.25 f.125/2; b.27 f.125/3; b.27 f.125/1. A number of individuals identified in the UCEI archive are not found in Briganti's published database.

Table 2 Italian-Jewish servicemen by branch of service

Combat roles		Non-combat roles	
Air Force	12	Accounting	2
Alpine troops	12	Drivers	31
Artillery	200	Chaplaincy	4
Bersaglieri	26	Commissariat	29
Military police	21	Finance police	2
Cavalry	40	Medical and Red Cross	139
Engineers	70	Telegraphists	5
Grenadiers	12		
Infantry	555		
Navy	30		
Total	978	Total	212

Data from UCEI, Archivio Consorzio [hereafter AC], b.27 f.125/1

almost 60% of all servicemen were part of the infantry by the war's end[23] (Tables 2 and 3).

Orvieto's directory also permits analysis of servicemen's regional origins.

In total, 25% of Jewish servicemen came from Rome itself or the Lazio region, 17% from Tuscany, 16% from Piedmont, and around 11–12% each from Emilia Romagna and the Veneto region. This distribution broadly corresponds with the general distribution of the Jewish communities within Italy. The substantial Italian Jewish presence in Egypt is also indicated—most of these were the sons or grandsons of Jews who had fled there after the failed 1848 revolutions or emigrated to work as labourers on the Suez Canal—while in Tunisia there was an even larger community. However, no figures were returned from much of the South or the islands, areas from which the Jews had been expelled in the fifteenth century; if any families did retain their faith in these regions, they did so in secret and there was no way to identify their wartime service. By contrast, within the Italian army as a whole, southerners were over-represented, since northerners were somewhat more likely to work in reserved occupations (such as military-related industry) whereas in the south there were relatively few justifications for exemption from service.

---

[23] Ufficio Statistico (1927), *Statistica dello sforzo militare italiano nella guerra mondiale* (Rome, Provveditorato Generale dello stato).

Table 3 Origins of 1268 Italian-Jewish servicemen, January 1916

Alessandria	14
Ancona	27
Asti	22
Bologna	90
Bulgaria	1
Chieti	1
Cuneo	7
Egypt	7
Ferrara	56
Florence	106
Genoa	42
La Spezia	3
Livorno	88
Lugo	9
Macerata	1
Milan	36
Modena	12
Naples	32
Padua	28
Parma	35
Pesaro	2
Pisa	3
Pitigliano	11
Reggio Emilia	8
Rome	322
Siena	11
Trieste	3
Tunis	3
Turin	153
Urbino	6
Venice	83
Vercelli	7
Verona	28

Data from UCEI, AC, b.27 f.125/1

In some cases, local community groups gave information on the civilian status or occupation of the individuals, giving a clear sense of the bourgeois, educated profile common to these servicemen. Orvieto's 1915 list includes 25 engineers, 24 doctors, 15 lawyers, seven surveyors, two rabbis, two rabbi's sons, six professors, nine unspecified graduates and no fewer than 17 with the title 'Cavaliere', loosely equivalent to a knighthood. All those described as 'Cavalieri' held commissioned rank, several at mid to senior level, and were most likely career officers.

Of those listed as graduates, only one was serving as an enlisted man, and only two were in the infantry, with the others all serving in specialist arms of the military. Engineers had a good chance of using at least some of their civilian skills, with a third of Jewish officers in engineer units and others serving often as junior or mid-ranking officers in the artillery or air force. Lawyers, by contrast, were more likely to hold lower status positions, perhaps because there were relatively few opportunities for their professional skills to be used in a military context.

These figures show that the distinctive geographical, social and educational profile of the Italian Jewish community shaped the parameters of wartime service, but that the overall impact of service was broadly in line with that of the Italian population as a whole. Given the structure of the Italian army there was little likelihood of serving with fellow Jews or even with people from one's home town, since the army practiced a system of non-regional recruitment and paid little attention to Judaism or Jewish culture at a formal level. Once Jewish men were recruited and mobilised there are two core areas which stand out in the archival records as distinguishing their experience from that of other Italians: interactions with rabbis serving as military chaplains, and the celebration of major religious festivals.

Jewish Chaplains

In May 1915, Angelo Sacerdoti proposed the creation of a scheme of Jewish military chaplaincies for the armed forces, consisting of 12 rabbis (one attached to each army or autonomous corps) who could travel around that unit's hospitals, collaborating as appropriate with the Red Cross.[24] On 2 June 1915 the official go-ahead was received from Vittorio Zupelli, the Minister of War:

> Soldiers belonging to the Jewish faith may also have spiritual comfort from ministers of their religion, and, in honour of the sense of patriotism displayed by Italian Jews, it is permitted that four rabbis may join the army as military chaplains.[25]

[24] Ilaria Pavan (2008), 'I rabbini italiani e la prima guerra mondiale', in Alberto Caviglion, Lucetta Levi Momigliano, and Isabella Massabò Ricci, eds. *Una storia del Novecento: il rabbino Dario Disegni (1878–1967): Torino, 10 dicembre 2008 - 30 gennaio 2009* (Turin, Archivio ebraico B. e A. Terracini), 139–40.

[25] UCEI, AC, b.27 f.150 Corr. dal Maggio 1915 al Marzo 1917: Ministero della Guerra Segretario Generale Div. Stato Maggiore, sezione 3. N. 2367.

After further negotiation, Zupelli agreed that five rather than four rabbis might be appointed. However, despite enthusiastic support from the *Comitato delle Università Israelitiche Italiane* (Committee for Italian Jewish Universities—the chief national Jewish institution) and its president Angelo Sereni, it initially proved hard to recruit the necessary figures. This was in sharp contrast to the Catholic chaplaincy, which was besieged by applicants and was forced to turn away huge numbers of aspiring military chaplains. Of the 28 local groups which belonged to the Committee, only 23 responded to Sereni's appeal, and their replies were disappointing to the patriotically minded organisers of the initiative. Most communities, even in large cities, such as Naples and Bologna, had only one rabbi available; six wrote that it would simply be impossible to abandon their community; four pleaded old age and four ill health; three wrote that they were already engaged in vital local services in support of the war effort, another that he could not leave his nine children. Only five rabbis responded with even partial or conditional agreement to the request for military chaplains.[26] Even those who agreed to undertake the role did not necessarily display any great enthusiasm for the task, as this letter from Elia Artom, Chief Rabbi of Turin, demonstrates:

> I consider myself authorised to express my views on an initiative which in my opinion presents no Jewish benefits. However I would consider myself to be failing in my duty if, once the initiative has been undertaken, it could not be completed owing only to the lack of my contribution, especially since it is an activity which, however useless, I do not consider to be actively damaging to Judaism.
>
> If, therefore, it is impossible to do without me without creating a very poor impression of our community and giving yet another sign of our complete disorganisation (which however real should not always be publicly displayed), then I am available to do whatever I can.[27]

While Sacerdoti was gratified by the enthusiastic response of Professor Rodolfo Levi of Pitigliano (Tuscany), who sent an immediate telegram expressing his desire to serve, he was bitterly disappointed with the

---

[26] UCEI, AC, b.27 f.150 Corr. Dal Maggio 1915 al Marzo 1917.

[27] UCEI, AC, b.27 f.150 Corr. Dal Maggio 1915 al Marzo 1917; letter dated 15 June 1915.

reaction of the rabbinical community as a whole and shocked by what he saw as a failure of both religious and patriotic duty. Most of those who declined excused themselves by arguing that they would be busy visiting Jewish soldiers in local military hospitals, but Sacerdoti was unimpressed, noting tartly that he had never imagined that any rabbi would fail in his duty to visit the sick and wounded in hospital so this did not seem like any extraordinary wartime sacrifice.

Once the team of five chaplains had finally been assembled, they were sent out to major military hospitals attached to each of the five main armies, where, for the most part, they remained for the duration of the war (though the reluctant Artom was replaced in November 1915 and all were permitted to take on assistants as the scale of the conflict and the number of casualties grew, for a total of 12 rabbis). By 1917, when the reality of the war's brutality had set in and hopes of a quick victory had faded, many more candidates for the chaplaincies came forward: if military service could not be avoided, better to serve as a chaplain than in the ranks, many considered.[28] The military authorities were unwilling to further increase the number of positions available, however. Unlike Catholic chaplains, rabbis were not permitted into the front-line areas to conduct services. They would not, in any case, have been very useful in this capacity as, owing to the organisation of the Italian army, few Jewish soldiers served in the same units as their co-religionists, and there were no units with large Jewish groups which might have clearly warranted such a system. Instead, Sacerdoti's team worked in hospitals in major towns in the rear of the war zone, collaborating with the Red Cross, the army medical service and their Catholic colleagues, who would often notify them of Jewish sick or wounded men awaiting a pastoral visit. Along with visiting hospitals, the chaplains performed a vital service in communicating with families at home, helping them to trace missing soldiers or reporting on the nature and extent of wounds when men could not write themselves owing to their physical conditions. Soldiers also wrote to chaplains, particularly to rabbis they had previously met either in hospital or at a religious celebration, to ask for help. In particular they hoped for assistance in tracing lost relatives, and in supporting Italian prisoners of war in Austrian or German camps via the *Magen David Adom* (Red Star of David) in Lucerne. This work became

[28] UCEI, AC, b.27 f.154 Corrispondenza Varia della Dir. del Rabb. Mil., letters from April and May 1917.

particularly important after the Italian defeat at Caporetto in October–November 1917, when nearly 300,000 prisoners were lost in under a month. Military rabbis in the field travelled in person to try to find widely dispersed units and chase up enquiries about specific soldiers who may or may not have been taken prisoner. When prisoners captured during the defeat were successfully located in Austro-Hungarian camps, the *Magen David Adom* would liaise with Austrian rabbis to secure visits and pastoral care for them.[29]

As well as working with the wounded and with prisoners, chaplains developed ongoing relationships with serving soldiers. Men often wrote requesting practical assistance, such as money for travelling home on leave or simply for supplementing depressing army rations. For instance, G.L.[30] of the 77th Infantry wrote to Rodolfo Levi in November 1916 when he was considering applying for promotion to corporal; he had hitherto served as a medical auxiliary, but if promoted would be transferred to a different branch of service, and he wanted to know whether the rabbi had any advice as to whether this would be worthwhile. The archive preserves only Levi's side of the correspondence, but it is clear that with advice and support G. L. went ahead and applied for promotion. By August 1917 he was interested in applying for an officer cadetship and wrote asking that the chaplains find out the minimum educational requirements and send him information about the administrative procedures for securing this new position.[31] While he noted that 'receiving letters from you all gives me great pleasure since I have no co-religionists here', it is clear that he wanted practical support for his military career as much as devotional or spiritual guidance.

Along with this generalised pastoral support many soldiers requested, and received, more specifically religious assistance. Requests for prayer books and shawls were common as were anxious enquiries about the possibilities of acquiring matzos for Passover. This last was a recurrent problem for the chaplaincy which struggled to procure and to pay for the necessary quantities, especially as the war went on. As large numbers of

[29] See, for example, Letters from Rabbi of IV Army, Padova, November–December 1917, UCEI, AC, b.27 f.151; Corr. dal Luglio al Dicembre 1917.

[30] In accordance with Italian archival privacy regulations, private individuals are identified only by initials.

[31] UCEI, AC, b.27 f.152 Corr. Varia di militari; see letters dated 11 November 1916 and 11 August 1917.

Austro-Hungarian prisoners fell into Italian hands, Italian military chaplains were made responsible for their religious needs. Of course, these prisoners included many Jews (at least 2200 by March 1917, and significantly more in 1918) who required practical support and supplies.[32] Sacerdoti and his team worked hard to persuade families to provide their own relatives with matzos and other essentials as well as carrying out major fundraising in the various Jewish communities in the run-up to Passover each year. The rabbis were also regularly asked to intervene with the military authorities to ensure that religious obligations could be adhered to. A Jewish soldier born and raised in Egypt wrote to Sacerdoti in March 1917 anxious about the imminent Passover celebrations. Since no winter leave had been granted for overseas soldiers in 1915–1916, and in 1916–1917 it was announced but then cancelled, he had not been home for nearly two years and had more or less abandoned hope of seeing his family again before the end of the war. He now hoped to spend his religious leave in an Italian city, just to get away from the front, and wrote asking if he could come to Rome to stay with the Chief Rabbi himself, and at least spend Passover correctly with someone of his own faith.[33] Along similar lines, Corporal Major C. P. wrote as he was discharged from hospital in September 1917: he had mislaid his personal ID booklet, but with no proof of his Jewishness he feared he might not be granted leave for Yom Kippur, and asked that the chaplains might intercede on his behalf.[34] As well as needing help with navigating the unfamiliar structures of army life, such requests reveal soldiers' fears that the army did not take the obligations of Judaism very seriously. Other letters simply sought to exchange religious greetings; extensive correspondence exists from an extremely devout machine gunner, M. F. H. from Alessandria (Egypt), who wrote every week to one or more of the chaplains, praying for peace and salvation, requesting prayer books and religious reading materials, and discussing the religious context of the war. Indeed, he was unusually demanding in his need for spiritual support, as references to him in letters between the various chaplains attest.

---

[32] UCEI, AC, b.27 f.154 Corrispondenza Varia della Dir. del Rabb. Mil., letters from Rodolfo Levi.

[33] UCEI, AC, b.27 f.152 Corr. Varia di militari.

[34] UCEI, AC, b.27 f.152 Corr. Varia di militari. (Later when C.P. was killed in action, his family contacted Sacerdoti to request help in bringing his body home for appropriate burial.)

Rabbi Michele Amar described him, with some exasperation, as 'religiosissimo'.[35] In June 1917, the chaplaincy of 3rd Army even received a request in English from a British artilleryman serving in Italy who was anxious to find a local synagogue for regular Shabbat services (though there was ultimately little the chaplains could do to help him).[36] However the vast majority of Jewish servicemen were focused less on the daily or weekly obligations of their faith than on the major annual observances of Passover and Yom Kippur.

Religious Holidays

Perhaps the most common requests from soldiers to the team of Jewish chaplains was for support in securing leave for religious celebrations. This correspondence perforce represents the more devout element since those men who were indifferent to their faith did not write to the chaplains, but there is enough evidence to suggest that for many Jewish soldiers the chance to celebrate the major festivals in the company of their co-religionists was extremely important, even if they were unable to go home and share the holiday with their family, which was always the ideal. Participation in the army's centrally organised events close to the war zone was still welcomed, and it is clear that (however much men hoped to go home) the driving concern was genuinely spiritual. In general, the army granted a day of rest for important festivals, but only for Yom Kippur was there opportunity to travel away from the front for a collective celebration. In 1915 this happened in a rather ad hoc way but as the war progressed it became more efficient and systematic. The successful organisation of Rosh Hashanah and Yom Kippur in 1917 is a useful example of the achievements of the chaplaincy and proved a highlight of the year for Jewish servicemen.

Men from 1st, 6th and 7th Armies gathered in Verona, hosted by the Provincial College, and received generous support from the local civilian authorities as well as the army itself. Yom Kippur became a surprisingly 'nationalistic' occasion, according to the report which Rabbi Ugo Massiach sent back to Angelo Sacerdoti in Rome, since unlike previous years the organisers had decided to invite senior officers

---

[35] UCEI, AC, b.27 f.153; b.27 f.156 sf. 3/sf. 4/ sf. 6.

[36] UCEI, AC, b.27 f.152 Corr. Varia di militari.

(of all faiths)—something which as Massiach noted would have been hard to imagine just a short while before. Officers and men were united in what appears to have been a distinctly military event, while Italy and the Allied nations were loudly cheered by the assembled men, and the report claimed that 'in every heart is the fervent hope that with the triumph of the Allies' righteous cause, the millenial dream of Israel will be fulfilled'.[37] Thanks to the support of the authorities, and to fundraising from Jewish communities in Rome, Verona, Turin, Asti and Mantova, gifts were distributed to the participants. Both officers and men participated in readings from the Sefer Torah, and prayers were well attended, while Zionist pamphlets and printed prayers were distributed widely, calling for 'the victory and the health of Italy, Israel and humanity'. After the fasting, dinner was organised by a local volunteer committee of young Jewish women, in a hall decorated with Jewish, Italian and Allied flags and featuring a huge portrait of the king. Although officers had been prepared a separate meal, many chose to mingle fraternally with the men on both evenings, while the young ladies presented them with flowers. When divisional general Giorgio Bompiani, not himself Jewish, arrived with his staff, the national anthem (royal march) was played on the piano and applauded vigorously.[38] The participation of army authorities was significant, symbolising the extent to which Jewish servicemen were fully acknowledged as an integral part of the national community; the patriotic and indeed royalist trappings of the event suggest that, along with its religious function, the celebration of Yom Kippur in Verona was conceived of as a morale-boosting occasion at which dedication to the national war effort would be reinforced.

Meanwhile the officers and men of 2nd, 4th and 5th armies were meeting not far away in Padua, where dedicated patriot Rodolfo Levi delivered a notable speech (subsequently widely published in the Jewish press). After opening with thanks to the local Jewish community, who

---

[37] UCEI, AC, b.27, f.149, report from Lt. Rabbi Ugo Massiach [b.1890] to Angelo Sacerdoti.

[38] UCEI, AC, b.27, f.149. HQ of 7th army sent out orders to all Jewish soldiers to gather in Brescia where the health services had put rooms at their disposal in the local branch of the Society for Garibaldians and Veterans, which also successfully held Rosh Hashanah services. Again, a close working relationship between the rabbinate, the army authorities and local patriotic institutions is revealed; on other occasions the nearest 'Casa del Soldato'—an official army leisure space for soldiers—was used for religious events.

had 'welcomed our heroic soldiers all dedicated to the holy cause of ITALY IN ARMS', he praised the assembled soldiers:

> The chosen ranks of our youth, the hope of Jewish renewal, temper your spirits with steel and endure with determination the harsh endeavours of this terrible war and in the midst of continual dangers, remaining always faithful to your leaders, fight for the honour of Italy and the achievement of her longed-for destiny.[39]

Everyone, including families at home, he added, was making sacrifices for the shared goal of 'law and justice achiev[ing] lasting triumph over brute force and lawless violence. To this end the Jewish soldier fights with love and with rigorous obedience'. For who, he asked, more than the Jewish people 'who have lived among so many nations during their tragic existence, through numerous persecutions' should value and endorse the quest for law and justice, in a war fought to end foreign domination and assure freedom for all? Although the conflict had ground on for well over two years, the idea of a just and righteous 'war for peace' was still alive. Already many had 'immolated their proud, ardent youth on the altar of the Nation to return it to those legitimate borders which God and nature have assigned to her'. However, this Risorgimento-inspired understanding of Italy's natural borders was not the only focus of Levi's irredentist vision. When speaking of 'assassinated Belgium, prostrate Serbia', one should also remember 'that *other* people [...] which has awaited its place among the peoples of the earth for centuries'. This link between the wartime occupation of established nation-states and the redemption of the people of Israel helped to give the war not only a moral but a specifically religious purpose. Thus, in fighting for Italy and helping to bring her honour and respect, he argued, men were also fighting for the Jewish cause: 'your sacrifices, the blood that you shed, will come to bear in the days in which the destinies of all peoples are decided'. He offered a transnational, racial definition of Judaism, saying 'in the peace to come you will recognise in every fellow Jew from whatever nation a brother, a friend, a blood relation, animated by your own purpose and working towards your own goals'. Zionism

---

[39] UCEI, AC, b.27 f.155 Rabbinato Militare IV & VI armata, 1916–1917–1919, typed copy of Levi's speech.

and Italian nationalism were, in Levi's impassioned rhetoric, perfectly intermingled; religious and national duty were as one.[40]

However, not all Jewish soldiers chose to actively participate in these events; a number went 'incognito', failing to declare their faith on their official army papers and never seeking out the support of rabbis or identifying themselves to community leaders.[41] This was a major cause for concern for the Jewish chaplains and press, especially as the war went on.[42] Complaints came in from some chaplains that they identified sick or wounded Jews in the hospitals only when they heard surnames such as Coen or Levi mentioned by nurses; one wrote that 'when they are among their fellow soldiers they abstain from any word or act which could reveal that they belong to a different faith; when sick or wounded they don't seek our care and even on occasion refuse to see the rabbis who visit the hospitals where they are'.[43] Indeed in some cases the chaplains were shocked to stumble across headstones in hospital cemeteries where men with identifiably Jewish names had been buried under crosses—evidently having failed to identify their faith either on their military service documents or in person, and consequently being buried with Catholic rites. This was perhaps inevitable given the practical difficulties under which burial teams operated both in the field and in hospitals as well as the impossibility of dying or unconscious men communicating their religious denomination to medical personnel. It is also possible that a few men were genuinely converted by the determined missionary activities of Catholic chaplains at the front.[44] Months after the Armistice, the team were still visiting burial grounds, trying to track down Jewish war dead for exhumation and proper reinterment. By 1916 the press was lamenting empty synagogues: after the crowded enthusiastic services of the opening months of the war, attendance was declining and seemed increasingly to consist only of women and the poor. Complaints about "Kipur-juden" who marked only the most important holidays abounded, along with accusations of absenteeism and a widespread indifference

---

[40] UCEI, AC, b.27 f.155 Rabbinato Militare IV & VI armata, 1916–1917–1919.

[41] Pavan (2008), 'I rabbini italiani', 138–139.

[42] L. Ravenna (1916), 'Guerra e Religione', *Il Vessillo* 15–30, 543.

[43] Cited in Toscano (1993), 'Gli ebrei italiani e la prima guerra mondiale', 293–294.

[44] I am grateful to Edward Madigan for his observations on this point.

of civilians to their faith, mirroring the problem of men in the military choosing to remain incognito. Rabbis complained about the high levels of religious ignorance and poor practice which they encountered (though strict observation was scarcely possible in the trenches) and that the young in particular seemed only loosely attached to their faith.

Was this in response to hostility or prejudice? It seems from the archival record that antisemitism was feared by the rabbinical authorities and ordinary servicemen alike but was in fact relatively rare; on the contrary, the demonstrable patriotism of the Jewish community appears to have continued the general acceptance of Italian Jews into national life, building on the assimilationist tendency of the nineteenth century. Explicit complaints about antisemitism were rare indeed—the only example I have found was from one private in the 162nd anti-aircraft battery in Ferrara, C. S., who wrote to a chaplain asking to be transferred to the 163rd battery. He claimed that he was being mistreated by officers and NCOs in his unit, where he had been stationed for the previous seven months, 'perhaps for reasons of personal antipathy or perhaps for other motives (probably because I am a Jew)'.[45] Rabbis and community leaders were in fact relentlessly positive about the support received from both military and civilian authorities, not only in their public declarations, as might be expected, but even in their private correspondence with one another.[46] Given the evidence of military rank, it seems highly unlikely at least that there was any official discrimination; whether fellow soldiers were as free from discriminatory attitudes in their interactions with Jewish peers is impossible to say. To many of those who have left specific written records, it may have seemed more appropriate in wartime to ignore episodes of open antisemitism. There were plenty of other reasons why soldiers might fail to declare their faith publicly within the armed forces, including simple convenience or a desire to blend in, and in particular a fear of conversion attempts being made by Catholic chaplains, which appear to have taken place on a number of occasions when

---

[45] UCEI, AC, b.27 f.152 Corr. Varia di militari.

[46] UCEI, AC, b.27 f.154 Corrispondenza Varia della Dir. del Rabb. Mil. The chaplains complained a great deal in their private correspondence about their personal circumstances (such as the provision of leave and the duration of service) and about Sacerdoti's management of the Jewish chaplaincy as a whole, but almost never about the army's treatment of Jewish servicemen or the provision of religious support.

men were sick or dying.[47] In some cases it may have reflected a crisis of faith in response to combat or to the nature of the war itself. Most commentators saw it as a symptom of the existing level of assimilation and the ongoing crisis of religion and culture which afflicted Italian Judaism in these years—a repeated theme in the Jewish press in 1916–1917.

CONCLUSION

The experience of Jews in the Italian armed forces sheds valuable light on the debate over assimilation, integration and cultural identity, as well as showing an often overlooked dimension of the secular, liberal Italian state. Many of the ways in which this experience differed from that of Jews in other combatant nations simply reflected the nature of the Italian community itself—a small, generally well educated and often prosperous group. Shortages of rabbinical candidates for chaplaincies or the high rates of service in the officer corps and specialisation among Jewish servicemen reflect the demographics of Italian Jewry as a whole. However, the specific cultural and political context also influenced the ways in which wartime service was conceived of and understood. Clearly a division had emerged even before the war within the Italian-Jewish community, between an 'assimilationist' majority and a youthful revivalism which was leaning towards Zionism. Nonetheless, from May 1915 both sides committed themselves energetically to patriotic war service. Italy's aims in the war—to 'liberate' the so-called 'unredeemed lands' of Trento, Trieste and their hinterlands from Austrian domination— were compared explicitly to the Zionist cause by revivalists, so that to be Italian and to be a Zionist were presented as intrinsically similar, related ideas. At the same time, participants reserved the right to weigh up the situation and to manage separate duties in their own way; Italianness and Jewishness were fully compatible identities but not necessarily identical, and this composite, integrated identity had, to some extent, to be constructed and also defended in wartime.

In 1918, Austro-Hungarian Jewish prisoners of war held in Italian camps began to lobby for recognition as a distinct nationality in line with the status granted to Czechs and other national groups within

---

[47] Pavan (2008), 'I rabbini italiani', 140.

the Habsburg Empire. Jewish prisoners, chiefly officers, wished to be put into separate prison camps on this basis and asked the Italian chaplains to forward their request to the secular authorities.[48] This request placed the Italian rabbis in an awkward position; having fervently used their own wartime service to demonstrate once and for all the compatibility of Jewishness and patriotism, how could they support a claim of Jewish nationhood in this way? Logically, it should have been as possible to be a loyal Austrian Jew as it was to be a loyal Italian Jew; thus, to say that Jews from the Habsburg Empire owed no duty to that state was to fundamentally risk validating the claims which Italian Jews had been so keen to defend themselves against. While these appeals were made to the chaplaincies on the basis of Zionism, they met with little in the way of a positive response (though Rodolfo Levi, who had visited the Austro-Hungarian prisoners in question, was impressed by their levels of education and religious culture). Zionist activities were in any case a minority trend within Italy before 1915 and had largely been put to one side during the war in favour of a strong patriotic adherence, part of a very practical integrationist approach which ensured that army authorities would continue to grant special leave for religious festivals. But any expression of Jewish nationhood had been carefully tailored to be perfectly compatible with Italianness and above all with military service which validated citizenship as part of the Italian nation. To posit a kind of Jewishness which explicitly worked *against* service in the armed forces of the state of one's birth—as these Habsburg prisoners were doing—was unthinkable for the army chaplains and these requests made little headway.

Instead, the war experience validated a patriotic understanding of self and community in which, for the majority, Judaism was a matter of personal faith rather than cultural or political identity. It was thus fully compatible with Italian patriotism, and military service on behalf of the state and the 'oppressed' minorities of Trento and Trieste was read as the culmination of the narrative of integration and emancipation within the structures of a secular liberal state. These distinct and yet compatible visions of the war are perfectly summarised in the inscription on a war memorial erected in the Cemetery at the Venice Lido by Chief Rabbi Adolfo Ottolenghi:

---

[48] UCEI, AC, b.27 f.157 s.f.4—1918.

Per la Grandezza d'Italia,

Per l'onore d'Israele.[49]

Acknowledgements My thanks go to Gisele Levy at the Centro Bibliografico of the *Unione delle Comunità Ebraiche Italiane*, Rome, whose assistance in conducting this research was invaluable.

---

[49] Briganti (2009), *Il contributo militare degli ebrei italiani*, 237.

'The March of the Judeans': The London Recruits of the Jewish Battalion in the First World War

Christopher Smith

In July 1917, the British Government created the 38th Battalion of the Royal Fusiliers. The unit was to be recruited mainly from the Russian Jewish population of London's East End and became known colloquially as the Jewish Battalion.[1] The decision conveniently solved an increasingly contentious wartime issue, specifically the Government's dilemma of how to deal with the 30,000 Russian Jews residing in Britain who were not serving in either the British or Russian armed forces.[2] The majority of East End 'Russian' Jews of military service age, although born in England to first-generation immigrant parents, were not naturalised

---

[1] The unit was also referred to by several different names including the Jewish Legion, the Jewish Regiment and the Judeans. For simplicity this chapter will refer in the most part to the unit as the Jewish Battalion.

[2] David Cesarani (1990), 'An Embattled Minority: The Jews of Britain During the Great War', in Tony Kushner and Kenneth Lunn, eds. *The Politics of Marginality. Race, the Radical Right and Minorities in Twentieth Century Britain* (London, Frank Cass), 66.

C. Smith (✉)
London, UK

© The Author(s) 2019
E. Madigan and G. Reuveni (eds.),
The Jewish Experience of the First World War,
https://doi.org/10.1057/978-1-137-54896-2_10

citizens and therefore exempt from conscription.[3] British born but not regarded as officially British, and not generally integrated into wider English society, non-naturalised East End Jews vigorously resisted calls to voluntarily enlist. The government hoped that the prospect of fighting with their co-religionists for the recovery of the Jewish homeland would represent a more compelling cause than 'King and Country', a notion that simply did not resonate with most non-naturalised Jews. This chapter will argue that, although it was bitterly resented at the time, the government ultimatum succeeded in physically and psychologically incorporating the population of the Jewish East End into Britain's war effort and led the community to feel as if it had a meaningful stake in the outcome of the war.

The testimonials of the veterans of the Jewish Battalion stored at the Beit Hagdudim Museum in Avichail, Israel, provide the primary source base for this chapter. These primary narrative documents offer us invaluable insights into the men's motivations for enlistment but are rendered problematic as sources by the many years that passed between the experience of service they describe and the writing of the testimonials in the late 1950s. They nonetheless offer us illuminating clues as to the soldiers' personal and political interest in the Battalion and their experiences of active service as Jewish men fighting for Britain. Crucially, moreover, the collection of over 1600 accounts of Jewish soldiers fighting in the same unit allows for a more thorough assessment of these collective experiences for the purposes of demographic data than the relatively sparse and unconnected voices of Jewish soldiers scattered across the various battalions of the British Army. The testimonials allow us to tally up collective information on important themes such as motivations for enlistment, attachment to Zionism before and after service, and engagement in post-war London society.

In assessing the testimonials, the use of these sources in Martin Watts' comprehensive 2004 history, *The Jewish Legion and the First World War*, has been taken into account.[4] In his evaluation of the social impact of the battalions on the East End, Watts concludes from the Avichail testimonials that Zionism was not a strong motivating factor for joining the

---

[3] See RJQ Adams (1986), 'Asquith's Choice: The May Coalition and the Coming of Conscription', *Journal of British Studies* 25:3, 243–263.

[4] Martin Watts (2004), *The Jewish Legion and the First World War* (Basingstoke, Palgrave Macmillan).

unit amongst East London recruits, and that service in the battalions did not encourage any particular interest in Jewish nationalism.[5] This chapter will reassess the role Zionism played in the connection between the Jewish Battalion and the East End recruits and argue that the testimonials reveal a complex picture; whilst coercion was an important factor in the enlistment of most East London Jews, a high number of the soldiers who served in the unit expressed a later interest in and involvement with Zionism which can be directly linked to their experiences of serving in the Jewish battalions in Palestine.

There were in fact three main 'Jewish' battalions in the Fusiliers: the 38th, consisting mostly of British-based recruits; the 39th, which was recruited almost exclusively in North America; and the 40th Battalion, recruited amongst the Jewish population of Palestine. The Jewish battalions have been identified as an important catalyst for Jewish nationalism amongst the American and Canadian volunteers who joined the 39th Battalion of the Royal Fusiliers in 1918.[6] Yet although the East London Jewish recruits lacked the collective zeal for Zionism of their North American comrades, the cause of Jewish nationalism was an important motivation for some London recruits and a direct consequence of their service in the unit for others. This chapter seeks to show that the Battalion had a lasting impact on social and political relations within the Jewish community of London that continued to be felt long after its official disbandment in 1922, not least by the men who served in it. It will examine their motivations for enlisting in an all-Jewish unit tasked with liberating the Holy Land and will explore the degree to which service shaped their attitudes not just towards Zionism but to Britain as their adopted home. For Jewish transferees and recruits from the East End alike, the Jewish Battalion provided meaning for their involvement in the war and instilled in many a layered set of identities: a community-based identity centred on their professions, but also a Jewish identity built on pride in participation with a Jewish cause and concurrently a British identity shaped by service—however reluctantly for many—in the British Army.

[5] Ibid., 130–131.

[6] For an account of the American and Canadian volunteers in the 39th Battalion, see Michael Keren and Shlomit Keren (2010), *We Are Coming, Unafraid: The Jewish Legions and the Promised Land in the First World War* (Plymouth, Rowman and Littlefield). For the most part, the use of 'Jewish Battalion' in this chapter will be in reference to the 38th Battalion, unless specifically stated otherwise.

LONDON JEWRY: A TALE OF TWO CITIES

The demographic make-up of London Jewry during the First World War was marked by a clear distinction between the older and more established Jewish community, which maintained a strong English identity and was heavily integrated within English society, and the more recent immigrant Jewish population, whose residence in London began predominantly after 1881 and can be characterised in 1914 as still in the process of transition between the eastern European culture of their origin and the British society of their current residence. The Jewish population of London, approximately 46,000 before the 1881 pogroms in Tsarist Russia, had risen to 135,000 by 1900, of which an estimated 120,000 lived in the East End.[7] By the turn of the century, the heavy concentration of newly-arrived immigrants in the east of the city gave rise to a situation in which about nine-tenths of the entire Jewish population of Britain lived in an area of less than two square miles.[8]

Upon arrival in London, the so-called sweated trades—usually clothing industries structured around small workshops employing cheap and plentiful low-skilled labourers—provided the only means of employment for many immigrant Jews, swallowing up as many as 70% of new arrivals. The majority found residence in the crowded streets of Whitechapel, in which a high proportion of the workshops were situated.[9] The influx of thousands of Jewish immigrants over a relatively short period of time had a major impact on the district, and by 1914, Whitechapel alone boasted four daily Yiddish newspapers. As Julia Bush has argued, 'Despite dialect variations which reflected divisions of culture and nationality amongst the Jewish East Enders, Yiddish was a unifying factor because it was universally understood'.[10] There were no fewer than 35 synagogues in East London by 1914, which formed the basis of an integral community network that not only provided daily support and catered for the religious needs of their congregations but also ensured the perpetuation

---

[7] Geoffrey Alderman (1992), *Modern British Jewry* (Oxford, Clarendon Press), 117–118.

[8] David Englander (1994), *A Documentary History of Jewish Immigrants in Britain 1840–1920* (London, Leicester University Press), 63.

[9] Todd Endelman (2002), *The Jews of Britain 1656 to 2000* (London, University of California Press), 128.

[10] Julia Bush (1980), 'East London Jews and the First World War', *London Journal* 6, 147.

of Judaism and knowledge of Hebrew through religious education.[11] This transfer of culture allowed for an imagined construction of the lost homeland to be created within the alien and hostile environment of East London in which a collective identity could be continued, albeit one which could be attacked for isolating itself from the host society.[12]

However, this was far from a crystallised process. As Anne Kershen has shown, the reimagined homeland was continually shaped by the forces of assimilation, a process that was most evident in the classrooms and playgrounds of East London schools.[13] Only 20% of immigrant Jewish children attended Jewish schools, the rest attending nondenominational state-supported schools where they interacted and socialised with English children and were introduced to the language, customs, literature, and traditions of their adopted country.[14] Born and schooled in England and with a greater grasp of English and the finer nuances of British society, the second generation of Jewish immigrants were also heavily influenced by the cultural customs and expectations of the older generation. This younger generation of immigrant Jews in the East End—the majority of whom were of military age by the later stages of the war—would become the subject of intense national pressure and local hostility during the conscription crisis of 1917. Overall, and despite their exposure to English culture, Jews of Russian origin in the East End of London were largely indifferent to concepts of British patriotism and were generally hostile to attempts to mobilise them for Britain's war effort. For although the fifteen years or so before the outbreak of the Great War saw a gradual process of acculturation within the Jewish East End, the community in 1914 could still be broadly characterised as a community in transition.

The majority of English Jews in London, those who belonged to the longer-standing community, resided in the central western districts of the metropolis. Many, if not quite all, of these Jewish 'West Enders' considered themselves to be English in nationality and culture.[15]

[11] Ibid., 147.

[12] John Marriott (2012), *Beyond the Tower: A History of East London* (London, Yale University Press), 231.

[13] See Anne J. Kershen (2004), 'The Construction of Home in a Spitalfields Landscape', *Landscape Research* 29:3, 261–275.

[14] Endelman (2002), *Jews of Britain*, 149.

[15] Alderman (1992), *British Jewry*, 200–205.

As Sam Johnson has argued 'in terms of Anglo-Jewish ambition, the greatest achievement was to be wholly unrecognisable as a Jew'.[16] Chaim Lewis, a Jewish resident of Soho at the beginning of the twentieth century, recalled: 'Many of the Jews who came into the West End began to show early signs of assimilation. They no longer observed the Sabbath. Well, it happened in the East End too, but because they had greater numbers there was always a stronger reservoir of orthodox Jews who adhered to the strict tenets of Judaism. Whereas in the West End you saw the loosening of religious ties even among the newly arrived immigrants'.[17] Tellingly, Lewis also recalled that his father regarded this community as distinctly Anglo-centric and 'used to call them the *Englischer Yehudim*, the English Jews'.[18] The indistinctive features of the integrated Jewish community in early twentieth-century London were thus in fact a point of distinction, and the product of a nuanced but concerted process of 'de-emphasising foreignness' within London Jewry.[19]

The acceleration of Jewish immigration into Britain from Russia and the Tsarist-controlled lands after 1881 threatened to reverse this process. This great influx of Eastern European Jews prompted the established London-Jewish community to create and shape social institutions such as the Jewish Board of Guardians, the Jews' Free School, and the Jews Temporary Shelter, as well as the Board of Deputies of British Jews 'through which to introduce to poor and alien Jews the values of the English middle class'.[20] The Anglo-Jewish Association and other philanthropic institutions were genuinely committed to nurturing the new arrivals on humanitarian grounds, but anxiety remained within Anglo-Jewry regarding British concerns about such issues as poverty, crime, and degeneration. This anxiety was heightened by the popular British perception that it was Anglo-Jewry's responsibility to police the immigrant

[16] Sam Johnson (2011), *Pogroms, Peasants Jews: Britain and East Europe's 'Jewish Question', 1867–1925* (Basingstoke, Palgrave Macmillan), 207.

[17] Chaim Lewis (1965), *A Soho Address. [An Autobiography]* (London, Victor Gollancz), 23–26.

[18] Ibid., 23–26.

[19] Susan Tananbaum (2014), *Jewish Immigrants in London, 1880–1939* (London, Pickering & Chatto), 24.

[20] Juliet Steyn (1999), *The Jew: Assumptions of Identity* (London, Cassel), 75.

population.[21] The majority of this 'West End' Jewish community overwhelmingly felt themselves to be English, and thus engaged in the war effort with unqualified patriotism from the earliest days of the conflict. Importantly, however, the repeated controversies during the war that placed emphasis on their status as Jews rather than Englishmen and women tended to diminish this patriotism.

The prospect of a Jewish Battalion formed of Russian Jews was opposed by the majority of the Jewish establishment, and was met with indifference and occasional hostility from the men that were meant to fill its ranks.[22] An all-Jewish unit was at odds with the discreet policy of integration the Anglo-Jewish leadership had followed since emancipation in 1858, and also threatened to define Anglo-Jewry's response to the war, distracting attention from the above average enlistment of English Jews since August 1914.[23] For many in the established Anglo-Jewish community, the Jewish Battalion was thus the antithesis of the proud assertion made by the *Jewish Chronicle* at the beginning of the war: 'We Jews are serving in the King's Forces at this time of strife and strain for the Empire shoulder to shoulder with our British fellow-citizens without distinction of race or creed'.[24]

RELUCTANT ZIONISTS: THE JEWISH BATTALION, 1914–1917

Efforts to raise a Jewish Battalion in Britain first emerged just weeks after Britain's declaration of war on Germany. In August 1914, an energetic Jewish army officer, Captain Walter Joseph Webber, attempted to mobilise the interest of East London's Russian Jews by campaigning to recruit 2000 of them for service in a Jewish unit. At a crowded gathering at the Pavilion Theatre in Whitechapel at the end of August, Webber attempted to persuade his audience by playing on their sense of obligation to the country that had sheltered them from persecution, specifically those who

---

[21] Yael Granot-Bein (2010), 'An Urgent Social Problem? Jewish Juvenile Delinquents in Turn-of-Twentieth-Century London', *Journal of Modern Jewish Studies* 9, 369.

[22] Watts (2004), *Jewish Legion*, 47–52.

[23] David Feldman (1994), *Englishmen and Jews: Social Relations and Political Culture 1840–1914* (London, Yale University Press), 16.

[24] *Jewish Chronicle*, 2 October 1914, 5.

had fled the Tsarist pogroms in Bialystok, Kishinev and Odessa between 1903 and 1908.[25] Webber argued that the most effective way to demonstrate this gratitude and counter accusations of Jews 'shirking' their duty was to enlist in a British Army battalion specifically made up of their co-religionists, which would serve as a shining symbol of the immigrant Jewish community's commitment to Britain's cause.[26] Webber's campaign sought to emphasise the 'Jewishness' of the proposed brigade, and was supported by Yiddish recruitment posters printed in favourable publications.[27]

Despite his energy and organisation, Captain Webber's efforts were doomed to failure when the War Office curtly pointed out at the beginning of September that the men could not enlist in the British Army as they were not naturalised citizens.[28] Indeed, many Russian Jews eager to enlist in the British Army had already been refused on the grounds of their nationality. *The Jewish Chronicle* reported on 28 August 1914 that Russian Jews were being turned away from a recruitment station in Tower Hill: 'A large proportion of the Jewish population of this country are of foreign birth, and, as such, are not eligible for enlistment. The recruiting sergeant at Tower Hill mentioned in fact, that an 'enormous lot', of foreign born Jews had come forward but had to be refused on that account'.[29]

Later in 1914, a Russian Jewish journalist called Vladimir Jabotinsky would renew Captain Webber's efforts to recruit a Jewish military unit. Jabotinsky saw the formation of a Jewish Battalion as a means to an end, specifically as a tool for forging a Jewish homeland. For Jabotinsky, the Battalion idea was an extension of Zionist policy and a weapon with which the movement could arm itself in an increasingly militarised world. Born into an assimilated and relatively secular middle-class family in Odessa in 1880, Jabotinsky developed a fierce Jewish nationalism after witnessing the Kishinev pogrom in 1903. He was later active in promoting the Zionist cause as a journalist and helped in

[25] *JC*, 4 September 1914, 5.

[26] Ibid.

[27] *JC*, 4 September 1914. Recruitment poster on p. 4, repeated regularly until the end of the year.

[28] David Cesarani (1994), *The Jewish Chronicle and Anglo-Jewry 1841–1991* (Cambridge, Cambridge University Press), 114.

[29] *JC*, 28 August 1914.

establishing the Jewish self-defence organisations across Russia during the pogroms.[30]

Arriving in Alexandria in December 1914 on the pretext of reporting on the local response to the Sultan's Jihad against the British Empire, Jabotinsky found a willing and politically uncontroversial source of Jewish men to serve in what would become the Zion Mule Corps. Learning from a British customs official that almost a thousand Jews had recently arrived from Jaffa from where they had been expelled by the Turkish authorities, Jabotinsky immediately dropped his journalistic mission and became a recruiter. At a meeting he organised with local Jewish businessmen and enthusiasts for the project on 2 March 1915, the decision was made to 'recruit from the young men in the camps a Jewish unit to fight on the side of the British Army on the Palestinian front'.[31] According to Elias Gilner, there were approximately 1200 Jewish refugees from Palestine in the British camps at Alexandria. Within a week of the meeting, more than 200 men had pledged to join the Jewish unit.[32]

Very little information regarding the men who served in the Zion Mule Corps exists outside of the Avichail testimonials, with the ad hoc nature of their recruitment meaning that no official unit records, such as war diaries or intelligence logs, were kept.[33] The *British Jewry book of Honour*, compiled by the Anglo-Jewish army chaplain, Michael Adler, lists the volunteers as mainly 'students and workmen'.[34] Some, such as Isaic Mouchkatine—a native of Vitebsk in Belorussia—had been forced to leave the Russian Empire 'due to revolutionary activity'.[35] Others were fleeing from persecution, such as Jack Knopp, whose family survived the first and second pogroms in Kishinev before emigrating.[36] The British military authorities in Egypt would only agree to use the men

[30] See Shmuel Katz (1996), *Lone Wolf: A Biography of Vladimir Jabotinsky* (New York, Barricade Books).

[31] Elias Gilner (1969), *War and Hope: A History of the Jewish Legion* (New York, Herzl), 36.

[32] Ibid., 35.

[33] Watts (2004), *Jewish Legion*, 27.

[34] Michael Adler (1922), *British Jewry Book of Honour* (London, Caxton 1922), 63.

[35] Isaic Mouchkatine, Avichail Testimonial.

[36] Jack Knopp, Avichail Testimonial.

as a supply corps as their experience best matched handling and equipping mules for transport.[37]

The importance of the Zion Mule Corps to the future prospects of recruiting a regiment of British Jews was ultimately subtle but significant. The *Jewish Chronicle* was the only British paper to report on the establishment of the regiment in April 1915.[38] However, the undeniable existence of a British Army unit formed from an exiled and nationless group of refugee Jews would provide powerful evidence of the possibilities of success for Jabotinsky's vision, and the bravery of the corps under fire served as a clear collective disavowal of the old slur of Jewish cowardice.

After leaving the Zion Mule Corps in April 1915, Jabotinsky settled in London to continue his campaign.[39] The War Office announced in December 1915 that British-born Jews of friendly alien parentage, and thus the majority of East End Jews of military age, were now eligible for service.[40] As the new year dawned, the British Government became increasingly concerned by the growing public resentment against non-enlisted Russian Jews in Britain, which accelerated rapidly following the introduction of conscription in January 1916. In the spring and summer of 1916, the Home Secretary, Herbert Samuel, Britain's first nominally-practising Jewish cabinet minister, laid the groundwork for a Military Convention with Russia which would present friendly aliens in Britain (mainly Russian Jews) with a choice between conscription into the British Army or deportation to their country of origin (or that of their parents) or enlistment in their own army.[41] Ultimately, the need to consult with the Russian Government and to test the legislative viability of the proposal delayed the implementation of the Convention until July 1917.[42] In the meantime, the ominous threat of future deportation back to Russia was expected to boost the voluntary enlistment of Russian Jews into the British forces.

---

[37] Watts (2004), *Jewish Legion*, 23–24.

[38] *JC*, 30 April 1915.

[39] Cited in Vladimir Jabotinsky (1945), *The Story of the Jewish Legion* (New York, Bernard Ackerman), 50–56.

[40] War Office communique 18 December 1915, Cited in Watts (2004), *Jewish Legion*, 56.

[41] Englander, *History of Jewish Immigrants*, 327–329.

[42] Watts (2004), *Jewish Legion*, 64.

However, the proposed Convention met with open hostility from both the immigrant community, with the formation of the Foreign Jews Protection Committee, as well as criticism from within established Jewry, including the *Jewish Chronicle*, which complained that the Convention 'would be an exchange of freedom for oppression' and argued that 'the formation of a Jewish Battalion on the lines of the Zion Mule Corps would adequately meet the case of the Russian Jews'.[43] Samuel still held out hope that the compulsion or deportation of Russian Jews would not be necessary and that the threat of deportation would help encourage voluntary solutions.[44] Hoping to boost volunteerism within the immigrant Jewish population, the Home Secretary approved (without officially backing) Jabotinsky's recruitment drives for a Jewish unit in the East End in the summer and autumn of 1916. However, in a series of public meetings and rallies during October 1916, the recruitment drive for a Jewish Battalion received only three hundred firm pledges to enlist.[45] Recruitment may have been hampered by efforts from within the community to prevent enlistment over the preceding months; in August the *Jewish Chronicle* reported the arrest of three men circulating the Yiddish language newspaper *The Worker's Friend* which urged Jews not to enlist.[46] Jabotinsky himself suspected that elements within established Jewry such as the arch anti-Zionist Claude Montefiore—the president of the Anglo-Jewish Association— were using their network of informers and agitators to disrupt meetings and misinform the Russian Jewish community about the feasibility of a Jewish Battalion.[47] The diverse opposition Jabotinsky encountered reveals the complexity of the Battalion's impact on Jewish politics in London during the war. *The Worker's Friend* and Claude Montefiore agreed on little beyond a mutual desire to render the Jewish Battalion scheme unworkable, so both sought to stir up anti-military sentiment within the Jewish East End.

The decisive reason for the campaign's failure, however, was that it was simply deeply unpopular with Russian Jews. Special Branch agent

---

[43] *JC*, 14 April 1916.
[44] Watts (2004), *Jewish Legion*, 64.
[45] Ibid., 77.
[46] *JC*, 4 August 1916.
[47] Jabotinsky (1943), *Jewish Legion*, 77; On Montefiore see Watts (2004), *Jewish Legion*, 62.

Sergeant Albers was sent to monitor recruitment meetings held on 16 and 17 October and reported:

> The audience at both these places consisted of the Jewish element, chiefly Russians of military age. From the commencement of the proceedings in each case, they were antagonistic towards the speakers and a considerable amount of booing and hissing greeted them ... At both the meetings it was found necessary to have the hall cleared by police. In my opinion it appears useless to hold these gatherings as the Jewish folk seem to greatly resent the arguments put forward, and in view of the hostile attitude of the crowd, no good purpose could be served by continuing to advocate Mr. Jabotinsky's propaganda.[48]

A sizeable number of Russian Jews had been keen to enlist in the excitement of the first weeks of the war in 1914, but rejection by the Army of those who attempted to sign up on naturalisation and fitness grounds led to resentment and indifference to the idea of serving, which was reinforced by increasing awareness of the grim reality of a soldier's lot on the Western Front.[49] The lack of a push factor of friends' enlistment, a sense of patriotic duty, family pressure, or, crucially, conscription, all militated against enlistment, but the relative success of the Jewish trades in wartime may have represented the major disincentive to volunteering.[50] According to the minutes of a Board of Guardians meeting that took place in December 1915: 'The Working Classes have had a more prosperous time than for many years past'.[51] As Eugene Black has argued, Russian Jews 'regarded recruitment as a thinly disguised scheme to take away their hard-won East End homes, jobs and sanctuary'.[52]

After one particularly hostile public meeting in Whitechapel that October, Jabotinsky was told by a Jewish anarchist: 'How much longer do you intend to knock your head against the wall? You do not understand a thing about our boys. You explain to them they should do this thing "as Jews" that thing "as Englishmen" and that other "as men".

---

[48] PRO HO 45/10819/318095/112a Special Branch Report, 18 October 1916.

[49] See John Rodker (1932), *Memoirs of Other Fronts* (London, Putnam), 112.

[50] Anne J. Kershen (2004), *Landscape Research*, 261–275.

[51] Board of Guardians minutes 1915 cited in Bush (1980), *Behind the Lines*, 170.

[52] Eugene C. Black (1988), *The Social Politics of Anglo-Jewry 1880–1920* (Oxford, Basil Blackwood), 374.

Nonsense. We are not Jews. We are not Englishmen. We are not men. What are we? We are tailors'.[53] Whilst there was increasing Zionist sympathy in radical and intellectual Jewish circles, Zionism had not penetrated sufficiently amongst the majority of male Jewish youths to encourage them to give up their hard-won jobs.[54] That East End Jewish youth rejected a national identity in favour of a professional one fits with the evolution process of a displaced ethnic minority and the traditional importance immigrants place on financial security over integration. Jabotinsky would be forced from his experiences in the East End in the autumn of 1916 to admit the majority of the recruits to the Jewish Battalion would have to be compelled to join rather than volunteer for service.[55]

Following the agreement of the Military Service Convention between Britain and Russia on 16 July 1917, the Government was under greater pressure than ever to be seen to be enforcing this policy.[56] The closure of the Foreign Jews Protection Committee and the arrest of its leader Abraham Bezalel in July 1917 indicate the adoption of a tougher approach.[57] Then, in short order, and despite the hostility of the Jewish East End to the scheme, the War Office issued the following press-release on 27 July:

Arrangements are now nearing completion for the formation of a Jewish Regiment of Infantry. Experienced British Officers are being selected to fill the higher appointments in the unit, and instructions have already been issued with a view to the transfer to this unit of Jewish soldiers, with knowledge of Yiddish or Russian languages, who are now serving in British Regiments.[58]

The Government's endorsement of the Jewish Battalion project was born of the pragmatic realisation that it offered the best resolution to the drawn-out affair of the non-enlistment of Russian Jews, which was

---

[53] Jabotinsky (1943), *Jewish Legion*, 61.
[54] See William J. Fishman (2004), *East End Jewish Radicals, 1875–1914* (Nottingham, Five Leaves).
[55] Watts (2004), *Jewish Legion*, 82.
[56] Ibid., 97.
[57] Watts (2004), *Jewish Legion*, 97.
[58] *JC*, 3 August 1917.

increasingly provoking the resentment of the wider population. On 17 July, *The Times* reported that in Stepney alone, there were 4000 Jewish absentees 'avoiding service by every conceivable means' and just over a week later, the paper ran a report on the local unrest caused by the issue amongst the Gentile population:

> Eight thousand Jewish aliens of military age are still living as civilians in Stepney and Hackney alone... "The ferment down here," a well-known Hackney resident said yesterday, "is rapidly becoming serious, and if the Government deals with the situation with a strong hand they will have the full support of the British population... [On the Russian Jews] They do not want to go to Russia. They do not want to fight for anybody ... Conscience has not prevented them from making money out of war contracts and war work".[59]

The difficulties of incorporating large numbers of non-naturalised men of a minority culture, religion, and language into the British Army rendered the idea of the Jewish Battalion quite attractive to the War Office. In effect, Russian Jews were presented with a third option: if deportation back to Russia or serving in the main British Army proved undesirable, they had a final choice of serving in an all-Jewish Regiment. This was as close to volunteerism as Jabotinsky could hope for, but Russian Jews clearly faced compulsion to choose one of these three options.

THE RECRUITS: MOTIVATIONS AND EXPERIENCE

At the end of August 1917, the War Office sanctioned the creation of a depot at Crown Hill in Plymouth to which the Jewish conscripts would be sent to create the first unit: the 38th Battalion of the Royal Fusiliers (the 39th and 40th battalions would be recruited in North America and Palestine respectively). Despite initially sluggish numbers of recruits and transfers,[60] the Battalion reached its required target of 1200 members by November, and, after intensive training, was ready for deployment overseas by the beginning of February.[61]

[59] *The Times*, 17 and 25 July 1917.
[60] Jabotinsky (1943), *Jewish Legion*, 101.
[61] Watts (2004), *Jewish Legion*, 123.

It is worth considering the factors that motivated the men who chose to join the 38th battalion in 1917. Only a fifth of the 7000 soldiers, recorded as serving in the various battalions of the Jewish Legion, are represented in the archives of the Beit Hagudim Museum, but this is still a significant number. The Museum houses 1672 testimonials, of which 425 were made by soldiers, or the relatives of soldiers, who served with the 38th battalion to which the majority of the London-based recruits were sent. As an overview, the testimonials of the London recruits reveal some expected and some rather more surprising pieces of information. Martin Watts' account of the testimonials affirms that over two-thirds of the men recruited in Britain were in fact born in Britain. Watts also gives the average age of the recruits as 20 years old. This appears to correspond with the evidence that the vast majority of Jewish immigration from Russia took place in the late Victorian period and certainly before the Aliens Act of 1905. He also states that the recruits from Britain demonstrated little or no allegiance to Zionism.[62]

However, a different picture emerges when only troops recruited directly from London are examined. From a random selection of 54 veterans who had been living in London in 1917 and who served in the 38th Battalion, 24 were born in England, 21 were listed as born within the Russian Empire and a further 9 did not list their country of birth. Less than half, therefore, were born in Britain and the majority of these had served in the British Army before transferring into the Jewish Battalion (16 out of 24, who listed prior service with other British Army regiments). These figures reveal that Russian Jews from the East End of London were actively prominent in the first drafts of the Jewish Battalion and cast doubt on the suggestion made by David Cesarani that the majority of males of military age returned to Russia in August following the Military Service Convention, or were interned in enemy alien camps on the south coast.[63] The impression that the Battalion contained many non-naturalised foreign Jews is further evidenced by the fact that a significant number of the men in its ranks had difficulty understanding English. According to a post-war report issued by The Jewish Regiment Committee (formed in August 1917 to raise donations to alleviate the

<hr>

[62] Ibid., 130–133.

[63] Cesarani (1990), *Embattled Minority*, 68. Watts has shown that the *JC* report of 25 January 1918 that 8000 Russian Jews were being held at an internment camp in Maidstone was incorrect and that the figure was nearer to 800. See Watts (2004), *Jewish Legion*, 126.

needs of the new recruits), it was necessary to send out text books to the camp in Plymouth and later to Palestine 'For the teaching of English to foreign-born members of the Regiment'. The report also stated that many of the literary materials sent to the Battalion had to be translated into Yiddish, Russian, and other Eastern European dialects.[64]

What is also revealing is that, contrary to Watts' assertion of a lack of Zionist affiliation on behalf of the recruits, 17 of the 54 London recruits from the same survey make at least some reference to Zionist activity in their testimonials.[65] These range from relocation to Palestine after demobilisation, such as in the case of Frederick Phillips, whose testimonial lists him as 'a member of an old Anglo-Jewish family and the only member sympathising with the Zionist cause'[66]; or Mark Kerstein, a 'bespoke gentleman's tailor' from Whitechapel referred to as 'A staunch Zionist at heart' who 'had a deep love of his Jewish religion and its traditions'.[67] Others mention more direct involvement in Zionist politics. Captain Samuel Barnet, for example, found employment as a military judge in the British protectorate of Palestine after the war but resigned after accusing the administration of anti-Zionist bias.[68] Whilst this does not reveal a collective Jewish nationalism on the part of the London recruits to rival that of the American and Canadian recruits of the 39th Battalion, it would suggest that the Jewish Battalion attracted and nurtured proactive Zionist supporters from the East End of London, but for the most part only after compulsion had been threatened.[69]

In addition, there were high levels of transfers of Jewish soldiers serving in other units into the new battalion, with about half of the men who joined the regiment in 1917 having transferred from other units, the majority of whom were English Jews.[70] Indeed, the circular letter to representatives of the Jewish community sent by Myer Landa, the official

[64] *The Jewish Regiment Committee August 1917 to August 1919* (London 1919), 13.

[65] Of the 54 London-based recruits identifiable from the testimonials for the 38th, 17 mention Zionist activity, 14 displayed activity alluding to a strong British patriotism before and after service, and 14 did not display signs of either.

[66] Frederick Phillips Testimonial, Avichail.

[67] Mark Kerstein Testimonial, Avichail.

[68] Samuel Barnet Testimonial, Avichail.

[69] Shlomit Keren and Michael Keren (2007), 'The Jewish Legions in the First World War as a Locus of Identity Formation', *Journal of Modern Jewish Studies* 6:1, 69–83.

[70] Avichail Testimonials.

secretary of the Jewish Battalion, alluded to these transferees, states: 'The large number of applicants from officers, non-coms, and men for transfer to the regiment indicates a strong sentiment in favour of the scheme on the part of those affected - those in the army or due to join. It proves also that English-born Jews of all classes are anxious to be associated with their Russian brothers'.[71]

There was a clear desire on the part of the transferees to serve with their co-religionists and, on the whole, an easy coexistence between Russian and English Jews prevailed in the camp at Crown Hill and later on campaign.[72] Importantly, Russian Jews already serving in the British Army expressed an interest in the Jewish Battalion project. One such serving soldier was Private J. Lancle, who wrote the following to Landa in September 1917: 'Being of Jewish birth, Polish born in Wilna, Poland, Russia, of Russian parentage and descent, I would very much like to transfer to the Jewish regiment amongst my co-religionists as I am at present the only Jewish private in our battalion'.[73] Others such as 2nd Lieutenant H. V. Oleef sought permission from their commanding officer to transfer to the Jewish units, his CO, Jack Davidson, writing to Landa on his behalf that he was 'desirous of joining the Jewish Regiment. He is a splendid fellow full of sympathetic interest in the Jewish cause and widely experienced in East End Jewish club life'.[74] Whilst most Jewish transferees were British born, these examples are a reminder that some Russian Jewish men had enlisted or sought commissions in the British Army before the issue of Russian Jewish conscription reached a crisis point in 1917. The experiences of isolation and loneliness hinted at in the reasoning of private Lancle's desire to join the unit corresponded with the difficulties and occasional experiences of antisemitism suffered by Jewish soldiers serving in the British Army.[75]

---

[71] Circular letter 24 August 1917, AJA MS 185.

[72] J.H. Patterson (1922), *With the Judeans in the Palestine Campaign* (London, Hutchinson), 23.

[73] Pte J Lancle 58th T.R.B glamp, letter to Landa 3 September 1917, Anglo-Jewish Archive (Southampton University) AJA MS 185.

[74] Letter to Landa from Jack Davidson 27 August 1917, AJA MS 185.

[75] For an example of antisemitism in the British Army during the Great War, see Myer (1979), *Soldiering of Sorts* (London, Imperial War Museum), 28. For the broader difficulties of Jewish soldiers in the British Army see Gavin Schaffer (2012), 'Unmasking the 'Muscle Jew': The Jewish Soldier in British War Service 1899–1945', *Patterns of Prejudice*, 46.

The men who transferred voluntarily into the unit are important in reveal-ing the symbolic and actual appeal of the Jewish Battalion. For these Jewish soldiers already serving in the British Army, the motivation for service in the Jewish Battalion ranged from the desire to be part of a momentous Jewish movement, or, more simply, as in the case of David Dobrin from Hackney who had served in the Duke of Cornwall's Light Infantry, to serve with fellow Jews. As Dobrin recalled, 'This was the happiest time of my army service amongst my own people'.[76]

Of course, the response to Landa's letter calling for Jewish soldiers to join the Jewish Battalion from regular British Army units was not univer-sally positive. One man wrote to him in November 1917 stating, 'I am not in sympathy with the movement which created a Jewish Regiment. I have two sons serving as officers in the army and as they and other Jews are on an equal footing with every other denomination I fail to see why the army should be divided into religious sections'.[77] One officer who shared similar doubts regarding the Jewish Battalion project was one of the transferees, Henry D. Myer. Born in 1892 to a wealthy Jewish family in the affluent London district of Bayswater, Myer rejected his father's offer to send him to the Jewish House at Clifton College, opting instead for the altogether more Anglican traditions of Westminster School.[78] By his own admission, he had little interest in his Jewish heritage and con-sidered himself a fervently patriotic Englishman with a particular pen-chant for the English military tradition fostered by childhood memories of Kitchener's march on Sudan and the wild excitement of the relief of Mafeking.[79] Myer joined the Territorial Army in 1908 and served with them initially in France upon the outbreak of the Great War before gain-ing a commission with the City of London Rifles and was wounded at the Battle of Loos in September 1915 and later witnessed the full hor-ror of the war in the Passchendaele offensive during the summer and autumn of 1917. Whilst convalescing after another injury, Myer received a telegraph from the War Office requesting his transfer into the Jewish Battalion.[80] Despite accepting the commission, Myer had his doubts: 'I felt that every anglicised, or even partly anglicised Jew would have long

---

[76] David Dobrin Testimonial, Avichail.
[77] Hillient Hoch letter to Landa 22 November 1917, AJA MS 185.
[78] Myer (1979), *Soldiering of Sorts*, 4.
[79] Ibid.
[80] Ibid., 93.

ago joined the Armed services, for this had been my experience and that of my older cousins and friends doing social [work] among these communities. I reckoned that in London, Leeds, Manchester, Glasgow, Cardiff and the like, the men would be of poor material in a military sense'.[81]

Myer joined too late to sail with the 38th Battalion in March 1918 but was assigned as an officer of the 40th Battalion. Whilst praising his fellow officers, he was scathing of the regular Jewish recruits, who, in March 1918, consisted of 400 men left over from the 38th. Many of these rankers had been tailors, cobblers, or cabinet makers in the East End, and Myer was condescendingly doubtful about their aptitude for soldiering:

> [T]hese men were types to whom soldiers and soldiering were anathema and were to be evaded at almost any cost. The daily sick parade consisted on average, of 100 men ... It would have reflected badly on the Anglo-Jewish community had it been ventilated in the National Press, because few people would have understood how men, who and whose relatives owed so much to the hospitality they had enjoyed in the United Kingdom, could have refrained from showing gratitude in the form of sharing burdens, which fell upon all Britishers.[82]

Myer was merely repeating the concerns expressed by Anglo-Jewish leaders that the Russian Jewish recruits and their poor performance in action would taint the Jewish community as a whole. But his repeated assertion that the recruits were 'poor material' suggests that at least some British Jews shared Gentile stereotypes of the weak nature of immigrant Jewish manhood and were concerned that this would feed wider caricatures of Jewish physical weakness on the part of the community at large.

Before embarkation to Palestine, the regiment was granted the honour of a march through the East End of London, from Tower Hill through Aldgate and Whitechapel and ending in Stepney. The *Jewish Chronicle* celebrated the upcoming parade with unbridled enthusiasm and hyperbole: 'It will be the first time that a Regiment consisting entirely of Jews will have tramped the streets of England, and the march of the Judeans will be a picturesque reminder of how history is being

---

[81] Ibid., 79.
[82] Ibid., 98.

made in these days, here and in Palestine'.[83] On Monday 4 February 1918 the Battalion paraded through the heart of the Jewish East End, and in contrast to the hostile reception that greeted Jabotinsky in the dark days of failed recruitment meetings, the Russian Jewish community greeted the Battalion with overwhelming support. According to a report that appeared in the *Jewish Chronicle*:

> There were tens of thousands of Jews in the streets ... women crying with joy, old Jews with fluttering beards murmuring, 'shehechianu' [the thanksgiving prayer for 'reaching this day'] ... the boys ... shoulder to shoulder, their bayonets dead level ... proud, drunk with the national anthem, with the noise of the crowds, and with their sense of a holy mission.[84]

This is not the response we might expect from a community that had vainly resisted a war eventually thrust upon it, and reveals, at least after the event, a good degree of communal support for the Battalion and its cause. The enthusiastic public response to the march past mirrored the positive reception enjoyed by the 17th Stepney and Poplar Battalion during the unit's marches through the East End in August 1914.[85] However, the crowds cheering the 38th battalion in February 1918 were not the optimistic and excitable masses of August 1914 that steadfastly supported Britain's cause, but members of a nationally maligned immigrant community that had shown indifference to Britain's war aims and were by 1918 generally very aware of the horror of modern industrial warfare. Despite this, the Battalion's commander J. H. Patterson recalled: 'As we approached the Mile End Road the scenes of enthusiasm redoubled, and London's Ghetto fairly rocked with military fervour and roared its welcome to its own. Jewish banners were hung out everywhere, and it certainly was a scene unparalleled in the history of any previous battalion'.[86]

After the march, the 38th Battalion embarked from Portsmouth and sailed via Italy to Egypt. The experience of the Jewish battalion was mixed and certainly did not live up to the expectations of Jabotinsky

---

[83] *JC*, 1 February 1918.

[84] *JC*, 8 February 1918.

[85] *East London Observer*, 15 August 1914.

[86] Patterson (1922), *With the Judeans*, 33.

and the project's supporters at home.[87] The men of the 38th acquitted themselves well on active service, particularly during the Jordan Valley offensive in June 1918, but were repeatedly side-lined and given inconsequential and laborious tasks, something Patterson attributed to an element of prejudice towards the Battalion within the Egyptian Expeditionary Force and influenced by certain elements within established Jewry hostile to the Battalion—revealing that the deep divisions opened up by the Jewish Battalion scheme within the community had never fully healed.[88] The Battalion had also missed sharing in the glory and publicity of the fall of Jerusalem the previous November, and the whole Middle-Eastern theatre was, to a large extent, overshadowed in the British public's perception of the war by the dramatic and decisive developments on the Western Front. Following the Armistice with Turkey in November 1918, the three Jewish battalions acted as a peace-keeping force in the newly established British Protectorate of Palestine before becoming surplus to military requirements and disbanding in 1922.

CONCLUSION

The majority of the recruits raised in Britain returned there after demobilisation and never went back to Palestine. This has been contrasted with the high proportion of American and Canadian troops who remained in Palestine, and has been cited by Watts and by Michael and Schlomit Keren as evidence that the Jewish recruits from Britain were not interested in Palestine or Jewish nationalism and had been compelled into service.[89] The reality was more complex: although the majority of non-naturalised 'Russian' Jews living in Britain avoided enlistment until the Convention forced their hand, they chose to serve in the Jewish Battalion over returning to revolutionary Russia or serving elsewhere in the British Army. Service in the Jewish Battalion, moreover, awakened in many a Jewish nationalism, that was revealed in examples of involvement in Zionist organisations and activities upon returning to England and declarations of solidarity with the Jewish settlers in Palestine and

[87] Watts (2004), *Jewish Legion*, 198–200.
[88] Patterson (1922), *With the Judeans*, 57.
[89] Keren (2007), *The Jewish Legions*, 69–83.

lamentations that circumstances had not allowed them to return that litter the testimonials at Avichail. For instance, Israel Bernswig, whose testimonial stated that he returned to England after he was demobilised in 1920, sadly 'intended to make his home in Israel, but death prevented [the] realisation of his plans'.[90] David Dobrin's account also reveals a wistful desire to settle in Palestine: 'I visited the then Jewish colonies and was greatly impressed with them ... I liked the country and if only [I] had a little encouragement would have settled there. However, that was not to be'.[91] The period of service in Palestine between 1918 and 1922 represented for the vast majority of the Battalion's overseas recruits their first experience of visiting the Holy Land, and their interaction with the local Jewish communities and exposure to the activities of Zionist groups in the region helped shape their political and personal connection to the future state of Israel after their return to Britain.

The testimonials also hint that service in the British Army and pride in victory won bred a certain amount of British patriotism in a number of the recruits, with involvement in wider society outside of the traditional spheres of the immigrant community listed in post-war activities, including, importantly, a sense of pride in performing air raid warden and firefighting services during the Second World War. According to Julius Bernstein, for example, 'I also served as an air raid warden throughout the Second World War with the London Civil Defence', and Jack Bieckler, who arrived in London from Poland only in 1912—working as a master tailor before and after service in the Jewish Battalion—who also served as an Air Raid Precautions officer during the later conflict.[92]

One of the more surprising transformations affected by service in the Jewish Battalion was experienced by Henry Myer. Myer had reluctantly transferred to the Battalion out of a sense of duty but was impressed by the commitment of the Palestinian recruits with whom he came in contact in the 40th Battalion, describing them as 'well developed mentally, and physically they are men' and 'worthy representatives of the race', and was impressed with their commitment to Zionism.[93] Writing to his fiancée

[90] Israel Bernsweig Testimonial, Avichail.

[91] Dobrin, Avichail Testimonial.

[92] Julius Bernstein, Avichail Testimonial; Jack Bieckler Testimonial, Avichail.

[93] Myer (1979), *Soldiering of Sorts*, 125.

Louie Solomons in January 1919, he insisted, 'I am only a sympathizer with their views and not an active Zionist', but sympathy with Zionism represented quite a turnaround for the ultra-patriotic Englishman who had previously shown only muted acknowledgement of his Jewish ancestry.[94] This might also be explained, to an extent, by his earlier experience within the British Army in France: 'there was a substantial number of Gentiles who either did not understand or did not want to associate with, or even disliked British Jews, no matter how assimilated they were, or appeared to be'.[95]

Antisemitism within the British Army dimmed for those British Jews who experienced it a previously strong sense of Britishness, which was replaced in the case of Henry Myer by a lost Jewish identity nurtured by his experiences with the Jewish Battalion in the Holy Land. The issue of the Jewish Battalion further widened the already deep divisions opened by the war between the established community and the immigrant population of London, and brought into the open conflict between the pro- and anti-Zionist camps that would dominate Jewish politics in the interwar years.[96] The legacy of the Jewish Battalion proved to be neither the disastrous humiliation of the whole community that opponents of the project feared nor the crowning glory of the Jewish war effort that Jabotinsky and others had hoped for, and the unit was largely lost in the euphoria and upheavals of the end of the war.

The Jewish Battalion did, however, represent a tangible watershed for the immigrant Jewish community of London and contributed to the painful process of integration into British society through its belated sacrifice in the war, attested by the many recruits who did not return home.[97] Its existence proved a powerful source of civic pride for the Jewish community, and inspired a sense of shared struggle alongside the wider Gentile society that proved a baptism of fire for a community previously in transition.

[94] Letter to Louie Solomons 16 January 1919. *Soldiering of Sorts*, 159.

[95] Ibid., 79.

[96] See Mark Levene (1992), *War, Jews, and the New Europe: The Diplomacy of Lucien Wolf 1914–1919* (Oxford, Oxford University Press).

[97] See Jewish war dead listed in Adler (1922), *British Jewry Book of Honour*.

PART III

Post-war Memory and Commemoration

The Female Side of War: The Experience and Memory of the Great War in Italian-Jewish Women's Ego-Documents

Ruth Nattermann

When first considering the question of how Jewish women in Italy experienced the Great War, one might spontaneously think of one of the most prominent Italian-Jewish women of the period, Mussolini's mistress Margherita Sarfatti, whose transformation from nationalist to fascist adherent had its origin precisely during the years of the First World War. This sophisticated writer and art critic, who originally had been an opponent of the war, followed Mussolini's ideological development when, as a supporter of Italian intervention, he left the Socialist Party in 1914 and founded the journal *Il popolo d'Italia* as the principal organ of the faction

R. Nattermann (✉)
Bundeswehr University, Munich, Germany

© The Author(s) 2019
E. Madigan and G. Reuveni (eds.),
The Jewish Experience of the First World War,
https://doi.org/10.1057/978-1-137-54896-2_11

of Socialist interventionists. Sarfatti was soon appointed an editor of the journal, which became the official organ of the Fascist Party in 1922.[1]

In addition to Sarfatti, contemporary evidence reveals an extraordinary commitment to the war effort on the part of many Italian-Jewish women who nursed soldiers, assisted war orphans, and organized relief funds. In contrast to this widespread support, there was also the activity and rhetoric of a comparatively small group of female pacifists who remained true to their ideals despite stiff opposition.[2] This staunch pacifism notwithstanding, however, the majority of Jewish women appear to have viewed the Great War, at least in the early phases of Italian involvement, as the last act of the Risorgimento that would eventually seal Italian independence, freedom, and unity. We find a striking example of this attitude in an article by the Trieste-born, Italian-Jewish writer Anna Errera, published in November 1916 in the journal *Per Il Nostro Soldato* [*For Our Soldier*]:

> Again it is Mazzini's voice who demands to purge from the heart everything that is not ideal, who demands that Italy should be independent, free and united ... and again it is the fascination of Garibaldi who calls our youth to war.[3]

In the same year, an anonymous authoress described the war in *Cordelia*, one of the most popular contemporary journals of the Italian women's movement, as follows:

> [...] the fire of war has its remote origins in revenge and competition. Nation against nation, people against people, man against man, it is all an accumulation of turbulent rancour that ... produces destruction and

---

[1] On Margherita Sarfatti, see Stefania Bartoloni (2014), 'Margherita Sarfatti. Una intellettuale tra Nazione e Fascismo', in Maria Teresa Mori et al., ed. *Di generazione in generazione. Le Italiane dall'Unità ad Oggi* (Rome, Viella), 207–220; Simona Urso (2003), *Margherita Sarfatti dal mito del Dux al mito americano* (Venice, Marsilio); and Karin Wieland (2004), *Die Geliebte des Duce. Das Leben der Margherita Sarfatti und die Erfindung des Faschismus* (Munich, C. Hanser).

[2] See Monica Miniati (2008), *Le 'emancipate'. Le donne ebree in Italia nel XIX e XX secolo* (Rome, Viella), 211–224.

[3] Anna Errera (19 novembre, 1916), 'L'Antica Fiamma', *Per il nostro soldato* II, 24. On Anna Errera, see Achille Norsa (1975), 'Tre donne che hanno onorato l'Ebraismo italiano: le sorelle Errera', *La Rassegna mensile di Israel* XLI, 1–2, 42–55. Errera's statement as well as all the following quotations from contemporary Italian journals and ego-documents have been translated into English by Ruth Nattermann.

death. Yet our war is so beautiful that it rises limpidly from the pains of all these years: it is a sacred war of freedom, and almost an act of justice that remains firmly within the circle of national claims.[4]

The underlying identification with Italian war aims and a general idealization of the Great War as such could not be more evident. Indeed, the traditional association of women with peace, and men with war, has been increasingly questioned in the relevant historiography.[5] Compared to the war experience of men, however, the wartime ideological positioning, everyday experiences, and, ultimately, the memorialization of the Great War on the part of women have been rather neglected. This applies especially to Jewish women in Italy, whose history tended to remain, in the words of historian Anna Foa, 'unknown territory'.[6]

This chapter thus focuses specifically on Italian-Jewish women's experience and memory of the so-called *Grande Guerra.*[7] It deals with the break between the hopes most Jewish women pinned on Italy's decision

[4] 'Tra le fiamme della guerra', *Cordelia* 35, 20 (14 maggio 1916).

[5] See Jean Bethke Elshtain (1987), *Women and War* (New York, Basic Books). Only recently, historians have become aware of the attitudes, experience, and participation of Italian women in the First World War. See Perry Willson (2010), 'On the 'Home Front': World War One and Its Aftermath, 1915–20', in idem, *Women in Twentieth Century Italy* (Basingstoke and New York: Palgrave Macmillan), 43–60; Allison Scardino Belzer (2010), *Women and the Great War. Femininity Under Fire in Italy* (Basingstoke and New York, Palgrave Macmillan); Matteo Ermacora (2014), 'Women Behind the Lines: The Friuli Region as a Case Study of Total Mobilization, 1915–1917', in Christa Hämmerle, Oswald Überegger, and Birgitta Bader Zaar, eds. *Gender and the First World War* (Basingstoke and New York, Palgrave Macmillan), 16–35; Augusta Molinari (2014), *Una patria per le donne. La mobilitazione femminile nella Grande Guerra* (Bologna, Il Mulino); Dacia Maraini, ed. *Donne nella Grande Guerra* (Bologna: Il Mulino, 2014); and Emma Schiavon, *Interventiste nella Grande Guerra. Assistenza, propaganda, lotta per i diritti a Milano e in Italia (1911–1919)* (Milan, Le Monnier).

[6] Anna Foa (1999), 'Le donne nella storia degli ebrei in Italia', in Claire E. Honess and Verina R. Jones, eds. *Le donne delle minoranze: le ebree e le protestanti d'Italia* (Turin, Claudiana Editrice), 11–29, here 11. On the widely neglected history of Jewish women in Italy, see the collection of essays *Donne nella storia degli ebrei d'Italia*, ed. (2007), Associazione Italiana per lo Studio del Giudaismo (Florence, La Giuntina).

[7] On the conceptual trinity 'Expectation, Experience, Memory' with regard to the First World War, see Petra Ernst (2009), 'Der Erste Weltkrieg in deutschsprachig-jüdischer Literatur und Publizistik in Österreich', in Siegfried Mattl, ed. *Krieg. Erinnerung. Geschichtswissenschaft* (Wien, Köln and Weimar, Böhlau), 47–72, here 62–68.

to enter the war alongside the *Entente* powers and their experience of the eventual horror and tragedy of the conflict they ardently supported. It also explores recollections of the war within different personal and political contexts. The chapter is divided into four sections and focuses on several activists of the early women's emancipation movement whose social and cultural commitment to the Italian war effort deserve particular attention. The first section outlines the self-understanding of Jewish women in the Italian women's movement and their attitudes toward the Great War, considering ideological developments from pacifism to interventionism. The second section focuses on the personal experience of the *Grande Guerra* and is based on the unedited wartime correspondence of the playwright Amelia Rosselli, whose eldest son Aldo fell in the war. The third section discusses perceptions and representations of Jewish-Christian relationships in the First World War, which were often glossed over in the writings produced by Italian-Jewish women during the war. The ego-documents and articles that have been incorporated, among them the diary of the Red Cross nurse Silvia Treves,[8] will be read against the backdrop of the actual conflicts and antipathies between Jewish and Catholic women in Italy at the time. Finally, the last section looks at the way the First World War was remembered. The focus will be on Amelia Rosselli's and Laura Orvieto's recollections, which were both published in edited volumes in 2001, as well as on the commemoration book for the Red Cross nurse Emilia Contini Ancona, published by her family in 1938.[9] The particular processes and transformations of these recollections will be discussed in a broader context, taking into account both private experience, such as the deaths of family members and friends in the Great War, as well as the political dimension, i.e. Italian fascism and anti-Jewish legislation, which formed the temporal background of these works. The underlying contention is that the experience of antisemitism during the fascist period led to a delusive memorialization of the Great War as a moment of national unity and complete integration of the Jewish minority into Italian society.

---

[8] Silvia Treves (1974), 'Diario di una crocerossina fiorentina, 1917–1918', *Rassegna storica Toscana* XX, 2, 233–278.

[9] Laura Orvieto (2001), *Storia di Angiolo e Laura*, ed. Caterina Del Vivo (Florence, Leo S. Olschi); Amelia Rosselli (2001), *Memorie*, ed. Marina Calloni (Bologna, Il Mulino); and Clemente Ancona (1938), *In memoria di Emilia Ancona Contini nel primo anniversario della morte* (Ferrara, private publication). The author of this article expresses her sincerest thanks to Emilia's and Clemente's great-granddaughter Sara Ancona (Padua) for a copy of the commemoration book, as well as numerous pieces of information on Emilia Contini and her commitment in the First World War.

BETWEEN PACIFISM AND INTERVENTIONISM: JEWISH WOMEN IN ITALY AND THE GREAT WAR

The Italian historiography of the First World War reveals a striking marginalization of the discourses and sociopolitical activities of Jewish women during the conflict. This failure to incorporate the Italian-Jewish female experience is at least partly a result of the disparate state of the relevant source material. It is also, however, a consequence of the long-time concentration on the political and military contribution of Italian-Jewish men to the war effort.[10] In her work on Jewish women in Italy, Monica Miniati has focused mainly on their engagement in social welfare in Jewish communities.[11] The approach taken in this chapter is somewhat more complex, as Jewish identities are viewed as fluid and movable. Protagonists from Jewish backgrounds with liberal, secular convictions, whose relationships to the Jewish communities were either weak or nonexistent, have been deliberately included. The important role played by Jewish activists in the political and social construction of the Italian nation is well established, and it should be emphasized that nineteenth-century patriotic sentiment and a strong sense of Italian consciousness were to remain outstanding characteristics of Italian Jewry until well into the twentieth century.[12] Participation in religious life,

[10]On the participation of Italian-Jewish men in the Great War, see the standard monograph by Felice Tedeschi (1921), *Gli israeliti italiani nella guerra 1915–1918* (Turin, Ferruccio Servi), as well as the more recent studies by Mario Toscano (2003), 'Gli ebrei italiani e la prima guerra mondiale (1915–1918): tra crisi religiosa e fremiti patriottici', in idem, *Ebraismo e antisemitismo in Italia. Dal 1848 alla guerra dei sei giorni* (Milan, Franco Angeli), 110–122; idem (2003), 'Ebrei ed ebraismo nell'Italia della grande guerra. Note su una inchiesta del Comitato delle comunità israelitiche italiane del maggio 1917', in idem (2003), *Ebraismo e antisemitismo in Italia. Dal 1848 alla guerra dei sei giorni* (Milan, Franco Angeli), 123–154; and idem (2005), 'Religione, patriottismo, sionismo: il rabbinato militare nell'Italia della Grande Guerra (1915–1918)', *Zakhor* 8, 77–133.

[11]Miniati (2008), *Le 'emancipate'*, 211–224.

[12]Among the recent studies on Italian Jewry, especially in the period of emancipation, see Carlotta Ferrara degli Uberti (2011), *Fare gli ebrei italiani. Autorappresentazione di una minoranza (1861–1918)* (Bologna, Il Mulino); Elizabeth Schächter (2010), *The Jews of Italy, 1848–1915. Between Tradition and Transformation* (London, Vallentine Mitchell); David N. Myers, ed. (2008), *Acculturation and Its Discontents: The Italian Jewish Experience Between Exclusion and Inclusion* (Toronto, University of Toronto Press); and *Ebrei e nazione. Comportamenti e rappresentazioni nell'età dell'emancipazione* (storia e problemi contemporanei n. 45, a XX, maggio-agosto 2007).

on the other hand, was altering and began to diminish in tandem with growing Jewish engagement in Italian political, social and cultural life. The process of secularization resulted in individual, occasionally alternative lifestyles and sometimes even the rejection of religion and the abandonment of the community.[13] Yet for many people who chose one of these options, some sense of Jewish identity persisted. In the vast majority of cases which were examined for this study, the secular orientation of the women in question did not lead to the abandoning of Jewish identities. This can above all be demonstrated by their conscious and continuous involvement in far-reaching Jewish family networks. As Guri Schwarz and Barbara Armani have pointed out, even nonreligious Italian Jews maintained a distinct 'family identity' which stayed alive in their families and was based on a common cultural memory and heritage.[14]

Regarding the early Italian women's emancipation movement, protagonists of Jewish origin were overrepresented in many of the relevant associations, especially in the most prominent one, the Milan-based, socialist-inspired *Unione Femminile Nazionale* (UFN).[15] There were less Jewish women in the more conservative *Consiglio Nazionale delle Donne Italiane* (CNDI) in Rome, which was dominated by members of the Italian aristocracy.[16] It should be stressed that the secular orientation

[13] On this argument, see also Tullia Catalan (2007), 'Juden und Judentum in Italien von 1848 bis 1918', in Gudrun Jäger and Liana Novelli-Glaab, eds. *denn in Italian haben sich die Dinge anders abgespielt. Judentum und Antisemitismus im modernen Italian* (Berlin, trafo), 71–86, here 72–73.

[14] See Barbara Armani, and Guri Schwarz (2003), 'Premessa', Ebrei borghesi. Identità famigliare, solidarietà e affari nell'età dell'emancipazione, *Quaderni storici* 14, 621–651, here 627, 632.

[15] Regarding the high percentage of Jewish women within the Italian women's emancipation movement, see also Liana Novelli-Glaab (2007), 'Zwischen Tradition und Moderne. Jüdinnen in Italien um 1900', in *...denn in Italien haben sich die Dinge anders abgespielt*, 107–128, here 113. On the UFN, see Annarita Buttafuoco (1986), 'Solidarietà, Emancipazionismo, Cooperazione. Dall'Associazione Generale delle Operaie all'Unione Femminile Nazionale', in Fabio Fabbri, ed. *L'Audacia insolente. La cooperazione femminile 1886–1986* (Venice, Marsilio), 79–110; Fabio D'Amico (2010), 'Per l'elevazione materiale e morale della donna e del genere umano. L'Unione Femminile Nazionale di Milano dall'impegno sociale allo scioglimento (1908–1939)' (Tesi di laurea, Università Statale di Milano); and Fiorella Imprenti (2012), *Alle origini dell'Unione Feminile. Idee, progetti e reti internazionali all'inizio del Novecento* (Milan, Biblion Edizioni).

[16] On the CNDI, see Beatrice Pisa, ed. (2003), *Cittadine d'Europa. Integrazione europea e associazioni femminili italiane* (Milan, Franco Angeli); Elisabetta Solinas (2001), 'Il Primo Congresso nazionale delle donne italiane. L'immagine dei quotidiani e dei periodici femminili' (Tesi di laurea, Università Statale di Milano).

both of the UFN and the CNDI was crucial for women of Jewish origin who sought to join these organizations.

Whereas for a long time the early Italian women's movement has had the image of a generally pacifist, united body, remaining true to the idea of a democratic unified Europe modeled on the vision of Giuseppe Mazzini,[17] recent research has offered a more nuanced picture. According to the historian Laura Guidi, the First World War actually precipitated a crisis within the Italian women's movement that eventually led to a profound disruption.[18] Jewish women participated in and bore witness to these developments in much the same way as non-Jewish protagonists. Only a small group of pacifists remained, among them the longtime president of the *Unione Femminile Nazionale* Ersilia Majno, whose mother was of German-Jewish origin. In contrast, numerous activists signed an appeal against what they viewed as a form of 'national self-abandonment'.[19] Even prominent, self-proclaimed pacifists such as the academic Paolina Schiff, who was of German-Jewish origin, had turned, by 1917, toward interventionist positions.[20] She followed the

[17] See Franca Pieroni Bortolotti (1985), *La Donna, La Pace, L'Europa. L'Associazione internazionale delle donne dalle origini alla prima guerra mondiale* (Milan, Franco Angeli). On Mazzini's influence on the contemporary ideas of women's emancipation, see Federica Falchi (2012), 'Democracy and the rights of women in the thinking of Giuseppe Mazzini', *Modern Italy* 17, 1, 15–30.

[18] See Laura Guidi (2007), 'Un nazionalismo declinato al femminile', in *Vivere la guerra: percorsi biografici e ruoli di genere tra Risorgimento e primo conflitto mondiale*, ed. idem (Naples, Cliopress), 93–118, here 94.

[19] Concetta Brigadeci (2001), *Forme di resistenza al fascismo. L'Unione femminile nazionale* (Milan, UFN), 3; Guidi (2007), 'Un nazionalismo declinato al femminile', 94. On Ersilia Majno's family background and her role in the UFN see Ruth Nattermann (2014), 'Weibliche Emanzipation und jüdische Identität im vereinten Italien. Jüdinnen in der frühen italienischen Frauenbewegung', in Gabriele B. Clemens and Jens Späth, eds. *150 Jahre Risorgimento – geeintes Italien?* (Trier, Kliomedia), 127–146, here 142. On her biography, see Cinzia Demi (2013), *Ersilia Bronzini Majno. Immaginario biografico di un'italiana tra ruolo pubblico e privato* (Bologna, Pendragon); Fiorenza Taricone (1995), 'Ersilia Bronzini in Majno', in Rachele Farina, ed. *Dizionario biografico delle donne lombarde* (Milan, Baldini&Castoldi), 223–227; and Franca Pieroni Bortolotti (1974), *Socialismo e questione femminile 1892–1922* (Milan, Mazzotta).

[20] On Schiff and her ideological development, see Ruth Nattermann (2015), 'Vom Pazifismus zum Interventionismus. Die italienische Frauenrechtlerin Paolina Schiff (1841–1926)', in Franziska Dunkel, and Corinna Schneider, eds. *Frauen und Frieden? Zuschreibungen – Kämpfe – Verhinderungen* (Opladen and Toronto, Budrich), 73–85.

lead of her ideological companions, the socialists Filippo Turati and Anna Kuliscioff, a feminist pioneer of Russian-Jewish origin, who from 1915 onwards gave priority to the defense of the Italian 'Fatherland' and supported Italian interventionism. Kuliscioff declared that 'she felt a vivid consciousness for the reality that Italy had to face. The country must not shrink back from the overall conflagration.'[21]

The interpretation of the Great War as a 'just war of liberation' from Austrian rule in northern Italy and thus the completion of the Risorgimento dominated the contemporary press of the Italian women's movement.[22] Whereas many working-class women protested against the conflict, as it meant a further deterioration of their already difficult living conditions, most outspokenly pro-interventionist women came from middle- or upper-class backgrounds.[23] The great majority of Jewish women who were engaged in the women's movement and supported an Italian intervention—among them, prominent activists such as Anna Errera, Laura Orvieto, and Amelia Rosselli—also belonged to the educated, liberal middle class. Their social and cultural backgrounds reflected the specific features of contemporary Italian Jewry. They thus tended to be urban dwellers, residing in north-central parts of the country, literate, and generally secular.[24] In contrast to devout Italian

---

[21] Marina Addis Saba (1993), *Anna Kuliscioff. Vita privata e passione politica* (Milan, Mondadori), 288.

[22] See e.g. *Natale di Guerra: Numero unico a favore dei feriti* (19 dicembre 1915); *Cordelia* 35, 20 (14 maggio 1916), *Per il nostro soldato*, II, 24 (19 novembre 1916), 26 (17 dicembre 1916), III, 1 (14 gennaio 1917).

[23] See Willson (2010), 'On the Home Front', 48.

[24] In contrast to the majority of the Italian population, who were involved in agriculture, most Italian Jews were engaged in commerce, worked in offices, or practiced a profession. Their professional choices and fields of economic activity were frequently associated directly with their high educational level and their urban status. See Eitan Franco Sabatello (1989), 'Trasformazioni economiche e sociali degli ebrei in Italia nel periodo dell'emancipazione', in *Italia Judaica: Gli ebrei nell'Italia unita 1870–1945. Atti del IV convegno internazionale (Siena, 12–16 giugno 1989)* (Roma, Ministero per i Beni Culturali e Ambientali), 114–124. A countrywide survey commissioned by the central Committee of the Jewish communities in Italy in 1917, gave evidence for the fact that Italian Jews tended to neglect the rites, especially dietary rules, and that they rarely frequented the synagogue. At the same time, the results reflected a continuity of a profound 'Jewish sentiment' (*sentimento ebraico*). See Toscano (2003), 'Gli ebrei italiani', 295–297.

Catholics, Jewish men and women tended to hold on to the ideals of the Risorgimento and the secular orientation of the Italian unitary state until well into the twentieth century.[25]

For Italian-Jewish activists, the discursive connection between the Risorgimento and the First World War, as expressed in Anna Errera's text *L'Antica Fiamma* [*The Ancient Flame*], quoted above, assumed a particular symbolic quality. With Italian unification in 1861, more than fifty years before, Jews had been granted emancipation.[26] In the eyes of most Italian Jews, the Great War thus represented the first concrete and outstanding opportunity to prove their national solidarity toward the *patria e gran madre Italia*, as well as their gratitude toward the royal house of Savoy, which had emancipated Italian Jewry.[27] Italian-Jewish feminists, in particular, hoped that the war would not only continue and further the process of Jewish integration in general, but would also eventually lead to the emancipation of (Jewish) women as well.[28] Interestingly, the women in question often came from families that had been closely involved in the Italian wars of independence.[29] The fascination which interventionism and irredentism exerted on them was above all based on the memory of their ancestors' commitment to Italian unification with its inherent project of Jewish emancipation. This attitude did not always stay the same, however, but often changed in the course of wartime experience.

[25] See Catalan (2007), 'Juden und Judentum', 82.

[26] As early as 1848 the Jews in the kingdom of Sardinia-Piemont had been emancipated; eleven years later the Jews in Lombardy and Tuscany were granted civil rights. With the Italian unification in 1861, emancipation was extended to all the Jews residing in the newly founded state. Only in 1870, however, after the defeat of the Papal State, the Jews in Rome were granted civil rights as well.

[27] See Toscano (2003), 'Gli ebrei italiani', 285, 289f., 292. On the 'specifically Jewish aspects' of the First World War in the German, Austria-Hungarian and French context, see Derek Penslar (2013), *Jews and the Military. A History* (Princeton, Princeton University Press), 170.

[28] See Miniati (2008), *Le 'emancipate'*, 224–229.

[29] See for example Gina Lombroso Ferrero (1921), *Cesare Lombroso. Storia della Vita e delle Opere* (Bologna, Zanichelli Editore), 68–94; Orvieto (2001), *Storia*, 52; and Rosselli (2001), *Memorie*, 53.

CHANGING EXPERIENCE IN THE MIRROR
OF WARTIME CORRESPONDENCE

A striking example of a woman with an initially ardent interventionist attitude coming, over time and through personal experience, to a desperate realization of the war's extraordinary brutality and apparent absurdity, is provided by the case of Amelia Rosselli (née Pincherle). The popular Italian-Jewish playwright, mother of the future resistance fighters Carlo and Nello Rosselli, descended from a liberal, patriotic Venetian family. She had been brought up in a profoundly anti-Austrian climate, which continued to influence her political attitude as well as the upbringing of her three sons in Florence, where the family resided from 1903 onwards. Rosselli took an active part in the Italian women's emancipation movement and became head of the literary section of the Florentine Lyceum, an important cultural association for women.[30]

Her outlook reflects the views of many Italian-Jewish women and men, who idealistically perceived Italy, in direct contrast to the Habsburg Empire, as a place of freedom and tolerance, where antisemitism had no place. This general attitude also explains the considerable number of Italian-Jewish activists who supported irredentist ideas and the Italian conquest of cities such as Trieste and Trento as acts of so-called 'liberation' from Austrian dominance.[31] In her memoirs, written mainly in exile in Switzerland and the US in the 1930s and the 1940s,[32] Rosselli makes direct references to these ideas as she describes the interventionist outlook of her family at the beginning of the Great War:

---

[30] On Amelia Rosselli, see Dolara Vieri (2012), 'Amelia Rosselli Pincherle', *Quaderni del Circolo Rosselli* 3; Giovanna Amato (2012), 'Una donna nella storia. Vita e letteratura di Amelia Pincherle Rosselli', *Quaderni del Circolo Rosselli* 1.

[31] The notion of Italy as a 'safe harbor' for Jews has had a long tradition; see Stanislao Pugliese (2002), 'Israel in Italy, Wrestling with the Lord in the Land of Divine Dew' in idem, ed. (2002) *The Most Ancient of Minorities: The Jews of Italy* (Westport, CT, Greenwood Press), 1–10, here 1. On irredentist positions among Italian-Jewish activists, see Ruth Nattermann (2016), 'Zwischen Pazifismus, Irredentismus und nationaler Euphorie. Italienische Jüdinnen und der Erste Weltkrieg', in Petra Ernst and Eleonore Lappin-Eppel, eds. *Jüdische Publizistik und Literatur im Zeichen des Ersten Weltkriegs* (Innsbruck, Studienverlag).

[32] See Marina Calloni (2001), 'Introduzione', in Rosselli, ed. *Memorie*, 7–26, here 17.

In this fatal year 1914 we and our friends were all interventionists. [My eldest son] Aldo, who studied medicine in the first year, showed a vivid interest in the students' demonstrations against Austria. The hope for a war of liberation for Trieste and Trento exerted a horrible fascination on young and old ... It was difficult to hold out under this heavy cover of neutrality which hung over Italy: the atmosphere was too charged with passion ...[33]

The author thus offers us what appears to be an authentic account of her ideological and emotional positioning at the outset of the war. The feelings she describes in her memoirs can also be found in her correspondence with her sons as well as with her dear friend, the Italian-Jewish writer and journalist Laura Orvieto, wife of the famous Florentine poet Angiolo Orvieto.[34] In the letters, which can be found in the Rosselli papers as well as the Orvieto family archives in Florence, Rosselli quite stridently supports Italy's intervention in the war. And although she foresaw the horrors of the conflict, she stuck to her interventionist conviction, at least in the first year of the war. On 3 August 1914, the day Germany declared war on France, Rosselli wrote to her fourteen-year-old son Carlo:

My dear Carlo, I am really horrified by this atrocious news, and I am unable to believe that it is true that we should be attending one of the most gruesome and murderous wars ever. With those new weapons of destruction, it will be a real massacre. I am very sorry for France which was taken by surprise, and I fear that it is bound to end in disaster for them.[35]

---

[33] Rosselli (2001), *Memorie*, 139.

[34] Angiolo founded the Florentine literary journal 'Il Marzocco' in 1896 and became its first director. Later on, Laura Orvieto wrote for 'Il Marzocco' as well. On her biography and opus, see in particular 'Laura Orvieto. La voglia di raccontare le 'Storie del Mondo'', *Antologia Vieusseux* 18:53–54 (2012); Ruth Nattermann (2015), 'The Italian-Jewish Writer Laura Orvieto (1876–1955) Between Intellectual Independence and Social Exclusion', in Tullia Catalan and Cristiana Facchini, eds. *Portrait of Italian Jewish Life (1800s–1930s)*, Quest. Issues in Contemporary Jewish History. Journal of Fondazione CDEC, 8, URL http://www.quest-cdecjournal.it/focus.php?id=368; Claudia Gori (2004), 'Laura Orvieto: un'intellettuale del Novecento', *Genesis* III, 2, 183–203; Giuliano Treves Artom (1983), 'Ricordando Laura Orvieto', in Caterina Del Vivo, and Marco Assirelli, eds. *'Il Marzocco'. Carteggi e cronache fra Ottocento e Avanguardie, 1887–1913* (Florence, Arti Grafiche C. Mori); and Carla Poesio (1971), *Laura Orvieto* (Florence, Le Monnier).

[35] Amelia to Carlo Rosselli, August 3, 1914, Archivio dell'Istituto della Resistenza in Toscana, Fondo Maria Rosselli: Lettere di Amelia Rosselli.

Amelia's inner tension became even more evident in a letter she wrote three weeks later to Laura Orvieto from a small mountain town in Piedmont where she spent the summer alone. The uncertain situation of Italy, which, at that time, was still officially an ally of Germany and Austria-Hungary, weighed continuously upon her mind:

> [...] these catastrophic events have made me numb and deprived me of any joy ... waiting for the news that one receives only every 24 hours becomes more and more frightful because of the solitude ... Two million men are about to throw themselves against each other, and the uncertainty for our Italy weighs on me like a monstrous nightmare.[36]

Rosselli's nervousness, her worry about Italy's fate, and her horror at the atrocities of war all pervade the text of the letter. Toward the end, though, she blows off some steam by openly expressing her resentment against the German warmonger: 'I fervently hope that the Germans get hit from all sides. They have deserved it so much!'[37]

From this moment onwards, Rosselli's antipathy for Germany and Austria, together with her profound sense of belonging to the Italian nation, strengthened her desire for Italy to join the war on the side of what she regarded as the democratic powers of France and Great Britain. Ultimately, Rosselli, along with Laura Orvieto and many other Italian Jews, reacted with something close to euphoria to Italy's decision in May 1915 to enter the war on the side of the *Entente*.

The initial exaltation, however, soon began to give way to practical maternal concerns. Rosselli's eldest son Aldo was only nineteen years old when he went to war in 1915, and indeed the tone of his mother's letters changes considerably over the following months. As early as September 1915, she wrote to Orvieto, alluding to the contemporary discourse about the alleged 'beauty' of the Italian war, mentioned at the beginning of this chapter:

> [Something] has become certain inside myself: the horror of war. The beautiful war preached by the nationalists does not exist ... And I am blushing, as if for a crime, because of the lightness with which I spoke

---

[36]Amelia Rosselli to Laura Orvieto, August 21, 1914, Gabinetto G.P. Vieusseux, Firenze, Archivio Contemporaneo 'Alessandro Bonsanti' (in the following: ACGV), Fondo Laura Orvieto, F.Or.1.2059.

[37]Ibid.

before and I thought, that yes, the war was an element of strength, a necessity in peoples' lives."[38]

The most decisive change in Rosselli's attitude, however, occurred with the death of her son. The twenty-year-old Aldo fell in March 1916 in the region of Carnia on the Italian-Austrian front. Since December 1915, the young lieutenant had been serving in the *Messina* regiment in Tolmezzo. Upon his own request, Aldo Rosselli was sent at the beginning of 1916 to the front lines in the area of the *Pal Grande* on the Italian-Austrian border. He fell in action during an Austrian attack on the Italian positions in the night of 26–27 March. Half a year later, he was posthumously awarded the military silver medal for bravery.[39] The news of his death did not reach Rosselli until the beginning of April. In her memoirs, she dedicates a long passage to her reluctant and unbearably painful realization of his passing.[40]

From this point onwards, there are no nationalist undertones in Rosselli's letters and writings. When in July 1919 she traveled to Bolzano, which had been annexed by Italy after the Austrian capitulation, she stated:

> I cannot say that I feel at home; at home in the sense of being in Italy. We are in somebody else's home ... We need to want and accept this appropriation as an inevitable necessity: but there is no joy at all. As you see, I am honestly impartial, in spite of my nationalist past.[41]

Rosselli thus certainly appears to have distanced herself from nationalism after Aldo's death.[42] Interestingly though, her patriotism seems unaltered, maybe even strengthened by this personal experience. When in 1919 Orvieto became interested in Zionism, she reacted almost harshly,

[38] Amelia Rosselli to Laura Orvieto, September 21, 1915, ACGV, Fondo Laura Orvieto, F.Or. 1.2059.

[39] His colonel had actually suggested Aldo for the golden medal for bravery. At the end of the war, he still remembered how courageous Aldo had been in action while defending the Italian positions; see Leo Valiani (1997), 'Introduzione', in Zeffiro Ciuffoletti, ed. *I Rosselli. Epistolario familiare 1914–1937* (Milan, Mondadori), VII–XXVII, here X.

[40] Rosselli (2001), *Memorie*, 151–155.

[41] Amelia Rosselli to Laura Orvieto, July 31, s.a. (1919?), ACGV, Fondo Laura Orvieto, F.Or. 1.2059.

[42] In this context, see also Amato (2012), 'Una donna nella storia', 112.

defining her own identity as Italian and referring explicitly to her son's death for his homeland: 'I have suffered the same pain exclusively as an Italian of today, most of all as an Italian mother of an Italian soldier who died for Italy.'[43]

The identification with the Italian people and an intense feeling of belonging, of being an integral part of the Italian nation characterizes the majority of ego-documents by Italian-Jewish women which have been examined in the course of research for this chapter. Amelia Rosselli's letters represent an important and quite representative case of the experience of an Italian-Jewish mother who lost her son in the war, fighting for what he clearly perceived as his homeland. It was this experience that caused a change in her political outlook but not in her patriotism.

PERCEPTIONS, REPRESENTATIONS, AND REALITIES OF JEWISH-CHRISTIAN RELATIONSHIPS

We find similarly patriotic expressions in the writings of Italian-Jewish women who experienced the war as nurses. One of the most significant examples are the diaries of Silvia Treves, a young woman from a learned and affluent Florentine family. Despite her privileged background, however, her writings are almost unknown even in Italy, although they represent one of the few surviving witness testimonies of an Italian-Jewish nurse during the Great War.[44] In her diaries, Treves, who was in her mid-twenties during the war years, writes on several occasions about the profound relationship that developed between herself and the wounded Italian soldiers with whom she came into contact. The young nurse interprets her own feelings as the result of a complete community, a mirror of a seemingly perfect sense of solidarity between Jews and non-Jews in the face of a common experience. In September 1916, she wrote:

---

[43]Amelia Rosselli to Laura Orvieto, s.d. (1919?), ACGV, Fondo Laura Orvieto, F.Or. 1.2059.

[44]A long excerpt has been published in Silvia Treves (1974), 'Diario di una crocerossina fiorentina, 1917–1918', *Rassegna storica Toscana* XX, 2, 233–278. Monica Miniati has quoted some central passages of the diaries in her work on Jewish women in Italy, see Miniati (2008), *Le emancipate*, 217; so does Stefania Bartoloni (2003) in her study about Italian nurses in the First World War: *Italiane alla Guerra. L'assistenza ai feriti 1915–1918* (Venice, Marsilio), see especially 191, 217.

When I look back on some evenings among the seriously wounded in the darkness of the patients' wagons, on their suffering and my desire to help them, to ease their pain, and on my instinctive impulse to give them the strength that arose from my affection for them ... and my deep admiration for what they suffered for us [Italians] ... then I realize that I have never experienced similar moments of such a sensitive community and trembling sympathy for them as I felt inside myself.[45]

The closeness of Jewish women to invariably non-Jewish Italian men in the extreme circumstances of war appears to have contributed to a deeper mutual knowledge and feelings of human as well as national solidarity. What is more, it allowed for quite meaningful encounters between Jewish nurses and Catholic nuns working together in hospitals and hospices. In her autobiography, Laura Orvieto, who committed herself to the Samaritan nurses during the war, remembers the collaboration with Catholic nuns in terms of appreciation and solidarity.[46]

The desire to show solidarity with Catholic Italians can also be clearly perceived in an article the Jewish writer Ada Cagli della Pergola[47] published in December 1916 in the journal of the *Consiglio Nazionale delle Donne Italiane*. Sympathizing with Italian soldiers who had to celebrate Christmas for the second time in the ongoing situation of war, Cagli della Pergola identified with their melancholy and homesickness on this special day, alluding to the soldiers' memories of the 'feast of the nativity' and the 'prayers' of their childhood.[48]

Yet this seemingly ideal image of Christian-Jewish solidarity, which we find in Treves's, Orvieto's, as well as Cagli della Pergola's writings, obscures the fact that there were distinct anti-Catholic tendencies among certain Jewish activists in the period before the First World War. Their attitude in part reflected the generally anticlerical discourse of the liberal Italian nation-state, but it was also an expression of deeply rooted

---

[45] Silvia Treves, *Diari inediti*, September 1916, in Miniati (2008), *Le emancipate*, 217.

[46] See Orvieto (2001), *Storia*, 117.

[47] Ada Cagli Della Pergola was born in Ancona and had studied with the writer Eugenia Levi at the *Magistero Superiore* in Florence. She wrote for the press of the Italian women's movement as well as literature for children, mostly under the nom de plume 'Fiducia'.

[48] Ada Cagli della Pergola ('Fiducia'), 'Natale di guerra', in *Attività femminile sociale* IV, 12 (December 1916). On this article, see also Miniati (2008), *Le emancipate*, 224.

resentment against the Church and what they regarded as the backward approach adopted by institutions such as orphanages and children's homes run by Catholic nuns.[49] Even the relationship between nuns and Jewish nurses in hospitals was apparently not always as harmonious as Orvieto suggests in her autobiography. The Friulian Fanny Luzzatto, who at the beginning of the century undertook a training programme for nurses, stated in a letter to Ersilia Majno that the nuns working in hospitals 'were rather more occupied with following the rules of their Order than following [the rules of] reason'.[50]

In the first years of the twentieth century, at precisely the time when Catholic culture was beginning to reassert its considerable influence in Italian society, critical remarks concerning Catholicism were increasingly present in the correspondence of Italian-Jewish women.[51] Overt tensions between Catholic and Jewish women also became dramatically evident in the context of the Italian women's movement during this period. In 1908, during the first national congress of Italian women in Rome, a clash occurred between Catholic and secular Italian women over the question of whether to abolish instruction in the Catholic religion in Italian primary schools. The large contingent of Jewish congress participants, Laura Orvieto, Amelia Rosselli and Paolina Schiff among them, unanimously supported the relevant motion, which was eventually accepted. On the initiative of the Pope himself, this conflict resulted in the almost immediate foundation of the Catholic women's organization, *Unione fra le Donne Cattoliche d'Italia* (UDCI), and its

---

[49] On anti-catholic tendencies among Jewish members of the Italian women's movement, see Nattermann (2014), 'Weibliche Emanzipation', 142.

[50] Fanny Luzzatto to Ersilia Majno, September 15, 1901, Archivio Unione Femminile Nazionale, Milan, Fondo Ersilia Majno, Cartella 12, fasc. 1. Fanny was the sister of the prominent doctor Oscar Luzzatto and the law professor Fabio Luzzatto (1870–1954). In 1931, the latter was among only twelve Italian university professors who refused to sign the oath of allegiance to Fascism; see Giorgio Boatti (2001), *Preferirei di no. Le storie dei dodici professori che si opposero a Mussolini* (Turin, Einaudi).

[51] On the increasing influence of Catholicism at the beginning of the twentieth century in Italy, see Oliver Janz (2004), 'Konflikt, Koexistenz und Symbiose: Nationale und religiöse Symbolik in Italien vom Risorgimento bis zum Faschismus', in Heinz-Gerhard Haupt and Dieter Langewiesche, eds. *Nation und Religion in Europa. Mehrkonfessionelle Gesellschaften im 19. und 20. Jahrhundert* (Frankfurt a.M., Campus Verlag), 231–252, here 243.

definite dissociation from secular institutions and activists.[52] Over the next number of years, religiously devout and anti-Jewish positions in the Catholic women's organization began to merge into a dangerous compound. This phenomenon is particularly evident in the writings of the influential Catholic activist Elena Da Persico. In a notorious paper presented in Genoa in 1916 and republished in Turin in 1925, Da Persico made extensive use of openly antisemitic stereotypes such as the 'Jewish-Masonic conspiracy'.[53]

The complete and mutual sense of community between Jewish and non-Jewish Italians, between Catholics and Jews, as Treves, Orvieto and Cagli della Pergola perceived it, was thus in reality a rather partial, subjective and short-lived idyll, caused by the extreme situation of the conflict and bound to lose its base again after the end of the war. In the context of the specifically Jewish experience of the war, it is worth exploring the impermanence of wartime solidarity further by examining the way the war was remembered by Italian-Jewish women, during the Fascist era.

REMEMBERING THE GREAT WAR DURING FASCISM

The Jewish memory of the First World War in Italy has been widely neglected in historiography and in collective memory. As in the German and Austrian context, Italian Jews' recollections of the Great War were overlain or even destroyed by the devastating experience of the Second World War and the Shoah.[54] Regarding Italian-Jewish women, there have thus far been no studies which analyze their memories of the Great War. In fact, only very few of their written testimonies have been handed down to us. Laura Orvieto's and Amelia Rosselli's recollections of the war, which form part of their more extensive autobiographical texts, are therefore highly relevant, not least because of their literary merit. They represent a vivid expression of the complex relationship between (war) experience and memory, especially with

---

[52] On the origins and the development of the UDC, see Liviana Gazzetta (2006), "Fede e fortezza'. Il movimento cattolico femminile tra ortodossia ed eterodossia', in Nadia Maria Filippini, ed. *Donne sulla Scena Pubblica. Società e politica in Veneto tra Sette e Ottocento* (Milan, Franco Angeli), 218–265.

[53] Elena Da Persico (1925), *Moda e carattere femminile* (Turin, L.I.C.E. Berruti & C.).

[54] On the long-time neglect and forgetting of the Jewish experience and memory of the First World War especially in Austria, see Ernst (2009), 'Der Erste Weltkrieg', 57.

regard to the transformation and fragmentation of the latter against the background of current political events and present human needs for meaning.[55]

Orvieto's autobiography and Rosselli's memoirs were written at a considerable temporal remove from the *Grande Guerra* and the knowledge of deaths of Aldo Rosselli and many of his young friends in the fighting. Amelia worked on her memoirs between 1932 and the late 1940s. The central section was written during her exile in Switzerland and the United States (1938–1944), where she had fled after the assassination of her younger sons Carlo and Nello by fascist henchmen.[56] Orvieto, on the other hand, wrote her autobiography in 1938 and 1939, mostly in Cortina D'Ampezzo, outside her Florentine place of residence.[57] Their hopes for a long-term continuation of the integration processes, both as Jews and as women, had been dashed in the postwar upheaval in Italian society. Only four years after the ending of the war, Mussolini had come to power and, with the advent of increasing state repression, the activities of the Italian women's movement and numerous initiatives of Jewish activists were brought to a standstill. While the *Consiglio Nazionale delle Donne Italiane* aligned itself with the fascist regime and continued its existence, the *Unione Femminile Nazionale* in Milan was increasingly marginalized and finally closed down in January 1939 on the orders of the ministry of the interior because of its high number of Jewish members.[58] Already from the beginning of the 1930s

---

[55] On the memory of the Great War and the development of the various forms of its memory, especially in France and Great Britain, see Jay Winter (2006), *Remembering War. The Great War between Memory and History in the Twentieth Century* (New Haven, Yale University Press). For the German-Jewish context in particular see Tim Grady (2012), *The German-Jewish Soldiers of the First World War in History and Memory* (Liverpool, Liverpool University Press).

[56] On the history and the origins of Rosselli's memoirs see the introduction by Marina Calloni, in Rosselli (2001), *Memorie*, 7–30, in particular 16.

[57] See Caterina Del Vivo (2001), 'Introduzione', in Orvieto, ed. *Storia*, VII–XI, here VII.

[58] See 'Decreto del prefetto di Milano riguardo allo scioglimento dell'UFN', Milano, Archivio UFN, Busta 1, fasc. 5. On women and women's organizations in Fascist Italy see especially Victoria De Grazia (1992), *Le donne nel regime fascista* (Venice, Marsilio); Perry Willson (1993), *The Clockwork Factory. Women and Work in Fascist Italy* (Oxford, Clarendon Press). On Catholic women's organizations during Fascism see Liviana Gazzetta (2011), *Cattoliche durante il fascismo. Ordine sociale e organizzazioni femminili nelle Venezie* (Rome, Viella).

onwards, Jewish men and women had been increasingly excluded from Italian society.[59]

In view of the fascist race laws that were introduced in November 1938, bitterness and a sense of isolation are clearly perceptible in Orvieto's writing. Meanwhile, the tragic undertone in her and Rosselli's narratives reveals a belated realization of the initially often underestimated horror of the Great War. Rosselli dedicated a whole chapter to her son Aldo who died before his time in a war he had joined on a patriotic impulse.[60] Whereas she remembered her son's parting, his military training, his ambition to be sent to the front and also the moment when she received the news of his death, Rosselli banished the concrete circumstances in which Aldo had died from her memory.[61] Having lost even her younger sons in the fight against fascism, being in exile and unable to take part in commemorative practices, she internalized the memory of Aldo's death. Looking back at her own ideals of justice and freedom, as well as those of her son, which the war had not been able to fulfill, Rosselli stated:

> The soldiers who returned saw that their sacrifice, instead of being appreciated, was mocked as a useless effort. And so in the heart of every mourning mother grew the terrible and almost monstrous question: Why? Why so much blood, so much pain, and a whole generation sacrificed?[62]

Unlike Rosselli, Orvieto still lived in Italy when she wrote her autobiography. She directly witnessed the increasingly violent antisemitic course of the fascist regime and experienced the transition from the attack on Jewish equality to the attack on Jewish rights. Between 1936 and 1938, the fascist government had removed almost all Jews from public positions in Italy, while the fascist press had intensified its anti-Jewish

---

[59] On the antisemitic course of Fascist Italy and the Racial Laws of 1938, see especially Enzo Collotti (2004), *Il fascismo e gli ebrei. Le leggi razziali in Italia* (Rome and Bari, Laterza); Michele Sarfatti (2006), *The Jews in Mussolini's Italy. From Equality to Persecution* (Madison, The University of Wisconsin Press); and idem (1994), *Mussolini contro gli ebrei. Cronaca dell'elaborazione delle leggi del 1938* (Turin, S. Zamorani).

[60] This concerns the second part of her memoirs, 'A Firenze', which deals to a considerable extent with Aldo and his death; Rosselli (2001), *Memorie*, 107–174.

[61] See ibid., 146–155.

[62] Ibid., 163.

campaign.[63] As a consequence of the race laws introduced in November 1938, Orvieto was expelled from the Florentine *Lyceum*, an important cultural association for women to which she had been committed since its foundation in 1908.[64] In the face of this drastic personal experience, the sense of resentment is more overt in Orvieto's autobiography as she alludes to Fascism and the consequences of the race laws for Italian Jews, who had given their lives in large numbers during the Great War. Referring to Rosselli's son Aldo, she writes:

> Aldo has given his glorious life over the Italian alps. Lucky Aldo, because if he was still alive today, he would be expelled from the army, in spite of the bravery medal that was given to his mother at that time.[65]

The memories of the First World War that formed the base of Amelia Rosselli's memoirs and Laura Orvieto's autobiography differed considerably from the euphoric national celebrations and irredentist passion that had influenced the writings of Italian-Jewish women at the beginning of the conflict. Out of temporal as well as spatial distance, the mourning for their fallen family members and friends dominated the images, thoughts, and emotions associated with the Great War. At the same time, Rosselli's and Orvieto's experience of exclusion, persecution, and exile during the years of fascist rule intensified their memory of the First World War as the last moment in which they had been able to act and feel part of the national community.

We find another interesting reaction toward the antisemitic course of the fascist regime in a book published by Clemente Ancona, a Jewish stockbroker from Ferrara, in June 1938 in memory of his late wife Emilia Contini Ancona. She had been a Red Cross nurse during the war and had distinguished herself through her extraordinary social commitment. Among many other accomplishments, Emilia had participated in the foundation of the day nursery known as 'Cavour' in Ferrara for children of frontline soldiers.[66] The commemorative book was based on personal

---

[63] See especially Sarfatti (2006), *The Jews*, 100–129.

[64] Orvieto (2001), *Storia*, 126.

[65] Ibid., 115.

[66] Monica Miniati, too, mentions Emilia Contini Ancona among the founders of the day nursery 'Cavour'. The group of altogether eleven Jewish initiators carried the costs for the institution by themselves; see Miniati (2008), *Le emancipate*, 216.

accounts of Emilia's commitment to various social projects during the Great War, letters of thanks to her and her family, obituaries by representatives of the Jewish community as well as Italian ministries and the army. In the introduction, Clemente Ancona wrote of his wife: 'This Italian citizen, who was filled with fervent patriotism, wanted to be useful and was confirmed in her benevolence.'[67]

Ancona's emphasis on Emilia's commitment to the Italian war effort, her patriotic fervor, as well as her Italian citizenship (which in reality was incomplete anyway, as Italian women still had no right to vote), reveals his need to represent his wife as an integral part of the Italian nation. The publication was addressed in the first place to Clemente's children and grandchildren, but against the backdrop of the now openly antisemitic attitude of the fascist regime, it was also certainly aimed at a wider Italian audience. In a rather desperate and almost apologetic way, Clemente Ancona apparently tried to prove his wife's national belonging (as well as that of his family) by highlighting her commitment and national solidarity during the national crisis of the First World War, as an image of a perfect national community.

The historical reality looked quite different. The passing of the race laws in November 1938 meant the definite judicial as well as factual 'revocation' of Jewish emancipation in Italy.[68] Similarly to Clemente Ancona, Laura Orvieto responded to this violent exclusion with an extenuation of her memories of the Great War. What is more, she made no mention of antisemitism but instead idealized the relationship between Jews and non-Jewish Italians during the war. In view of the brutal experience of fascist antisemitism, she remembered the period of the First World War in spite of all its tragedy once again as an era of a strong national community, in which Jews and non-Jews had worked in harmony to support the Italian cause:

> [...] at that time we believed in an unconditional battle for Italy's independence, so that the enemy could be expelled from Italian territory, from the alps, so that he would not any longer command a people that was

---

[67] Ancona (1938), *In memoria*, 8.

[68] Enzo Collotti, 'La politica razziale del regime fascista' (paper presented at the conference 'L'invenzione del nemico. Sessantesimo anniversario della promulgazione delle leggi razziali', organized by the Istituto Nazionale per la Storia del Movimento di Liberazione in Italia and the Ministero della Pubblica Istruzione, December 3, 1998), 3.

finally free, free in their own will, their own strength, their own sacrifice. This is what we believed at that time, this is what we desired, all of us united, we Italians, without racial discrimination and difference, in a common love and a common belief.[69]

CONCLUSION

The hopes of Italian-Jewish women as to what might be achieved by Italian involvement in the Great War, concerning the completion of Italian independence and unity, as well as the desired 'liberation' of the *terre irredente*, were dashed by the gruesome experience of the conflict. An important example is Amelia Rosselli's ideological and personal transformation, for which her wartime correspondence provides clear evidence. At the same time, Italian-Jewish women frequently perceived the relationship between Jewish and Catholic Italians in the extreme situation of war as a perfect community. This positive image, however, stood in sharp contrast to the actual conflicts and resentments on the side of Jewish and Catholic activists close to the Italian women's movement. There were clearly antisemitic tendencies present within the Catholic women's organization and we find evidence of anti-Catholic sentiment in the writing of Jewish activists. The perception and representation of Jewish-Christian solidarity thus differed considerably from reality or rather depicted only a small detail of the actual overall situation.

Ultimately, the experience of antisemitism during the fascist period led to a delusive memorialization of the Great War as an era of complete national unity. In response to their exclusion from Italian society, historical actors such as Amelia Rosselli, Laura Orvieto, and Clemente Ancona turned toward the past. In their memories, the First World War assumed the nimbus of a distant era, in which antisemitism among Italians had not existed. The success with which the race laws in Italy were implemented only two decades after the ending of the *Grande Guerra* tells quite a different story.

[69] Orvieto (2001), *Storia*, 119.

Once 'the Only True Austrians': Mobilising Jewish Memory of the First World War for Belonging in the New Austrian Nation, 1929–1938

Tim Corbett

On 3 November 1918, a group of Habsburg military officers assembled around the gravesite of a deceased colonel high up in the Karawanks, near the front between Austria and Italy. One by one, the officers threw a handful of earth into the open grave, symbolising the soil of their respective homelands in the crumbling Habsburg Empire, saying in turn: 'Soil from Hungary [...] Soil from Poland [...] Soil from Carinthia [...] Soil from Carniola [...] Soil from Bohemia [...] Soil from Trento [...]'. Finally, it was Doktor Grün's turn. Grün, a regimental field doctor and also a Jew, hesitantly said: 'Soil from... Soil from... Austria!' This scene occurs in the iconic play *Dritter November 1918* by the Viennese dramatist Franz Theodor Csokor, which eulogises the end of the First

T. Corbett (✉)
Museum of Jewish Heritage, New York, USA

© The Author(s) 2019
E. Madigan and G. Reuveni (eds.),
The Jewish Experience of the First World War,
https://doi.org/10.1057/978-1-137-54896-2_12

World War and the collapse of the old order in Central Europe.[1] What is striking in this depiction of the constellation of peoples that made up the disintegrating Habsburg Empire is the peculiarity of the Jew: having no homeland—literally, no soil to call his own—he instead invokes the spiritual soil of 'Austria'. Csokor hereby draws our attention to two profound questions emerging in the aftermath of the First World War, namely what, if anything, was 'Austria' in the post-Habsburg world, and to what the Habsburg Jews could claim their loyalty, if not to Habsburg Austria.

In November 1918, with group after group declaring sovereignty in new 'national' states, even the German-speaking Austrians disavowed 'Austria' in the form of the multicultural Habsburg Empire, and overwhelmingly sought to unify as one 'nation' with Germany.[2] The Proclamation of the Republic of *Deutschösterreich* on 12 November 1918 exclaimed that 'German-Austria is a constituent part of the German Republic'.[3] The Austrian Constituent Assembly voted almost unanimously for an *Anschluß* (understood in 1938 as annexation, but in this context more akin to union) with the new German Republic and, thereby, against an independent Austria—with one exception: Robert Stricker, the only Zionist representative in the Assembly, who would later be murdered in Auschwitz, was also the only delegate to vote against the union of Austria to Germany.[4] In this climate of irredentist nationalism,

---

[1] Franz Theodor Csokor (1936), *Dritter November 1918: Ende der Armee Österreich-Ungarns* (Vienna, Zsolnay), this scene 60–62. All translations, unless otherwise stated, are my own.

[2] A plethora of work on the relationship between nationalism and the collapse of the empire has emerged since the earliest trailblazing works on this question such as Oscar Jászi (1936), *The Dissolution of the Habsburg Monarchy* (Chicago, University of Chicago Press). More recently, both the extent of nationalist sympathies and the inevitability of their corroding impact on the empire have been increasingly called into question. See for example Johannes Feichtinger and Gary Cohen, eds. (2014), *Understanding Multiculturalism: The Habsburg Central European Experience* (New York, Berghahn); Pieter Judson (2016), *The Habsburg Empire: A New History* (Cambridge, MA, Harvard University Press).

[3] Cited in Hans Rauscher, ed. (2005), *Das Buch Österreich: Texte, die man kennen muss* (Vienna, Braumüller), 293.

[4] As observed by George Berkley (1988), *Vienna and Its Jews: The Tragedy of Success 1880s–1980s* (Cambridge, Cambridge University Press), 166. Berkley elsewhere described the assembly as 'consisting solely of German-Austrians (including Socialist Jews who believed themselves to be such)', 142. The paradigm opened up here—differentiating among other things between Jews and Germans or between Zionists and

in a time of rupture often accompanied by virulent, even violent, outbursts of antisemitism, contemporaries and later historians alike remarked that the 'only true Austrians' were the Jewish Austrians.[5]

This is a compelling but complicated notion, and a trope which can be found surfacing repeatedly in disparate texts relating to Austria's Jews after the collapse of the Habsburg Empire. The Jew as the 'only true Austrian' is a provocative epithet which seems especially pertinent as a departure point for an investigation into the related questions of Jewishness and Austrianness in the early twentieth century. The earliest such statement I have identified was made by Heinrich Schreiber, a functionary of the Vienna Jewish community organisation, who commented in 1918 that 'we Jews were without exception and without differentiation [...] true and real Austrians'.[6] Then in 1936, Max Grunwald, a prolific Viennese rabbi and historian who had witnessed the collapse of the empire first-hand, wrote that 'the Jews showed themselves to be the only loyal Austrians'.[7] In 1971, years after the Holocaust and the destruction of Austrian Jewry, which for a long time eclipsed the eventful history of the early twentieth century, the Austrian-born Israeli military historian Wolfgang von Weisl commented that 'the only "Austrians" [had been] the Jews'.[8] More recently, in 1988, a time when mainstream Austrian society was beginning to 'rediscover' its Jewish past, Erika Weinzierl, one of the most prolific Austrian contemporary historians, remarked

Socialists—pre-empts some of the discussion at the heart of this paper, whereby Berkley's conclusions should be approached with caution.

[5] This is the first paper to emerge from my on-going postdoctoral project, provisionally entitled *Once the 'Only True Austrians': Jews and the Transformation of Austrian Culture Through the Twentieth Century*. It is based on a paper presented at the conference *Contesting Jewish Loyalties: The First World War and Beyond* at the Jewish Museum in Berlin on 16 December 2016, and draws on the research undertaken during a Prins Foundation Postdoctoral Fellowship at the Center for Jewish History in New York in 2015/2016.

[6] Cited in David Rechter (2014), 'Die große Katastrophe: Die österreichischen Juden und der Krieg', in Marcus Patka, ed. *Weltuntergang: Jüdisches Leben und Sterben im Ersten Weltkrieg* (Vienna, Jüdisches Museum Wien), 25.

[7] Max Grunwald (1936), *Vienna* (Translated by Solomon Grayzel, Philadelpha, Jewish Publication Society), 156.

[8] Wolfgang von Weisl (1971), *Die Juden in der Armee Österreich-Ungarns—Illegale Transporte—Skizze zu einer Autobiographie* (Tel Aviv, Olamenu), 1.

that the empire's Jews were 'the only actual "Austrians"'.[9] Finally, Erwin Schmidl, an Austrian military historian, observed in 1989 that 'in the Old Monarchy, the Jews had often been called the only truly 'supra-nationals', the only truly Austrian element'.[10] This assessment of being 'true', 'real', or 'actual' (not to mention loyal) Austrians is a compelling and enduring characterisation of early twentieth-century Austrian Jews, espoused by contemporaries and historians, Jews and non-Jews alike, including in more implicit forms, as in the Csokor play. The import of this notion for the study of twentieth-century transformations in cultural and national identities in Central Europe is evidently deserving of deeper exploration.

One of the key premises of my research concerns the inherent malleability of various forms of Jewish belonging articulated in early twentieth-century Austria, a complex issue that is the topic of on-going scholarly discussion in both its theoretical and empirical dimensions.[11] An integrally related but less widespread premise is that the very concepts of 'Austria' and 'Austrianness' have been no less malleable over the course of the twentieth century than the notion of 'Jewishness', and have in fact been actively bound up in the fate of Austria's Jewish population through various incarnations of Austria—be it in the cultural genesis of Habsburg Austria and of the First Austrian Republic, or in the cultural genocide of the Nazi *Ostmark* and the conflicted politics of memory in the Second Austrian Republic.[12] As this juxtaposition already implies,

---

[9] Erika Weinzierl (1988), 'Der jüdische Beitrag zur österreichischen Kultur der Jahrhundertwende', in Wolfgang Plat, ed. *Voll Leben und voll Tod ist diese Erde: Bilder aus der Geschichte der jüdischen Österreicher 1190–1945* (Vienna, Herold), 208.

[10] Erwin Schmidl (1989), *Juden in der k. (u.) k. Armee 1788–1918/Jews in the Habsburg Armed Forces* (Eisenstadt, Österreichisches Jüdisches Museum), 146.

[11] Key works of recent years emphasising malleability over essentialist understandings of Jewishness include Klaus Hödl (2006), *Wiener Juden—Jüdische Wiener: Identität, Gedächtnis und Performanz im 19. Jahrhundert* (Innsbruck, Studienverlag); Lisa Silverman (2012), *Becoming Austrians: Jews and Culture Between the World Wars* (Oxford, University Press). Silverman and Hödl made a major contribution to the field with their concept of 'Jewish difference', in which 'Jewishness' is understood as an analytical category, like gender or class, according to which Jewish and non-Jewish Austrians defined themselves through the last century.

[12] The study of the construction of an Austrian national identity has mostly been limited to the post-1945 Republic. See for example Oliver Rathkolb (2006), *Die Paradoxe Republik: Österreich 1945 Bis 2005* (Vienna, Donauland).

the First Republic occupied a pivotal place in these convoluted developments, and has only recently begun to gain traction in scholarship, as a field in its own right and not merely as an epilogue to Habsburg Austria or a preamble to the Holocaust.[13] Modern Austrian history—a history defined more by vicissitude than continuity—witnesses a tumultuous succession of transformations in the political realities and even the very concept of 'Austria' itself. 'Austria' can in this sense be seen as a mutable historical term, a transformative ideological and cultural concept through modernity. Unfortunately, and much to the detriment of scholarly research, the writing of history today largely still follows the contrived identity politics of the early twentieth century, whereby—among other shortcomings—a history of Jews in Austria is seen as essentially separate from the history of Austria itself.[14]

The First Republic, as this chapter argues through recourse to the mobilisation of memory of the First World War in the 1930s, should be understood as a specific but not unique modern exercise in building a nation and forging a cultural identity, underlining moreover the significant role that Jews and Jewish micro-cultures, whether as active participants or passive subjects, have played therein. The rump state left over when the Entente had finished dissecting Central Europe—following which they forbade an *Anschluß* with Germany and even the name *Deutschösterreich*[15]—was a far cry from the multicultural Habsburg conglomeration of peoples, and was regarded by most of its bitterly divided populace 'not [as a] liberation but [as a] punishment for losing

---

[13] This point was also made recently by John Boyer (2010), 'Introduction: Boundaries and Transitions in Modern Austrian History', in Günter Bischof, Fritz Plasser, and Peter Berger, eds. *From Empire to Republic: Post-world War I Austria*, Contemporary Austrian Studies Vol. 19, 15.

[14] Aside from the widespread omission of Jews in Austrian historiography and national consciousness, this problem is exacerbated in much of the scholarly literature on Austria's Jews, which with its inability to overcome outdated narratives such as that of 'Jewish assimilation' perpetuates the notion of Jewish otherness in Austrian society, past and present. See the discussion in Steven Beller (2003), 'Knowing Your Elephant: Why Jewish Studies Is Not the Same as Judaistik, and Why That Is a Good Thing', in Klaus Hödl, ed. *Jüdische Studien: Reflexionen zu Theorie und Praxis eines wissenschaftlichen Feldes* (Innsbruck, Studienverlag).

[15] Article 88 of the Treaty of Saint-Germain-en-Laye, 10 September 1919. See the full text under https://www.ris.bka.gv.at/GeltendeFassung.wxe?Abfrage=Bundesnormen& Gesetzesnummer=10000044. Accessed 30 January 2017.

the war'.[16] The vast majority of Jews remaining in this new Austrian republic resided in Vienna, some 180,000 people, self-defined as Jews, who constituted a kaleidoscope of cultural, political, social, religious, and other milieus, and including some 30,000 veterans of the recent war. Vienna in the 1920s was one of the major Jewish metropolises of its era, and a bastion of Social Democracy in a country overwhelmingly supporting authoritarian rule, and thus became the theatre for the conflicts that would finally reach their devastating climax under National Socialism.[17] Austria's Jews became instrumental in defining the character of the short-lived First Republic, be it in the arts and sciences or in the attempt to create a new Austria.[18] To epitomise this point, the central figure in Vienna's Monument to the Foundation of the Republic on the Ringstraße is none other than the Jewish-born (but decidedly secular) Social Democrat, Victor Adler.[19] Indeed, Vienna, and the independent Austrian republic more generally, were often attacked by their detractors, and especially by those who belonged to the burgeoning Nazi movement at home and abroad, as essentially 'Jewish' phenomena.[20] In this context,

[16] Bruce Pauley (1981), *Hitler and the Forgotten Nazis: A History of Austrian National Socialism* (London, Macmillan), 3–4.

[17] As discussed by Wolfgang Maderthaner (2010), 'Utopian Perspectives and Political Restraint: The Austrian Revolution in the Context of Central European Conflicts', in Bischof, Plasser, and Berger, eds. *From Empire to Republic*, 56–58.

[18] The creative genius of Vienna's Jews is a perennial topic of discussion: see for example Steven Beller's (1990) now classic *Vienna and the Jews, 1867–1938: A Cultural History* (Cambridge, Cambridge University Press). This is also a favourite topic for Jewish Austrians in exile: see for example John Emanuel Ullmann (1993), *The Jews of Vienna: A Somewhat Personal Memoir*, unpublished memoir, Leo Baeck Institute, AR 10682. The compulsion to quantify Jewish 'contributions' to Austrian culture (see the title of the above-cited work by Erika Weinzierl), however, often runs the risk of evaluating Jewish history purely on the merits of its cultural productivity while discursively reducing Jews to a group of outsiders who merely 'contribute' to a dominant—usually portrayed as disinterested—non-Jewish culture.

[19] Adler was appointed Foreign Minister of the new republic but died on 11 November 1918. Other Jewish-born individuals to hold prominent positions in the newly founded republic include Otto Bauer, who succeeded Adler as Foreign Minister, and Julius Deutsch, who became Defence Minister. Berkley (1988), *Vienna*, 142.

[20] Illustrating this point, the popular perception by non-Jews of the number of 'racial Jews' living in interwar Vienna by far exceeded reality, with estimates ranging from 300,000 to as high as 583,000. Bruce Pauley (1990), 'Politischer Antisemitismus im Wien der Zwischenkriegszeit', in Gerhard Botz, Ivar Oxaal, and Michael Pollak, eds. *Eine zerstörte Kultur: Jüdisches Leben und Antisemitismus in Wien seit dem 19. Jahrhundert* (Buchloe, Obermayer), 224.

the memory of the recent war was increasingly mobilised to support competing narratives of the past and ideas about how the present and future should be formed, especially with regard to Austrian nationhood.

This chapter analyses the memory discourses concerning Jewish participation in the First World War as they emerged around two memorial sites in Vienna: the *Kriegerdenkmal* (Soldiers' Memorial), a Jewish memorial created in the Jewish part of the Central Cemetery on the outskirts of Vienna in the late 1920s and emerging within a specifically Jewish memory discourse, and the *Heldendenkmal* (Heroes' Memorial), an Austrian state memorial, but more specifically an Austrofascist memorial, created at the Heldenplatz in central Vienna in the early 1930s in the context of a short-lived and only partially successful attempt to secure Austrian independence, statehood, and a sense of 'nation' through the means of a home-grown form of militant nationalism.[21] For all their obvious differences, these two sites offer some remarkable parallels in discourse. The interplay of Jews and the state therein reflected the complex interaction of Jewishness and Austrianness as they were negotiated in the short-lived First Republic. The discourses concerning these sites reveal lines of both continuity and rupture, first between the Austria of the Habsburg past and the Austria of the republican present, and second between Jewish Austrians and non-Jewish Austrians, as a platform from which to open up a more fundamental discussion into the transformative nature of Austrianness in the interwar period and the role of Jewish memory discourses therein.

Some 300,000 of the altogether 1.5 million Jews who fought in the First World War fought for the Habsburg army, which Oscar Jászi described as one of the most 'centripetal' forces in the empire.[22] The Habsburg army had been a principal vehicle for Austria's Jews to realise their emancipation, to pursue a career in an atmosphere relatively free of antisemitism, and to demonstrate their loyalty to the Austrian

---

[21] For an overview of Austrofascism, see Tim Kirk (2003), 'Fascism and Austrofascism', in Günter Bischof, Anton Pelinka, and Alexander Lassner, eds. *The Dollfuss/Schuschnigg Era in Austria: A Reassessment,* Contemporary Austrian Studies Vol. 11. Kirk argues (in brief summary) that this movement could best be described as an alliance between 'fascist' and 'fascisant' elements. While acknowledging the complexity of discussions surrounding Fascism generally and the problem of definition in the Austrian case specifically, I nevertheless employ the term 'Austrofascist' here, partly for simplicity but also in the interest of not euphemising what was a violent and authoritarian movement.

[22] Jászi (1936), *The Dissolution,* 134.

'fatherland'.[23] The memory of their service thus subsequently became as central a medium through which Jews asserted their belonging in the new Austrian nation as the memory of the military and of the Habsburg Empire generally was a vehicle for the Austrian state to attempt to consolidate its nationhood—albeit unsuccessfully, as it turned out. Although both memorials, and the broader memory discourses surrounding them, have been the object of previous study,[24] this chapter offers a novel attempt to connect these hitherto segregated historiographies, and, in so doing, to open new grounds for discussion of the interplay between Jewishness and Austrianness in the dynamics of cultural genesis and genocide in early twentieth-century Austrian history.

THE JEWISH *KRIEGERDENKMAL* AT THE CENTRAL CEMETERY

The spatial—and therefore mnemonic—separation of Jewish and non-Jewish war graves and later memorials appears to correlate with the segregation of Jews in Austrian historiography and more generally with their absence in the state and civil self-understanding of Austria. However, the separation of Jewish and non-Jewish graves—and by extension or implication of Jewish and non-Jewish memory—only happened gradually, with fallen Habsburg soldiers being buried together in the opening stages of the war. In Vienna, the Jewish community organisation

[23] See among other contributions the chapter by Erwin Schmidl (2014), 'Jüdische Soldaten in der k.u.k. Armee', in Patka, ed. *Weltuntergang*. The origins of Jewish service in the Habsburg army and its significance as a vehicle for emancipation were explored by Michael Silber (2006), 'From Tolerated Aliens to Citizen-Soldiers: Jewish Military Service in the Era of Joseph II', in Pieter Judson and Marsha Rozenblit eds. *Constructing Nationalities in East Central Europe* (New York, Berghahn).

[24] On the *Kriegerdenkmal*, see the seminal papers by Martin Senekowitsch (1994), *Ein Ungewöhnliches Kriegerdenkmal: Das jüdische Heldendenkmal am Wiener Zentralfriedhof* (Vienna, Militärkommando Wien); Gerald Lamprecht (2014), 'Erinnern an den Ersten Weltkrieg aus jüdischer Perpektive 1914–1938', in Gerald Lamprecht, Eleonore Lappin-Eppel, and Heidrun Zettelbauer, eds. *Der Erste Weltkrieg aus jüdischer Perspektive: Erwartungen, Erfahrungen, Erinnerungen* (Innsbruck, Studienverlag). On the *Heldendenkmal*, see the seminal paper by Peter Pirker, Magnus Koch, and Johannes Kramer (forthcoming), 'Contested Heroes, Contested Places: Politics of Remembrance in Vienna', in Jörg Echternkamp and Stephan Jaeger, eds. *Views of Violence: Representing the Second World War in Museums and Memorials* (New York, Berghahn). I wish to thank the authors, for whom I translated this paper, which provides a welcome history of the politics of memory at this most conflicted memorial landscape in contemporary Vienna, and which allowed for many opportunities to consider the links between Jewish and Austrofascist commemorative practices in the preparation of this chapter.

originally rejected proposals for a separate Jewish war section in its cemetery, preferring to cooperate with the City Council in the creation of a general soldiers' section in the Central Cemetery. Ultimately, a separate Jewish soldiers' section was created after all, largely as a result of the wishes of many families to bury their fallen relatives in a Jewish cemetery, but also due to more symbolic considerations. As early as 1915, Jewish newspapers began publishing opinion pieces which lauded the egalitarian intentions underlying the communal burial of fallen soldiers, yet called for the separate burial of at least some Jewish soldiers in order to set a symbolic statement for posterity, lest visitors pass the Jewish cemetery and wonder why there were no soldiers' graves or war memorials to attest to the sacrifices of Jewish servicemen.[25] Considerations of ritual purity, Jewish religious tradition, and the rejection of Christian symbolism in the general soldiers' cemeteries were also significant.[26]

Questions concerning the collective or segregated burial of fallen soldiers during the war foreshadowed the schisms in memory that were to follow after its end. Both during and after the war, numerous publications aimed solely to highlight Jewish sacrifices to the war effort, above all quantitatively.[27] Such discourses can be seen as much as evidence of Jewish patriotism as they can of the popular contestation of Jewish loyalty to or belonging in the Austrian state. Gerald Lamprecht has moreover pointed to parallels between Jewish and non-Jewish memory discourses of the war, involving tropes such as 'the willingness to sacrifice, the love of the fatherland, and comradeship', while simultaneously these memory discourses constituted 'fields of conflict' when attached to notions of ethnicity and religious or social difference, above all reflecting the pervasive sense of 'Jewish difference'.[28] It ultimately took close to a decade to erect and dedicate a Jewish war memorial in Vienna. This was also the case with the general war memorial commissioned by the City Council, which, like the Jewish memorial, would be located in the city's

[25] See for example Hermann Stern (1915), 'Ein jüdisches Kriegerdenkmal', *Oesterreichische Wochenschrift*, 8 January, 24–25.

[26] See for example a complaint about the 'religious neglect' of burying Jewish soldiers in non-Jewish cemeteries in 'Die jüdischen Opfer des Krieges', *Jüdische Volksstimme*, 20 January 1915, 5.

[27] See for example the *Jüdisches Kriegsgedenkblatt, Nummer 1, November 1914* (Vienna, Halm & Goldmann, 1915), and subsequent issues, which lobbied its readership to send in information on 'Jewish officers, cadets, and doctors who fell before the enemy'.

[28] Lamprecht (2014), 'Erinnern an den Ersten Weltkrieg', 247.

Central Cemetery. These delays reflected the more pressing financial and material concerns reigning in Vienna in the desperate years after the end of the war. The Jewish community would not finally turn its attention to a memorial until 1926, when its leaders unanimously agreed to locate it in the soldiers' section of the Jewish part of the Central Cemetery on the outskirts of the city, as was generally customary with Jewish war memorials of the time. The origins of the memorial as a statement to Jewish belonging in the state paralleled the ideology underlying the creation of the Jewish parts of the Central Cemetery, resulting however paradoxically in a spatial segregation that seems to belie this very belonging, a point I shall return to later.[29]

The memorial was inaugurated on 13 October 1929 in the presence of Chancellor Johann Schober and other representatives of the republic, the army, and the Catholic Church, as well as military delegations from Hungary, Poland, and Germany.[30] As Lamprecht has discussed, the memorial is demonstrative of an interesting parallel discourse between 'love of the fatherland' and 'loyalty to Judaism' which characterised Jewish memory discourses throughout the interwar period.[31] Also, and importantly, the memorial evinced a decidedly pacifist message through the prominent inscription of Isaiah 2:4, in Hebrew and German: 'Nation shall not take up sword against nation; they shall never again know war'. State recognition of Jewish commemoration was regarded as a crucial acknowledgement and legitimation of the place of the Jewish community in the Austrian republic, in a climate of burgeoning Fascism, paramilitarism, and antisemitism, and was emphasised as such at every given opportunity in both the Jewish and the non-Jewish press. The inauguration was referred to as an 'impressive celebration' by various leading Austrian newspapers, which also highlighted the long list of state functionaries who participated in the event.[32] Not surprisingly, the conservative and frequently antisemitic Austrian press carried no such reports.

[29] See Tim Corbett (2016), 'Culture, Community and Belonging in the Jewish Sections of Vienna's Central Cemetery', in *Austrian Studies*, 24 (2016): Jews, Jewish Difference and Austrian Culture.

[30] Martin Senekowitsch (2006), "Ich hatt' einen Kameraden': Gedenkfeier für die im Ersten Weltkrieg gefallenen und im Holocaust getöteten jüdischen Soldaten Wiens', *Österreichisches Schwarzes Kreuz Kriegsgräberfürsorge* 123:2, 17.

[31] Lamprecht (2014), 'Erinnern an den Ersten Weltkrieg', 245.

[32] For example in 'Ein Kriegerdenkmal für die jüdischen Kriegsgefallenen', *Arbeiter-Zeitung*, 14 October 1929, 3; in 'Kriegerdenkmälerenthüllung auf dem Zentralfriedhof',

The memorial was originally maintained directly by the Jewish community organisation. In the early 1930s, however, the administrative and commemorative responsibility for the memorial was taken over by the *Bund jüdischer Frontsoldaten* (Union of Jewish Front-Line Soldiers), which was founded in 1932 in response to the rise in support of National Socialism in Austria.[33] The creation of such a militant defensive organisation is indicative of the increasingly perilous situation of Jews in the First Republic and the widespread contestation of their belonging in the new Austrian nation. This had been demonstrated from the outset by their exclusion from right-wing veterans' organisations, and by the increasing number of antisemitic attacks on Jewish civilians.[34] Conceived as a non-partisan organisation,[35] the *Bund*'s first president, General Emil Sommer,[36] was a Habsburg legitimist whose attempts to steer the *Bund* in this direction led to a schism in 1934, whereupon he seceded to found the *Legitimistische jüdische Frontkämpfer* (Legitimist Jewish Front-Line Soldiers).[37] He was succeeded as president by Captain Sigmund

Wiener Zeitung, 15 October 1929, 5; in the longer article 'Enthüllung der Kriegerdenkmäler für jüdische Soldaten: Eindrucksvolle Feier auf dem Zentralfriedhof', *Neue Freie Presse*, 14 October 1929, 4. The latter underlined the pacifist message of the memorial, which was also espoused by speakers at the event, while simultaneously emphasising Jewish fulfilment of 'duty to the *Volk* and *Heimat*' of Austria.

[33] See their own publication: Sigmund Friedmann (1935), *Drei Jahre Bund jüdischer Frontsoldaten Österreichs* (Vienna, Bund jüdischer Frontsoldaten), and a brief history of the organisation: Martin Senekowitsch (1994), *Gleichberechtigte in einer grossen Armee: Zur Geschichte des Bundes jüdischer Frontsoldaten Österreichs 1932–38* (Vienna, Militärkommando Wien).

[34] The *Frontkämpfervereinigung Deutsch-Österreichs* (Association of Front-Line Soldiers of German-Austria) for example, founded in 1920, was only open to 'former front-line soldiers of German-Aryan origin'. Lamprecht (2014), 'Erinnern an den Ersten Weltkrieg', 251. The need to mobilise against violent antisemitic attacks was evident from the earliest days of the First Republic, with attacks increasing dramatically in number and severity in the 1930s. See Berkley (1988), *Vienna*, 212.

[35] As in the mission statement: 'We do not fight for any party, we fight for our rights!' Flyer of the *Bund jüdischer Frontsoldaten Oesterreichs*, Vienna, July 1932, digital copy in author's collection kindly supplied by the *Österreichisches Schwarzes Kreuz*.

[36] In 1921, Sommer had led a successful defensive manoeuvre against Hungarian forces attempting to retain control of the ceded Burgenland, making him 'Austria's first postwar military hero'. Berkley (1988), *Vienna*, 163.

[37] Lamprecht (2014), 'Erinnerung an den Krieg: Der Bund jüdischer Frontsoldaten Österreichs 1932 bis 1938', in Patka, *Weltuntergang*, 202–203.

Friedmann, who led the *Bund* until its dissolution in 1938. Friedmann wrote of the organisation: 'The Bund immediately took a positive position towards the fatherland. Its members proudly wore the decorations won in the war at a time when the majority of the population did not yet feel themselves to be Austrian'.[38] He thereby emphasised the widespread contestation of Austrian nationhood which endured in some circles right into the 1930s, and which stood in stark contrast to the steadfast loyalty of many Austrian Jews to the new Austria, beyond the collapse of the empire. Simultaneously, the *Bund* also supported Jewish settlement in Palestine and maintained transnational links with Jewish veterans' organisations from across Eastern and Western Europe and as far afield as the USA, indicative of the kind of parallel discourse discussed earlier, namely loyalty to both the Austrian state and to Jewish peoplehood (*das jüdische Volk*).[39] This ambiguity in political loyalties was fairly typical of the Austrian Jewish population of the time, among whom political Zionism had become a growing force, yet where conceptions of Jewish peoplehood did not necessarily preclude the sense of belonging in the Austrian nation, a condition to a large degree inherited from the Habsburg era.[40]

The *Bund* quickly allied itself to the Austrofascist regime of Engelbert Dollfuß after it seized executive power in 1933, joining Dollfuß' political organisation, the *Vaterländische Front* (Fatherland Front), despite the implicit antisemitism of the movement.[41] Antisemitic rhetoric was

---

[38] Friedmann (1935), *Drei Jahre*, 17.

[39] The *Bund*'s dual loyalty was evident in its mission statement in Friedmann (1935), *Drei Jahre*, 4, while the transnational dimension of Jewish war commemoration is evident in the letters from various organisations abroad, 10–16.

[40] See the overview of the politics of the era in Harriet Freidenreich (1991), *Jewish Politics in Vienna 1918–1938* (Bloomington, Indiana University Press).

[41] During its short-lived rule, the Austrofascist state practised a quiet policy of attrition against Jews in the public sector, not to mention the intellectual and artistic exodus of Jews that had already begun with the Austrofascist seizure of power in 1933. See John Warren (2009), 'Weiße Strümpfe oder neue Kutten': Cultural Decline in Vienna in the 1930s', in Deborah Holmes and Lisa Silverman, eds. *Interwar Vienna: Culture Between Tradition and Modernity* (Suffolk, Camden House), 32–37. On Austrofascism and antisemitism, see Pauley (1990), 'Politischer Antisemitismus', 240–244. With the increasing dominance of both religious orthodoxy and political Zionism in the Jewish community of the 1930s, some of the segregationist policies of the Austrofascist state were even welcomed by the community organisation, as demonstrated by Sara Yanovsky (2010), 'Jewish Education in Interwar Vienna: Cooperation, Compromise and Conflict Between the Austrian State and the Viennese Jewish Community', in Bischof, Plasser, and Berger eds. *From Empire to Republic.*

near ubiquitous in Austria in the volatile interwar period, especially among the right, with Jews significantly being characterised in right-wing media as both inherently un-Austrian and as cynical masterminds behind the detested democratic system.[42] The *Bund*'s questionable political choice, which was shared by the leadership of Vienna's Jewish community organisation,[43] and even by such unlikely individuals as Joseph Roth and Karl Kraus,[44] has been widely interpreted as a calculated strategy based on the perception of the Austrofascists as the final bulwark against the Nazis within Austria and against Nazi Germany beyond its borders.[45] The same could of course be said in reverse, meaning that the Austrofascists could not eschew the support of a large segment of the Jewish population in an otherwise deeply fragmented society.[46] By the time Dollfuß banned the Nazi Party in Austria, the country was in a state of near civil war, with as many as forty bombings per day perpetrated by Austrian Nazis in early 1934, often targeting Jews.[47] Dollfuß was himself murdered by Austrian Nazis in a failed putsch attempt on 25 July 1934. As Bruce Pauley has demonstrated, support for both National Socialism and Austrofascism in Austria was strongest among the 'front generation', which associated 'democracy with military defeat and parliamentarianism with frustrating ideological conflict'.[48] The same could be said of Jewish support for Austrofascism, of the sort espoused by members

[42] See for example the Nazi-leaning weekly *Kikeriki* from 20 October 1929, which led on the front page with a Heimwehr militiaman in a Tyrolean hat kicking stereotyped Jewish men out of the parliament in Vienna, with the caption in Austrian dialect: 'Dear God, is the Heimwehr man powerful! What a kick!'.

[43] Berkeley wrote that that the Jewish community organisation greeted the creation of the Austrofascist state with 'enthusiastic approval', while the *Bund* cheered the end of Austrian 'pseudo-democracy'. Berkeley (1988), *Vienna*, 219. The community organisation was thereafter purged of Social Democrats in what resembled a 'witch-hunt'. Freidenreich, *Jewish Politics*, 165–166.

[44] Roth wrote a tribute to Austrofascism: 'An den » Christlichen Ständestaat«', reproduced in Hermann Kesten, ed. (1976), *Joseph Roth Werke*, Vol. 4 (Cologne, Kiepenheuer & Witsch), while Kraus regarded Austrofascism as 'the only effective barrier against the rising power of the Nazis'. Frank Field, *The Last Days of Mankind: Karl Kraus & His Vienna* (London: Macmillan, 1967), 72.

[45] See for example Pauley (1981), *Hitler*, 84; Freidenreich, *Jewish Politics*, 195.

[46] See Pauley (1990), 'Politischer Antisemitismus', 240.

[47] Berkley (1988), *Vienna*, 212.

[48] Pauley (1981), *Hitler*, 91.

of the *Bund*. Jewish support for Austrofascism was, however, later also exploited by the Nazis as evidence of a Jewish conspiracy to thwart the aspirations of German unity. This forms a striking contrast but also an interesting parallel to the allegations of a Judeo-Bolshevik conspiracy during the heyday of Red Vienna in the 1920s.[49]

By 1935, the *Bund* boasted over 20,000 members, making it the second-largest Jewish organisation in Austria after the Vienna Jewish community organisation. Although founded as a commemorative and defensive organisation, it expanded rapidly, branching into dozens of subsidiaries all over Austria which dealt with youth work, charity, education, and similar matters, and becoming ever more a representative umbrella organisation of Austrian Jewry[50]—albeit not of the significant Social Democratic milieu, which had largely been forced underground. Importantly, the *Bund* became instrumental in this context in maintaining and even expanding the Jewish war memorial at the Central Cemetery, using the site to stage commemorative events for the Great War, which functioned simultaneously as demonstrations of loyalty to the new Austrian state. Gerald Lamprecht has argued that the appeal of the *Bund* was its invocation of continuity with the Habsburg past—an authoritarian, militant past to be sure—serving as a pillar for the reformulation of Jewish Austrian identity, with mobilisation of the memory of the First World War serving a narrative of equality and belonging in Austrian society.[51] As we shall see, this evinces significant parallels to the memory discourses espoused by the Austrofascist movement.

The first commemorative event staged by the *Bund* at the Jewish war memorial took place on 18 June 1933. It was attended by around 10,000 people, including 2000 members of the *Bund*, numerous military and government representatives, along with delegations from the United Kingdom, Hungary, and Bulgaria. Naturally, there was no delegation from Germany on this occasion. The Minister of Education and '*Reichsführer*' of the *Ostmärkische Sturmscharen* (Stormtroopers of the Eastern March, an antisemitic paramilitary organisation notably modelled on the SA in Nazi Germany)[52] Kurt Schuschnigg, who

[49]See for example Werner Bergmann (2004), *Geschichte des Antisemitismus* (Munich, C. H. Beck), 79–81.

[50]See Lamprecht (2014), 'Erinnern an den Ersten Weltkrieg', 257.

[51]Lamprecht (2014), 'Erinnerung an den Krieg', 207.

[52]Walter Goldinger and Dieter Binder (1992), *Geschichte der Republik Österreich, 1918–1938* (Vienna, Verlag für Geschichte und Politik), 252.

would eventually become Chancellor after Dollfuß' assassination, sent a spokesperson to read a speech. The event was also attended by a delegation from the *Zionistische Landeskomitee* (Zionist Committee of Austria) under the leadership of Desider Friedmann, the new President of the Jewish community organisation, a Zionist and also a member of Dollfuß' State Council who would later be murdered in Auschwitz. A notable shift in emphasis from previous commemorative ceremonies is discernible in the speeches and reports of the event, reflecting the changing political realities of the time.[53] In his speech, Sigmund Friedmann called for 'equal rights in death, but also equal rights in life',[54] while the rabbis Israel Taglicht and Arnold Frankfurter (the latter a military rabbi who had served in the war and was later murdered in Buchenwald) emphasised the Jewishness of the fallen soldiers first, comparing them with Jewish warriors of old and seeing their fulfilment of military duty as the fulfilment of a 'commandment of their religion'. Rather than constituting a natural sacrifice for love of the fatherland, which had previously been the dominant trope, the actions of the Jewish war dead were now interpreted as serving 'equal rights [...] in this state', with General Emil Sommer stating 'our brothers *shall not have died in vain*' (emphasis in the original).[55] Notably, the *Christlich-Soziale Arbeiter-Zeitung*, in effect the party newspaper of the nascent Austrofascist movement, did not report on Jewish war commemorations, although it did report on a Christian memorial event to which only 'the Christian working people of Vienna' were invited.[56] The Labour Zionist weekly *Der jüdische Arbeiter*, meanwhile, also declined to report on the Jewish memorial event in Vienna, instead running extensive reports on the assassination and burial of the Zionist leader, Haim Arlosoroff, in Tel Aviv, demonstrating the exclusion from within and without of left-wing Jewry in the Austrofascist state.[57]

---

[53] The article 'Heldengedenkfeier der jüdischen Soldaten', *Neues Wiener Journal*, 19 June 1933, 2, for example, is framed by articles discussing Austria's position in Europe alongside articles on the Nazi bombing terror in Vienna, while highlighting as usual the Jewish 'love for the fatherland'.

[54] Friedmann (1935), *Drei Jahre*, 43.

[55] Cited in 'Heldengedenkfeier des Bundes jüdischer Frontsoldaten: Kundgebung für Gleichberechtigung und Frieden', *Neue Freie Presse*, 19 June 1933, 4.

[56] 'Heldensonntag', *Christlich-Soziale Arbeiter-Zeitung*, 24 June 1933, 4.

[57] See the issue from 23 June 1933.

THE AUSTROFASCIST *HELDENDENKMAL* ON THE HELDENPLATZ

A significant opportunity for the *Bund* to demonstrate its loyalty to the Austrian state to the wider public occurred with the inauguration of the new *Heldendenkmal* (Heroes' Memorial) on the Heldenplatz in central Vienna on 9 September 1934. The Heroes' Memorial, incorporated into the nineteenth-century Burgtor in front of the former Habsburg imperial palace, represented the appropriation of a central square in the Austrian capital—no longer Red Vienna—by the Austrofascist movement. The dedication of the memorial also established a military commemorative practice that was very much in keeping with older, anti-democratic forms of memory inherited from the Habsburg Empire, and linked, for example, with the crushing of the 1848 revolts. The honorary committee for the creation of the Heroes' Memorial included among a long list of functionaries Vienna's Chief Rabbi David Feuchtwang and the President of the Jewish community organisation Desider Friedmann.[58] The inauguration was widely celebrated in the Austrian press, both Jewish and non-Jewish, with the *Jüdische Front* commenting on how the uniformed Jewish veterans 'attracted attention in general through their sturdy conduct and their impeccable parade march. At many points on the Ringstraße, they were greeted by the population with joyous cheering'.[59]

Such reports evoke an apparent success story of the inclusion of the Jewish populace in Austrian society, but an exploration of Vienna's major non-Jewish broadsheets on the relevant date reveals not one mention of the *Bund*, of Jewish functionaries, or of Jewish veterans in any capacity. To cite a representative example: The *Neue Freie Presse*—before 1934 Austria's pre-eminent liberal newspaper but thereafter little more than a mouth organ for the Austrofascist state—reiterated at length the rhetoric of the state leaders, expounding 'Austria's historical mission' as a bulwark of order in Europe and tracing continuities from the Habsburg Austria of yesteryear into the present, specifically in the form of authoritarian leadership and the institution of the military.[60] Colonel General

---

[58] *Gedenkschrift anläßlich der Weihe des österreichischen Heldendenkmales am 9. September 1934* (Vienna: Vereinigung zur Errichtung eines Österreichischen Heldendenkmals, 1934), 14.

[59] 'Der B.J.F. bei der Heldengedenkfeier am 9. September 1934', *Jüdische Front*, 15 October 1934, 16.

[60] 'Die Weihe des Heldendenkmals', *Neue Freie Presse*, 10 September 1934, 2–3.

Viktor Dankl von Krásnik proclaimed that 'the old Austrianness' of the Habsburg Empire had been honoured once more and had 'proven its invincible power in the battles of this year'—a reference to the brutal crushing of Social Democracy in February and defeat of the Nazi putsch attempt in July. Chancellor Schuschnigg spoke of a 'new era', with a 'new *Volk*, a new country, and a new form of state', but emphasised that the Heldenplatz had 'a thousand-year historical message that we must not forget, for then we should never understand our new fatherland'. Federal President Wilhelm Miklas finally called Austria 'the sole bulwark of Europe' and, echoing Joseph Roth, 'the redemptive idea for all of Europe'—albeit that the *völkisch*, pseudo-Germanic, and arch-Catholic nationalism promoted by the Austrofascists had little else to do with Roth's conception of a multicultural Austrian role model for Europe.[61] In any case, there was no space in the rhetoric of the state leaders or in non-Jewish press reports to mention Jewish participation, either in the war or in its commemoration at the Heldenplatz.

The perplexing blur of definitions between the 'Austria' of the Habsburg past and the 'Austria' of the Fascist present also manifested itself in a publication of the memorial committee following the inauguration of the site, for example in the words of Chancellor Schuschnigg: 'For the construction of our historic German Ostmark we can find no better role models or shining examples than in the ranks of those men who are now finally granted an honourable commemoration.'[62] The paradox here extends beyond the identification of the empire with the Austria of the 1930s, with Schuschnigg appealing to an independent state which he then referred to as the 'German Ostmark', employing a term that today is more usually associated with Nazi German discourses on Austria. The authenticity of the 'German' nationalism of the Austrofascist movement is the focus of intense discussion and a topic which requires more sustained research in the future.[63] There were, in any case, numerous such blurred boundaries between Austrofascism

---

[61] See for example his essays on the destruction of Austria following the *Anschluß*: Joseph Roth, 'Totenmesse' and 'Huldigung an den Geist Österreichs', in Kesten (1976), *Joseph Roth Werke* (Vol. 4).

[62] *Gedenkschrift* (1934), 4.

[63] See Julie Thorpe (2010), 'Pan-Germanism After Empire: Austrian 'Germandom' at Home and Abroad', in Bischof, Plasser, and Berger, *From Empire to Republic*.

and National Socialism, both in terms of ideology and personalities.[64] Detailed elaboration on this exceeds the scope of this chapter, but, to offer a representative example, the crypt of the Austrofascist Heroes' Memorial—which was unsurprisingly co-opted as a memorial site by the Nazis from 1938 to 1945 and thereafter used to commemorate convicted Nazi war criminals in the Second Republic—was after many decades of rumour excavated in 2012 to confirm that the sculptor, Wilhelm Frass, who it later turned out had been a member of the illegal Nazi Party all along, had indeed buried a dedication to National Socialism and an appeal for an *Anschluß* to Nazi Germany here, at a site that was supposed to underscore Austria's nationhood and independence.[65] Viewed today from one angle, the memorial stands before the balcony of the Hofburg where Hitler announced Austria's *Anschluß* with Germany on 15 March 1938, while viewed from another angle it stands before one of the flak towers built during the disastrous war launched by German and Austrian Nazis. The square in which it stands is framed by the seat of Austrian power: the President's offices, the Chancellery, and the Parliament. Arguably, no other site in contemporary Austria so viscerally encapsulates the paradoxical interconnectivity of twentieth-century Austrian history.

Despite these contextually and, to some degree, retrospectively reconstructed patterns of ideology evinced by the Austrofascist movement, the ostensibly mutual support between the *Bund* as a Jewish umbrella organisation and the Austrofascist state was once again put on display during the annual commemorative service at the Jewish war memorial only eight days later. Held on 17 September 1934, with some

---

[64] George Berkley recounted a joke from the interwar period that characterises the paradoxes of political sentiments in the First Republic: Chancellor Schuschnigg asks the mayor of an Austrian town about its political makeup: 'How many of your people are Christian Socials? About fifty per cent. How many are Social Democrats? Some forty percent. Well, then, how many are Nazis? Approximately one hundred per cent'. Berkley (1988), *Vienna*, 241, see also the discussion of the '180-degree turn' from Austrofascism to National Socialism, 301–303. In terms of discourse alone, Austrofascism was deeply reminiscent of National Socialism, which would also be deserving of closer study.

[65] See Peter Diem, 'Das Äußere Burgtor: Ein österreichisches Heldendenkmal?' http://austria-forum.org/af/Wissenssammlungen/Symbole/Burgtor_-_Heldendenkmal (accessed 31 January 2017).

30,000 people in attendance, this was to be the largest such Jewish commemorative event of the First World War in the history of the First Republic.[66] The ceremony was attended, as usual, by representatives of the state, the army, the *Vaterländische Front*, the *Ostmärkische Sturmscharen*, the Vienna City Council, and numerous Jewish organisations, not to mention veterans and their relatives. After heaping praise on the murdered Chancellor Dollfuß, the *Bund*'s President Sigmund Friedmann made an interesting appeal to 'Austrianness': 'It has been twenty years since Austria's peoples were called up to defend the fatherland. All Austrians, whether Christian or Jew, joyfully answered the call to fulfil their duty as citizens of the state. They moved out to protect Austria's honour and Austria's borders'.[67] Time and cultural space were here, as in Austrofascist rhetoric, collapsed in on themselves; the Habsburg Empire became synonymous with the Austrofascist state, and while all the 'peoples of Austria' were ostensibly collectivised, only Christians and Jews were explicitly included in this appeal to Austrianness[68]—bearing in mind, of course, that the contemporaneous discourses concerning the Heldenplatz did not mention Jews at all. And yet Friedmann's speech, like that of Chief Rabbi Feuchtwang after him, once more decried antisemitism and invoked the memory of service in the war as proof of 'Jewish loyalty to the fatherland'. Even Desider Friedmann, a Zionist, proclaimed that the Jewish soldiers had 'fallen as sons of Austria, they sacrificed their lives for Austria'. These speeches by Jewish leaders were followed by speeches from Austrian military dignitaries, who mostly just rehashed the Austrofascist state discourse analysed above.

Non-Jewish newspaper coverage of the event was much the same as it had been the year before—the same titles, the same lists of

---

[66] A detailed account can be found in 'Friedhofs- und Beerdigungswesen', in *Bericht des Präsidiums und des Vorstandes der Israelitischen Kultusgemeinde Wien über die Tätigkeit in den Jahren 1933–1936* (Vienna, Verlag der israelitischen Kultusgemeinde in Wien, 1936).

[67] 'Die Feier auf dem Zentralfriedhofe', *Jüdische Front*, 15 October 1934, 3–8.

[68] This also excluded other participants in the Habsburg military, such as Muslims, of whom 14,000 served in the First World War. Christoph Neumayer (2014), 'Muslimische Soldaten in der k.u.k. Armee', in Patka ed. *Weltuntergang*, 98.

prominent attendees, the same appeal to Jewish sacrifices to the father-land.[69] The same was true of the next annual commemoration, held on 22 September 1935,[70] and of the small annual commemoration on 20 September 1936.[71] The final event before the *Anschluß* and the destruction of Vienna's Jewish community which followed in its wake was held on 12 September 1937. This time, however, a change of tone was evident, with Sigmund Friedmann stating that it was not up to Jews to draw the right conclusions from their service in the war, explicitly imploring the 'Christian comrades from the front' to 'remember the mutual aid and support in the battlefield, and help us also now, in the hour of our need', referring specifically to the pervasive 'Jew-hatred' in Austrian society.[72] Exactly six months later, on 12 March 1938, German troops marched unhindered into Austria. According to an unverified legend, General Emil Sommer, the former President of the *Bund*, was granted permission by the SA in March 1938 to appear in full military uniform to scrub the Austrofascist propaganda off the streets of Vienna during a citywide pogrom.[73] He died in Massachusetts on 10 April 1947, his ashes being returned to Austria and buried at the Central Cemetery in a ceremony attended by state, military, and community leaders. Some managed to escape, including Sigmund Friedmann, who changed his name to Eitan Avissar and henceforth became a leading figure in the *Haganah* and later Israeli Defence Forces, while still maintaining contact with his former comrades of the Habsburg imperial army until his death in 1964.[74] No records allowing for exact statistics survived the

[69] For example 'Heldengedenkfeier des Bundes der jüdischen Frontsoldaten', Neue Freie Presse, 17 September 1934, 6. Note that the title is almost word for word the same as in the report of the previous year.

[70] See for example 'Heldengedenkfeier des Bundes jüdischer Frontsoldaten', Neue Freie Presse, 23 September 1935, 8.

[71] See 'Grabgang zu den jüdischen Heldengräbern im Zentralfriedhof', *Neue Freie Presse*, 21 September 1936, 6.

[72] Cited in 'Heldengedenkfeier des Bundes jüdischer Frontsoldaten', *Neue Freie Presse*, 13 September 1937, 8.

[73] Martin Senekowitsch (2014), 'Emil Sommer: Bundesheer-Generalmajor, BJF-Gründer, Kultusrat', in Patka, ed. *Weltuntergang*, 225.

[74] Peter Steiner (2014), 'Sigmund Edler von Friedmann / Eitan Avissar: BJF-Präsident und israelischer Brigadegeneral', in Patka, ed. *Weltuntergang*, 221.

destruction of the Nazis, who wanted to eradicate any evidence of Jewish soldiery or sacrifice for the Central Powers in the First World War, but at least 238 Jewish Austrian soldiers, mostly officers, were forcibly retired in March 1938, most of whom later fell victim to the Holocaust.[75] They survived the front as Austrians, and died in the gas chambers and killing fields as Jews.

CONCLUSION

The Nazi era, among its numerous atrocities, witnessed the attempt to eradicate 'Austria' from the political and cultural map, to be absorbed as merely a constituent part into a newly conceived 'Nazi German' culture. The creation of this new and idealised construct of 'German' culture was to be achieved largely through the monstrous, genocidal removal of Jews, as much a physical genocide as it was cultural in intention and impact. If we follow the idea of Austria's Jews going into the interwar period as, in some sense, the 'only true Austrians'—after all, many of the Austrofascists, even if they were not secret Nazis already, were quick to jump ship and join the ranks of Nazi Germany after the *Anschluß*—then the creation of a new, idealised 'Nazi German' culture was to be achieved, at least within the borders of Austria, through the destruction of the most Austrian of Austrians.

What I have briefly sketched here is an outline of a topic that promises deep insights into the conflicted, and largely failed, attempt at creating an Austrian nation after the First World War. This nation was not only supposed to be inclusive of perceived minorities such as Jews, but was in fact largely shaped and defined by them, although we would have to look elsewhere, for example in the burgeoning literary culture or among the cosmopolitan socialites of 1920s Vienna, for positive and constructive interactions between Jewishness and Austrianness. What we have seen here, rather, is a great parallelism of discourse running through the commemoration of war, but where the participation and belonging of Jews ended up as discursively marginalised as the Jewish war memorial is spatially removed on the outskirts of the city, by contrast to the central, and today still deeply contested, Heldenplatz. For all that National

---

[75] Schmidl (1989), *Juden*, 90.

Socialism and the Holocaust have eclipsed the formerly illustrious world of Jewish Austria and the unsuccessful attempts at nation-building in the First Austrian Republic, this preliminary examination demonstrates that the memory of service in the First World War, and by extension the memory of the vanished world of Habsburg Central Europe, served for a short period for Jews and non-Jews alike as a meaningful and unifying platform on which to attempt the construction of a new nation by consensus, and moreover that the relationship between Jews and nascent Austrian nationhood in its modern, republican form was far more interactive than has hitherto been acknowledged.

The Iron Shield of David: The First World War and the Creation of German-Jewish Markers of Patriotism and Memory

Michal Friedlander

When war was declared in 1914, citizens of the Austro-Hungarian Empire and the German Reich were quick to express their patriotic zeal. Four years later, they were shocked and sobered by defeat. The appalling death toll numbered in the millions and the populations of the Eastern and Central European nations that had been embroiled in the conflict were forced to reflect on the grim results. As in the victor states, a commemorative culture developed and monuments to fallen soldiers were erected in their thousands across the territories of the former Habsburg and Hohenzollern Empires. 'Rolls of Honour' were compiled, listing the names of fallen soldiers, and became the basis for permanent wall-hanging tablets that could be found—and may still be found—in schools, banks, meeting halls, pubs and churches, to name just a few examples.

The German-Jewish community had never experienced human loss and bereavement on such a massive scale and the *Reichsbund Jüdischer*

M. Friedlander (✉)
Jewish Museum Berlin, Berlin, Germany
e-mail: m.friedlander@jmberlin.de

© The Author(s) 2019
E. Madigan and G. Reuveni (eds.),
The Jewish Experience of the First World War,
https://doi.org/10.1057/978-1-137-54896-2_13

Frontsoldaten (RJF), an organization of Jewish war veterans, compiled a memorial book listing the number of fallen Jewish soldiers. In 1929, they published the numbers of German Jews in military service during the recent war, thereby challenging a perceived lack of Jewish participation, a subject that had been a matter of contention throughout the war period and thereafter. According to their figures, of the 540,000 Jews in the German Reich, more than 100,000 men had served in the military, with 80,000 of them serving at the front and 12,000 falling in the field.[1] German Jews thus very much shared in the wave of grief that coursed through their country and began to consider appropriate forms of memorialization.

As Tim Grady has noted, Jewish and non-Jewish German soldiers had often attended the same schools, shared workplaces, and were members of the same clubs and organizations. This led to a variety of intertwined groups of mourning and forms of commemoration and shows how Jews were part of a wider community of collective remembrance.[2] However, many German-Jewish communities also erected their own collective war memorials and created commemorative objects. A broad survey of First World War memorials and memorial objects for German-Jewish soldiers is much needed, but regrettably beyond the scope of this chapter.[3] This large and complex body of material includes grave markers for soldiers buried in military cemeteries or on the battlefield; hometown tombstones for individual soldiers in cases where it was possible to repatriate and reinter remains; and commemorative graveyard inscriptions when repatriation proved impossible. This chapter will focus on distinctively Jewish objects of remembrance in the form of commemorative plaques that were placed in the intimate, indoor prayer space of synagogue sanctuaries. It will also examine a particular group of patriotic 'nailed' emblems connected to the First World War that were created by Jews. In Gerhard Schneider's epic

[1] See *Gemeindeblatt der Israelitischen Gemeinde Frankfurt am Main*, Heft 7, March 1929, 224.

[2] See Tim Grady (2008), 'A Common Experience of Death: Commemorating the German-Jewish Soldiers of the Great War, 1914–1923', in Alon Confino, Paul Betts, and Dirk Schumann, eds., *Between Mass Death and Individual Loss: The Place of the Dead in Twentieth Century Germany* (New York, Berghahn), 185–187.

[3] Ulrich Knufinke concurs on the regrettable absence of a scientific overview in this research area and lists relevant, extant publications. See Ulrich Knufinke (27 June 2017), 'Sie haben gestritten und sind gestorben fürs Vaterland und fürs Judentum', in *Friedhöfe für jüdische Gefallene des Ersten Weltkriegs im Deutschen Reich*, RIHA Journal 0157, footnote 8.

2013 monograph on this highly distinctive form of patriotic object, which documents approximately one thousand 'nailed' emblems, the author mentions that he only discovered a small number of the emblems that must have existed.[4] While Schneider's work greatly enriches our understanding of German First World War patriotic culture, and the phenomenon of *Nageln* in particular, the author generally overlooks the German-Jewish use of the distinctive medium of 'nailing' emblems. This chapter will add some largely unknown cases of Jewish nailed objects and perhaps provide new insights and broaden our understanding of this medium.

Support on the Home Front—The Patriotic Act of 'Steeling' War Symbols

During the early years of the war, civilians on the home front were keen to demonstrate solidarity with the war effort and express their hopes for victory. This is evidenced by a peculiar practice that spread through the German Reich and Austro-Hungary from 1915 to 1916 known as *Nageln* or 'nailing.' The phenomenon was inspired by a section of spruce tree displayed in Vienna called the *Stock im Eisen* (staff in iron),[5] a piece of wood that had been pounded with nails, ostensibly for good luck, for centuries.[6] The idea of hammering nails into wood to release (protective) powers can be found in many ancient cultures, for example in the Congo, where nails were driven into Nkondi idols to arouse a spirit into action when petitioning for help.[7] The *mezuzah*, which is nailed to the doorpost of a Jewish home, has been viewed in Jewish folk culture as a 'house amulet' with apotropaic qualities, even if rabbinic authorities have sought to provide rationalist explanations for the custom.[8]

On 6 March 1915, a wooden figure of a medieval knight, designed by sculptor Josef Müllner, was set up in Vienna's Schwarzenbergplatz.

---

[4] Gerhard Schneider (2013), *In eiserner Zeit: Kriegswahrzeichen im Ersten Weltkrieg* (Rödelheim, Wochenschau Verlag), 5.

[5] All German and Hebrew translations in this text are by the author.

[6] The origins of this relic are discussed by the naturalist, Franz Unger (14 July 1859), the *Wiener Zeitung*, 13.

[7] See Wyatt McGaffey (2000), *Kongo Political Culture: The Conceptual Challenge to the Particular* (Bloomington, Indiana University Press), 97.

[8] For further discussion of this subject, see M. L. Gordon (1977), 'Mezuzah: Protective Amulet or Religious Symbol?', *Tradition: A Journal of Orthodox Thought* 16:4, 7–40.

For a prescribed sum, anyone could hammer an iron nail into the figure and the accumulated proceeds were designated for the aid of war widows and orphans. At the end of April 1915, the first nailing in the German Reich, which took the form of a large Iron Cross, was set up in Darmstadt. The idea was initiated by Fürstin Marie zu Erbach-Schönberg, a writer and the wife of a local count, who had been living in Vienna and witnessed the *Wehrmann in Eisen*.[9] The city of Heilbronn in northern Baden-Würtemberg followed suit and erected a nailing emblem only a month later.[10] It was the figure of a knight—*Der Eisenhart*—whose soft wood would become as hard as iron (and hence unassailable), just like a German in times of adversity, as proclaimed in rhyme on a postcard from 1915.[11]

The fund-raising for these monuments, which was very much a communal practice, captured the public imagination and was taken up throughout the German Reich, without any form of national, centralized organization. There were both official, civic initiatives and private efforts, usually on a far smaller scale. Germans of all backgrounds and ages were soon hammering iron nails into wooden forms (with pre-bored holes) of heraldic lions, eagles, griffins and civic coats of arms; military motifs included swords, submarines, grenades, torpedoes and ships, although the Iron Cross was the most prevalent. They nailed motifs into tables, church and town hall doors. They drove nails into three-dimensional figures of legendary heroes and saints and, in 1915, a 13-metre-high alder wood figure of the revered general, Paul von Hindenburg, was unveiled on Königsplatz in Berlin to be nailed by the masses. The dedication on September 4 took place a few days after the first anniversary of the victorious Battle of Tannenberg that had been led by Hindenburg.[12] The war hero became a national symbol and in the form of a colossus, a literal embodiment of German hopes for victory in war.[13]

---

[9] Michael Fischer and Aibe-Marlene Gerdes, eds. (2016), *Der Krieg und die Frauen: Geschlecht und populäre Literatur im Ersten Weltkrieg* (Münster, Waxmann), 298.

[10] Gerhard Schneider (1999), 'Zur Mobilisierung der 'Heimatfront': das Nageln von Kriegswahrzeichen im Ersten Weltkrieg', *Zeitschrift für Volkskunde* 95, 37.

[11] 'Weich Holz zuerst // dann Eisenhart //so ward in Not //die deutsche Art', 25 March 2017.http://www.ebay.de/itm/191992926985?clk_rvr_id=1110493900853&rmvSB=true.

[12] *Berliner Tageblatt und Handels-Zeitung*, Berlin Mosse, 4 September 1915, 4.

[13] Jesko von Hoegen (2007), *Der Held von Tannenberg—Genese und Funktion des Hindenburg-Mythos*, Stuttgarter Historische Forschungen, vol. 4. (Stuttgart, Böhlau), 143.

The organization of a nailing project was a visible sign of patriotism and societal engagement in the local community. The July 1916 issue of the monthly Jewish periodical *Im Deutschen Reich* mentions the unveiling of the figure of a knight, the *Stadtritter*, in the northern Bavarian town of Bamberg.[14] It describes how in October 1915, the first golden nails were hammered into the figure by Archbishop Dr. von Hauck, the Mayor of Bamberg and the donor of the figure.[15] Photographs document the event, which took place in front of the town hall on the Maximillianplatz. The figure was set up under a roofed shelter in the centre of the crowded square. There was a band, local organizations displayed their banners and many uniformed military servicemen were present.[16] As in Darmstadt, a woman was at the centre of this highly charged civic event, but, in this case, the donor of the figure was a Jewish woman, Emma Hellmann. Born in Verona in 1867, she was the wife of a local Jewish banker and businessman,[17] Hermann Hellmann. Jews had a significant presence in the commercial life of Bamberg at the time, particularly in the field of banking, and it was a Jewish hop-dealer, Samuel Rosenfelder, who suggested the use of the motif of the Bamberg heraldic knight for the nailing. Emma Hellmann donated the figure itself, while her husband's bank managed the donations (which ultimately totalled around 20,000 Marks) that were devoted to aiding the Red Cross and purchasing war provisions.[18]

One indication of the confident Jewish presence in Bamberg at this time was the city's large and imposing synagogue, which had been built in the years before the war at a cost of 500,000 Marks. The synagogue tower was 37 metres high and a prominent city landmark. The dedication ceremony for the new building, which took place on 11 September 1910, concluded with a prayer for King and Fatherland and a song.[19]

---

[14] Schneider (2013), *In Eiserner Zeit*, 131.

[15] *Im Deutschen Reich: Zeitschrift des Centralvereins Deutscher Staatsbürger Jüdischen Glaubens*, Heft 7–8, July 1916, 182.

[16] A photographic series, documenting the dedication ceremony, is held in the collections of the Staatsbibliothek Bamberg, Sig. V Bxb 2–10a.

[17] Hellmann held the title of 'Kommerzienrat', an honour awarded in the German Reich until 1919 to successful businessmen who were generous public patrons.

[18] Regina Hanemann, ed. (2013), *Jüdisches in Bamberg* (Bamberg, Michael Imhof Verlag), 296.

[19] *Allgemeine Zeitung des Judenthums*, Beilage, 16 September 1910, 3.

Members of the Jewish community were thus clearly prepared to voice their patriotism within the walls of their place of worship, and were witnessed doing so by their non-Jewish neighbours. According to a contemporary Jewish press report, 'The participation of church and civil authorities makes it clear that the dragon seed of antisemitism happily has few roots here.'[20]

While the Jewish press emphasized the positive atmosphere at the Bamberg synagogue dedication ceremony, which apparently reflected the harmonious relations between Jews and non-Jews in the area, the *Im Deutschen Reich* report also hinted at a certain insecurity in the Jewish community. The use of the phrase 'the dragon seed of antisemitism' suggests an underlying feeling that antisemitism could potentially sprout and grow in Bamberg at any time. Such fears would prove to be valid concerns.

Five years after the synagogue dedication, Emma Hellmann's public act of striking a golden nail into a *Kriegswahrzeichen* (emblem of war) in front of the assembled Bamberg community, made for a major demonstration of personal and Jewish support for the war effort and an expression of identity and values shared with other German patriots.[21] In spite of this clear demonstration of patriotism, Emma Hellmann was deported to Theresienstadt some twenty-seven years after the nailing of the Bamberg *Stadtritter*. On 9 September 1942, at the age of 75, she was murdered in Treblinka.

JEWISH NAILED MOTIFS

The participatory public nailing of a symbolic, community object can also illustrate the ambivalence and distrust with which Jews were regarded in some German communities and their social exclusion from the German mainstream. For instance, Moritz Sender, President of the Jewish community in Biebrich (Wiesbaden) in Hessen, wrote to the local

---

[20] *Im Deutschen Reich*, Nr. 10, October 1910, 692.

[21] It should be noted that this was not an isolated case of Jewish involvement in creating local patriotic war emblems to help fund the war effort. For example, a Jewish factory owner, Karl Ullmann, donated 3000 Marks towards the construction of the Fürth nailing column that was installed in 1916 (see Simon Rötsch 2017), Spuren jüdischen Lebens in Fürth während des ersten Weltkriegs, 37, http://www.stadtheimatpflege-fuerth.de/wp-content/uploads/2017/04/Fiorda-14-18.pdf.

mayor in 1915 complaining that the participation of the Jewish population in the nailing of the Iron Cross was clearly unwelcome.[22]

Jewish individuals and communities took the initiative to create their own nailed monuments and motifs, although it is impossible to establish if the creation of such monuments was in any way motivated by feelings of exclusion from public events. There are references to the nailing of distinctively Jewish wooden icons taking place in a specifically Jewish social context. In the *Jüdische Turn- und Sportzeitung* of 1919, for example, the Hamburg division of the Zionist sport club, Bar Kochba, reviewed events from the recent war period. They mentioned collecting and sending care packages to soldiers in the field, creating a field library, as well as nailing the wooden motif of a seven-branched candelabrum (*menorah*): 'In February 1916, Lotte Hecker donated our iron menorah, which had been nailed so eagerly, proving how closely we Bar Kochba members hold together. The use of this nailing fund is yet to be decided.'[23]

The long-standing German-Jewish publication, *Allgemeine Zeitung des Judenthums*, also gives a detailed and very revealing report of the nailing of a *Magen David* (Shield of David) in Ulm in Baden-Württemberg in 1915.[24] At the time, Ulm was a garrison town with a large military presence. On Sunday 5 December, all available Jewish soldiers were given the day off to participate in a special synagogue service, to be followed by a Chanukkah celebration. Several hundred soldiers, in military dress, attended the prayer service. Rabbi Dr. Treitel delivered a sermon that highlighted the particular relevance of the Chanukkah story in a contemporary German context, given the current 'revival of a Maccabean spirit.' The Chanukkah festival celebrates the military triumph of Judah Maccabee and his followers in 164 B.C.E. and, in Jewish

---

[22] Paul Arnsberg (1971), *Die jüdischen Gemeinden in Hessen. Angang – Untergang - Neubeginn*, vol. 1 (Frankfurt a. Main, Societäts-Verlag), 72. This type of social exclusion would surface again when nailing projects were revived in German schools to encourage membership in the Hitler Youth organization. Select (non-Jewish) school children would be told to buy a nail that they could then hammer into a Hitler Youth insignia. See Heinz 'Coco' Schumann's description in Tina Hüttl and Alexander Meschnig (2013), *Uns kriegt ihr nicht: Wie jüdische Kinder versteckt überlebten* (Munich, Piper ebooks), 126.

[23] *Jüdische Turn- und Sportzeitung: Organ des Deutschen Kreises der jüdischen Turnerschaft*, 2. Jahrgang, Heft 2, 1919, 19. Reprinted in Manfred Lämmer, ed. (1977), *Jüdische Turnzeitung: 1919–1921*. Jg. 20–22 (Walluf, Sändig Reprint Verlag).

[24] *Allgemeine Zeitung des Judenthums*, Beilage, Heft 51, 17 December 1915, 3.

lore, the Maccabees are associated with tactical skill, exemplary military leadership and heroic deeds.[25]

Following the service, the soldiers marched to a local inn, the Gasthof Mohren zu Ulm,[26] and lit and blessed innumerable Chanukkah candles that were placed on a table. The ostensible highlight of the evening occurred when a certain Corporal Marks set a wooden form on the table to be nailed.[27] The shape to be nailed was a *Magen David* and the word *Chanukkah* was written in colourful Hebrew letters in the centre. The term *Magen David* is generally translated as 'Star of David' but it is clear that the literal meaning of the term is intended here, i.e. 'Shield of David.' The symbol is of course associated with the figure of King David, a valorous warrior who united the people of Israel and led them to military victory. Apparently, Dr. Treitel also expounded on the meaning of the *Magen David* at the soldiers' Chanukkah party when dedicating this Jewish war emblem. We are fortunate that the magazine printed an illustration of this ephemeral object in a later article that refers to the event[28] (Fig. 1). The image shows a six-pointed hexagram, the lines of which are made up of four rows of nails set within a circle that is also delineated with four rows of nails. The Jewish and Gregorian years are written between the points of the star element. The overall composition suggests a shield and a direct comparison can be made with popular wooden nailing forms for the Iron Cross, which was also often set within a circle, suggesting the form of a shield.[29]

---

[25] The use of the Maccabees and the Chanukkah story to promote national military pride among Jews was not unique to Germany. The Rev. (rabbi) Francis L. Cohen had instituted a special, patriotic Hanukkah service for British Jewish soldiers in 1893. The London Borough synagogue was decorated with trophies and military memorabilia for the occasion (see *The Graphic*, No. 1256, vol. XLVIII, 23 December 1893, cover page, with ill.) and it became a regular event (see also 'Chanucah Celebrations—Annual Military Service', in *The Jewish Chronicle*, 10 December 1915, 21).

[26] The Gasthof zum Mohren was located on 23 Weinhof, Ulm from 1600 until a bombing raid in World War II destroyed the building. The local Israelitische Lese-Verein, founded in 1855, convened here prior to 1920. One can therefore assume that this inn was a place that welcomed Jewish group gatherings. My thanks to Matthias Grotz, Stadtarchiv, Stadt Ulm, for this information.

[27] Corporal Marx is most likely to have been Ernst Marx (1878–1917), son of the prominent Ulm industrialist Leopold Marx. He died in a military hospital in Belgium while on active service.

[28] *Allgemeine Zeitung des Judenthums*, Heft 16, 21 April 1916, 185, ill., 186.

[29] For a number of examples see http://www.kriegsnagelungen.de/von-der-1-klasse-bis-zur-oberprima-schulnagelungen-im-deutschen-reich/, accessed 25 March 2017.

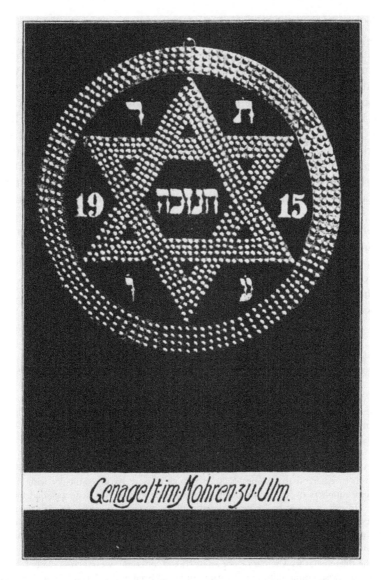

Fig. 1 'The nailing of a Mogen Dovid.' *Allgemeine Zeitung des Judenthums*, 21 April 1916, ill., 186. © Allgemeine Zeitung des Judenthums/Jewish Museum Berlin

First awarded in 1813, the Iron Cross was a well-established military decoration by the outbreak of the First World War, and it commanded considerable public esteem. The decoration was awarded primarily for valour in combat and Jewish newspapers proudly reported every Iron Cross awarded to a Jewish serviceman and were quick to note if Jewish recipients of the medal were mentioned in the mainstream press.[30] Its acceptance by Jews is exemplified by a memorial 'stele' commemorating Julius Reis, a Jewish soldier from Heilbronn, who was serving with a field artillery unit in northern France when he was killed in June 1918. The stele is carved in relief with a portrait of Reis by the Karlsruhe artist Hugo Dohm and shows the bespectacled soldier in uniform, his chest demonstrably emblazoned with an Iron Cross[31] (Fig. 2). Despite the acceptance of the Iron Cross by Jews as a military decoration,[32] a particular Jewish community may nevertheless have been uncomfortable to select any form of cross, with its Christian associations, as a symbol to represent them.[33] In Ulm, they chose instead to create an 'Iron Star' as their nailing emblem: a crossover object inscribed with both Jewish and secular dates.

The Ulm nailing project raised the charitable sum of close to 2000 Marks for troops in the field and their families. A newspaper report notes

---

[30] *Allgemeine Zeitung des Judenthums*, 11 December 1914, 590: cites a report in the *Berliner Tagesblatt*: 'A private survey on the participation of Jews in the War reveals interesting information. To date, 710 soldiers of the Jewish faith have received an Iron Cross, including three of the First Order.'

[31] Reis's mother immigrated to England in August 1939 at the age of 65, taking this cumbersome memorial stone with her. It is now in the collection of the Jewish Museum Berlin, inv. no. 2016/27/0.

[32] Jewish pride in the Iron Cross decoration is reflected in a commentary from 1917 (*Mitteilungen aus dem Verein zur Abwehr des Antisemitismus*, 7 February 1917, 24). The author remarked that some '*Nörgler*' (whiners) were having difficulty with the fact that large numbers of Jews were in active military service and had been awarded the Iron Cross. He was incensed by ironic comments in the publication *Auf Vorposten*, suggesting that Jews should be awarded an 'Iron Star of David' in its stead, viewing such comments as both an insult to Jewish recipients of the Iron Cross as well as to 'the most beautiful of all decorations.'

[33] The dilemma as to whether or not a Jew should, or could, wear a cross symbol was not unique to Jewish communities in Germany. In Great Britain, the *Jewish Chronicle* reported a debate that transpired in (pre-war) 1914 concerning the wearing of the Red Cross by Jewish women in the military hospital corps and the related question of whether or not a Jew should wear a Victoria Cross that he had been awarded. See *The Jewish Chronicle*, 30 January 1914, 15.

Fig. 2 Memorial stone for Julius Reis, a Jewish soldier killed in France in 1918, by Hugo Dohns, 1921. Height: 71.5 cm. © Collection of the Jewish Museum Berlin/Jens Ziehe (photographer)

that this effort represented 'Yet another testament to the self-sacrifice and patriotism of German, Jewish citizens …' and that 'All of the participants had the impression of being part of a lovely family gathering, celebrated in a truly patriotic as well as Jewish spirit.'[34] Through the example of this distinctively Jewish nailing motif, we see how Jews reinterpreted and used their own historical narratives and cultural symbols to underscore their patriotic fervour for Germany and sought to demonstrate that German and Jewish identities were complementary rather than contradictory. As such, the nailing in Ulm was a proud demonstration, by Jewish soldiers, of dual national and Jewish affiliation.

The need for a pro-active stance in the Jewish community becomes more understandable when viewed in a general societal context. This specific nailing project, for example, was attacked by Heinrich Pudor, a German nationalist who regularly expressed fiercely anti-Jewish views in self-published journals. A series of Pudor's antisemitic statements were repudiated in the *Allgemeine Zeitung des Judenthums* and his comments on the Ulm nailing project reviled as the 'highest point of ignorance and malice'.[35] Pudor had read the magazine's report of the Ulm nailing event[36] and circulated part of the article under the heading 'The Auctioning off of an "Iron"' ('Versteigerung eines "Eisernen"') with reference to the following passage:

'The sizable sum [raised by the nailing] was increased even more by the auctioneering of the *Benschen*, a custom that has been introduced to Southern Germany, which brought in over one hundred Marks.'[37]

Pudor seems to have understood the word *Benschen* as referring to the nailed object and that Jewish soldiers were disrespectfully auctioning off and abusing a patriotic war symbol.[38] He uses the opportunity

---

[34] *Allgemeine Zeitung des Judenthums*, Beilage, Heft 51, 17 December 1915, 3.

[35] *Allgemeine Zeitung des Judenthums*, Heft 13, 31 March 1916, 147.

[36] See footnote 24.

[37] See footnote 35: *AZJ*, Heft 13, 31 March 1916, 148.

[38] War symbols were held in extraordinarily high regard and any perceived abuse was found extremely offensive. The Berlin police, for example, stepped in to stop civilians and children from wearing Iron Cross replicas. See Bayerischer Kunstgewerbe-Verein. *Kunst und Handwerk: Zeitschrift für Kunstgewerbe und Kunsthandwerk*, vol. 65, 1914–1915, 55.

to discredit Jewish soldiers and to drum up suspicion and general mistrust towards the Jewish community. In fact, *Benschen* is a Judeo-German word meaning 'to bless'. It refers to the honour of leading the Grace after Meals (*Birkat ha-Mazon*) and it was this privilege that was auctioned off, the proceeds of which were then added to the soldiers' charitable fund.

Evidence of another specifically Jewish *Nagelung*, most likely from Oldenburg, can be found today as a photographic motif on a postcard. It shows a wooden form in the shape of a Star of David, the lines of the hexagram studded with nails (Fig. 3). There is a dedicatory text in the centre, as well as a Hebrew text made up of six words: a single word appearing in each point of the star. The dedication states that it (presumably the collected proceeds) was intended for Jewish soldiers and the wounded in the war year of 1915. The dedication continues that it (presumably the form) was a gift from Landrabbiner Mannheimer and his wife, on the occasion of their silver wedding anniversary on 22 October 1915. David Mannheimer was an orthodox rabbi, married to Mathilde Jaffé, who served as Landrabbiner for the district of Oldenburg. Three of their sons served in the First World War and their son Max was the first soldier from Oldenburg to fall in action, on 29 August 1914.[39] The Oldenburg yearbook of 1915 lists local men who fell in battle, commemorating them with photographs, biographies, poems and extracts from letters written at the front. However, Max Mannheimer is not included in the list of 'our heroes' for 1915,[40] or in subsequent volumes. Such pointed exclusion would have been reason enough for Rabbi Mannheimer (a passionate patriot and Jewish naval chaplain) to commission a conspicuously Jewish *Kriegswahrzeichen*.

The Hebrew text on the nailed *Magen David* form is taken from Jeremiah 31:13: 'For I will turn their mourning into joy and will comfort them and make them rejoice for their sorrow.' This biblical quotation relating to mourning and loss shows that already by late 1915,

---

[39] See a death notice from the Mannheimer family for their son and brother Max Mannheimer in *Nachrichten für Stadt und Land: Oldenburger Zeitung für Volk und Heimat*, Oldenburg, 17 September 1914.

[40] Oldenburger Verein für Altertumskunde und Landesgeschichte Oldenburg, ed. (1915), 'Unsern Helden zum Gedächtnis' in the *Oldenburger Jahrbuch für Altertumskunde und Landesgeschichte, Kunst und Kunstgewerbe*, Stalling, vol. 23, 2–163. I thank Dr. Matthias Nidal of the Niedersächisches Landesarchiv for confirming this information.

Fig. 3 'The First Jewish War memorial.' Postcard, 1915 (Courtesy of the William A. Rosenthal Judaica Collection, College of Charleston Libraries)

only seven months after the first war emblem was nailed for German glory and victory, and some years before the Armistice, an emblem was being used as a memorial object in a Jewish context. The post-card is titled 'The First Jewish War Memorial' and was issued as number 16 in the series *Jüdische Kriegskarten*, published by Louis Lamm in Berlin some time in 1915 or 1916.[41] By designating this nailing as the first 'Jewish war memorial,' implying that there would be other such memorials, Lamm was staking out a specifically Jewish heroic war narrative. As well as creating 'Jewish war postcards', a new category of First World War souvenir ephemera, Lamm also published a series of booklets intended for Jewish soldiers at the front. In 1915, he brought out a collection of inspirational literary texts entitled *Makkabäa*. Here again, the Jewish soldier of the First World War is linked in a Jewish context to the heroic Jewish freedom fighters of antiquity. But unlike the Maccabees, German Jews were not fighting for Jewish independence; they were fighting for Germany.

JEWISH NAILING MOTIFS POST-1918

As mentioned above, German nailing emblems were hammered enthusiastically from the spring of 1915, driven by a widespread emotional need on the home front to demonstrate community pride, unity and patriotism. When hope of a German victory diminished and feelings of despondency began to set in, nailing a patriotic emblem no longer functioned as a tool to whip up public support and money. Towards the end of the conflict, nailings thus vanished from central public showplaces and nailing projects were no longer initiated. Although originally intended to record wartime sentiments for posterity, First World War nailings would ultimately disappear from local cultural memory as well. Some have survived as museum curiosities, but many went the way of the formidable *Eiserne Hindenburg* in Berlin. The headless body was put into storage and became a useful source of firewood.[42]

Given the virtual disappearance of this vibrant form of patriotic devotion by the end of the war, it is intriguing to learn of two Jewish nailings

---

[41] A list of the first 22 postcards in this series can be found in Louis Lamm (1916), *Verzeichnis jüdischer Kriegsschriften*, vol. 1 (Berlin, Louis Lamm Verlag), 14.

[42] Schneider (1999), *Mobilisierung*, 55–57.

that were made after 1918. In early 1919, the Jewish press reported the return of soldiers to their hometowns and the special synagogue services of thanksgiving that were held in their honour.[43] The *Allgemeine Zeitung des Judenthums* describes the return of native soldiers to the city of Laupheim in Baden Württemberg and their jubilant reception by the Jewish community. A nailed *Magen David* was specially created and dedicated for the occasion. It was sponsored by community members and listed almost one hundred names.[44]

According to the magazine, 'Both Chebroth [Jewish community societies] donated a nail for every combatant and his name was inscribed for eternal memory.'[45] Rabbi Mannheimer's nailed *Magen David* from Oldenburg commemorated the fallen, but in Laupheim, we find a nailed *Magen David* that venerated the living. Through this honour, the community both dignified the Jewish war veteran and demonstrated their ongoing commitment to the Fatherland.

In the closed inner courtyard of the synagogue in the Swabian city of Augsburg, one can still see a nailed iron form embedded in one of the walls (Fig. 4). This is particularly notable as it is the only Jewish nailing emblem connected to the First World War that is known to have survived into the twenty-first century. The plaque features a large seven-branched nailed candelabrum (menorah) in the centre. Above the menorah are two Hebrew words in relief: *Le-Zecher Olam* (for eternal memory), a standard phrase in Jewish memorial culture,[46] and in relief below the menorah's foot are the dates '1914–1918'. The menorah motif is covered with hand-forged iron nails and rows of nails serve to frame the inscriptions and the plaque as a whole.

The menorah motif has seven flames, a three-tiered foot, and the arms are detailed with rosettes ('buds and blossoms') alluding to the candelabrum that was lit in the ancient Jerusalem Temple.[47] The menorah has

---

[43] For example, celebrations for returning soldiers were held in Düsseldorf and Hörde i. M, *Beilage zur AZJ*, Heft 4, 24 January 1919, 3; in Göttingen, *AZJ*, Beilage, Heft 7, 14 February 1919, 3; in Stettin, *AZJ*, Beilage, Heft 6, 7 February 1919, 3, etc.

[44] *Allgemeine Zeitung des Judenthums*, Beilage, Heft 6, 7 February 1919, 4.

[45] Ibid.

[46] The phrase is derived from Psalm 112:6. 'For he shall never be moved; the righteous shall be remembered for eternity.'

[47] For a biblical physical description of the Temple menorah, see Exodus 25:31–40.

Fig. 4 War memorial, Augsburg Synagogue. © Jüdisches Kulturmuseum Augsburg-Schwaben; photo: Franz Kimmel

been a Jewish symbol since antiquity and serves as a *lieu de mémoire*, an object that is loaded with historical significance and meaning for collective Jewish memory, linking the place in which it stands to the ancient Temple in Jerusalem. There is a traditional Jewish belief that when the Messiah arrives, the Jerusalem Temple will be rebuilt and Temple activities resumed. This menorah motif, whose lights have been (re)kindled, may represent the hope for a messianic age of peace. The flames may also symbolize a form of victory in the eternal flame of the soul. As such, it is a symbol of both historical memory and future continuity. An interesting detail is the suggestion of an Iron Cross motif at the conjunction of the lowest pair of lamp arms, which is very subtly delineated, but surely intentional. To the right of the menorah's foot is a palm tree motif, set in a circle. The date palm was a symbol of ancient Judea and a motif that was minted on coins from the First Jewish-Roman War,[48] a first-century nationalist rebellion against Rome with the goal of restoring an independent Judean state. The palm tree here references the timeless connection of the Jewish people to the Promised Land and to a history of brave and zealous Jewish warriors. To the left of the menorah's foot is a horn instrument, surmounted by a small *Magen David* motif, and also set in a circle. In this context, the horn is immediately associated with the Jewish ram's horn instrument, the shofar. The shofar is an ancient Jewish symbol and appears, for example, on Jewish coins and ossuaries. The shofar has always served as an instrument for religious praise and was used in Temple ritual, as well as being implemented in war.[49] In this ambiguous depiction however, the form of the mouthpiece and the hanging straps that are draped over the instrument seem to also suggest a more generic kind of military horn. Perhaps this is referencing the non-Jewish, military 'Last Post' bugle, which is ceremonially sounded in remembrance of fallen soldiers.

In short, this nailed plaque, densely packed with Jewish imagery, is a war memorial to Jewish soldiers who fell in the years 1914–1918. It was clearly created for the Jewish community and was not intended as a

---

[48] Ya'akov Meshorer (2001), *A Treasury of Jewish Coins: From the Persian Period to Bar Kokhba* (Jerusalem, Yad Ben-Zvi 2001), 149–150, illus., 339–341, 347–348. The 'year four' coins have depictions of palm trees with nine branches (p. 339, no. 212), as found on the Augsburg plaque.

[49] The most well-known biblical example is the blowing of rams' horns at the battle of Jericho. See Joshua 6:4–12.

public monument. The dominant motifs on the plaque are Jewish symbols, but secular military motifs have been merged into them. When walking through the synagogue courtyard, members of the congregation would have understood at a glance that this fusion of worldly and religious symbols echoed a distinctively German-Jewish identity.

It seems that in the post-war years, the symbolic act of nailing forms could still serve certain needs for the Jewish community. As a group, there was an urge to demonstrate pride in their active participation in the German war effort. During the conflict itself, and continuing into the post-war period, Jewish military service and the personal sacrifices made within the wider community were undermined, questioned and belittled by the public voices of 'völkisch' antisemitic nationalists and as a consequence of the so-called *Judenzählung*. This was a form of census instituted by the German government in October 1916. The survey aimed to establish the number of Jews who were in some sort of military service, and, importantly, the numbers of those serving at the front, and who had fallen in action. The Jewish community saw this as a clearly antisemitic measure and as an attempt to prove that German Jews were shirking their military duty and were trying to avoid frontline service. The results of the census did not prove these points and, crucially, the statistics were not officially published during the war period, an act that would have publicly exonerated the community. This only added fuel to antisemitic sentiment and fed a growing sense of insecurity within the Jewish community.

THE RISE OF THE SYNAGOGUE MEMORIAL PLAQUE

As with the nailing of patriotic wooden forms, the commissioning of synagogue memorial plaques may also have been somewhat motivated by the desire to make a politically charged statement in response to hostile, antisemitic attitudes regarding Jewish military service. The majority of plaques listing the names of local fallen Jewish soldiers were originally situated in buildings frequented primarily by members of the Jewish community, and were often placed in the synagogue sanctuary.

German commemorative culture, and the celebration of individual war heroes, became particularly widespread after the capitulation of France in the Franco-Prussian war and Germany's unification into a nation state in 1871. Many monuments were also erected after the death of Kaiser Wilhelm I in 1888 and the monument industry boomed towards the end of the nineteenth century. A metalwork company, the *Württembergische Metallwarenfabrik* (WMF) in Geislingen, a small town situated south-east of Stuttgart, led the field in creating statues, busts, reliefs and medallions of major public figures. A subsidiary division of the firm was the *Abteilung für Galvanoplastik* (electroplating department), where the manufacture of war memorial plaques was one area of specialization. During the 1920s, many German communities and organizations wished to honour their fallen sons as local heroes and commissioned large numbers of plaques. The plaques had no standardized format and the client generally hired an artist to design a suitable motif, which was then submitted to the WMF for production.

One such WMF plaque was manufactured for the Jewish community of Hamelin in Lower-Saxony. Designed by the (non-Jewish) Berlin-based sculptor, August Kattentidt, it was dedicated on 12 December 1920.[50] Religion teacher Salomon Bachrach spoke at the dedication ceremony, and his somewhat defensive words demonstrate the wish for the wider community to insist that Jewish soldiers were as German as any other soldiers of the Fatherland and had made the same sacrifices as their non-Jewish comrades:

> No one has the right to say that German Jews shirked their duties in the war. There are six names on our plaque. One can put up comparable plaques in every Jewish community of our Fatherland, and each one will bear the names of fallen Jews. We will not tolerate the defamation of their memory. In spirit, we are standing before a single mass grave. Those who slumber within it are Germany's sons. They died for us.[51]

In 1926, WMF issued a brochure with illustrated examples of war memorial plaques produced since the end of the war.[52] Among the twenty-five plaques selected are two that were dedicated to fallen Jewish soldiers. These are from the communities of Limburg an der Lahn in Hesse in 1919 and from Crailsheim in Baden-Württemberg, dating from 1920.[53]

[50] See Bernhard Gelderblom (1996), *Sie waren Bürger der Stadt: die Geschichte der jüdischen Einwohner Hamelns im Dritten Reich: Ein Gedenkbuch* (Hameln, C. W. Niemeyer), 14.

[51] *Diester- und Weser Zeitung*, 12 December 1920, cited in Gelderblom (1996), *Sie waren Bürger*.

[52] Württembergische Metallwarenfabrik. *Ausgeführte Krieger-Gedenktafeln*. Geislingen: Württembergische Metallwarenfabrik, 1926.

[53] See Württembergische Metallwarenfabrik. *Krieger-Gedenktafeln*, 21 (Limburg a. d. Lahn) and 25 (Crailsheim).

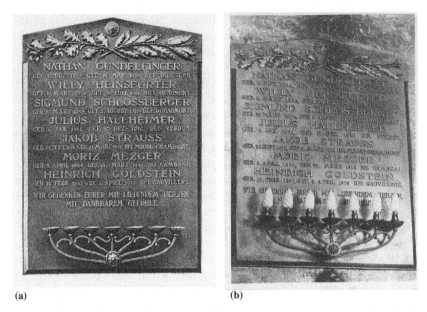

(a)   (b)

Fig. 5 Memorial plaque for the fallen Jewish soldiers of Crailsheim produced by the Württembergische Metallwarenfabrik (WMF) in Geislingen,
1920. Height: 97 cm. The image on the right shows the later electrification
of the candelabrum (a *Ausgeführte Kriegergedenktafeln*, Württembergische
Metallwarenfabrik 1926/1927, by permission of WMF Group GmbH,
Geislingen; b Collection of the Jewish Museum Berlin, donated by Steven and
Hilary Anson)

A memorial plaque commissioned by a Jewish community did not
have to be designed or made by a Jew, nor was there any kind of prescribed format or motif. While a list of soldiers' names remained the central element, the plaques varied a great deal with respect to the material,
size, text, typography, language combination (German and/or Hebrew)
and decorative symbols. The Crailsheim plaque has a particularly remarkable feature—a seven-branched candelabrum, affixed below the soldiers'
names and the dedication text (Fig. 5). The candelabrum symbolically
references the Temple menorah (the seven arms of which, in this case,
opportunely match the number of fallen soldiers), but it also served a
ritual memorial function. This function can be understood through a
comparable example mentioned in *Der Israelit* of 18 May 1915, which

reports on the decision to place memorial plaques (*Ehrentafel*) in the Oldenburg synagogue. A design was approved which included '... a light which should be lit on the anniversary date of death for each individual fallen soldier'. An article describing the dedication ceremony mentions that there were two plaques in the Oldenburg synagogue and that each plaque was surmounted by a single electric lamp.[54] It is common Jewish practice to kindle a memorial candle (*ner neshamah* a 'light of the soul')[55] on the anniversary of a person's death (*yahrzeit*) and at other times set in the Jewish calendar. This custom has been linked to the biblical verse of Proverbs 20:27: 'The soul of man is the lamp/candle of God.'

From the form of the Crailsheim candelabrum in the WMF catalogue, one can infer that long-burning memorial candles would have been lit on the candelabrum on the *yahrzeit* of one of the named soldiers. However, the realities of ritual practice sometimes diverge from the original intended usage of an object. An undated photograph, taken prior to 1933, shows the Crailsheim plaque after it had been installed onsite and reveals that the candelabrum was electrified at some point[56] (Fig. 5). This appears to have been done without much sensitivity to the original design, as the bulbs conceal part of the dedicatory inscription. The effort and expense involved in electrifying the existing candelabrum suggest that someone considered it a liability to leave naked flames unattended overnight in the synagogue sanctuary.[57]

---

[54] *Allgemeine Zeitung des Judenthums*, Beilage, Heft 2–3, 17 January 1919, 4.

[55] Light or flames were recurrent motifs in Jewish war memorial plaques. The *Hattingen Zeitung* of 9 September 1926 notes that on the Hattingen Jewish soldiers' memorial plaque the '... six small flames symbolically refer to the eternal light of the soul'. See also the eight stylized flames on the memorial plaque designed by Jewish sculptor, Arnold Zadikow, for the Jewish community of Würzburg: 'Kriegertafel in Würzburg,' photograph 5560 from the former Art Collection of the Jewish Community of Berlin, now in the collection of the Jewish Historical Institute (ŻIH) in Warsaw.

[56] Collection of the Jewish Museum Berlin (inv. no. 2009/204/163) donated by descendants of the fallen soldier Sigmund Schlossberger, who is listed third on the plaque.

[57] The Crailsheim memorial plaque is the only surviving remnant of the Crailsheim synagogue after its interior was destroyed in the pogrom of 1938 and the building bombed in 1945. The plaque is now situated in the local Jewish cemetery. A local initiative led to the renewal of the lamp in 2009, approximating the original form. It is no longer electrified and has bowl form candleholders once again. Karl W. Schubsky (1997), *Jüdisches Leben in Crailsheim: Der jüdische Friedhof* (*Crailsheim*, Hohenloher Druck), 104.

The Crailsheim *yahrzeit* memorial plaque was originally hung and used in the communal prayer space of the synagogue. Soldiers were of course mourned by their immediate families, but these *yahrzeit* memorial plaques show that Jewish soldiers were also honoured and mourned by the whole community. It should be emphasized that *yahrzeit* memorial plaques were not limited to the examples mentioned above, but could be found in other Jewish communities as well.[58]

PLACEMENT IN THE SANCTUARY

Documentary photos reveal that it was not unusual for pairs of Jewish First World War memorial plaques to be placed in the synagogue sanctuary on either side of the Torah Ark, as found in synagogues in Ichenhausen in Bavaria, Detmold in North-Rhine Westphalia and Rexingen in Baden-Württemberg.[59] Single plaques were placed to one side of the Ark, often to its right, if space allowed (e.g. in the communities of Westheim and Ahlen).[60] The Torah Ark, housing the sacred Torah scrolls, is the focal point of any Jewish prayer room. As the direction of Jewish prayer is towards Jerusalem, Torah Arks in Germany are usually situated on the eastern sanctuary wall, where the attention of the synagogue worshippers would be focused. The decision to place memorial plaques in the synagogue sanctuary and adjacent, moreover, to the Torah Ark, shows the extraordinarily high regard in which they were held by

---

[58] For example, a photograph of the Fulda synagogue interior, ca. 1926–1938, shows a pair of candleholders affixed to the foot of the black marble synagogue memorial plaque (Jüdisches Museum Frankfurt am Main, Sammlung Dr. Paul Arnsberg, Hessen, F87-G238). The plaque had gold Hebrew and German lettering, listing the names of eighteen fallen soldiers, and was dedicated in May 1926, *Der Israelit*, 1 July 1926.

[59] For documentary photographs of the plaques see: Ichenhausen—Postcard of synagogue interior before 1922, reproduced in *Juden auf dem Lande—Beispiel Ichenhausen* (Munich, Haus der Bayerischen Geschichte), 41; Mathias Schafmeister (2014), *Detmold 1918-1933* (Gilching, Sutton Verlag), 53; and Joachim Hahn and Jürgen Kruger (2007), *Synagogen in Baden-Württemberg, vol. 2, Orte und Einrichtungen* (Stuttgart, Konrad Theis Verlag), 219.

[60] Theodor Harburger (1998), *Die Inventarisation jüdischer Kunst- und Kulturdenkmäler in Bayern* (Fürth, Jewish Museum Franken); Günter Birkmann, Hartmut Stratmann, and Thomas Kohlpoth (1998), *Bedenke vor wem du stehst, 300 Synagogen und ihre Geschichte in Westfalen und Lippe* (Essen, Klartext-Verlag), 242, with a sketch reconstructing the synagogue interior from memory.

the community. As might be expected, the placement of such plaques in the sanctuary was not universally accepted. Tim Grady remarks that Berlin's Adass Jisroel community advised the Jewish community in Halle against placing a memorial plaque above the Torah Ark. As 'This most sacred place ... is dedicated solely to the honour of God.'[61]

War memorial plaques nevertheless became central and significant features of synagogue sanctuaries, as well as ubiquitous elements of German-Jewish memorial culture. Dedication ceremonies were major community events and the plaques were often adorned with laudatory laurel leaf garlands or funerary black ribbons.[62] When two marble war memorial plaques were dedicated as part of commemorative event in Ichenhausen in the summer of 1922, the interior decoration of the sanctuary was described in *Der Israelit* as follows: 'The synagogue was decorated with small spruce and laurel trees and decorated with garlands, both plaques were wound with laurel wreaths and mourning ribbons.'[63] Annual memorial prayers ensured that the military service and sacrifice of so many Jewish soldiers became deeply embedded in the historical narrative of German Jews.

The commissioning of a pair of WMF memorial plaques for the synagogue of Limburg an der Lahn was initiated by the synagogue President (*Kultusvorsteher*) and the non-Jewish artist and drawing teacher Peter Assmann, who produced the preliminary design. A report in the local *Limburger Anzeige* of 29 September 1919 mentions that all of the (six) fallen Jewish soldiers had been his pupils. The article goes on to say that Fritz Ducker[64] modelled the forms in the style of 'Middle Age epitaphs ... referencing the late Baroque, but modern throughout ...' The relief menorah motif at the foot of the plaques is intriguing, as it is clearly the design on which the Crailsheim, three-dimensional candelabrum was based and produced one year later! The *Limburger Anzeiger* article mentions that the copper plaques with 'real bronze patina' would be on

---

[61] Letter, Adass Jisroel Berlin to Rabbiner Dr. Kahlberg Halle, 9 March 1920, CJA, 2A2, Nr. 1214. Cited in Grady (2008), *A Common Experience of Death*, 188.

[62] For a photograph of the memorial plaque from the Gelsenkirchen synagogue decorated with garlands and black ribbons, see Leo Baeck Institute, Gelsenkirchen Jewish Community Collection, AR 2424.

[63] *Der Israelit*, 27 July 1922.

[64] Drucker was Director of the Decorative Arts vocational training school in Limburg. See Württembergische Metallwarenfabrik. *Krieger-Gedenktafeln*, 21.

Fig. 6 Interior view of the synagogue Limburg a. d. Lahn, showing the pair of memorial plaques hanging on the walls on either side of the Torah Ark (Courtesy of the Stadtarchive Limburg a. d. Lahn. See Fig. 7 for a detailed image of one of the plaques)

exhibit for public viewing in a local antique store before their transfer to the synagogue: 'The plaques will be put on the choir wall on either side of the Torah Ark and in so doing, the Jewish community honors their honorably fallen, their synagogue building and themselves.'[65]

It is nevertheless surprising to find the two Limburg memorial plaques, with their stark depiction of the contemporary soldier's equipment—rifle, bayonet and steel helmet—flanking the Torah Ark (Fig. 6). There is a Jewish custom to avoid using base metals (such as iron, steel or bronze) when making a Torah scroll, as they are used to forge instruments of war.[66] It is therefore very striking that such overt glorifications of weaponry, as symbols of valour, are positioned next to the Torah Ark (Fig. 7) and underscore the strong, albeit contested, identification of the Jewish community with the German nation and her armed forces.

---

[65] *Limburger Zeiger*, 29 September 1919.

[66] The custom not to use base metals when making the holy Torah scroll may derive from an interpretation of Deuteronomy 27:5, where it is explicitly forbidden to use a base metal tool to create an altar: 'There you shall build an altar for the Lord, your God, an altar of stones; *you may not wield an iron tool on them.*'

Fig. 7 One of a pair of memorial plaques dedicated to the fallen Jewish soldiers of Limburg a. d. Lahn produced by the Württembergische Metallwarenfabrik (WMF) in Geislingen, 1919. Height: 107 cm. *Ausgeführte Kriegergedenktafeln*, Württembergische Metallwarenfabrik ca. 1926/1927 © used by permission of WMF Group GmbH, Geislingen

The two plaques were evidently a source of general local pride, indicating a good relationship between the Jewish and non-Jewish residents of Limburg. It is worth noting here that the town also commissioned a pair of memorial plaques for the fallen soldiers of Limburg (ca. 1919–1930). The plaques were hung, most likely, in the town hall and are preserved today in the collection of the Limburg city archive. The town's hand-calligraphed plaques included the names of fallen Jewish soldiers. However, when viewing the plaques today, one can see that the names of the Jewish soldiers have been carefully pasted over with paper labels. These labels conceal the Jewish names and bear the names of non-Jewish soldiers.[67]

During the 1920s, and in common with the other former belligerent states, First World War public memorials became features of cities, towns and villages throughout the German Reich. Sometimes Jewish fallen soldiers were included on these plaques and monuments and sometimes they were omitted, depending on local politics and attitudes. In the novel *The Black Obelisk*, which is set in 1923, Erich Maria Remarque describes the resistance to including Jewish soldiers' names on a village memorial:

> Unfortunately, there were two Jews among the fallen, the sons of the cattle dealer Levi. [...] His son had died in 1918 of the flu in the reserve military hospital in Werdenbrück. He wanted him to appear as a hero on the memorial and therefore explained that death is death and a soldier is a soldier – and so the Levis got the lowest two places on the back of the memorial, there on the part where dogs would probably piss on it.[68]

Such negative attitudes towards Jews, while not held by all, may conceivably have influenced members of the Jewish community to be sure to situate their memorials in safe community spaces, where it was possible to ensure that their fallen sons would be honoured with respect. The act of concealing Jewish names on the Limburg town plaques probably took place during the later National Socialist era, when questions

---

[67] I would like to thank Dr. Christoph Waldecker, Director of the Limburg city archive, for kindly sharing information and documentary photographs with me.

[68] Erich Maria Remarque (1980), *Der schwarze Obelisk* (Berlin, Aufbau), 119. First published in 1956. I am grateful to Dr. Christoph Kreuzmüller for introducing me to this novel and for his helpful comments.

were raised about the ongoing memorialization of Jewish soldiers who had died (as proven patriots) in the service of the Fatherland. A 1935 edict from Joseph Goebbels, Reich Minister for Propaganda, ordered that while it was not permitted for any new world war monuments to include the names of Jewish soldiers who had served at the front; names that were already to be found on existing monuments did not have to be effaced.[69] This statement emitted an ambiguous message and suggests a reluctance to order citizens to deface their local war monuments. The result of the order was a certain confusion and inconsistency as to how, and if, it should be carried out, which could very well explain the concealment of Jewish names on the Limburg town plaques.

CONCLUSION: THE ATTEMPTED DESTRUCTION OF A MEMORIAL CULTURE

The National Socialist regime tried to erase Jewish contributions to German society from national cultural memory, which included the eradication of the memory of heroic, German-Jewish soldiers. The destruction of synagogue memorial plaques took place due to systematic, violent attacks against German Jews, their property and their houses of worship. In the pogrom of 9 and 10 November 1938, synagogues throughout Germany were attacked, vandalized and sometimes set on fire. Synagogue sanctuaries were demolished and ransacked and, in most cases, the war memorial plaques were destroyed or looted for the value of the metal. These criminal and brutal acts, violating the private prayer spaces of the Jewish community, are the reason why there are almost no nailed objects and very few indoor Jewish war memorial plaques in existence in Germany today.

The November pogrom was a signal to even the proudest German-Jewish war veterans that they had no future in Germany and that they and their families were in physical and possibly mortal danger. Pogroms also took place in the city of Danzig on 12 and 13 November 1938

---

[69] 'When building new monuments for those who fell in the world war, the names of Jewish front fighters should no longer be listed. However, if their names are found on monuments erected earlier, these need not be removed.' 24.10.35 RMfProp in Joseph Walk, ed. (1996), *Das Sonderrecht für die Juden im NS-Staat* (Heidelberg, C. F. Müller Verlag), 137.

and many in the Jewish community urgently sought ways to emigrate. In 1939, the community shipped its entire inventory of Jewish ceremonial objects to the Jewish Theological Seminary in New York for safe keeping, with the hope of re-establishing the community in the future. Within this group of treasured objects was a marble First World War memorial plaque that originally hung in the sanctuary of the Great Synagogue in Danzig. It is extraordinary to think that this weighty stone slab, of little monetary value, was so invested with meaning and historical memory that the community saw fit to ship it to the United States, where it survived intact.[70]

The creation of the early Jewish nailed forms was motivated by an unbridled sense of patriotism and loyalty to the German Reich, an allegiance that would be constantly challenged. The many synagogue memorial 'Roll of Honour' plaques that followed, whether decorated with a simple *Magen David* or with a complex pictorial programme, reflect the way in which German-Jewish communities tried to reconcile Jewish and national identities and to express them in a symbolic form. The plaques were objects of ritual mourning for communities and bereaved individuals, but they also served as mirrors in which communities could reflect, within the apparent safety of their own walls, on their self-image as German-Jewish patriots. An image that would ultimately be truly and irrevocably shattered.

[70]Vivian B. Mann and Joseph Gutmann (1980), *Danzig 1939, Treasures of a Destroyed Community* (Detroit, Wayne State University Press), 33. For an image of the memorial plaque, see the on-line collection of the Jewish Museum, New York (http://thejewishmuseum.org/collection/5816-memorial-plaque-of-the-great-synagogue-of-danzig).

'Thou Hast Given Us Home and Freedom, Mother England': Anglo-Jewish Gratitude, Patriotism, and Service During and After the First World War

Edward Madigan

In his eloquent address to the first International Zionist Congress at Basle in 1897, Max Nordau argued that Western European countries had adopted Jewish emancipation not out of a sense of heartfelt conviction but because the intelligentsia in the West regarded religious and ethnic freedom as one of the hallmarks of a culturally evolved society. Along with other core elements of the modern liberal state, such as freedom of the press and trial by jury, emancipation, he claimed, was much more the 'imitation of a political fashion' than a genuine expression of sympathy for Jewish citizens. As the co-founder of the World Zionist Organisation, it suited Nordau's agenda to paint a picture of Western Europe as a region in which the status of Jews was, at best, precarious. Yet at a time

E. Madigan (✉)
Department of History, Royal Holloway, University of London,
London, UK
e-mail: edward.madigan@rhul.ac.uk

© The Author(s) 2019   307
E. Madigan and G. Reuveni (eds.),
The Jewish Experience of the First World War,
https://doi.org/10.1057/978-1-137-54896-2_14

when the Dreyfus Affair was still ongoing, few Jewish commentators would have disputed the existence of fairly widespread antisemitism in ostensibly enlightened countries such as France, Germany, and Austria.[1] Significantly, however, the Hungarian-born Nordau made a point of highlighting England as an exception to the rule of failed emancipation and illusory assimilation. 'In England', he insisted, 'emancipation is a truth. It is not alone written, it is living ... Consequently, in England, antisemitism is only noticeable in a few instances, and then only it has the importance of an imitation of Continental fashion.'[2]

Some two decades later, in January 1920, the English Zionist Federation held a reception in Nordau's honour in London. After being introduced by the Federation's president, Chaim Weizmann, and receiving a rapturous welcome from the audience, the now elderly activist delivered an impassioned speech in which he painted a vivid picture of the international menace of antisemitism. Just over a year had passed since the end of the Great War and Nordau asked those in attendance to consider how Jewish veterans of the conflict were being repaid for the extraordinary sacrifices they had made:

> Can they now indulge the idea that having gallantly done their bit, and considerably more, they have at last vindicated the Jewish name and heightened the position of the Jewish people in the world? Look around you. Your eyes everywhere meet the answer to these questions. Even in the advanced and highly cultivated countries of the West we see a huge wave of antisemitism welling up from the darkest, most secluded depth of atavistic prejudice and of hereditary injustice; asphyxiating gas rises from deep abysses like a cloud, condensing like an irrespirable mist round the Jewish population, surrounding them with suspicion, ill-will, and a hatred which, in many cases, degenerates into absolute persecution.[3]

Nordau went on to praise the British Government for its professed commitment to the foundation of a Jewish homeland in Palestine, the British seizure of which from the Ottoman forces in 1917 had given a major

---

[1] For an early account of the emergence of ideological antisemitism in Western Europe in the last decades of the nineteenth century, see Lucien Wolf (1934), *Essays in Jewish History* (London, The Jewish Historical Society of England), 413–460.

[2] *Jewish Chronicle*, 3 September 1897, 7.

[3] *Jewish Chronicle*, 16 January 1920, 23.

boost to the international Zionist movement.[4] He made no attempt, however, to suggest that England should be regarded as relatively free of anti-Jewish sentiment, as he had done in Switzerland at the end of the previous century. Indeed, his contention that, despite their staunch patriotism and service during the war, Jewish communities were facing an aggressive post-war wave of antisemitism, would have resonated with many in the Anglo-Jewish community, irrespective of their views on Zionism. Jewish men and women from well-established families that had prospered in England in the decades before the war would, in particular, have noticed a contrast between the relative security and acceptance they had enjoyed before 1914 and the colder, more hostile atmosphere of the early 1920s.

Although there remains a great deal to explore and understand, the recent historiographical record concerning the Anglo-Jewish experience of the First World War is reasonably rich. In a pioneering 1991 article, David Cesarani demonstrated the degree to which the ultra-nationalistic atmosphere that prevailed in Britain during the conflict combined with other factors to heighten divisions between Anglo-Jewry and the Christian majority.[5] Two more recent explorations of Anglo-Jewish history, Todd M. Endelman's *The Jews of Britain, 1656–2000* and Aaron M. Kent's *Identity, Migration and Belonging: The Jewish Community of Leeds, 1890–1920* contain chapters on the war and shed valuable light on the character and composition of Jewish communities in Britain in the decades before 1914.[6] With regard to Anglo-Jewish military service during the war years, Martin Watts's account of the formation and deployment of the Jewish battaltions of the Royal Fusiliers and highlights an important but much-overlooked episode in British military history.[7]

---

[4] The Allied states would formally recognise Britain as the mandatory power in Palestine at the San Remo Conference in April 1920, less than four months after Nordau's speech. Stuart A. Cohen (1982, 2014) *English Zionists and British Jews: The Communal Politics of Anglo-Jewry, 1895–1920* (Princeton, Princeton University Press), 20–21.

[5] David Cesarani (1991), 'An Embattled Minority: The Jews in Britain During the First World War', *Immigrants and Minorities* 8:1–2, 60–81.

[6] Todd M. Endelman (2002), *The Jews of Britain, 1656–2006*.

[7] Martin Watts (2004), *The Jewish Legion During the First World War* (Basingstoke, Palgrave); For a transnational overview of Jewish engagement with military service during the war, see Derek J. Penslar (2013), *Jews and the Military* (Princeton, Princeton University Press), 152–165.

Finally, Tony Kushner's highly enlightening *Anglo-Jewry Since 1066*, first published in 2009, takes an ambitiously long view of Jewish settlement in, and migration within, Britain, and, although the author offers little in the way of detail concerning the First World War, his nuanced portrayal of modern Anglo-Jewish identity helps us better understand Jewish responses to the conflict.[8]

Yet while this body of literature has done a great deal to enhance our understanding of the complexities of Anglo-Jewish engagement with the First World War, historians have had relatively little to say about the ways in which English Jews interpreted the conflict as it unfolded. Although most of these accounts acknowledge the significant numbers of Jews who served in the British armed forces, moreover, the rhetoric used to frame this service, and later to remember it, has been largely overlooked. This chapter seeks to add to the layered but elliptical historiography on Anglo-Jewry and the First World War by exploring the distinctive and revealing ways in which Jewish commentators in England responded to the war in 1914 and tracing the degree to which Anglo-Jewish patriotism and Englishness were subsequently denigrated before considering one of the key ways in which the Anglo-Jewish community attempted to counter these attacks.

Pre-war Jewish Englishness

The widespread popular support and affection for the 'ordinary' British soldier that was so much in evidence throughout the First World War were not without precedent. During the Second South African War, or Boer War, the common serviceman was idealised and romanticised in the national press and on the music hall stage in much the same way as he would be in the later conflict. With titles such as 'Tommy Atkins, You're A Dandy', 'A Medal or A Bullet', and 'He Isn't Sleeping Now',[9] the songs of the Boer War lionised the British soldier and exemplified the sort of naïve patriotic fervour that could be indulged in a war of relatively limited liability. 'The Jewish Soldier', a ballad published at the

---

[8] Tony Kushner (2009), *Anglo-Jewry Since 1066*.

[9] Arago Easton (1900), *Tommy Atkins, You're a Dandy* (London, Nolan & Easton); Blanche Eryl (1900), *A Medal or a Bullet* (London, Novello & Company); and James Fax (1900), *He Isn't Sleeping Now* (Toronto, Anglo-Canadian Music Publishers Association).

height of the conflict in 1900, sheds rare light on the way the war was interpreted by the more affluent and well-established members of the Anglo-Jewish community. The song's lyrics, written by the Jewish poet and social activist, Alice Lucas, paint a highly idealised picture of a soldier who is determined to defend the country that has granted his people the kind of acceptance and freedom they have been denied elsewhere. The final two verses convey this message very clearly:

> Thou hast given us home and freedom, Mother England,
> Thou hast let us live again,
> Free and fearless, 'midst thy free and fearless children,
> Sharing with them, as one people, grief and gladness,
> Joy and pain.

> For the Jew has heart and hand, our Mother England,
> And they both are thine to-day –
> Thine for life and thine for death – yea thine for ever!
> Wilt thou take them as we give them, freely, gladly?
> England, say![10]

Lucas's words now seem almost absurdly romantic and sentimental, but the central message of the ballad—that English Jews should be prepared to fight and make any sacrifice for the country that had allowed them to 'live again'—genuinely spoke to many in the Anglo-Jewish community at the turn of the century. For despite their cosmopolitanism and their international family ties, a sharp sense of patriotism came quite naturally to the members of the Jewish elite whose families had prospered in England in the decades before 1914.

By the turn of the twentieth century, the more assimilated sections of the various Anglo-Jewish communities had become wealthy, influential, and highly anglicised. Nathan de Rothschild and Henry de Worms had been elevated to the peerage, the sons of affluent Jewish families commonly held high office in government and the civil service, and middle-class Jews were thriving in a variety of professions.[11] Anglo-Jewish businessmen and financiers also made vast fortunes during this period

---

[10]Mrs. Henry Lucas and Arthur M. Friedländer (1900), *The Jewish Soldier* (London, Edwin Ashdown), 2–6.

[11]Colin Holmes (1979, 2016), *Anti-semitism in British Society, 1876–1939* (London, Routledge), 108–109.

and Jews were disproportionately represented among the nation's millionaires in a world in which wealth tended to pave the way to social acceptance.[12] Popular antisemitism was by no means unheard of, and seems to have been quite pronounced in Bethnal Green and other parts of London's East End where there were large populations of Jewish immigrants from Eastern Europe.[13] Importantly, however, antisemitism in Britain in the years before the war, as Todd Endelman has observed, 'was neither as virulent or explosive as in other European states and not as successful in derailing Jewish integration'.[14] Indeed, writing in the 1960s, the historian William Rubinstein referred to the period from 1870 to 1914 as 'the golden age of the Jewish people in Britain'.[15] The notion that they enjoyed a degree of acceptance, and, importantly, a more authentic sense of belonging than Jews in any other country was thus widely accepted among more affluent English Jews and they often felt a deep sense of pride in their nationality.[16]

One of the ways in which this national pride expressed itself was in their general indifference or hostility to Zionism, which was very much a fringe movement in Britain in the years before 1914.[17] The Anglo-Jewish upper-class were certainly interested in Jewish settlements in Palestine and were willing to lend financial and moral support to Jewish refugees from Eastern Europe, but they tended to be quite disdainful of the suggestion that their true homeland should be anywhere other than England.[18] In a speech she gave to a group of Jewish girl guides in London in March 1907, Lady Aline Sassoon, the French-born artist

---

[12] Todd M. Endelman (2002), *The Jews of Britain, 1656–2000* (London, University of California Press), 155; Colin Holmes (1979, 2016), *Anti-semitism in British Society, 1876–1939,* 109.

[13] Colin Holmes (1979, 2016), *Anti-semitism in British Society, 1876–1939,* 110.

[14] Ibid., 162.

[15] William D. Rubinstein (1972), 'Jews Among Top British Wealth Holders, 1857–1969: Decline of the Golden Age', *Jewish Social Studies* 34:1, 76–77.

[16] On the gratitude engendered among English Jews by their sense of enjoying privileges that other communities in the diaspora did not, see especially William D. Rubinstein (2002), 'The Decline and Fall of Anglo-Jewry?', *Jewish Historical Studies* 38, 16.

[17] Todd M. Endelman (2002), *The Jews in Britain, 1656–2000* (London, University of California Press), 189.

[18] William D. Rubinstein (2002), The Decline and Fall of Anglo-Jewry?, 18; Jonathan Schneer (2010), *The Balfour Declaration: The Origins of the Arab-Israeli Conflict* (London, Bloomsbury), 110–112.

and wife of Liberal MP Edward Sassoon, stressed the compatibility of Englishness and Jewishness. The Zionist dream of a Jewish homeland was all very well, she felt, for 'our poor coreligionists in Russia' but had little to offer English Jews:

> We do not chafe for the freedom of tomorrow while we are enjoying the freedom of today. We cannot be sufficiently grateful to our countrymen for their loyalty and friendly feeling. Our religion does not prevent us from being loyally English.[19]

Lady Sassoon's message to her young audience was clear: while they should, of course, feel sympathy for Jews fleeing persecution in Eastern Europe, the Anglo-Jewish homeland was England, not an imagined Israel in the Middle East. Crucially, moreover, English Jews owed their Christian compatriots a debt of gratitude for the acceptance and 'freedom' they had been accorded. This view seems to have been quite widely shared among the Anglo-Jewish elite in the early 1900s. The eminent biblical scholar, Claude Goldsmid Montefiore, although personally very interested in Palestine, was staunchly opposed to Zionism on the grounds that it emphasised difference and felt that those Jews fortunate enough to be born in England should consider England their national home.[20] He was very much in favour of Anglo-Jewish military service in the Boer War and strongly encouraged Jewish enlistment during the First World War.[21] As scion of one of the more notable Anglo-Jewish families and author of numerous books on Judaism, Montefiore was quite an influential figure and his belief in the compatibility of Englishness and Jewishness was shared by at least some members of the community who fought in the war. Basil Henriques was educated at Harrow and Oxford and served as a subaltern on the Western Front, where he commanded a tank during the final phase of the Somme Offensive in 1916. Writing in the 1930s, he recalled that his mother had taught him to 'realize the splendid combination of English citizenship and Jewish religion, and how much richer the former became when based upon the latter'.[22]

---

[19] *Jewish Chronicle*, 1 March 1907, 17.

[20] H. A. L. Fisher in Lucy Cohen (1940), *Some Recollections of Claude Goldsmid Montefiore* (London, Faber & Faber), 14.

[21] Ibid., 89.

[22] Basil Henriques (1937), *The Indiscretions of a Warden* (London, Methuen), 12.

He was also greatly inspired as a young man by Montefiore's writings and felt that there could 'be no grander combination than to be an Englishman of the Jewish religion'.[23] Given the world of refined privilege and culture in which they had been brought up, it was perfectly natural for Henriques and other Englishmen and women of his class to want to demonstrate their loyalty, and their gratitude as Jews, to Britain and the empire.

The tens of thousands of Jewish immigrants that had begun arriving in Britain from Russia and elsewhere in Eastern Europe in the early 1880s were much less integrated, and certainly less prosperous, than their native-born co-religionists, who tended to be of Iberian or German descent. By the eve of the Great War, as many as 150,000 Eastern European Jews had settled in Britain and, in the process, divided the broad community between 'established' and 'newly-arrived' with all of the cultural and social tension that that division entailed.[24] Their general poverty, their distinctly orthodox forms of dress and worship, their occasional political radicalism, as well as their tendency to speak Yiddish, meant that these 'Russian' Jews were subject to a marked degree of 'othering', not only by the Christian majority, but also, to some extent, by the Jewish establishment.[25] Although their communities were relatively insulated from wider British society, and they were possessed of a limited sense of English identity, the sons of Jewish immigrants from Eastern Europe nonetheless showed some willingness to volunteer for military service in 1914 and 1915. Significant numbers of non-naturalised Russian Jews would also see active service in specially formed Jewish units from the middle of 1917.[26] The Anglo-Jewish community, in all its

---

[23] Ibid., 93.

[24] Gisela Lebzelter (1978), *Political Anti-semitism in England, 1918–1939* (Basingstoke, Macmillan), 136. A much greater number of Jewish immigrants—perhaps as many as one million—spent some amount of time in Britain or Ireland before moving on to the United States, see Tony Kushner (2009), *Anglo-Jewry Since 1066*, 184.

[25] Todd M. Endelman (2002), *The Jews of Britain, 1656–2006*, 156–158; Mark Levene (1992), *War, Jews, and the New Europe: The Diplomacy of Lucien Wolf, 1914–1919* (Oxford, Oxford University Press), 23. Levene points out that Lucien Wolf and certain other members of the Anglo-Jewish elite felt that Jewish immigration from Eastern Europe drew unwanted negative attention on the wider community and should be discouraged.

[26] For an account of the raising of the five Jewish battalions of the Royal Fusiliers that became known as the Jewish Legion, see especially Martin Watts (2004), *The Jewish Legion During the First World War* (Basingstoke, Palgrave).

diversity, and through the participation of both civilians and servicemen, was thus very much engaged in the British war effort throughout the conflict.

ANGLO-JEWISH RESPONSES TO THE WAR

The British state that declared war on Germany in August 1914 had a relatively small standing army, and, alone among the belligerents, could not rely on a system of military conscription. Importantly, moreover, British territory had not been invaded and was under no realistic threat of invasion. The need to present the conflict to the public as a just war by highlighting its moral dimension was thus especially pressing in Britain. Jewish clergymen, journalists, and other public figures engaged in this process of 'cultural mobilisation' with just as much energy as their Christian counterparts. In so doing, they frequently echoed Lucas's vision of the Boer War, interpreting the conflict as a great opportunity for the Jewish community to repay a country, and an empire, that had granted them such a comparatively high degree of emancipation and assimilation.

The clergy of virtually all of the major religious communities across Britain and Ireland played an active role in promoting the moral case for war in 1914 and many of them publicly encouraged young men to volunteer for military service.[27] English rabbis were very much part of this wave of clerical support for mobilisation, and, despite their often pronounced doctrinal differences, they offered a remarkably consistent interpretation of the conflict as a just war in which Anglo-Jewry was duty-bound to participate. In a sermon delivered at the Great Synagogue in Aldgate in central London, the spiritual home of the Ashkenazi community, on 21 September 1914, rabbi Michael Adler read the same two verses of 'The Jewish Soldier' quoted above. For Adler, Lucas's lyrics captured the sentiments of English Jews regarding military service and sacrifice 'with wondrous beauty and vigour' and the war offered Anglo-Jewry 'a glorious opportunity to repay in some slight degree the measure of our devotion to the land we love'.[28] Adler's status as a Territorial

---

[27] Edward Madigan (2011), *Faith Under Fire: Anglican Army Chaplains and the Great War* (Basingstoke, Palgrave), 41–42; Edward Madigan (2015), "Their Cross to Bear': The Church of England and Military Service, 1914–1918', *Annali di Scienze Religiose* 8, 168–172.

[28] Michael Adler (1914), *Anglo-Jewry and the Great War* (London), 8.

Army chaplain, and the only Jewish clergyman then officially attached to the British forces, lent his sermon a particular weight. Yet he was by no means the only rabbi to cast the war as an opportunity for British Jews to repay a debt of gratitude by demonstrating their loyalty to king and country. Preaching at the West London synagogue on 15 August, the influential reformist scholar, Morris Joseph, emphasised the moral imperative for English Jews to fight to defend English interests. In language very similar to that being used by many of his Protestant counterparts, Joseph emphasised the glory of dying for such a righteous cause. He also suggested that, in this time of great national crisis, English Jews should be more conscious of their nationality than their faith and culture:

> ... to fight in such a cause is a duty; to fall in it – if indeed we are destined to fall (which Heaven forfend!) – is glory. We of this congregation will keep this truth in mind. The broadest spirit shall actuate us. We are Jews, but Englishmen too: and, in this crisis, we are Englishmen first. Nay, in showing ourselves Englishmen, we are proving ourselves Jews, faithful to the grand conceptions of righteousness for which Judaism pre-eminently stands.[29]

In another sermon delivered on the same day, Ephraim Levine reminded the orthodox congregation at the Hampstead Synagogue that Judaism was essentially a religion of peace but was quite clear about Jewish fealty to England and the Jewish obligation to support the war. The *Jewish World* paraphrased his words as follows:

> Jews especially owed her a debt above all other countries in the world: They joyed with England. They were a part of England, loyal and faithful ... The Jew preached peace but he did not shirk war. They had received well of England: they would show that they were not ungrateful.[30]

Preaching on the theme of 'Jewish Patriotism' at the West London Synagogue the following month, rabbi Isidore Harris spoke of the 'opportunity' that the war offered English Jews to act on their love for their homeland. With the outbreak of war, he told the congregation, 'the opportunity had been given them to prove that Jewish loyalty was no

---

[29] *Jewish World*, 19 August 1914, 10.
[30] Ibid., 10.

mere lip profession, but a very real sentiment inspiring them to offer up all that they held most precious for love of their Empire'.[31]

In their generally staunch support for the war and their use of dramatic language with reference to the national crisis, English rabbis were little different to the tens of thousands of Christian clergymen who addressed the British public in the late summer and autumn of 1914. Nor were Jews the only religious minority in Britain who interpreted the war as an opportunity to demonstrate their patriotism. The English Catholic community was still regarded with a degree of distrust by the overwhelmingly Anglican or evangelical majority, and Catholic priests often stressed the patriotism of their community in much the same insistent tone employed by Jewish commentators.[32] Their status as clerical representatives of the only significant non-Christian minority in the country put rabbis in a much more potentially suspect position in the eyes of the wider population, however, and goes some way towards explaining the tenor of their support for the war in 1914. The pointed emphasis they placed on the gratitude that Jews owed to Britain, and their positive interpretation of the war as a moment in which Anglo-Jewry could demonstrate its essential Englishness, were also quite distinctive.

Although their rhetoric was naturally somewhat less religious, Jewish journalists interpreted the war in a similar light and Jewish press commentary during the early months of the war very much echoed the patriotic 'debt of gratitude' refrain of the clergy. The Anglo-Jewish press in 1914 was dominated by two weeklies, the *Jewish Chronicle* and the *Jewish World*. The former had acquired the latter in 1913, both were produced from the same office in London's East End, and, under the energetic management of their editor and proprietor, Leopold J. Greenberg, they exerted an extraordinary influence over the Anglo-Jewish community. Greenberg, the son of a wealthy Manchester jeweller who had made his

---

[31] *Jewish Chronicle*, 18 September 1914, 26.

[32] Oliver Rafferty (2011), 'Catholic Chaplains to the British Forces in the First World War', *Religion State and Society*, 39:1, 37–38. See, for example, Msgr. Bernard Ward (1915), *Thoughts in War Time* (London, Catholic Truth Society), 22–24. On Anti-Catholic mentalities in nineteenth century Britain, see Diana Peschier (2005), *Nineteenth-Century Anti-Catholic Discourses: The Case of Charlotte Brontë* (Basingstoke, Palgrave). On the degree to which English Catholics interpreted the war, at least partly, as an opportunity to assert their patriotism, see Keith Robbins (2008), *England, Ireland, Scotland, Wales: The Christian Church, 1900–2000* (Oxford, Oxford University Press), 112–115.

own fortune in advertising, was a committed Zionist and close friend and correspondent of Chaim Weizmann.[33] Yet while both papers were certainly sympathetic to Zionism, they also displayed a genteel English patriotism and a respectful deference for English institutions. To begin with, both were highly circumspect about the prospect of a British alliance with Tsarist Russia and quite equivocal about British mobilisation. Indeed, the editorial that appeared in the *Jewish World* on 5 August, which was clearly written—probably by Greenberg himself—when a British declaration of war was likely but still undecided, was emphatically opposed to British intervention on moral grounds. Crucially, however, it also offered a stirring and revealing expression of patriotic love for 'our beloved England, England to whom all the Jews of the world, and not of England alone, have learnt to point with pride and thankfulness as the home of freedom'.[34] The following week's editorial very much reversed the anti-interventionist stance of the paper, insisting that German aggression had simply left 'this country no option, save dishonour or the arbitrament of the sword'.[35]

After expressing a somewhat premature desire for the Central Powers to prevail over the Russian Empire in the *Jewish Chronicle* on 31 July, Greenberg performed an abrupt about-face and robustly denounced German aggression and called on all British Jews to support the national war effort in his editorial of 7 August. In a highly evocative phrase that seemed to capture perfectly the spirit of appreciative Anglo-Jewish loyalty, he declared, no fewer than three times, that 'England has been all she could be to Jews, Jews will be all they can be to England'.[36] An anonymous member of the Anglo-Jewish community had these words printed on a giant placard which, in a very public display of patriotism, was hung outside the *Jewish Chronicle* building on Finsbury Square for the duration of the war (see Fig. 1).[37]

Throughout the late summer and autumn of 1914, both the *Chronicle* and the *World* followed their initial endorsements of the war

[33] For a detailed portrait of Greenberg during his tenure as editor of the *Jewish World* and the *Jewish Chronicle*, see David Cesarani, *The Jewish Chronicle and Anglo-Jewry*, 103–114.

[34] *Jewish World*, 5 August 1914, 5.

[35] *Jewish World*, 12 August 1914, 3.

[36] *Jewish Chronicle*, 7 August 1915, 5.

[37] David Cesarani (2005), *The Jewish Chronicle and Anglo-Jewry, 1841–1990* (Cambridge, Cambridge University Press), 115; *Jewish World*, 19 August 1914, 7.

Fig. 1 Placard outside the office of *Jewish Chronicle*, Finsbury Square, London, 1914, *Jewish World*, 19 August 1914

by consistently highlighting the righteousness of the British cause and praising the self-sacrificing spirit of the Anglo-Jewish community. The dramatic and laudatory language the Jewish press employed to describe Jewish enlistment in the armed forces both reminded those who had not yet joined up of their obligation to enlist and notified the Christian majority that Anglo-Jewry was doing its bit. On 14 August, for example, barely a week after the British declaration of war, the *Jewish Chronicle* gave a vivid account of the patriotic volunteerism of young Jewish men:

> The Jewish manhood is responding with alacrity and enthusiasm to the call of England ... There is not a Jew in this country who cannot tell of friends enlisted, or relatives enrolled in one or other of the British legions, of youthful zeal that will not be denied, of love of the Motherland exquisite in its tenderness, boundless in strength, unsurpassed in all the wonderful annals even of British loyalty and enthusiasm.[38]

---

[38] *Jewish Chronicle*, 14 August 1914, 10.

Just five days later, the *Jewish World* praised the Jewish zeal to enlist in similar terms, reporting that 'there has been something approaching a panic anxiety on the part of our young men of all classes to take their places in the ranks of England's fighting'.[39] In a striking example of its determination to persuade Jewish men of military age that they should be in uniform, the *World* printed a recruitment poster with a very explicit message in the first week of October. The poster draws both on the popular perception of Britain's historically fair treatment of its Jewish population and the ancient martial spirit of the Maccabees to encourage young men to join the army (see Fig. 2). 'Since the days of Oliver Cromwell', reads the text, 'Great Britain has meted out the fairest treatment politically, socially and in every way to Jews. Now is the time for the Jews to reciprocate and show that the old spirit of the Maccabees is not dead.'[40] The use of both English and Yiddish text reflects the designer's intention to appeal to as broad a swathe of the community as possible, and while the poster's presentation of military service as a moral obligation was in no sense unusual, its emphasis on reciprocity to England for traditionally fair treatment was highly distinctive. In March of the following year, the message that Jewish men should repay their debt to a benevolent nation was printed on a more public recruitment poster that displayed Greenberg's stirring pledge of Jewish loyalty under a billowing Union Jack (see Fig. 3).

As the months passed and the British Expeditionary Force became mired in a war of attrition on the Western Front, reports of volunteerism in the Jewish press were increasingly accompanied by accounts of Jewish heroism in combat and letters from Jewish soldiers on active service. Stories of German atrocities on the western and eastern fronts were also consistently reported, and a 'shilling fund' for the relief of Belgian-Jewish refugees launched jointly by the *Chronicle* and the *World* at the end of October 1914 drew direct attention to the plight of civilians who had been forced to flee from the zone of war.[41] The narrative of German violence against civilians, based on a combination of authentic eye-witness accounts and embellished or fabricated stories, was central to the

[39] *Jewish World*, 19 August 1914, 3.
[40] *Jewish World*, 7 October 1914, 7.
[41] *Jewish World*, 28 October 1914, 12–13.

Fig. 2 Anglo-Jewish recruitment poster, *Jewish World*, 7 October 1914

Fig. 3 'Britain has been all she could be to Jews' recruitment poster. Printed by Hill, Siffken & Co., March 1915 (Alamy)

British process of cultural mobilisation in 1914.[42] The generally accurate atrocity reportage in the Jewish press very much fed into this narrative, offering particularly troubling testimony concerning the murder of Jewish civilians in Kalisz and other cities in Eastern Europe which were occupied by the German forces in the early months of the war.[43] Under Greenberg's close editorial guidance, the Anglo-Jewish weeklies thus helped to reinforce the resolutely anti-German climate that prevailed in Britain during the war years and contributed to the wider press interpretation of the war as a great clash between good and evil.

Jewish intellectuals and authors also actively contributed to the public discourse on the malevolence of the German state, which found expression in the first year of the war in a plethora of books and pamphlets that highlighted the apparently immoral worldview of German philosophers and writers, such as Friedrich Nietzsche, Friedrich von Bernhardi, and Heinrich von Treitschke.[44] In a pamphlet published in December 1914 and entitled *Jewish Ideals and the War*, the historian, journalist, and former editor of the *Jewish World*, Lucien Wolf, offered a distinctively Jewish take on the moral corruption of German society. In Wolf's view, the exaltation of the state that was such a key element in the more reactionary strain of German thought in the decades before 1914 ran contrary to Jewish ideals and most of the more prominent German thinkers of the pre-war period were antisemitic. He concludes that:

[42] On the extent and nature of atrocities committed by the German armed forces in the opening phase of the war on the Western Front, see John Horne and Alan Kramer (2001), *German Atrocities: A History of Denial* (London, Yale University Press). On the impact of reports of atrocities on the British home front see Adrian Gregory (2008), *The Last Great War: British Society and the First World War* (Cambridge, Cambridge University Press), 40–69; Catriona Pennell (2012), *A Kingdom United: Popular Responses to the Outbreak of the First World War in Britain and Ireland* (Oxford, Oxford University Press), 92–116.

[43] In the *Jewish Chronicle* see, for example, 'German Atrocities Against the Jews at Kalish', 28 August 1914, 11; 'The German Atrocities Against the Jews', 4 September 1914, 13. In the *Jewish World*, see 'The Unatoneable Sin', 2 September 1914.

[44] For a pioneering account of British intellectual responses to the war, see Stuart Wallace (1988), *War and the Image of Germany: British Academics, 1914–1918* (Edinburgh, John Donald). For contemporary criticism of the influence of German philosophy on German militarism see, for example, Joseph McCabe (1914), *Treitschke and the Great War* (London, T. Fisher Unwin); William Archer (1915), *Fighting a Philosophy: A Study of Nietzsche on Germany Policy* (Oxford, Oxford University Press).

> The makers of Anti-Semitism are the makers of the present war. Both are the logical outcome of the same order of barbarian ideas ... For the whole world, German militarism means perpetual anxiety and the exhausting burdens of tremendous armies and fleets. For the Jews, however, it means a perpetual menace to their civil and political rights; and its success would probably signify in one form or another the restoration of the Ghettos.[45]

The essence of Wolf's argument was that a German victory would be particularly bad for Jewish communities in Europe and the wider world, and that Jews thus had a very personal moral and material stake in the conflict. Up to the summer of 1914, Wolf had been a very public critic of the treatment of Jews in Tsarist Russia, publishing polemical articles in a weekly bulletin entitled *Darkest Russia*, which he had begun editing in 1912. With the outbreak of war, the production of the bulletin ceased and, in common with Leopold Greenberg, Wolf began focusing on the Hohenzollern rather than the Romanov Empire as the real threat to international Jewish security and well-being.[46]

English Jews and Military Service

It is difficult to gauge exactly the impact that the explicit support for the war voiced by Jewish clergymen, journalists, and intellectuals had on recruitment, but thousands of Jewish men of military service age, from a variety of different backgrounds and from across the United Kingdom, volunteered for service in the first year of the war. The wartime experiences and writing of the London-born rabbi Michael Adler offer us something of a window into the spirit with which these Anglo-Jewish men enlisted. By August 1914, Adler had been serving as a Territorial Army chaplain, combining this role with his duties as rabbi at the Central Synagogue in West London, for over five years. After war was declared, he quickly became regarded as an important liaison between Jewish civilians and the

---

[45] Lucien Wolf (1914), *Jewish Ideals and the War* (London, Buck & Wootton), 6.

[46] Mark Levene (1992), *War, Jews and the New Europe*, 32–36; David Cesarani (1994, 2005), *The Jewish Chronicle and Anglo-Jewry*, 115. For a detailed exploration of the content and impact of *Darkest Russia*, see Sam Johnson (2006), 'Darkest Russia, British Opinion and Tsarism's "Jewish Question"', 1890–1914', *East European Jewish Affairs* 36:2, 199–211.

armed forces.[47] In January 1915, he was granted a temporary commission as chaplain to the regular army and posted to the Western Front, where he served as senior Jewish chaplain until the final year of the war. Despite being in his mid-forties when he embarked on active service, he seems to have carried out his fairly onerous duties with energy and dedication and he was awarded the Distinguished Service Order in 1917.[48]

Adler tirelessly highlighted Anglo-Jewish volunteerism and self-sacrifice throughout the war, and, although he was clearly a somewhat biased observer, his writing from the period gives us a very well-informed impression of Jewish service in the British forces.[49] In an article written for a popular wartime magazine in January 1915, he emphasised the diversity of Anglo-Jewish enlistment, making clear that patriotism was not the sole preserve of the wealthier, relatively more assimilated members of the community:

> From all sections of the community they have come, fired by the same impulse – from the houses of the rich, and the middle classes, and the very poorest. From London, Leeds, Manchester, Liverpool, Glasgow, Birmingham, Glasgow, and Dublin they have come forward to offer themselves for King and country in a spirit of willing self sacrifice … so that it makes one feel proud to be able to minister to such a body of men.[50]

In a 1919 pamphlet entitled *The Jews of the Empire and the Great War*, Adler provided a fairly comprehensive account of Jewish military service in which he emphasised the very active role that Anglo-Jewish servicemen played in British campaigns from the earliest days of the conflict. Again, he stresses the diversity of Anglo-Jewish enlistment and mentions English Jews of Russian and Polish descent who saw active

---

[47] *Jewish Chronicle*, 14 August 1914, 10. Adler kept a diary throughout his years at the front and although the entries lack detail they nonetheless reflect the varied and demanding nature of his chaplaincy. See Papers of Revd. Michael Adler, University of Southampton Special Collections, AS/16.

[48] *The Times*, Michael Adler Obituary, 2 October 1944, 6.

[49] Articles and pamphlets published by Adler during and in the aftermath of the war include: 'The YMCA and Jewish Soldiers', *The Times*, 9 February 1915, 9; 'A Few Thoughts on Jews', *On Service*, vol. 4, June 1916, 6; and Michael Adler (1920), *A Jewish Chaplain on the Western Front* (Lewes, Lewes Press).

[50] Michael Adler, 'Jews in the War: Their Roll of Honour', *T. P. O'Connor's Great Deeds of the Great War*, vol. 1, 2 January 1915, 313.

service, stating that they 'contributed a large number to the ranks'. He is particularly keen, however, to highlight the volunteer spirit and natural patriotism of the sons of 'families of English birth', who he estimates enlisted at a rate of 90% of the eligible total. This figure is difficult to verify and seems quite high, but approximately 10,000 Jewish volunteers had joined the forces by the time conscription was introduced in Britain at the beginning of 1916.[51] Given that the overall Jewish population of the United Kingdom was then not much more than about 250,000, and that British Jews had no strong traditional connection to the army or navy, this represents a very high level of service indeed. Taking the entire British Empire into account, Adler estimated that approximately 50,000 Jewish men had seen service in the various branches of the British forces during the war years.[52] Many of these men evidently served with distinction under fire, moreover, with five Jewish servicemen being awarded the universally esteemed Victoria Cross and several hundred receiving other awards for gallantry and distinguished service. Finally, and importantly, Adler cites a figure of just over 2320 Jewish officers and men who died while on active service, offering an insight into the levels of bereavement experienced in Anglo-Jewish homes as a result of the war.[53]

Wartime and Post-war Antisemitism

There can be little doubt that Anglo-Jewish men served in the British armed forces in significant numbers, and often served with distinction, during the war. Indeed, their willingness to fight was publicised not just in the Jewish press but also in the mainstream national dailies during the war years. *The Times* printed several positive reports of Jewish servicemen's contribution to the war effort, including an account of Michael Adler's work at the front, and the *Daily Mail* also highlighted and praised Jewish service.[54] Yet despite this publicly acknowledged service and sacrifice, and the vocal support for the war expressed by Jewish

---

[51] Michael Adler (1919), *The Jews of the Empire and the Great War* (Hodder and Stoughton, London), 1.

[52] Ibid., 4.

[53] Ibid., 5.

[54] See *The Times*, 'Jews in the Firing Line', 4 December 1914, 5; 'Jews in the Fight', 13 March 1915, 11; *The Daily Mail*, 'British Jews Loyalty', 14 December 1914, 3; and 'Our Fighting Jews', 8 August 1917, 5.

leaders, the loyalty, and indeed the very Englishness, of the Anglo-Jewish community were called into question throughout the conflict. David Cesarani has emphasised the degree to which the *Jewish Chronicle* was forced to refute the popular misconception that most British Jews were of German descent or in some way connected to Germany, and the *Jewish World* regularly reported instances of this rather dangerous conflation in the opening months of the war.[55] Indeed, the unequivocal Anglo-Jewish support for the war was at least partly inspired by the need to counter accusations of Jewish profiteering, malingering or simple indifference to the war effort.

The emergence and often quite public expression of anti-Jewish sentiment in Britain during the war years has been quite well documented by historians.[56] In the context of Jewish wartime patriotism, it is nonetheless worth emphasising the extent to which Jewish service and sacrifice were respectively denied and denigrated both while the conflict was ongoing and in the years after the Armistice. The controversy caused by the non-enlistment, until 1917, of some 30,000 non-naturalised 'Russian Jews', mostly resident in London's East End, tended to overshadow the willing service of British-born Jews and greatly exacerbated an already tense situation for the Anglo-Jewish community.[57] As the British death tolls in the various theatres of war mounted, the suggestion, accurate or not, that a particular section of the civilian population was unprepared to make sacrifices met with extraordinary public indignation. Indeed, popular resentment against Jewish communities ultimately flared into quite serious disorder and violence; in June 1917, a crowd of thousands descended upon the Jewish quarter in Leeds where they destroyed property and looted shops.[58] The following September saw the eruption of a pitched battle between thousands of Jewish and

[55] David Cesarani (1994, 2005), *The Jewish Chronicle and Anglo-Jewry, 1841–1991*, 117.

[56] See Gisela Lebzelter (1978), *Political Anti-semitism in England 1918–1939*; Colin Holmes (1979), *Anti-semitism in British Society, 1876–1939*; Elkan D. Levy (1970), 'Anti-semitism in England at War, 1914–1916', *Patterns of Prejudice* 4:5, 27–30; and especially, Colin Holmes (1979), *Anti-semitism in British Society, 1876–1939*, 121–140. For an account of post-war antisemitism that adds to, and, in some ways, challenges this work, see Tony Kushner (1990), 'The Impact of British Anti-semitism, 1918–1945', in David Cesarani ed. *The Making of Modern Anglo-Jewry* (Oxford, Basil Blackwell), 191–208.

[57] David Cesarani, 'An Embattled Minority', 66–69.

[58] Aaron Kent, *Identity, Migration and Belonging: The Jewish Community of Leeds, 1890–1920*, 246–250.

non-Jewish workers in Bethnal Green.[59] Writing in the *Jewish Chronicle* in mid-March 1918, Leopold Greenberg commented on the wartime rise in anti-Jewish sentiment, which he linked directly to the exemption from conscription of non-naturalised Eastern European Jews: 'the whole of the unfortunate question of the position of the Russian Jew in relation to military service has ... tended to feed the spirit of resentment against our people, which certain classes are doing their best to encourage'. Importantly, he went on emphasise the disturbingly novel nature of these antisemitic attacks. 'I desire to warn the Community', he wrote, 'that these attacks are growing in virulence and that antisemitic feeling is being energetically fostered against us to an extent that has no precedence in modern times.'[60]

The prevalence of anti-Jewish sentiment that had so alarmed Greenberg and others in the final year of the war seems to have continued, and become more organised, in the year or so after the conflict ended. In March 1919, a poster denouncing Sir Alfred Moritz Mond as a traitor and accusing him of selling shares to the Germans during the war was publicly displayed in London. Mond was the son of a wealthy German-Jewish chemist and a prominent Liberal MP and this was not the first time he had been publicly accused of disloyalty to Britain.[61] He sued the creators of the poster, Henry Hamilton Beamish and Harry McLeod Fraser, and during the trial, which took place in December and was widely reported in the press, Beamish insisted that a man could not be both Jewish and English.[62] An Anglo-Irish veteran of the Boer War and the Great War, Beamish had co-founded an avowedly antisemitic nationalist pressure group called 'The Britons' towards the end of 1918.[63] He lost the Mond libel trial and left the country without paying the £5000 in damages demanded by the court, but the leaflets produced by The Britons in his absence, and the virulently antisemitic propaganda

[59] Todd. M. Endelman, *The Jews of Britain, 1656–2006*, 185–186.

[60] *Jewish Chronicle*, 15 March 1918, 10.

[61] Harry Percival Smith, a war veteran and future Archdeacon of Lynn, and David Davies, editor of the *South Wales Daily Post*, both accused Mond of wartime treason when he campaigned to retain his Swansea seat in the autumn of 1918. See *The Times*, 18 October 1918, 3 and 12 December 1918, 10.

[62] For a detailed account of what was said at the trial, see *The Times*, 2 December 1919, 5.

[63] *The Britons* (1952), [history of the society] (London, BPS Printing Co.).

contained in the organisation's monthly journal, *Jewry Über Alles*, reveal the malicious nature of post-war British antisemitism.

The organisation's motto was 'Britain for Britons' and its core objective was to exclude those who were not 'of British blood' from the political process in the United Kingdom.[64] Virtually all of its propaganda was designed to denigrate Anglo-Jewry and, in common with antisemitic groups in continental Europe, it sought to portray Jews as international conspirators who had secretly connived to bring about the Great War and the Russian Revolution. References to the lack of patriotism of the Jewish population of Britain during the war were quite common in the organisation's early propaganda and, although it should be stressed that The Britons were a relatively obscure group, this material gives us quite a vivid idea of the sort of attacks English Jews had to endure in the aftermath of the conflict. The editorial in the third issue of *Jewry Über Alles*, published in April 1920, made specific reference to the behaviour of Jewish citizens during the war and is worth quoting at length:

> ... there is one thing that the War has accomplished ... it has shown to the people of these islands that A JEW IS NOT AN ENGLISHMAN: he is a Jew, and there's an end on't. The flight of young Jews to Ireland when conscription was in the offing; the scenes in the tubes on raid nights; the flight of the tribe of Israel to Brighton – which town their private information bureau told them would never be raided; the rush of Jew "officers" to safe billets in the Strand and Whitehall. And of the privates to "work of national importance" in the clothing and food-contracts line – these moving pictures will never be erased from the mind of the Briton, and they, with many others of the like description, prove to him that the Jew is of another blood and another continent from his own.[65]

The war, in other words, had had the unintended but positive effect of highlighting the incompatibility of Englishness and Jewishness, which was something of an ongoing theme for The Britons. In her 1978 study of inter-war antisemitism in Britain, Gisela Lebzelter argued that although The Britons had little impact on the political landscape in the United Kingdom, the organisation helped to reinforce the idea of an

---

[64] *The Britons* (1920), [membership leaflet] (London, Judaic Publishing Co.), 4.
[65] *Jewry Über Alles* 1:3, April 1920, 2.

international Jewish conspiracy by consistently disseminating antisemitic literature.[66] Their dedication to printing and circulating the notorious *Protocols of the Elders of Zion*, a literary forgery that was promoted as authentic by the *Morning Post* and initially taken seriously by *The Times* when it appeared in Britain in 1920, is particularly notable. And, as with the British Union of Fascists in the 1930s, the negligible influence of The Britons on the wider culture does not negate the undoubted impact that the existence of such organisations had on the increasingly embattled Anglo-Jewish community. The ongoing and, for the West, quite threatening repercussions of the Russian Revolution, along with Britain's apparently more precarious position in the world gave rise to a post-war mood of suspicion and resentment, in which Jews, as a readily identifiable 'alien' group, were subjected to the sort of public denunciation that would have been hard to get away with before 1914. In this context, The Britons were simply more extreme exponents of the sort of 'respectable' antisemitism that could be found in the early 1920s in the pages of the *Morning Post*, in The Duke of Northumberland's weekly *The Patriot*, in Lord Alfred Douglas's periodical *Plain English*, and, perhaps more disturbingly, in the writings of popular and erudite authors such as Hilaire Belloc and G. K. Chesterton.[67]

Given the alarmingly antisemitic mood abroad in post-war Britain, the *British Jewry Book of Honour*, edited by Michael Adler and published in 1922, should be seen both as a communal memorial to the Jewish men who had lost their lives during the war and a rebuttal to the now more blatant and public denials of Jewish Englishness. In the context of post-war commemorative culture, this lavishly produced record of Jewish service and sacrifice is quite a unique document. The publishing of 'rolls of honour' citing the names and details of fallen members of particular religious or regional communities, prominent firms, schools or sports clubs, was a reasonably common practice in Britain in the years after the

---

[66] Gisela Lebzelter (1978), *Political Anti-semitism in England 1918–1939*, 67.

[67] Colin Holmes (1979), *Anti-semitism in British Society, 1876–1939*, 215–216; Thomas Linehan, *British Fascism, 1918–1939: Parties, Ideologies and Culture* (Manchester, Manchester University Press), 177. For Belloc's most detailed antisemitic statement, see Hilaire Belloc (1922), *The Jews* (London, Constable & Co.). On G. K. Chesterton's antisemitism, see Dean Rapp (1990), 'The Jewish Response to G. K. Chesterton's Antisemitism, 1911–1933', *Patterns of Prejudice* 24, 75–86; Adam Gopnik (2008), The Troubling Genius of G. K. Chesterton, *The New Yorker*, July 2008.

Armistice,[68] but the *British Jewry Book of Honour* was an altogether more ambitious project, and an ultimately more forceful statement, than a mere roll of honour. Over the course of more than 1000 pages, the book not only lists the names of the approximately 2000 Jewish soldiers and sailors who died while on active service during the war, but it also cites the names of the vast majority of Jewish men who served in the forces of the British Empire at any point between 1914 and 1918. These 'nominal rolls' of service, which have no parallel, at least in terms of sheer scale, in any other religious or special interest group in post-war Britain, cover some 421 pages and feature the names, ranks, and units of no fewer than 40,000 men. Importantly, moreover, the lengthy rolls are supported by detailed sections of text that highlight the depth of the Jewish commitment to the British war effort and the heroism and self-sacrificing spirit of Jewish servicemen.

The book opens with a series of statements made by eleven very eminent Jewish and non-Jewish figures that testify to the service and sacrifice of the Jews of the empire during the war years. The reader thus finds Lieutenant-General Sir John Monash, Commander of the Australian Corps and the most senior Jewish officer in the imperial forces, and Sir Herbert Samuel, the first ever Jewish cabinet member and then Commissioner of Palestine, joined by Field-Marshal Haig and Sir Winston Churchill, praising the Jewish contribution to the British war effort in the warmest terms. These powerful testimonies are followed by detailed accounts, written by Adler himself, of Jewish service in the various theatres of war, along with a section on the Jewish battalions that served in the Middle East by Ze'ev Jabotinsky.

The *British Jewry Book of Honour* made for a compelling response to the antisemitic commentary that had impugned the patriotism of British Jews since at least 1916, and which had become particularly malignant in the years since the war ended. Indeed, Adler and the other authors of the book's content clearly conceived of it, at least partly, as a document that would make an unassailable case in defence of Anglo-Jewish patriotism. In the opening lines of the text, the Chief Rabbi, Joseph Hertz, refers directly to attacks on the Jewish community:

[68]See, for example, E. H. D. Sewell, *The Rugby Football Internationals Roll of Honour*, London; *Linton House School. The Great War, 1914–1919 [A Roll of Honour]*, London, 1920; and *The National Bank of Scotland Roll of Honour*, Edinburgh, 1922.

This permanent written record of the part played by Anglo-Jewry in the Great War will help lovers of the Truth in their warfare against the malicious slander that the Jew shrinks from the sacrifices demanded of every loyal citizen in the hour of national danger.[69]

Adler, for his part, reiterated the stance he had taken in 1914, that the war provided English Jews with an opportunity to demonstrate their loyalty and to repay their homeland for the refuge it had offered their people:

> British Jews have vindicated, once and for all time, their right to British citizenship. They have proved in an unmistakable manner that they are part and parcel of the Empire. Great Britain was the first country in the world to completely emancipate the Jews. This was in 1854. The opportunity to justify that emancipation did not come for sixty years, but when it did come – in August, 1914 – the opportunity was seized with a spontaneity and enthusiasm that surprised even those who knew the loyalty of the British Jews.[70]

For Adler, then, the willing, and indeed enthusiastic, Anglo-Jewish engagement with military service during the war both 'vindicated' the Jewish claim to British citizenship and irrefutably demonstrated Jewish loyalty to England and the empire.

CONCLUSION

Anglo-Jewish clergymen, journalists, and intellectuals publicly interpreted the advent of the war in 1914 as a positive opportunity for English Jews to demonstrate beyond all doubt that they were deserving of full citizenship and that they were just as loyal to Britain and the empire as their Christian compatriots. Importantly, moreover, the patriotic obligations of the Jewish community were frequently framed in reciprocal terms, and military service, in particular, was presented as the repayment of a debt to a country that had traditionally treated Jews well. The unprecedented strain of a protracted total war would lead, however,

---

[69] Michael Adler, ed. (1922), *British Jewry Book of Honour* (London, Caxton Publishing Co.), ix.

[70] Ibid., 1.

to the emergence of mentalities and give rise to circumstances that transformed the social and cultural landscape in Britain and put intense pressure on minorities in general and on Anglo-Jewry in particular. Thus, despite the service of thousands of Jewish men, from all sections of the community, in the British forces, and despite the staunch and vocal patriotism of the Jewish establishment, the loyalty and commitment of the Anglo-Jewish community were continually called into question during the war years. In the final year of the conflict, moreover, English Jews had to contend with the emergence of a new, more overtly political form of antisemitism that would become even more pronounced in the years immediately after the Armistice. This anti-Jewish rhetoric consistently challenged the very Englishness of Anglo-Jewry and was particularly damaging, and indeed hurtful, to the assimilated elites whose families were well established in England by 1914.

Pre-war Britain was not quite the haven for Jews that some commentators suggested it was, but it had nonetheless been a place in which the Jewish community felt confident and self-assured and where antisemitism could generally be regarded as a nuisance rather than a pervasive threat. At the end of 1918, by contrast, English Jews emerged from the maelstrom of a war in which they had made extraordinary sacrifices and found themselves in a world from which old certainties seemed to have disappeared and where bigotry was very much off the leash. In such an environment, the war record of Jewish servicemen provided irrefutable proof of patriotic commitment. The *British Jewry Book of Honour* should thus be understood not simply as a memorial to the Anglo-Jewish dead but as a powerful statement of Anglo-Jewish patriotism and Jewish Englishness in a political and cultural climate in which these things were increasingly denied.

INDEX

© The Editor(s) (if applicable) and The Author(s) 2019
E. Madigan and G. Reuveni (eds.),
The Jewish Experience of the First World War,
https://doi.org/10.1057/978-1-137-54896-2

CPI Antony Rowe
Eastbourne, UK
November 26, 2019